Praise for *Havana Nocturne*

"Keenly researched history. . . . English describes a luscious island throbbing with sensuality."　　　　　　　　　　　　　—*Wall Street Journal*

"Engaging. . . . Clever. . . . English's brand of narrative is history, and he aims to set the record straight."　　　　　　　　　　—*Miami Herald*

"[An] entertaining new book . . . by veteran crime writer T. J. English."
　　　　　　　　　　　　　　　　　　　　　　　—*New York Post*

"Spellbinding prose. . . . *Havana Nocturne* is a powerful reminder of how the mob nearly achieved its biggest payday and how Castro beat the house, forever changing the course of history."
　　　　　　　　　　　　　　　　　—*San Antonio Express-News*

"Driven by the booming tourist industry, Havana's nightlife pulsed with music, dancing, liquor, drugs, and sex, and English ably captures the colorful rhythm. . . . Those glitzy days may be gone, but *Havana Nocturne* is a worthy reminder of a unique saga of politics, culture, and corruption."
　　　　　　　　　　　　　　　　　　　　—*St. Petersburg Times*

"True-crime writer English (*Paddy Whacked*) presents an empire-building saga in which the 'Havana mob' of American gangsters, led by visionary financier Meyer Lansky, controlled Cuba."　　　—*Publishers Weekly*

"English's engaging narrative reads with the gripping quality of fiction: the dark underworld of Havana comes to life. . . . Highly recommended."
　　　　　　　　　　　　　　　　　　　　　　—*Library Journal*

"Crime writer English (*Paddy Whacked*) unfolds a story whose main outline will be familiar to any fan of *The Godfather: Part II*, but whose twists and turns no screenplay could keep up with."   —*Kirkus Reviews*

"Combining extensive research with a poignant narrative, English has crafted a book that is both informative and entertaining. He neatly balances keen historical analysis, biographical detail, and journalistic insight, resulting in a compelling work of nonfiction that throbs with the feeling that you are actually in the middle of all that was happening during these exciting years in Cuba."   —*American Chronicle*

"Finally, the definitive book has been written on the mob's heyday in Cuba. *Havana Nocturne* is at once compelling and incisive—an entertaining page-turner that will both shock and inform."
     —Sam Giancana, author of *Double Cross*

"Sex and drugs and rockin' mambo! *Havana Nocturne* is a dazzling parade through the mob's interests in Cuba. A must for mob fans everywhere."
     —Legs McNeil, author of
     The Other Hollywood and *Please Kill Me*

"All the razzle-dazzle is here—Sinatra, the black sedans, the showgirls— but English goes further to show how gangsterismo permeated the politics of Cuba and influenced its destiny."   —*The Scotsman*

"Wonderful. . . . The book's tour de force might be the account of the early morning hours of January 1, 1959. . . . A well-researched page-turner, highly recommended."
     —Ned Sublette, author of *Cuba and Its Music*

ALSO BY T. J. ENGLISH

Paddy Whacked

Born to Kill

The Westies

HAVANA

How the Mob Owned Cuba . . .
and Then Lost It to the Revolution

NOCTURNE

T. J. ENGLISH

HARPER

NEW YORK • LONDON • TORONTO • SYDNEY

In memory of Armando Jaime Casielles
(1931–2007)

y para el pueblo cubano

HARPER

This book was originally published as *The Havana Mob* in the United Kingdom in 2007 by Mainstream Publishing.

A hardcover edition of this book was published in 2008 by William Morrow, an imprint of HarperCollins Publishers.

HarperCollins books may be purchased for educational, business, or sales promotional use. For information please write: Special Markets Department, HarperCollins Publishers, 10 East 53rd Street, New York, NY 10022.

Designed by Lovedog Studio

Library of Congress Cataloging-in-Publication Data is available upon request.

ISBN 978-0-06-171274-6

09 10 11 12 13 WBC/RRD 10 9 8 7 6 5 4 3 2 1

And in my imagination's dreams I see the nation's
representatives dancing, drunk with enthusiasm,
eyes blindfolded, their movements dizzying, their
momentum inexhaustible . . . Amid this sinister
splendor, a red specter lets out a strident cackle.
They dance . . . Dance now, dance.

—*José Martí, Cuban patriot*

She can wiggle her ass, but she
can't sing a goddamn note.

—*Meyer Lansky on Ginger Rogers,
opening night at the Copa Room,
Havana, Cuba, 1957*

CONTENTS

INTRODUCTION

ON STORMY DAYS AND NIGHTS IN HAVANA, CUBA, THE ocean batters the sea wall that rims the northern edge of the city. Waves crash against the rocks and splash upward, spraying the sidewalk, avenue, and cars driving along the famous waterfront promenade known as the Malecón. Briny saltwater rushes inward sometimes as much as a full city block. Huge puddles ebb and flow as the result of turbulent winds that sweep down from the north—Los Nortes, Cubans call them. Pedestrians and cars are forced to use inland streets to avoid the expanding pools. Water seeps into cracks and crevices, eating away at an already crumbling infrastructure. On days and nights like these, it is as if La Habana were under siege from a powerful, pounding deluge that threatens to undermine the very groundwork on which this glorious Caribbean city was founded.

Half a century ago, another kind of tempest swept across this storied island republic. Unlike the tropical squalls that form in the Gulf of Mexico and assault the city from the north, what happened in the decades of the late 1940s and '50s was initiated from within the country's political and economic structure.

At first, this upheaval appeared to have a positive side: if it was a malignant force, it was a malignant force that came bearing gifts. Over a seven-year period—from 1952 to 1959—the city of Havana was the beneficiary of staggering growth and development. Large hotel-casinos, nightclubs, tourist resorts, tunnels, and highways were constructed in a whirlwind of activity. Neon, glitter, the mambo, and sex became the hallmarks of a thriving tourist business. The allure of organized gambling, along with fabulous nightclub floor shows and beautiful women, brought an influx of money into the city.

The flash, ample flesh, and entertainment venues in Havana were the most obvious manifestations of the gathering storm. The gaudy gambling emporiums, racetracks, and back-door sex shows brought in the tourists and created a veneer of prosperity, but the true force behind the maelstrom was bicoastal in nature.

The fabulous nightlife was a lure used by the Cuban government to attract foreign investors, mostly from the United States. The country's most precious resources—sugar, oil, forestry, agriculture, refineries, financial institutions, and public utilities—were all up for sale. Foreign capital washed over the island. Throughout the post–World War II years and into the 1950s, direct U.S. business investments in Cuba grew from $142 million to $952 million by the end of the decade. Such was the extent of American interest in Cuba that this island, roughly the size of the state of Tennessee, ranked in third place among the nations of the world receiving U.S. investments.

The financial largesse that flooded Cuba could have been used to address the country's festering social problems. Hunger, illiteracy, subhuman housing, a high infant mortality rate, and the dispossession of small farmers had been facts of life in Cuba throughout the island's turbulent history. It is true that Havana had one of the highest standards of living in all of Latin America, but this prosperity was not spread evenly throughout the nation. And as the decade wore on, the gulf between the haves and the have-nots continued to widen.

To those who cared to look below the surface, it was apparent that Cuba's startling economic windfall was not being used to meet the needs of the people but rather to pad the private bank accounts and pocketbooks of a powerful group of corrupt politicians and American "investors." This economic high command would come to be known as the Havana Mob.

It is a historical fact—and also a subject of considerable folklore in Cuba and the United States—that the Havana Mob comprised some of the most notorious underworld figures of their day. Charles "Lucky" Luciano, Meyer Lansky, Santo Trafficante, Albert Anastasia, and other gangsters who came to Havana in the late 1940s and 1950s were men who had honed their craft and amassed or inherited their wealth during the "glory days" of Prohibition in the United States. These mobsters had always dreamed of one day controlling their own country, a place where they could provide gambling, narcotics, booze, prostitution, and other forms of vice free from government or law enforcement intrusion.

Gaming and leisure were only part of the equation. The idea formulated by Luciano, Lansky, and others was for Havana to serve as the front for a far more ambitious agenda: the creation of a criminal state whose gross national product, union pension funds, public utilities, banks, and other financial institutions would become the means to launch further criminal enterprises around the globe. The Havana Mob could then bury the profits from these criminal operations underneath the patina of a "legitimate" government in Cuba and no one would be able to touch them.

Political developments on the island would play a large role in determining the Mob's fortunes in Cuba, but its efforts were also shaped by events back home. Luciano and Lansky may have wanted to establish Cuba as a base of operation as far back as the 1920s, but history sometimes got in the way. Economic downturns, wars, and the efforts of U.S. law enforcement caused retrenchments and changes in strategy. The plan was not formulated in its final form until the postwar years of the late 1940s, and even then there were interruptions. Much of the onus would fall on Lansky, who would devote a good portion of his adult life to formulating the necessary relationships and providing the impetus.

By the 1950s, the plan appeared to be coming to fruition. Through force of will, shrewd organization, and the judicious use of political repression, violence, and murder, the mobsters seemingly achieved their dream. Havana seethed and sizzled. The money that flowed from huge hotel-casinos was used to construct nightclubs that attracted major performers, Cuban, American, and European. A fabulous epoch was created—perhaps the most organic and exotic entertainment era in the history of organized crime. Elaborate floor shows at places like the world-famous Tropicana nightclub set the standard for generations to come. Smaller cabarets allowed patrons to get closer to the dancers, who were scantily clad, voluptuous, and sometimes obtainable. Varying levels of burlesque clubs and bordellos were sprinkled throughout the city.

Havana had always been a place of great music, but in the era of the Havana Mob a generation of musicians found their voice. In the late 1940s, arranger Dámaso Pérez Prado and his band, along with other renowned orchestras, created a craze called "the mambo." The mambo was both a type of music and a dance, a sensual transaction between two people engaged in mutual seduction. The mambo was the unofficial dance of the Havana Mob, and the sultry Latin rhythms that inspired the phenomenon were to underscore the entire era.

Luciano, Lansky, Trafficante, and the other U.S. mobsters became local royalty. Since casino gambling was legal in Cuba, the gangsters operated more openly than was normally their custom. Various mobsters and their associates served on the board of directors for banks, financial institutions, and powerful corporations. Since Meyer Lansky & Co. were outsiders in Cuba, their operations had the look and feel of an act of prestidigitation, except that in truth none of it would have been possible were it not for the cooperation of the ultimate insider: El Presidente Fulgencio Batista y Zaldívar.

On March 10, 1952, Batista took over the government by force. It was a bloodless coup only because Batista, who had ruled the country before, from 1933 to 1944, was a well-known figure. A mostly self-educated man, with the physical appearance and bearing of a Hollywood matinee idol,

Batista owed his power to his "special relationship" with the military, from which he had risen through the ranks from private to sergeant to major colonel before becoming president.

As a leader, Batista was a classic strongman, an all-too-familiar postcolonial Latin American type. A brutal dictator who had assumed the position of president by hostile takeover—and would therefore never be seen as legitimate by many in the country—Batista embraced the dictates of the American mobsters. The casinos and nightclubs generated capital, which was used to build elaborate public works and attract investors, who were then fleeced by Batista and his underlings. All Batista had to do was keep the Cuban rabble in their place. It was his job to make sure that the revolutionary fervor that was as much a part of Cuba as sugar and rum did not spill over and threaten the Golden Goose. With intelligence operatives, soldiers, and secret torture squads within the police serving as his enforcers, President Batista was the muscle behind the Havana Mob.

Violent reprisals on Batista's part toward any and all "subversive activity" brought about a phenomenon well known to physicists: for every action, there is an equal and opposite reaction. Political upheaval had been a staple in Cuba since the island's nominal independence from Spain in 1898. The stench of colonialism lingered on, creating resentment, bitterness, and a strong sense of righteous indignation. Political leaders bullied their way into office and were then toppled, many of them more corrupt than those who came before. One president lasted a total of five days in office before being overthrown. Even among this cavalcade of despots, Batista achieved a new level of infamy. He had taken over the government by force, suspended the constitution, and was in the process of creating a capitalist Shangri-La in Havana. To those who opposed his fraudulent regime, the casinos, nightclubs, sex trade, and mobsterism in the capital city became a symbol of everything they despised about the plundering of Cuba by outside interests.

A showdown was destined to occur. In the interior mountains of the Sierra Maestra, revolution was brewing, with a small band of anti-Batista guerrilla fighters hunkered down in anticipation of the coming storm.

They were led by a charismatic lawyer and former political candidate named Fidel Castro Ruz.

It is impossible to tell the story of the Havana Mob without also chronicling the rise of Castro and the revolutionary movement he founded. For a time, these two stories ran on parallel tracks, with season after season of revelers gambling and partying in Havana while the revolutionaries starved and plotted in the hills. The inspiration for the resistance ran deep and could be located in the writings of José Martí, a poet, journalist, and activist who was one of the architects of Cuba's long-running struggle for freedom. Martí was killed during the War of Independence, but his writings, and the example of his life, lived on. Castro's revolutionary movement was inspired by Martí, and historical in nature, but it found its focus in the criminality and economic exploitation of the Batista regime.

Comandante William Gálvez Rodríguez was a young rebel leader entrenched in the Sierra Maestra during the Revolution. Years later, he recalled: "It would not be accurate to say that the [mobsters] in Havana were the reason for the Revolution—there were deeper reasons that went back to the beginning of Cuba's formation. But it is a fact that the casinos and the money—and most importantly the connections among the U.S. gangsters, U.S. corporations, and the Batista regime—became a symbol of corruption to us. Even though we were away in the mountains, we knew of the prostitution, the stealing of government funds, the selling of the country to outside interests. We vowed that *when*—not if; *when*—we were in power, this was going to change."

The revolutionaries had little in the way of soldiers, guns, or resources, but they did have a clandestine network of supporters spread throughout the island. *Fidelista* resistance fighters and spies infiltrated Batista's army and circulated in the casinos and resort hotels. Occasionally, the guerrilla war that was being fought in the outlying provinces erupted right in the middle of the mobsters' playground. People connected with the government—and by extension, the Havana Mob—were kidnapped and sometimes assassinated. Student protest rallies turned into occasions for armed combat with the police. Homemade bombs exploding in the night and the *rat-a-tat-tat* of gunfire sometimes sounded alongside the revelry that spilled out of the casinos and cabarets owned by the Mob.

How did Lansky and the gangsters react to the ominous trade winds? With more development: bigger hotel-casinos, flashier floor shows, and larger doses of "investment capital" designed to reinforce the status quo and drown out the forces of revolution. Havana became a volatile mix of Monte Carlo, Casablanca, and the ancient Spanish city of Cádiz all rolled into one—a bitch's brew of high-stakes gambling, secret revolutionary plots, violent repression, and gangsterism.

The legacy of these years has entered the realm of legend. In modern-day Havana, the remnants are everywhere. The gambling casinos are long gone, but many of the old hotels are still in existence, some ragged and faded, others shining monuments to the past. At the exquisite Hotel Nacional, where Luciano and Lansky once lived and held secret Mob conferences, there is a special room off the lobby called the Salón de la Historia. Its walls are adorned with life-sized murals of gangsters intermingled with celebrities and movie stars. At the Hotel Sevilla (formerly the Sevilla Biltmore), framed black-and-white photographs of the mobsters who once operated there line the walls of the Roof Garden alongside the panoramic view of the Malecón, the ocean, and beyond. In the streets, vintage American cars from the 1940s and '50s are everywhere, as are the flickering neon signs and air of insouciance that contribute to the city's allure. The effect is hallucinatory: on certain nights, it is as if the ghosts of the past are still alive, a spooky, spectral testament to the era of the Havana Mob.

Beyond Cuba, the story still resonates: the premise of the Mob in Havana has been fodder for innumerable novels and movies. A mythology has evolved over the years based largely on fictionalized accounts, most notably *The Godfather Part II* (1974), the venerable Hollywood movie that dramatized the last days of pre-Castro Cuba through the eyes of the Corleone family. More recently, Cuban-born Andy Garcia directed and starred in *The Lost City* (2005), which portrayed Havana in the 1950s as a kind of Paradise Lost. There have been other movies and more than a few crime novels, of varying quality, all of them based on a skimpy public record or pure imagination.

This book constitutes the first nonfiction, English-language attempt to tell the full story of the Mob's infiltration of Havana. It is impossible to understand the present-day stand-off between the governments of Cuba and the United States without first knowing the details of this era. For forty-six years the U.S. government has maintained an economic embargo of the island (referred to in Cuba as *el bloqueo* or "the block-ade"). Unprecedented in length, this act of economic strangulation has done little to alter the monolithic trajectory of Cuban politics, though it has succeeded in fostering decades of isolation, ignorance, and mistrust. The roots of this epic antipathy can be traced in part to the influx of mobsters and the plundering of Havana that took place in the late 1940s and '50s. For some, it was a time of diversion and fun. For others, it was a moneymaking proposition. To the revolutionaries and the government of Fidel Castro that followed, the era stands as an example of capitalist exploitation at its most venal.

However the story is viewed, the era of the Havana Mob represents a time in history that defines the current reality. Fifty years after the fact, the empire presided over by Lansky, Batista, and the rest is gone, but the consequences of that time are still very much alive. Ten U.S. presidents have come and gone; Fidel inches closer to a date with the Grim Reaper. But the legacy of the Mob's adventures in Cuba continues to inflame the imagination. The professional gamblers have all departed, but the sounds of the slot machines and the intoxicating rhythms of the mambo and cha-cha-chá linger on, still relished or denounced, depending on which side of the gaming tables you were on. Few are willing to forgive or forget.

—T. J. English
Havana, Cuba
April 2007

Part One

MOBSTER MAMBO

FEELING LUCKY

WHEN CHARLES LUCIANO OF NAPLES, ITALY, BOARDED A huge freighter in the autumn of 1946 and headed out to sea, he had many things on his mind but only one thing that mattered: Cuba. The Pearl of the Antilles was to be his salvation, the place where he would ascend once again to the top of the most powerful crime organization in the free world. After a long decade of prison and exile, he deserved nothing less.

Having been deported from the United States just seven months earlier, Luciano did not want to tempt the fates: his journey from Italy to Cuba was to be a secret known only to his closest criminal associates. Using an Italian passport and traveling under his birth name—Salvatore Lucania—he set out on a journey that would take nearly two weeks. The freighter that left Naples in mid-October reached port first in Caracas, Venezuela. Luciano remained there for a few days and then flew to Rio de Janeiro, where he stayed for a few more days. After he was certain that he was not under any kind of surveillance, Luciano flew on to Mexico City and then back to Caracas, where he chartered a private plane for the last leg of his trip—to Cuba.

He landed at the airport in Camagüey, in the interior of the island, on the morning of October 29. Arrangements had been made for the famous mobster to deplane on the far side of the airport. When he stepped out of the plane, Luciano encountered a Cuban government official. The first words out of his mouth to the official were "Where's Meyer?"

Luciano didn't have to wait long to see the familiar, taciturn grin of his childhood friend and longtime criminal associate. A car arrived from across the tarmac and stopped near Luciano's private plane. Out stepped Meyer Lansky.

Luciano and Lansky hadn't seen one another in months. Lansky, age forty-four, was trim and tanned, as usual. His 5-foot-4-inch stature had earned him the nickname "Little Man." It was meant ironically: in his chosen profession as an underworld entrepreneur who specialized in gambling, Lansky was anything but little. Luciano knew this to be true because he had partnered with Lansky on many of his most ambitious schemes.

Luciano was taller than Meyer, with a classic Sicilian mug that would forever be described in the press as "swarthy." At age fifty, his black hair had begun to gray at the temples and his many years in prison had softened his physique. Luciano spent nearly his entire forties behind bars, and much of the youthful swagger that had characterized his rise to power in New York City had now been tempered by the monotony and humiliation of prison life. "Lucky," as Luciano was sometimes known, was looking to get his mojo back, to reassert his power and rediscover his inner gangster. Cuba would be the place.

With Lansky at his side, the famous mafioso passed through Cuban customs in record time. Lansky was a big shot on the island, a friend of government officials going all the way to the top. It was Lansky who one month earlier had sent a cryptic note to Luciano in Italy that read: "December—Hotel Nacional." Luciano knew what it meant. He and Lansky's plans for Cuba went back decades.

Accompanied by a bodyguard and driver, the two men drove to the nearby Grand Hotel, the most renowned dining establishment in the country's interior. From the hotel's café terrace, they could see the entire city of Camagüey, with its winding streets, bell towers, and terra-cotta rooftops. The lunch was lavish and accompanied by sweet Santiago rum. Afterward, Luciano and Lansky continued on toward the capital city of Havana.

The celebratory lunch and two-hour drive across the island would have been a time of nostalgia and expectation for these two men raised on the Lower East Side of Manhattan island. That they were sitting in a car driving freely through Cuba was the result of a fantastical turn of events. Just seven months earlier, with Luciano buried away in Dannemora Prison and later Great Meadow Correctional Facility—or Comstock, as the prison in upstate New York was commonly known—life had looked bleak. Luciano was nine years into a thirty- to fifty-year prison sentence. There was seemingly no possibility that he would be seeing the light of day beyond prison walls anytime soon.

The manner by which Luciano and Lansky had finagled his early release was still largely unknown to the general public. Upon the commutation of Luciano's sentence and his deportation to Sicily, newspapers around the world alluded to a "secret relationship" between Luciano and U.S. naval intelligence during the Second World War. It was alleged that from inside his prison cell Luciano had helped the war effort, a claim that was given credence by New York governor Thomas E. Dewey, who recommended that Luciano's sentence be commuted and he be released. Dewey was the same man who, as special prosecutor, had put Luciano away on compulsory prostitution charges in the first place.

"Lucky Luciano Walks," read the headline in the *New York Daily Mirror* on the day the Mob boss was released. Other newspapers touted the event with headlines of a size usually reserved for wars and elections. Precious little was revealed about the details of Luciano's cooperation with the navy. The facts of his "deal" were still highly classified. The average citizen of the world was left with the impression that some nefarious relationship existed between the underworld and the government—in this case, the U.S. military. The fact that Luciano was immediately deported from the United States to Lercara Friddi, Sicily—the town of his birth—did not change the fact that he was a free man, somehow above the law.

Not surprisingly, Luciano had a different view. He was irate that he had been deported to Sicily. His only consolation was that he had no intention of staying put in Italy. From the moment he was exiled, it had been his aim somehow to return to the United States via Cuba.

Luciano and Lansky finally arrived at their destination, the regal Hotel Nacional, Havana's most prestigious address. Lansky was a partner in a corporation that owned a piece of the place. Situated on a bluff, with distinctive twin spires and a spectacular Caribbean view, the Nacional was the pride of Havana.

It was late afternoon. Meyer told his friend that he would not be coming in. That night he would be returning to the United States to begin circulating the word among their underworld pals that Luciano was in Cuba. Their presence would be requested at a major gathering of the tribe to take place at this very same Hotel Nacional in December. The conference would be the first major meeting in fourteen years of Mob bosses from throughout the United States. It was at this meeting that the New World Order would be established and Luciano would reassert his position as a high-ranking member of what was variously known as the Syndicate, the Commission, or the Mob.

The two men said their good-byes. Under the name Salvatore Lucania, Luciano signed the register and was led to his room. Years later, he recalled the moment:

When I got to the room the bellhop opened the curtains on them big windows and I looked out. I could see almost the whole city. I think it was the palm trees that got me. Everyplace you looked there was a palm tree and it made me feel like I was back in Miami. All of a sudden, I realized for the first time in over ten years that there was no handcuffs on me and nobody was breathin' over my shoulder, which is the way I used to feel even when I was wandering around Italy. When

I looked over the Caribbean from my window, I realized somethin' else; the water was just as pretty as the Bay of Naples, but it was only ninety miles from the United States. That meant I was practically back in America.

Luciano spent two weeks at the Hotel Nacional. In mid-November, he moved into a spacious house in the exclusive neighborhood of Miramar, among the estates and yacht clubs of wealthy Cubans and American residents. A few blocks from Luciano's Spanish-style mansion on 30th Street, near 5th Avenue, was the private estate of Cuba's president, Ramón Grau San Martín. Luciano wasted no time settling in:

I took it easy for the next few weeks. I had breakfast in bed and then I'd put on a pair of slacks and walk around my estate and supervise the four gardeners, as we would discuss the kind of flowers I wanted 'em to plant. The house was furnished with fantastic antiques and there must've been a thousand yards of all kinds of silk, from curtains to sheets. It was one helluva change from Dannemora and Great Meadow. The place was owned by a rich sugar planter, but it was the time when things were very low and I only paid eight hundred bucks a month for the whole joint, includin' all the servants and the gardeners.

Among the associates with whom Luciano reacquainted himself in Havana was a Cuban senator named Eduardo Suarez Rivas. Through Lansky, Luciano had known Senator Suarez for some time. In fact, the senator had been in New York City at the time of Luciano's deportation. The Cuban senator had been among the dozen or so guests who attended a going-away party held for Luciano aboard the SS *Laura Keene*, the ocean liner that transported the exiled mobster to Sicily. It was the contention of the U.S. Bureau of Narcotics that, in addition to his duties as a member of the senate in Cuba, Suarez Rivas was a *narcotrafficante*, specifically a peddler of cocaine, looking to do business with Luciano.

The American mobster was seen often with the senator in the early weeks after his arrival in Havana. Occasionally Luciano went on trips to the countryside with Suarez Rivas and his family. He was seen sunning himself at the pool at the Hotel Nacional with the senator, the senator's wife, and their children. At one point, Luciano sought to ingratiate himself with the senator by offering his wife the gift of a brand-new four-thousand-dollar Chrysler station wagon, ordered straight from Detroit. However, an import license for the car was denied. Luciano and Suarez Rivas had to have the car shipped to an associate in Tampa, Florida, who happened to be a prominent cigar manufacturer. The associate drove the car around the Tampa area for a few days until it had accumulated sufficient mileage to be declared a secondhand vehicle. It was then brought into Cuba for a declared value of five hundred dollars. Later, Luciano was able to import a car for himself—a Cadillac—that entered the country with no import tax at all.

In Havana the American Mob boss lived a life of leisure. Along with tending to his garden, his day trips with the Suarez Rivas family, and hanging out poolside at the Hotel Nacional, he made frequent trips to Oriental Park Racetrack in the suburb of Marianao. He also spent evenings at the elegant Gran Casino Nacional. Much of his time was either devoted to cultivating political contacts in Cuba that might be helpful in the future or trying to enjoy the many sensual pleasures that Havana had to offer.

One of those pleasures was women. As Lansky once put it: "Charlie liked pussy. It was one of his weaknesses." Of course, Luciano also had some catching up to do. He had been denied the pleasures of the flesh during his ten-year stretch in prison. In Havana, he frequently entertained prostitutes in an executive suite at the Hotel Nacional.

Mostly, Lucky was killing time until the main event in December, when his "friends" would begin to arrive for the scheduled Mob conference, and their long-held plans for an empire in Cuba could finally be put into place.

No one was supposed to know that Luciano was in Havana, but occasionally the word got out, or someone saw the mobster with his or her own eyes. Such was the case with Bernard Frank, a young attorney living in Miami at the time. One morning in December, Frank got a call at his home from Luciano's pal Meyer Lansky.

"Counselor, you awake?" asked Lansky.

The lawyer looked at a bedside clock: 6 A.M. "I am now," he answered.

Bernie Frank knew Meyer and his younger brother Jake. Five years earlier, the lawyer had appeared in the middle of the night at a bail hearing for some croupiers who worked at a gambling club affiliated with the Lansky brothers in Broward County, just north of the Miami city line. Frank secured the croupiers' release, so they didn't have to spend the night in jail. Meyer had always remembered the young lawyer for that.

"What's up?" Frank asked the Jewish Mob boss.

"Can you be at the airport by nine o'clock to fly with me to Havana? I got Carmen Miranda performing at the Colonial Inn and she needs a new set of maracas." The Colonial Inn was a popular "carpet joint," or casino-nightclub, on the outskirts of Miami owned and operated by the Lansky brothers.

Frank was about to ask, "Can't you go to the local ten-cent store and buy maracas?" when Lansky explained that Miranda, the temperamental Brazilian singer, actress, and star then at the height of her celebrity, was demanding a specific set of maracas she'd seen in a shop in Havana and would accept no substitutes. The young attorney rubbed sleep from his eyes and thought about it: he had only recently returned to the United States from a four-year stint in the army and had never been to Havana. Sure, he'd accompany Lansky on a trip across the Straits of Florida to buy maracas for Carmen Miranda. "I'll see you at the airport," he said.

After the hour-long flight to Havana, Lansky and Frank drove first to Oriental Park Racetrack. There, Lansky greeted a number of friends.

Then they drove on to a mansion in a nice part of town. The two men approached the door, knocked, and were greeted by a servant. The servant seemed to know Lansky. The man disappeared and when he returned he was accompanied by an Italian-looking gentleman in a silk bathrobe and leather slippers. Lansky said to the man, "Charlie, I want you to meet my lawyer, Bernie Frank." To Frank, Lansky said, "Bernie, meet Mr. Charlie Luciano."

Frank shook Luciano's hand. Then Lansky and Luciano disappeared into another room to talk privately. The young Miami lawyer sat in the foyer and waited. It dawned on him that the man he had just met was supposed to have been banished to Italy by the U.S. government. Later that night, it occurred to Frank that he was possibly one of the first Americans to know for a fact that the infamous Luciano was in Cuba. The next day—after he and Lansky had purchased the maracas for Carmen Miranda—Bernie got his ass back to Miami and kept his mouth shut.

NOBODY WAS SUPPOSED to know. Luciano was in Cuba, and the Mob was on the move. Only later, in the refracted glow of history, would it all make sense: the arrival of Lucky was a clarion call. For Luciano, Lansky, and the rest of the Mob, establishing Cuba as a base of operations was to be the next big scheme in their master plan of creating a multinational crime organization. The prospects were exciting, but the idea was not new; it went all the way back to the Lower East Side, when Charlie and Meyer first led the American Mob out of the dark ages and into the effervescence of the twentieth century

Ever since the underworld had emerged from a collection of street-corner gangs to become a corporate-style, multiethnic conglomerate, Luciano, Lansky, and other mobsters had dreamed of an offshore base of operations. The enticements were obvious. In the year 1919, Congress passed the Volstead Act, ushering in the era known as Prohibition. Henceforth, the manufacture, distribution, and imbibing of alcoholic beverages was a crime punishable by a fine or imprisonment. Bootleggers in New York, Chicago, Kansas City, Detroit, Boston, and many other U.S. cities got rich by giving the public what they wanted. Booze and gambling became the basis of a new underworld empire.

Cuba as an extension of the Mob's hegemony first entered underworld consciousness in the 1920s. Mobsters were well acquainted with the island: early in the Prohibition era, the Caribbean became an important conduit for illegal booze shipments. Rum, or molasses to make rum, was smuggled from the Leeward and Windward Islands along an outer stretch of the Atlantic Ocean that came to be known as Rum Row. Cuba was a primary transshipment point. The island's substantial craggy shoreline, with multiple coves and inlets, made it ideal for offloading contraband. Havana, in particular, became renowned as a kind of smuggler's paradise, a hotbed of black market commerce and international intrigue immortalized by Ernest Hemingway in his novel *To Have and Have Not*. The book is set in Havana and Key West, from which a skipper named Henry Morgan smuggles booze and other contraband between Cuba and the United States. The story ends with a smuggling operation gone bad: Henry Morgan is shot in the gut and left for dead.

Both Luciano and Lansky made trips to Havana in the 1920s to oversee their bootlegging operations, but the first mobster to set up shop in Cuba was from the city of Chicago. Alphonse "Big Al" Capone, the loudest and most notorious of the Prohibition-era gangsters, booked the entire sixth floor of the Sevilla Biltmore, an elegant hotel located in Habana Vieja (Old Havana), the city's colonial quarter. Capone stayed in room 615. He did not hide the fact that he was in Havana. He attended the racetrack and the opera house, where his favorite singer, Enrico Caruso, had once dazzled local audiences. In 1928 Big Al opened a pool hall in Marianao, near Oriental Park Racetrack. He closed it shortly thereafter, telling a reporter from the *Havana Post* that Cuba offered no field for "this particular class of business." It was no great loss: Capone's pool hall was most likely a front for his bootlegging operations.

With the Roaring Twenties in full swing, booze became the magic elixir that would transform Havana into a reigning example of the high life. Sugar, which had sustained the island since its inception as a country, had nearly doubled in price on the world market. Cuba was booming. Landowners, sugarmill owners, bankers, railroad magnates, and American companies grew at dizzying rates. The era was called *la danza de los millones*, the Dance of the Millions. Newspaper ads in New York, Chicago, and elsewhere around the United States touted Havana as a tourist destination, with the emphasis on alcohol. A popular guidebook of the era was entitled *When It's Cocktail Time in Cuba*. The appeal was not subtle: the most famous bar in Havana was called Sloppy Joe's. U.S. citizens went there to get "tight" on a popular new drink, the Cuba libre, a mix of Cuban rum, lime juice, and Coca-Cola. Gambling was also part of the equation. There was the racetrack and also the Gran Casino Nacional, at the time the most ornate gambling establishment in the Americas, with a majestic multilayered water fountain at the entrance that would set the standard in casino architecture for decades to come.

There was also sex. Mostly, male tourists left their wives at home.

Joe Stassi—a mafioso from the Lower East Side of Manhattan who would later become an important man in Havana—remembered his first trip to the city in 1928: "Beautiful young whores everywhere, every street corner, every bar. In one club, there were twenty-five girls. You picked the one you wanted to be in a live sex show."

Booze, gambling, and sex—what more could a Yankee tourist ask for?

To maximize the island's potential, capitalists circled the wagons: a "pleasure trust" of North American corporations and investors was established, aligned with certain Cuban political interests. The idea from the beginning was that some of the money earmarked for development would be used to "grease" local officials. In later years, this connection between U.S. corporate interests and corrupt local politicians would help to create the moral rot that would inspire a revolution.

The manner in which the pleasure trust would operate was made abundantly clear in January 1927, when popular New York mayor Jimmy Walker steamed into Havana's harbor to great fanfare. Among other things, the charismatic Walker was known for his tolerant relationship with the underworld. The mayor was first-generation Irish-American, a product of Tammany Hall, the vaunted political organization that was deeply intertwined with bootleggers and racketeers. Philosophically, the Mob was a product of this political-criminal axis, in which gangsters worked hand-in-hand with government officials, business interests, and law enforcement to stroke the underbelly of American capitalism.

In Havana, Walker was feted at a gala that included bank presidents, real estate developers, the president of the Cuban tourist commission, the city's mayor, and the chief of police. Beau James, as Walker was known to his admirers, attended Oriental Park Racetrack and later dined at the Jockey Club. At a ceremony the following day, he was awarded a key to the city of Havana.

Walker's appearance in Cuba was more than just ceremonial. It was intended as a symbol that business in Havana would be run on a par with business in New York City, where elaborate speakeasies, illegal gambling parlors, and swanky cabarets were the engine behind a prosperous nightlife, where the city's high society and mobster elite intermingled to create a glamorous facade.

Meyer Lansky was the first New York mobster to see the island's full potential. Sometime in 1928, he mentioned to his partner the idea of establishing Havana as more than just a transshipment point for booze. The plan was not yet fully formulated, but gambling, of course, would be part of it. A number of casinos and hotels could be financed, built, and operated by the Mob. And nightclubs and restaurants. And banks and financial institutions, which were great for laundering gambling proceeds. With a friendly government in Cuba, there was no telling what the Mob could accomplish. Perhaps they could one day establish the island as their own private fiefdom, a country into which they could funnel illegal proceeds from criminal rackets around the world, and no one could touch them.

Luciano liked the idea, but he and Lansky had a problem. The New York underworld—and by extension the underworld in most big cities in the United States—was still under the sway of the "Mustache Petes," the old-style mafiosi with roots in the Old Country. The two main Mafia bosses in New York—Salvatore Maranzano and Giuseppe "Joe the Boss" Masseria—were old-school Sicilians. They didn't like doing business with Irish-Americans and Jews, much less investing in operations based in a Spanish-speaking foreign country. There was no way a couple of young upstarts like Luciano and Lansky could go against the *unione siciliano*, or branch off on their own, without serious repercussions.

There was only one answer: the old-timers would have to be removed from the scene.

From 1928 to 1931, Luciano, Lansky, and a multiethnic amalgam of young bootleggers served as provocateurs in a bloody Mob war dubbed the Castellammarese War, after the town of Castellammare del Golfo where Maranzano and so many other mafiosi had been born. One near victim of the war was Luciano himself. On the night of October 17, 1929, he was "taken for a ride" by loyalists of Maranzano. In a warehouse on Staten Island, he was strung up, tortured, and gashed across his right cheek. Luciano was released, but the cut on his face left a nasty scar and resulted in muscle damage that caused a permanent droop to his right eye. It also provided him with a spiffy moniker. When Meyer Lansky came to visit him during his convalescence, Luciano told his friend the story of his abduction and torture, adding, "I guess I'm lucky to be alive."

"Yeah," replied Lansky. "That's you—Lucky Luciano." The name stuck.

By early 1932, the city's two old-time Mafia bosses had both been murdered in gangland hits engineered by Luciano and Lansky: Masseria was gunned down while eating pasta at a restaurant in Coney Island, having been lured there by Lucky. Maranzano was stabbed and shot to death in his Manhattan office by four Jewish gangsters disguised as New York City policemen. Beyond the Big Apple, a similar purging had taken place, a violent changing of the guard that would go down in history as the Night of the Sicilian Vespers. Across the land, old-style Sicilian mafiosi were replaced by a younger generation of mostly Italian-American, Jewish, and a few Irish-American mobsters. A new kind of Mob was born, based more on the philosophy of robber barons like Cornelius Vanderbilt, J. P. Morgan, Henry Ford, and the Rockefellers than on rural Mafia societies back in Sicily. Luciano, Lansky, and a few others in New York were seen as the masterminds of this dramatic new direction and were therefore established as prominent members of the Commission, a governing body composed of like-minded Mob leaders from Chicago, Cleveland, Kansas City, Philadelphia, Boston, New Orleans, and just about anywhere else where the American underworld enforced its will.

In the spring of 1933, Lansky came to Luciano with an astounding proposition. He was interested in approaching a possible contact in the Cuban government. He wanted to "buy in" with the Cubans so that the Mob could begin to develop its own gambling infrastructure on the island. The person Lansky had set his sights on was a young military man on the rise in Cuba named Fulgencio Batista.

It is not known if Lansky had actually met Batista at this point or merely designated him as a likely entry point into the volatile, complex world of Cuban politics. Either way, Luciano liked what he heard. The proposition made sense. With Prohibition coming to an end through government repeal, the Mob was looking to diversify and Cuba seemed like a smart move.

The Italian Mob boss convened a meeting of mafiosi at his plush suite at the Waldorf Towers, in the Waldorf-Astoria Hotel on Park Avenue in midtown Manhattan. To a handful of carefully selected regional Mob bosses from around the United States, Luciano explained, "We gotta expand someplace and we need a place to send our dough where it'll keep making money and also get those guys from Washington off our backs. Meyer's been down to Havana and he's made some good contacts. Within a couple months, by August or September, he's goin' back again and he'll probably make a deal. It could cost us a bundle up front, so everybody better get ready to put in at least half a million each."

Years later, Luciano recalled the reaction to this financial overture on his part:

It was like droppin' a bomb. Five hundred thousand bucks as an ante for a kitty in 1933 wasn't peanuts. Chuck Polizzi from Cleveland started screamin' and that kinda made me laugh. I told him that we was makin' so much money out of his place in Covington [a Mob-owned gambling casino in Kentucky] that plenty of guys were gettin' rich off it, so how could he complain about takin' a piece of income that taxes could never grab, to make even more. I laid it on him pretty damn hard and from then on there was no complaints.

Lansky took over from there. Over the next few weeks, the cash was gathered and placed in suitcases. Lansky made arrangements to fly to Havana with an associate, Joseph "Doc" Stacher, a fellow Jew whom he'd known since the early days on the Lower East Side. Stacher was a street-savvy, cigar-chomping loyalist who had been a close confidant of Lansky's and a trusted gofer, or errand boy, ever since Meyer first ran crap games on Delancey Street. According to Stacher:

Lansky and I flew to Havana with the money in suitcases and spoke to Batista, who hadn't quite believed we could raise that kind of money . . . Lansky took Batista straight back to our hotel, opened the suitcases and pointed at the cash. Batista just stared at the money without saying a word. Then he and Meyer shook hands and Batista left. We had several meetings with him over the next week and I saw that Meyer and Batista understood each other very well. We gave Batista a guarantee of between $3 and $5 million a year, as long as we had a monopoly on the casinos at the Hotel Nacional and everywhere else on the island where we thought tourists would come. On top of that he was promised a cut of our profits.

The Havana operation was now in place, though the timing could not have been worse. By the early 1930s, the effects of the Great Depression had set in and Cuba's tourism industry was hit hard. The number of visitors going to the island dropped precipitously. During the peak tourism years of 1928–29, foreigners visiting Cuba spent almost twenty-six million dollars. By 1933–34, revenues from tourism had slipped under five million. But more than that, political turmoil was sweeping across the island. Cuba's brutal strongman dictator, Gerardo Machado—who had ruled the country for eleven years—fled into exile. Violent reprisals against the remaining *Machadistas* gripped the country. People were kidnapped, tortured, and burned to death in town squares. Bodies were hung from lampposts and dumped on the side of the road. As had sometimes been the case in the past, the island became a tropical netherworld of revenge killings and political repression—not exactly the ideal climate for capitalist expansion.

As if all this weren't bad enough, the Mob had an even more pressing problem on its home turf. In New York City, an ambitious, aggressive district attorney named Thomas Dewey had designated organized crime as America's number one social ill. Using methods that had succeeded in bringing down Al Capone in Chicago, Dewey nailed a number of Mob bosses on federal income tax charges. In 1935 Dewey became special prosecutor for the state of New York; it was then that he went after Luciano, indicting him not on a tax charge but on ninety counts of compulsory prostitution.

Luciano made money from a wide assortment of rackets, some of which he ran directly and some from which he merely collected tribute for allowing others to operate. Few people beyond Tom Dewey and others in his office felt that Luciano was directly involved in prostitution. It didn't really matter. In the years since he had removed the old-time Mustache Petes, Luciano had become a celebrity in the press. He wore expensive suits, hung out on Broadway, and basically rubbed his notoriety in the noses of God-fearing, law-abiding citizens everywhere. He was a mobster boss, and everyone knew it. All Dewey had to do was show that organized prostitution in New York did, in fact, exist and then tie Luciano to it in some cursory way and he would have a guilty verdict.

The trial was a circus, with some sixty prostitutes and madams taking the stand. Luciano smirked and chatted with reporters through much of the trial. When he took the stand to testify in his own defense, Lucky came off as crude, with a surly disregard for the truth. He was shocked when the verdict of guilty on all counts was announced, and even more shocked when, on June 7, 1936, the judge socked him with a sentence of thirty to fifty years, the longest sentence ever given in the United States for compulsory prostitution.

Forever after, Luciano maintained that he was framed on a cooked-up charge. Many observers who knew him—even those who would willingly concede that he was a professional racketeer with vast criminal holdings—swore he was not guilty on the charges for which he was convicted.

Meyer Lansky stayed away from his friend's trial. The Little Man abhorred publicity. He and Luciano shared an attorney, Moses Polakoff. Through Polakoff, Lansky passed the word to his friend that, from this day forward, he would do everything in his power to get the sentence reduced or the conviction overturned. But Lansky was a professional gambling man; he knew the odds. Getting Luciano's conviction overturned was the proverbial million-to-one shot.

Luciano was an essential cog in the machine. With Lucky away in jail, Lansky's dreams of an empire in Havana appeared to be little more than a passing flirtation.

FOR THE AMERICAN UNDERWORLD—and, in particular, members of the New York Syndicate—the incarceration of Charlie Luciano was an inconvenience but not a decisive blow. For the most part, business continued as usual. Even though he was in prison, Lucky was still considered a high-ranking decision-maker and he still received his cut of various rackets. No one was supposed to slack off just because one of the bosses was "away at college." The person who stepped into Luciano's role as chairman of the board was Francesco Castiglia, alias Frank Costello, a close boyhood friend of both Luciano and Lansky. It was Costello's job to oversee the day-to-day operations of the Syndicate and to serve as Luciano's eyes and ears on the multicity governing body known as the Commission.

In the wake of major Mob prosecutions that had culminated in the stunning conviction of his longtime associate and pal, Meyer Lansky became scarce in and around New York City. He moved upstate and opened a lavish casino in Saratoga Springs, a horse-racing town with a long underworld history. He opened the Colonial Inn and other carpet joints in South Florida. As a partner with Costello, he made a small fortune by monopolizing the jukebox business, especially in the state of Louisiana. At the same time, he partnered with a group of mostly Jewish mobsters from Cleveland known as the Mayfield Road Gang. Together with this group and with his old friend Doc Stacher, Lansky established the Molaska Corporation, a company that ostensibly manufactured powdered molasses for distilling rum. Proving that old habits die hard, the company distilled its own booze to be sold—cheap and untaxed—to Lansky's old bootlegging outlets around the United States.

Lansky had a lot on his plate. Still, Cuba beckoned. As he said years later, "I couldn't get that little island out of my mind."

Sometime in the mid-1930s, Meyer cofounded a new corporation called Cuba National, which extended his partial ownership of the Hotel Nacional in Havana. Lansky, Frank Costello, and a notorious New Jersey Mob boss named Abner "Longy" Zwillman were on the company's board. Soon after being formed, Cuba National merged with the National Cuba Hotel Corporation, a larger company that would eventually become part of the Hilton Hotel chain. Lansky's new version of Cuba National was based in Miami, with offices on Flagler Street.

By establishing a business affiliation with Hilton Hotels, Lansky was paving the way for future developments in Cuba. It was the type of long-range thinking for which he would eventually become famous.

In late 1937, during a break in the racing season at Saratoga, Lansky was summoned to the Caribbean by Batista. The man he had singled out as his best bet in Cuba was now firmly in power as head of the Cuban military. Various puppet presidents came and went. With the tourist business on the island in remission during the years of the Depression, both the Gran Casino Nacional and Oriental Park Racetrack had fallen into disrepair. An old gambling contact of Lansky's named Lou Smith had been contracted to clean up and operate the racing at Oriental Park. At Colonel Batista's behest, Smith bequeathed the job of managing the track's two casinos to his friend and benefactor Meyer Lansky.

Lansky had by now become something of an expert on the running of casino operations. He had established a large network of gambling employees—dealers, croupiers, pit bosses, and floor managers—whom he could trust. He imported some of these people to Havana for the tourist season of 1938–39 and again in 1939–40.

Lansky also instituted some reforms and innovations. In 1939, to mark the opening of the renovated racetrack casino, he came up with the idea of presenting gamblers with a "Golden Ticket" to be handed out at a ceremony. Welcomed at a special reception was Colonel Batista, who was bestowed with his own complimentary key to the casino.

For the first time, Lansky stayed and got to know Cuba a bit. He brought his wife, Anne, and two young sons on one trip. He appreciated the country's old-world Spanish formality and languid atmosphere, but what he was most impressed by was the degree to which Cuba was ripe for development and open to political corruption. The entire island was there for the taking.

It must have been frustrating: although Lansky was now a gambling operator in Havana, it was not at the level he had once anticipated. He would have liked to initiate the visionary plan that he and Luciano originally discussed, but he was in a tight spot. As a Jew operating within a criminal universe that was highly Mafia-centric, he could not undertake such a grandiose scheme on his own. It required the financial backing and approval of the Commission. Given Lansky's attachments to the Mob, if he had tried to make an independent move there would most certainly have been violent consequences. Many people would have been shot, stabbed, or clubbed to death. Bodies would have been found in car trunks, sealed in 10-gallon drums, or rolled up in carpets and dumped along the New Jersey Turnpike. Lansky didn't like violence; in fact, his entire reputation was built on his ability to avoid unnecessary gangland upheavals. Lansky was known to organize and negotiate in such a way that everyone felt they were getting their fair piece of the pie.

His biggest single impediment was having Luciano locked away in upstate New York. Even if Lansky were to get the approval of the Commission, he could not go forward without his friend: the whole idea for the Cuba operation had been hatched by Lansky and Luciano together. And Charlie would never have allowed the plan to go forward without him. He had given in to an affliction common to many incarcerated mobsters: he believed he could somehow manipulate the system and get himself released.

Lansky thought Charlie was delusional. For a time, he had aided an effort to gather evidence that might get Luciano's conviction overturned, but it had gone nowhere. Privately, Lansky had given up hope and come to believe that Lucky was doomed.

And then the unthinkable occurred.

In April 1942, Lansky was approached by his and Luciano's attorney, Moses Polakoff, who had himself been approached with a startling proposition.

Apparently, with the United States now deeply embroiled in the war in Europe, U.S. naval intelligence had become unnerved at the number of U.S. and British ships being sunk by German U-boats. In the month of March alone, fifty ships had been incapacitated. Not only that, but sabotage in the Port of New York had reached crippling proportions. It seemed as though New York's waterfront was riddled with German, and possibly Italian, spies who were tipping off the enemy as to the whereabouts and capabilities of Allied naval forces.

This possibility had been underscored in dramatic fashion that February when the ocean liner *Normandie* went down in flames while moored on the West Side of Manhattan. The *Normandie* was in the process of being converted into a gigantic troop carrier, renamed the *Lafayette*. Its high speed would have made it a difficult target for the German submarines that were patrolling the Atlantic, sinking literally hundreds of Allied vessels.

Multiple fires burned all over the *Normandie*. It seemed as though arson had been committed in several parts of the ship. Despite the efforts of local firefighters to put out the flames, the huge ocean liner eventually rolled over on its side and lay in the water like a beached whale.

Whether or not the destruction of the *Normandie* was in fact an act of sabotage was never established; either way, it was a tremendous psychological victory for the Axis powers. The Nazis were already winning the war in the open seas; now, they seemed to have found a way to penetrate the New York waterfront and wreak havoc at will.

To counteract this assault, U.S. naval intelligence had come up with a novel strategy. Since it was commonly believed that the forces of organized crime controlled much of the commercial activity in the Port of New York, why not enlist the Mob as their eyes and ears on the waterfront?

Joseph "Socks" Lanza, a barely educated hood who was considered the Mob's main man at the Fulton Fish Market—the epicenter of the Port of New York—was astounded when he was contacted by the U.S. Navy. He was asked, point-blank, "As an American patriot, would you and your friends be willing to aid your country in its time of need and help us root out spies and saboteurs on the waterfront?"

Lanza answered that he did not have the authority to make such a decision on behalf of his "friends." The only man who could give that kind of order to the Mob's rank and file and have it followed was Lucky Luciano.

The navy then approached Moses Polakoff. Same question: would your client be willing to aid his country in its time of need? Polakoff sensed that Luciano would indeed be interested in mulling over the proposition, but he believed the overture would have to be made by someone within his tight circle of friends and associates. Polakoff recommended Meyer Lansky.

A meeting took place at Longchamps Restaurant, on West 58th Street in midtown Manhattan. The participants were New York assistant district attorney Murray Gurfein, who was head of the Rackets Bureau, Moses Polakoff, and Meyer Lansky. After explaining the situation to Lansky, as it had been explained to him by naval intelligence, the assistant D.A. asked the Mob boss, "Can Luciano be trusted?"

"Sure, he can," said Lansky. "I'll guarantee it."

Later that afternoon, in room 196 at the Astor Hotel in Manhattan, Lansky met Lt. Cdr. Charles Radcliffe Haffenden, head of the B-3 (investigative) section of the Third Naval District's intelligence staff. On a desk in front of Haffenden was a dossier on Meyer Lansky that read in part:

[Lansky] was a major figure in bootlegging operations and is concerned today with the manufacture, sale, distribution and the gathering of money from jukeboxes. He is a personal friend of every major Mafia leader and man of crime in America. He is deeply involved in illegal gambling.

Haffenden reiterated the navy's position to Lansky, who remembered:

He had obviously been well briefed on my background. I could see the dossier on his desk. He was very careful and polite with me. He said he knew I had a reputation as a gangster but he also knew I was strongly against the Nazis. He appealed to me to be a good American and to think of the Jews suffering in Europe.

Lansky did not hesitate. He shook the commander's hand and said, "You can count on me, and I believe Charlie Luciano will go along with the plan." Lansky suggested that in order to facilitate making the pitch to Luciano, the Mob boss should be moved from Dannemora Prison in the far northern reaches of New York State to Comstock, which was near Albany.

"I'll take care of it," said Haffenden.

One month later, Lansky and Polakoff were on a train to Albany, where they were met by a driver who took them the rest of the way to Comstock.

Charlie Luciano, meanwhile, had no idea what was happening. He had been moved from Dannemora to Comstock, he was told, for "administrative reasons." Late one morning in May, he was taken by the warden to a special interrogation room and instructed to wait for some visitors.

In the six years Luciano had spent in jail by this stage, he had had a few visits from his brother and sister, but he had not set eyes on his friend Lansky since his last days of freedom in New York City.

"When he saw us he could hardly believe his eyes," recalled Lansky. "He stretched out his arms and shouted, 'What are you doing here?' Charlie threw his arms around me and kissed me. He'd never done that before, but he was pretty carried away."

And so began one of the most unorthodox alliances in the history of the American underworld. In a series of meetings between the Mob and the military, Luciano pledged his full cooperation with the U.S. war effort. He ordered that the word go out along the waterfront for everyone to clamp down on "suspicious activity." The results were immediate. On June 27, 1942, the Federal Bureau of Investigations (FBI) announced that eight German secret agents had been arrested in New York and Chicago. They had landed by U-boat in Florida and Long Island and brought ashore explosives and more than $170,000 in cash, together with maps and plans for a two-year-long campaign of attacks on defense plants, railroads, waterworks, and bridges. The FBI took the credit, but a crucial role in tracking down the Long Island saboteurs had been played by Commander Haffenden's B-3 agents, using fishing fleet contacts supplied by Socks Lanza, Luciano, and Lansky.

There were similar arrests in the months that followed, and attacks on Allied ships at sea nearly came to a standstill. Later in the war, Luciano, at the behest of the navy, also supplied the U.S. Army with important logistical information in support of the July 1943 Allied invasion of Sicily. The go-between for Luciano and the military was always Lansky, who was even assigned his own code number as a naval intelligence contact. The entire project was given a code name: Operation Underworld.

In all the time of Luciano's top secret cooperation with military intelligence, there had never been a quid pro quo arrangement that the Mob boss would be released early from prison. The way the deal had been suggested to the lawyer, Polakoff, was that Luciano's cooperation would be made known to the powers that be when the time was right—presumably when the war was over. Which is why on VE Day, May 8, 1945, Moses Polakoff swore out a petition for a grant of executive clemency on behalf of his client, Charles Luciano.

Right away, there was a problem with the navy, which had decided that Operation Underworld was a subject not suitable for public consumption. A cover-up went into effect. It would be seven months before Polakoff was able to secure the necessary affidavits and present them to Governor Dewey.

By then Dewey still didn't have all the details, but he had enough to declare in a public statement: "Upon entry of the United States into the war, Luciano's aid was sought by the Armed Services in inducing others to provide information concerning possible enemy attack. It appears that he cooperated in such effort, although the actual value of the information procured is not clear."

On January 4, 1946, inmate number 15684 at Comstock Prison was told that his old nemesis, Tom Dewey, had granted him "special commutation of sentence." Luciano's euphoria was short-lived, however.

Within days, he also discovered that, as a condition of his commutation, he was being deported from the United States to Italy.

Meyer Lansky did not attend the famous going-away party that was held for Luciano aboard the SS *Laura Keene* and attended by, among others, Senator Eduardo Suarez Rivas of Cuba. Lansky knew there would most likely be reporters there. In all his years in the Mob, his picture had never once appeared in the papers, and his name was rarely mentioned along with those of better-known Mob bosses like Luciano, Capone, and Costello. That was just the way Lansky liked it.

Besides, he'd had his chance to say bon voyage to Lucky days earlier. At an Immigration and Naturalization Service (INS) facility on Ellis Island, where Luciano was being held before his deportation, Lansky brought cash and some personal belongings to his friend. Despite the fact that Luciano would be seeing freedom for the first time in nine years, he was in a sour mood. Given his contribution to the U.S. war effort, he felt it was an injustice that he was being deported as a common "undesirable."

It was then that Lansky soothed the savage beast by uttering the magic word.

Cuba.

THE FIRST TO ARRIVE for the December 1946 Mob conference in Havana was Vito Genovese. It was days before the gathering was officially scheduled to begin. Genovese had delivered a message to Luciano that he would be arriving early because he wanted to have a few days to lie around on the beach. Luciano didn't believe that for a second. At forty-nine years of age, Genovese was squat and leathery, a creature of the night. In the sunlight, he would wither and die like a vampire.

Genovese was a mobster from the old school who had known Charlie Lucky since before the Castellammarese War of the late 1920s. In the Mafia, there were many roles to be played: there were the tacticians, the moneymakers, and the killers. Genovese was a killer. Not a thuggish, mindless killer, but a cunning, tactical killer. Some murders he ordered his underlings to carry out. Others he preferred to do himself. His method was the shotgun, up close and personal; preferably a gory head shot.

Over the years, Genovese had undertaken murders on behalf of Luciano, particularly during the Castellammarese War. But this did not result in a special bond between the two men. On the contrary, Luciano never liked "Don Vitone," as he sometimes called Genovese when he wanted to make fun of him. Luciano believed that Genovese had designs on being *capo di tutti capi*. The position of boss of all bosses was something that Luciano, Lansky, and others on the Commission had done away with when the Mustache Petes were eliminated and the Syndicate was born. At the last major Mob conference, which took place at the Statler Hotel in downtown Chicago in 1932, Al Capone suggested that Luciano himself accept the top position. But Lucky turned it down flat. "None of that old-world Sicilian shit," he told Capone and the other two dozen Mob bosses gathered together at the time. "This is America. All of us bosses will be equal in stature, just like a corporation."

Upon his arrival in Havana, Genovese was set up in a penthouse suite at the Hotel Nacional, where the nearly two dozen men arriving for the conference would stay and the meetings would he held. The agreement was that there would be no private conferences. Everyone would meet together. The top item on the agenda was to be the Mob's plans for Cuba and Luciano's status now that he was out of prison, just ninety miles off the coast of the United States. Other items of interest to individual members could be discussed, but openly, with everyone in attendance.

Genovese had other plans. As Luciano remembered it:

It was a couple days before I was expectin' anybody, around the 20th of December, when Vito called me at my house. It was a private number and he got it from Lansky. Tells me he come down a little beforehand to get a couple days' rest on the beach. Now, I knew that little prick well enough to know he didn't come to Havana to get a suntan. That wasn't the way he operated. I knew he had somethin' in mind . . . so I told him to come over to my house for lunch.

At Luciano's mansion in Miramar, Genovese got right to the point: "Let me tell you what I think, Charlie. I think you oughta quit—I mean, retire. It's a good proposition. You'll have all the dough you can ever need. I give you my personal word on that. You won't have to worry about what's goin' on. You won't have to think up ideas on how to get back to New York—which is gonna be tough. And you'll still be the boss, the *capo di capi re*. Everybody'll think of you as the guy who put it all together back in the old days, and they'll still come to you when they need advice. It's like you'll be the head, but I'll be runnin' things on the spot. That's all there is to it."

Luciano wanted to take Vito's head off right there:

That guinea son of a bitch! I always knew he was a gutsy bastard, so I should've known that he'd have the nerve to stand up to me, to my face—just as long as no one else was around. All he really wanted was to take over and cut me out. His whole life he wanted to be boss . . . I looked at Vito very calm, like talking to a schoolboy, and I said, "You forget what happened in Chicago when I set this thing up. There is no Boss of Bosses. I turned it down in front of everybody. If I ever change my mind, then I will take the title. But it won't be up to you. Right now you work for me, and I ain't in the mood to retire. Don't you ever let me hear this again, or I'll lose my temper."

The next day, when Luciano told his pal Lansky about the meeting at his home with Vito Genovese, he did so in a jocular manner. But Lansky didn't see the humor in it. The thing Lansky was most concerned about was his baby—Cuba—and how to put into action the plan he'd had for years on how to develop and exploit the island. Here they were, days before the landmark conference at the Hotel Nacional, and already people were descending to the level of personal agendas and subterfuge.

This was not what the Little Man had in mind.

2

THE MOB'S PLAYGROUND

IN DIRECTOR FRANCIS FORD COPPOLA'S CINEMATIC CLASSIC
The Godfather Part II, the Mob conference in Havana is portrayed as a
kind of weekend sabbatical for the gangster elite. On a rooftop somewhere in the city (with Santo Domingo standing in for Havana), a cake
is presented to the gathered mafiosi. Atop the cake's frosting is a fac-
simile of Cuba drawn with sugary icing. The cake is cut into pieces and
distributed to the gathered guests. The image constitutes a forceful and
accurate metaphor—a valid representation of the thinking behind the
conference—with the mobsters literally carving up the island and dividing the spoils among themselves.

Meyer Lansky is loosely depicted in the movie as Hyman Roth. Unlike the real-life Lansky, who was forty-four years old and in his prime at
the time of the Havana conference, Roth is a man well into his seven-
ties, bothered by an assortment of medical ailments. Lee Strasberg, the
famous New York acting teacher cast as Roth, portrays the man as a
kind of Lion in Winter, a fatalist whose only regret is that he won't live
long enough to see the full fruition of his dream of a mobster's paradise
in Cuba.

At the rooftop gathering, the movie's protagonist, Michael Corleone, relates an incident he saw earlier that day. On a Havana street, a political revolutionary was being detained by the military police. Rather than be taken in, the revolutionary detonates a bomb, taking his own life and the life of a military captain.

"It occurred to me," says Michael Corleone, "that the soldiers are paid to fight. The rebels aren't."

"What does that tell you?" asks Roth.

"They can win," answers the Don.

The exchange suggests a remarkable prescience on the part of the Godfather. The rooftop conference and other events in the movie are presented as having taken place on the eve of New Year's Day 1959, when the government of Fulgencio Batista was to fall dramatically to rebel forces. In real life, the mobster conference of December 1946 took place while Batista was out of power, and many years before the revolutionary movement in Cuba began to coalesce around the then largely unknown figure of Fidel Castro.

The Godfather Part II is more faithful to historical reality than many Hollywood movies, but it is still a work of fiction. The degree to which the movie has become a cultural touchstone on the subject of the Mob in Cuba, creating the visual representation and mythology that exist in the imagination of many Americans, is an example of how the story has been relegated to the level of folklore rather than preserved as fact.

In reality, the biggest gathering of American mobsters in fourteen years almost didn't get off the ground. Luciano and Lansky had the power to summon two dozen high-ranking mobsters, but they had no control over the Cuban hotel workers' union, the Sindicato Gastronómico. Three weeks before the conference was scheduled to begin, 480 employees of the Hotel Nacional went on strike. Almost immediately, the bars and salons, the kitchen, and the garage and terrace were left unattended. The hotel's restaurant and café were only partly serviced. There was no one to clean the tables, serve drinks, or bring customers the world-famous Havana cigars. For the group of American mobsters who were scheduled to arrive at the hotel for an extended stay over the Christmas holiday, it was a potential disaster.

The union demanded a pay increase of 30 percent. The hotel management offered 25. Normally, labor negotiations in Cuba were handled through the courts. But on this occasion there was a high level of concern from above. President Ramón Grau San Martín and his prime minister, Carlos Prío Socarrás, took a special interest. They summoned the hotel management and strike representatives to the presidential palace and demanded a settlement. Eventually, the union got their 30 percent. Apparently there was intense political pressure to end the strike so that the upcoming gathering of American "dignitaries" could take place without a hitch.

From December 22 through December 26, the top two floors of the Hotel Nacional were closed to the public. Access to the grounds was guarded by a private security force. The hotel closed its doors to all outside interests other than those directly affiliated with the American mobsters. Nobody was allowed to enter the premises—not journalists, not the police, not bureaucrats of the Cuban government.

The gangsters came from far and wide, from Buffalo, New York City, Chicago, Cleveland, New Jersey, Louisiana, and Florida. Most, like Vito Genovese, were high-ranking members of the tribe. Albert Anastasia, who would later be dubbed by the New York press "Lord High Executioner of the Mob," was in attendance, as was Moe Dalitz, a Jewish mobster who had partnered with Lansky in the Molaska Corporation. Frank Costello, Luciano's stand-in as titular boss of the Syndicate while Lucky was away in prison and exile, was in attendance, as was Doc Stacher, Lansky's buddy who had helped deliver a secret cash bribe to Cuba's military leader Batista more than ten years earlier. Representing the city of New Orleans was Carlos Marcello, of Sicilian heritage. From Tampa, Florida, came Santo Trafficante, who at thirty-three years of age was the youngest mafioso at the gathering (see Appendix).

The first thing the "delegates" did was visit Luciano's mansion in Miramar to pay homage and deliver envelopes filled with cash. The money was an idea of Lansky's, who felt Luciano deserved the "tribute." That night $150,000 in cash was delivered to Luciano, who later gave the money to Lansky as an investment in the casino at the Hotel Nacional.

The first night, the group eschewed business and met at a special banquet room on the lower level of the hotel. A gourmet feast was prepared, made up mostly of local dishes. There were crab and queen conch enchiladas brought from the southern archipelago. For the main course, there was a choice of roast breast of flamingo, tortoise stew, roast tortoise with lemon and garlic, and crayfish, oysters, and grilled swordfish from the nearby fishing village of Cojímar. There was also grilled venison sent by a government minister from Camagüey who owned livestock and, the most obscure delicacy of all, grilled manatee. The guests drank *añejo* rum and smoked Montecristo cigars.

Later, the visiting delegates were encouraged to make the most of their inaugural night in Havana. A fleet of fifty cars with chauffeurs was at the ready. Dancers and showgirls from the city's three main nightclubs—the Tropicana, the Montmartre, and the Sans Souci—were selected and paid for their services, as were prostitutes from Casa Marina, the classiest and most renowned bordello in the city. A series of parties were held on the hotel's upper floors, and the more intrepid of the visitors ventured out to get a taste of Havana's vibrant postwar nightlife.

The following day, the first of three formal meetings took place on a top floor at the Hotel Nacional. Everyone was in attendance. Although Luciano was the guest of honor, it was Meyer Lansky who presented the Mob's plans for Cuba. According to Doc Stacher, "[Lansky] was handling most of [the mobsters'] finances and was the key figure in their gambling income. Meyer kept in the background as always, but nobody at that meeting was in the faintest doubt who held the whip hand."

Among the proposals Lansky presented that day was his idea to turn the entire Caribbean into the center of the greatest gambling operation the world had ever seen. For starters, land would be bought on the Isle of Pines, a small Cuban island near the western province of Pinar del Rio

that was presently serving as a penal colony. It was Lansky's plan to con-
vert the island into a kind of international Monte Carlo, with huge resort
hotel-casinos and its own private airport. It was a bigger scheme than Las
Vegas, bigger than anything the Syndicate had ever tackled before.

Most of the men at the conference considered themselves shrewd
businessmen, though few had more than an eighth-grade education.
With an underworld business, no one needed to see fancy flow charts or
hear complicated economic theories. All anyone needed to know was
whether or not the right people were in their pocket and, if not, who
needed to be bought off, intimidated, or killed. Everyone in the room
knew that Lansky had been cultivating Cuba as a source of plunder for
more than a decade. They were all in agreement that the island would
make a wonderful home away from home.

Given Luciano's long absence from the ruling Commission and the
vacuum it had created, there were other topics to discuss. The subject of
narcotics dominated the conference. Profits from heroin, cocaine, and
marijuana trafficking had the potential to be the biggest moneymaker
since bootleg booze, but the downside was substantial. There was an
entire division of the U.S. Justice Department devoted solely to combat-
ing drug trafficking: the Federal Bureau of Narcotics (FBN). Luciano, in
particular, was concerned that the head of the Narcotics Bureau, Harry
J. Anslinger, had for years been trying to pin a major narcotics charge on
him. By getting involved in dope, they would be giving "Asslinger"—as
Lucky always derisively called him—the ammunition. As the Mob boss
later recalled:

I must have talked for an hour, maybe more . . . I told 'em it had become clear to me that there was so much dough to be made in every-
thin' else we had, why ruin it with the dangers of playin' around with
junk that would only bring the federal guys down on us . . . I tried to
make 'em understand that everything was different now that the war
was over; we was businessmen runnin' businesses and givin' people
what they wanted in a way that didn't hurt nobody . . . Sure, here and

there we would squeeze some guys, but on the other hand, look at all the money we was puttin' in circulation just from other good businessmen buyin' our protection. I said there wasn't a politician or a cop who could hold on to none of the money we paid him off with, that they spent it as soon as they got it and that was very good for the American economy—to put money in circulation.

Putting money into circulation was a tactic any businessman could understand, and to most of the gangsters in attendance, there was no better way to circulate cash than through the burgeoning narcotics business. By and large, Luciano's protestations fell on deaf ears. Vito Genovese and others were making more on dope than on any other racket, and they felt Luciano's position was based more on his own personal problems with Harry Anslinger and the Narcotics Bureau than it was on sound business sense. Even Frank Costello, Lucky's lifelong crime partner and friend, cautioned him to back off.

"Charlie, don't hit your head against the wall," said Costello. "Go with the flow."

Luciano let it go, with one proviso. "For chrissake keep me out of it," he told the others, "or I'm gonna have to take out an ad in the *New York Mirror* and declare my position." That got a laugh from everyone in the room.

Another major item on the agenda had to do with Benjamin "Bugsy" Siegel.

In the entire history of the American underworld, there was no more significant mutual admiration society than the one between Ben Siegel, Luciano, Lansky, and Costello. These four men had come together as teenagers and begun a lifelong criminal partnership that changed the face of crime in the United States. Initially, Siegel and Lansky headed up a mixed Italian and Jewish gang of hooligans known to New York cops as "the Bugs and Meyer Gang." Later, when Luciano and Costello joined the group, they were among the founding fathers of the country's bootleg booze empire and the sundry other rackets that followed.

Siegel was always the wild card in the group. Devilishly handsome even at a young age, he was a ladykiller metaphorically, and a killer of men in a more literal sense. He was believed to have been one of the gunmen who murdered Joe "the Boss" Masseria in a Coney Island restaurant back in 1931. He had been charged and convicted of many crimes, including rape, hijacking, burglary, bookmaking, robbery, extortion, and numerous homicides. It was Siegel's overactive criminal habits that led Luciano, Lansky, and others in their gang to feel that he might be better off starting with a clean slate in another jurisdiction.

So in the early 1930s, Siegel was sent to Los Angeles to sniff out possible criminal rackets related to the movie business. It wasn't long before he fell in with the Hollywood crowd and befriended many famous actors, including Jean Harlow, Clark Gable, Gary Cooper, and Cary Grant.

In the early 1940s, Lansky had visited his boyhood pal in Los Angeles and pitched one of his grandiose schemes. Together, they flew to a dusty, nondescript Nevada town known as Las Vegas, rented a car, and drove through the desert. It was a hot, isolated location with little to offer, except for one thing—gambling was legal in the state of Nevada. Lansky asked Siegel: "What if we built a luxury hotel-casino out here and started a local gambling boom?"

It took Ben a while to warm to the idea, but once he did he went at it with gusto. With investment capital supplied by Lansky and other leading mobsters, Siegel was given the go-ahead to build an elaborate hotel-casino that he would eventually call the Flamingo.

Almost from the beginning, the Flamingo was plagued by cost overruns, some caused by unforeseen natural events such as bad weather, others by Siegel's megalomania. One of the problems seemed to be that Bugsy's plans for the hotel had become entangled with his romance with Virginia Hill, a precocious failed actress who had been the mistress of many other mobsters before Siegel.

By the time of the Havana conference in late December of 1946, the Flamingo project, which had initially been budgeted at one million dollars, had ballooned to six million and was still unfinished. Siegel's

investors felt that he had become a man out of control. More omi-
nously, they felt that his mistress, Virginia Hill, might have led him
into the dark world of deception and betrayal. Just weeks before the
Havana conference, it was revealed that Hill had been traveling to Europe and depositing sizable funds in a Swiss bank account. Mobster Joe
Adonis, brothers Rocco and Charles Fischetti from Chicago, and others in attendance at the Havana conference knew Virginia Hill. She
had at various times been mistress to all of them and they knew
firsthand of her charms and deceptions. All evidence seemed to suggest
that Siegel had fallen under the sway of Hill and that together they
were skimming money from the Flamingo for their own personal gain.

In the many years since the Havana conference, it is still not clear who
gave the order to have Ben Siegel whacked. In his posthumous autobiography, *The Last Testament of Lucky Luciano*, Luciano is quoted as saying:

There was no doubt in Meyer's mind that Bugsy had skimmed the
dough from his buildin' budget and that he was sure that Siegel was
preparin' to skip as well as skim, in case the roof was gonna fall in on
him. Everybody listened very carefully while Meyer explained it.
When he got through, somebody asked, "What do you think we
oughta do, Meyer?" Lansky said, "There is only one thing to do with a
thief who steals from his friends. Benny's got to be hit."

So it was put to a vote . . . The result was unanimous, and Bugsy
was as good as dead.

To his dying day, Lansky was adamant that it was not he who gave
the order to have Ben Siegel murdered. On the contrary, he tried to save
his life. According to Doc Stacher, who was quoted at length on the
subject in *Meyer Lansky: Mogul of the Mob* by Dennis Eisenberg, Uri
Dan, and Eli Landau,

Meyer did all he could to save his friend. He begged the men to be
patient and let Bugsy open the hotel "and then we can settle matters

with him if we find out he's been cheating us" . . . It was the first time I ever heard Meyer become so emotional . . . Meyer couldn't deny that Siegel had betrayed the trust placed in him, but he pleaded with everybody there to remember the great services that Bugsy had performed for all of them. They looked at him stonyfaced without saying a word, and Meyer realized that Bugsy's fate was sealed.

According to Stacher, it was later decided that Lansky should be given an opportunity to "resolve the problems that Bugsy had created for them." Lansky left the Havana conference and made a quick visit to California to see Siegel. But when he came back, he told Stacher, "I can't do a thing with him. He's so much in that woman's power that he cannot see reason."

Six months later, on June 20, 1947, Ben Siegel died in a hail of bullets while sitting on a sofa in the living room of Virginia Hill's Beverly Hills home. The coup de grâce was a shot that hit Siegel in the face, blowing his left eyeball out of its socket. The eyeball was later found—intact—14 feet away from the body. The gunmen were never identified and the murder remains unsolved to this day.

Thirty years after the hit, Lansky weighed in on the subject when he wrote a terse note to a would-be biographer: "If it was in my power to see Benny alive, he would live as long as Matusula [sic]. This was a terrible shock to me."

Given that all the participants are gone, it will never be known for certain who initiated the idea or gave the order to have Siegel killed. But one fact is clear: the collective decision that sealed his fate took place at the Hotel Nacional amid the splendor and "camaraderie" of the Havana conference.

AFTER THE CONFERENCE was over, some of the mobsters stayed put in Cuba, while others went their separate ways. The man who made it all happen—Lansky—had some messy personal problems to deal with.

After darting off to consult with Siegel in California, he headed to Miami, where his wife had filed for divorce.

Anne Lansky had always had problems with Meyer's chosen line of work. The more time he spent with his notorious underworld associates, the more Anne withdrew from her husband and the world. She became clinically depressed and at one point even submitted herself to electroshock therapy. Lansky became increasingly frustrated with his wife's "weak mindedness." In a Miami Beach courtroom just five weeks after the Havana conference, Anne testified that Lansky's opinion of her had deteriorated over the eighteen years of their marriage:

ANNE LANSKY: He didn't approve of anything I did, whether right or wrong. It was always wrong—it couldn't be right.

JUDGE: How did he act when he found fault?

ANNE LANSKY: As nasty as he possibly could, whether anyone else was there or not—in front of my friends, or the maid, or the butler, anybody. Nothing I ever did was right.

Lansky did not contest the case. In fact, it was Meyer who hired Anne's lawyer, Bernard Frank, the same attorney who had accompanied him to Havana to purchase maracas for Carmen Miranda. On February 14, 1947—Saint Valentine's Day—the Lanskys were officially granted a divorce.

Meanwhile, back in Havana, Luciano was basking in the glow of the Mob conference, which he deemed a smash success. The weeks that followed were filled with parties, trips to the racetrack, the cultivation of local political officials, and a visit by an esteemed friend of the Mafia—none other than Francis Albert Sinatra, the most popular recording star in America.

From early in his life and career, Sinatra had developed a fascination with the mafiosi he met in New Jersey, where he was raised, and through his travels as a singer and budding movie star. The first mobster he befriended was Willie Moretti, who was also an attendee of the Havana conference. Moretti was the influential bookmaker, extortionist, and killer who first "discovered" the skinny kid from Hoboken when he was performing in local roadhouses and clubs. In 1939 bandleader Tommy Dorsey signed Sinatra for what must have seemed at the time like a king's ransom—$125 a week. Sinatra's popularity skyrocketed, thanks primarily to the young bobby-soxers who packed his shows and screamed with adoration. The problem was, no matter how many hit records Sinatra recorded, he was locked into his contract with Dorsey—until the bandleader suddenly and inexplicably allowed Frank out of the deal.

According to gangland legend, Willie Moretti had visited Dorsey's dressing room, stuck a gun into his mouth, and demanded the bandleader reconsider the terms of Sinatra's contract.

From then on, the singer and star was a Mafia sycophant. Sinatra's friend and fellow crooner Eddie Fisher once observed, "Frank wanted to be a hood. He once said, 'I'd rather be a don of the Mafia than President of the United States.' I don't think he was fooling."

On the morning of February 11, 1947, Sinatra landed at the airport in Havana accompanied by Rocco and Charles Fischetti, friends of his and also attendees of the Mob conference at the Hotel Nacional. Sinatra was carrying with him a suitcase stuffed with two million dollars, the equivalent of sixteen million today. He allegedly delivered the cash to Luciano, who had rented a suite on the eighth floor of the Hotel Nacional, one floor above Sinatra's room.

The singer's arrival in Havana was part business, part entertainment. On the business side, he had begun to establish a pattern of investing in Mob enterprises that would continue throughout his life. With the Fischetti brothers, he owned a percentage of a car dealership. He was also believed to be a silent partner in a casino-nightclub that Willie Moretti planned to open in the Palisades, New Jersey, and he was thinking of investing in the building of a hotel-casino in Las Vegas.

The partnership between Sinatra and the Mob was a two-way street. According to Luciano, he and other mafiosi had invested in Sinatra's career from the very beginning. "When the time come when some dough was needed to put Frank across with the public, [we] put it up," Luciano recalled. "He needed publicity, clothes, different kinds of special music things, and they all cost quite a bit of money—I think it was about fifty or sixty grand. I okayed the money and it came out of the fund, even though some guys put up a little extra on a personal basis."

Sinatra showed his gratitude by occasionally acting as a cash courier for the Mob. He also brought assorted trinkets—a gold cigarette case, a gold watch, and other items—that he presented as gifts to Luciano and other mobsters in Havana.

According to a former member of the Hotel Nacional staff, Jorge Jorge, Sinatra also performed exclusively for a gathering of mobsters in the hotel's banquet room. Jorge, who was assigned to serve Luciano and his friends because he spoke English, sometimes brought breakfast to a special suite that had been set aside for Sinatra. Jorge recalled that he and other busboys often delivered room service in the presence of Sinatra, Luciano, and Lansky, who shuttled back and forth between New York, South Florida, and Havana on a regular basis. Said Jorge: "We would come with the tables, the tables with the little wheels. And there they'd be, Sinatra, Luciano, and Meyer Lansky. They thought I was going to listen to what they were talking about, so they would change the subject. They waited for me to serve breakfast . . . Once I had finished, they would look at me as if to say 'Good-bye,' and I would leave."

Sinatra had a special affection for Luciano. His Italian ancestors were from Lercara Friddi, the same village in Sicily where Salvatore Lucania was born. Although in later years Sinatra would deny that he was ever a close friend of Luciano, witnesses at the Hotel Nacional painted a different picture.

According to a report hidden away in the files of the U.S. Narcotics Bureau, at some point during Sinatra's stay in Havana, he and Luciano took part in an orgy together. The details were corroborated by Robert Ruark, a syndicated newspaper columnist who was the first to report on Sinatra's arrival in Cuba. In an in-house memorandum that Ruark wrote to his executive editor at the New York World-Telegram, Ruark noted, "I was told by Mr. Larry Larrea [Hotel Nacional general manager] that Frank Sinatra was vacationing in Havana and—to Mr. Larrea's evident horror—was spending most of his waking hours with Lucky Luciano, Mr. Luciano's bodyguard, and an assorted group of gamblers and hoodlums." In a face-to-face meeting with the general manager, Ruark was informed that Sinatra, at that very moment, was upstairs with Luciano.

"I wouldn't advise your going up there," Mr. Larrea warned the columnist. "The best you can expect is to get thrown out. They are pretty tough fellows. They've got a lot of women with them, and I don't know how much they've been drinking." Ruark remembered that he was also warned by the manager "not to file my stories concerning Sinatra and Luciano by Western Union. [The manager] said it was a practice of the Cuban wireless office to immediately call subject people in stories of the type I intended to write, and that there would be a good chance of the story being lost, badly garbled, or distorted. He also said that the writer of such a story might be likely to wind up with a 'knot' on his head."

The orgy at the Hotel Nacional caused quite a stir. An informant later told the FBI that "a planeload of call girls" had been sent to Havana courtesy of the Fischetti brothers. They were supplied for "a party at the Hotel Nacional attended by Sinatra." Along with Luciano, another guest at the party was Al Capone's younger brother, Ralph.

In the midst of a ribald bacchanalia, somehow a contingent of Cuban Girl Scouts escorted by a Catholic nun were allowed to visit Sinatra's suite. According to an account preserved in the files of the Narcotics Bureau, the Girl Scouts were there to present Sinatra with an award of some sort and had been allowed past security "through a series of disastrous mistakes by various personnel." The call girls were quickly hidden away in a back bedroom. When the Girl Scouts entered the suite, there were bottles on the floor, lingerie was hanging from lampshades, and the air was filled with the stench of stale perfume. Sinatra entered the front room in a robe and silk scarf as if nothing were wrong. The ruse was exposed when four naked bodies fell giggling into the front room. The nun and her charges quickly left the suite in a state of shock.

Sinatra and Luciano may have had a good laugh at the screw-up, but the fallout would prove disastrous. Columnist Robert Ruark filed a story, dateline Havana, which appeared in numerous American newspapers. Although he left out the part about the orgy, in his attack on Sinatra Ruark revealed for the first time in the media that Lucky Luciano was living in Havana:

> I am puzzled as to why Frank Sinatra, the fetish of millions, chooses to spend his vacation time in the company of convicted vice operators and assorted hoodlums . . . He was here for four days last week and his companion in public was Luciano, Luciano's bodyguard and a rich collection of gamblers . . . There were considerable speculations of a disgusted nature by observers who saw Frankie, night after night, with Mr. Luciano at the Gran Casino Nacional, the dice emporium and the horse track.

The article was explosive. Sinatra denied it all, saying, "Any report that I fraternize with goons and racketeers is a vicious lie." He later threatened to sue, complaining that his integrity had been impugned.

For Luciano, the consequences were worse. He had been outed as having left Italy and settled just 90 miles off the shores of the United States. Given his reputation as perhaps the world's premiere vice lord, the U.S. government was not likely to sit idly by while Lucky violated the terms of his release from prison and flaunted his freedom. Evil was on the loose. Something would have to be done.

FOR THE U.S. BUREAU of Narcotics, the fact that Luciano was living in Cuba was no secret. From almost the day he arrived in Havana, information had been filtering through to agents from at least two informants on the staff at the Hotel Nacional about his activities on the island. American authorities could have gone after the infamous Mob boss immediately if they had wanted to, but Harry Anslinger decided it would be better to place him under surveillance. A tracing device was put on Luciano's phone that allowed the Bureau to keep a log of calls to and from his house in Miramar. His whereabouts were reported upon by a number of informants, including Luciano's Cuban maid and members of the National Secret Police.

The narcotics agent in charge of the Luciano case was J. Ray Olivera, a fluent Spanish speaker. From November 1946 onward, Olivera filed a series of reports about Luciano's activities in Cuba. Through his network of Cuban informants Olivera heard about the many U.S. mobsters who passed through Havana. He also heard that a casino in the elegant Hotel Presidente was owned by Frank Costello, and that the former boxing champion Jack Dempsey frequently acted as a cash courier for the Mob, à la Frank Sinatra.

Among the events Olivera received information about was an attempt on the life of Luciano.

Apparently, on the night of either December 27 or 28, just a day or two after the conclusion of the Havana conference, gunmen came after Luciano inside the Gran Casino Nacional, located in the Havana suburb of Marianao. According to Agent Olivera, after the attempt was made on Luciano's life, "he was taken out by the servants' entrance of the casino and the killers, aware of the movement, jumped in their car and gave chase through the dark streets surrounding the casino. But Luciano was able to elude the killers since a Cuban radio car appeared on the scene and gave chase."

In a report to his district supervisor, Olivera stated that the following day Luciano was back at the casino. He was seated at a table with a number of Cuban dignitaries that included his friend Senator Eduardo Suarez Rivas; the senator's son Pablito Suarez Arostegui, who was a noted racketeer; Dr. Indalecio "Neno" Pertierra, a member of Congress whom Agent Olivera described as "the axle of Cuban and American gangsters"; and Senator Paco Prío Socarrás, older brother of the prime minister, whom the U.S. Narcotics Bureau believed to be a major *narcotrafficante* on the island. Also seated at the table was Chester Simms, floor manager at the Gran Casino Nacional, an American whom Meyer Lansky first brought to Havana back in the late 1930s to oversee reforms at the casino and who had stayed on to become a big shot in Cuban gambling circles.

While seated at their table, Luciano and his group were approached by a colonel and a major with the National Police. After briefly questioning Luciano and Simms, the policeman announced that they both were to be placed under arrest. The Cuban dignitaries at the table immediately protested. They pulled aside the two high-powered cops and a payoff was made. The cops left but not before warning Luciano and Simms: "Be careful. Those killers from last night are still out there, and they may try again."

After the policemen departed, Senator Paco Prío insisted that Luciano go to his private estate and hide out there.

"No," said Pertierra, the congressman. "He should go to my apartment at the Jockey Club, where there are armed men at all times."

"Nonsense," said Luciano's friend Senator Suarez. "Charlie will stay at my house, and Chester can go hide out at my farm."

One consequence of the attempt on Luciano's life was that he was assigned two Cuban bodyguards, Armando Feo and Miguelito Garcia. Feo, an expert gunman and former dealer at the Montmartre casino, was known to be exceedingly polite. Garcia, nicknamed "Trabuco," was a killer and legendary ladies' man. According to Luciano's maid, who was later interviewed by Agent Olivera, "Those bodyguards ate and slept with Luciano, although Luciano did not sleep every night at the house. Sometimes he would not come home for a week at a time."

Feo and Garcia worked as a team: one would drive Luciano's car while the other sat in the back with the Mob boss, a sawed-off shotgun lying within easy reach on the floor.

Another visible member of Luciano's security team was Clemente Carreras, nicknamed "Sungo," a former Havana baseball player of some renown. Sungo was in the employ of Congressman Indalecio Pertierra, who was also owner of the Jockey Club. Pertierra sometimes loaned

Sungo out as a personal assistant. The retired player was often seen eating meals in the kitchen of Luciano's home in Miramar and driving his car, though he denied being Luciano's chauffeur. He did, however, tell Agent Olivera a story that belongs in the American mobster Hall of Fame.

Sungo was driving for Luciano on the day the Mob boss heard the news that the most murderous gangster of all time, Al Capone, had died. Capone had been living in Miami and battling the effects of tertiary syphilis when he suffered a heart attack and passed away on January 25, 1947. According to Sungo, when Luciano received the news he sat in the backseat of his car and cried like a baby. He then looked at Sungo and said, "Al was a fine person."

The Narcotics Bureau would have been content to follow Luciano around, interview those who knew him, and compile a dossier on his dealings in Havana were it not for the article by Robert Ruark. In its wake, Harry Anslinger changed his tune entirely and, through the U.S. State Department, formally requested that the Cuban government deport Luciano to Italy.

The Cuban government balked. Inside the presidential palace, President Grau San Martín held a meeting with a group of powerful political figures. In attendance was Prime Minister Carlos Prío and also Alfredo Pequeño, minister of the interior. It was the opinion of all that Luciano was in Cuba on a legitimate Italian passport, that his visa was in order, and that he had done nothing illegal in Havana. There was no legislative requirement to expel Luciano as long as he continued to behave in a lawful manner.

In an internal memo, President Grau decreed that the Luciano matter was "of no importance." Interior Minister Pequeño held a meeting with the U.S. ambassador in Havana and explained the government's position—a position no doubt influenced by the fact that Luciano and Lansky had spread bribes far and wide in Cuba. From the beginning, their plan for Havana had involved laying the proper groundwork. Key government figures—congressmen, senators, and political operatives reaching into the presidential palace—were bought off and compromised the same way they had been in New York, Chicago, Miami, and other cities where the mobsters had long ago founded their underworld empire.

When the Cuban government declined to respond favorably to the State Department's request, Narcotics Bureau commissioner Anslinger turned to President Harry S Truman. He familiarized the president with Luciano's criminal history, which included narcotics arrests in his youth. He produced memos and reports from agents in the field that suggested narcotics smuggling in the region had increased and that Luciano was most likely a major player. He requested that Truman take whatever steps were necessary to force Cuba to deport Luciano, and he made sure his request received public attention in the *New York Times* and elsewhere. After further negotiations with the Cuban government stalled, Truman took an extraordinary step: he authorized the U.S. State and Treasury departments to cut off all supplies of legitimate medical drugs to Cuba until the American Mob boss was sent packing.

"U.S. Ends Narcotics Sales to Cuba While Luciano Is Resident There" read the February 22 page-one headline in the *Times.* An official with the Narcotics Bureau was quoted in the article:

There are hundreds of [Luciano's] old Mob just waiting for the day their master can return. It is an interesting coincidence that in the three months that Luciano has been [in Cuba] we received in this country the first large shipment of European heroin—$250,000 worth . . . We believe the best place for him is that place most distant from this nation. He should not be permitted to reside where he can exercise his dangerous influence over the American underworld.

The evidence that Luciano was directly involved in heroin smuggling in Cuba was slight. Commissioner Anslinger admitted as much in a confidential memo to the secretary of state in Washington on February 21. Anslinger wrote that he was acting "on suspicion," not hard evidence. Nonetheless, to the public, Luciano's narcotics involvement was presented as a conspiracy in full flower.

From his estate in the Miramar district of Havana, Luciano kept up with events. He couldn't help but begin to have that sinking feeling he'd had in the waning days of his prostitution trial back in 1936:

> I called Meyer and Frank Costello over to Havana and we talked about the situation. I knew that the American system where you're supposed to be innocent until proven guilty didn't hold up for me. Look what happened to me with Dewey. So, if somebody said that Charlie Lucky is runnin' junk out of Havana, well, them guys in Washington are sure I hadda be doin' it. Things didn't look good.

Luciano wasn't about to give up without a fight. When approached by officials in the Cuban government, who asked him to leave the country under his own volition, Lucky refused. Knowing that his future as leader of the American underworld hung in the balance, he hired a Cuban attorney to concoct a plan to counter the U.S. medical supplies embargo by having Cuba cut off sugar shipments to the United States. The plan never materialized.

On February 23—a Saturday afternoon—Luciano was having lunch at a restaurant in the Vedado neighborhood of Havana when six police officers arrived and placed him under arrest. Police Chief Benito Herrera, who was known to be in the pocket of Luciano and Lansky, was nowhere to be seen. "[He] didn't have the heart to do this to me personally," believed Luciano.

He was given a few days to settle his affairs and then incarcerated in the Triscornia Immigration Camp until his ultimate fate was decided. Luciano had seen it all before:

> [Triscornia] is the Cuban version of Ellis Island, but what a difference. It was surrounded by a big swamp, hot as a son of a bitch and so humid your clothes just stuck to your body. I knew I couldn't take that very

long. It was the same old story of what happened to me in Italy. When the big United States started to put the squeeze on a little country like Cuba, what choice did they have?

MEYER LANSKY had been following his friend's high-stakes diplomatic battle mostly from Hallendale, north of Miami, where he presided over the Colonial Inn gambling casino, and also from New York City, where he owned an apartment on Central Park West. The situation with Luciano was troubling for a variety of reasons. First, there was Lucky's overweening attempt to reestablish himself as "boss" and somehow get back into the United States—an issue separate from the development of Cuba as a base of operations. Then there was Luciano's counterproductive penchant for the high life. Among his many exploits in Havana, Lucky had struck up a romance with a beautiful New York socialite named Beverly Paterno. They made the rounds at all the Havana nightspots: the Sans Souci nightclub, the grand mansions on Paseo Street, the roulette wheels at the Montmartre casino. Miss Paterno was so proud of her dalliance with the famous mobster that she hired a public relations firm to plant gossip items in the *Havana Post,* the city's English-language daily newspaper. This, along with Luciano's highly publicized fraternizing with Frank Sinatra, had virtually sealed his fate.

Even though Meyer might have come to the conclusion that he was better off without Luciano in Havana, he dutifully approached Fulgencio Batista to see if anything could be done. Batista, who had left the Cuban presidency in 1944, was living in Daytona Beach, Florida, and also in a luxury suite at the Waldorf-Astoria in New York City. Although Batista was no longer resident on the island, both Lansky and Luciano believed he was still the puppet master when it came to Cuban politics. Lansky convinced Batista to put heat on the government of Ramón Grau San Martín, but nothing could be done. Cuba simply could not withstand the pressure of having all U.S. pharmaceuticals cut off. Luciano would have to go.

On March 29, Luciano was loaded onto a rusty Turkish freighter named the SS *Bakir*. The ship chugged out to sea, passing El Morro, the colonial fortress and lighthouse at the mouth of Havana Bay. After five months, Luciano's Cuban adventure ended as it had begun: on the high seas. Forever after, the memory of his time in Havana would live on, swathed in nostalgia for an era of lust, high life, and sweet corruption.

To Lansky, the banishment back to Italy of his lifelong pal and closest associate was a stunning turn of events. Publicly and with his business partners, he maintained the view that it was a great injustice. Luciano had done nothing wrong or illegal; he was being persecuted. But history shows that the removal of Lucky from Cuba was the best thing that could have happened to Lansky. With his penchant for high-profile skirt-chasing and cavorting in public with celebrities, Charlie Lucky had been more trouble than he was worth. The good news was that the Mob's plans for Havana had been inaugurated at the conference at the Hotel Nacional, and nobody could put that horse back in the barn. Even better for Lansky, with Luciano out of the picture he was now the undisputed top man in Cuba. He was free to organize and pursue the matter as he saw fit, the Lansky way—quietly, behind closed doors, in smoke-filled rooms, with no diversionary hassles from nosy entertainment reporters or meddling lawmen looking to bag a famous mobster.

If American mafiosi wanted to gamble on Havana and the hope that it would one day be a major source of revenue, they had no choice. They now had to put their money on one man and one man only: Lansky.

3

EL JUDIO MARAVILLOSO
(THE MARVELOUS JEW)

IN THE LONG HISTORY OF THE AMERICAN UNDERWORLD,
there had never been anyone quite like little Maier Suchowljansky. He
was a Jew surrounded by Italians, an interloper in the House of Rome.
Although he partnered with some of the most murderous individuals in
the history of organized crime, he is not known to have killed anyone
with his own hands, and he achieved what was an uncommon distinc-
tion for gangsters of his vintage: he lived into his golden years and died
of old age.

Born in 1902 in Grodno at a time when Poland was occupied by czar-
ist Russia, he was ten years old when his family fled the pogroms directed
at Jews and headed for New York City. There were tens of thousands of
immigrant Jewish families in the big city, and the Suchowljanskys were
just one of them. It was in America that the family name was changed
to Lansky. Meyer, three years older than his brother Jake, was an exemplary student. He loved arithmetic, geography, and science, and he always toed the line in the classroom. "Our teachers were strict," he
remembered years later. "They didn't tolerate nonsense. I loved school."

All his life, Lansky professed to have a great appreciation for formal
learning. He claimed that he had been taught to recite the Gettysburg

Address by memory and had learned "history from Roman to American." He also studied and memorized Shakespeare, especially *The Merchant of Venice*. Lansky's lifelong fascination with the play might have had something to do with the character of Shylock, the Jewish moneylender who would have his "pound of flesh." In the American underworld, the term *shylock*—derived from *The Merchant of Venice*—was interchangeable with *loanshark*, a person who lends money at usurious rates. In his lifetime, Lansky would come to know and do business with many shylocks. For a lover of Shakespeare, the irony was inescapable.

The classroom was a sacred place to Lansky, but life outside the classroom had a way of rearranging a kid's priorities. Like many in the neighborhood of Brownsville, Brooklyn, and later the Lower East Side, where the Lanskys lived in a crowded tenement, life was a struggle. Throughout his existence, Lansky remembered the day when his father learned that his parents, who he believed were wealthy, had died and left nothing behind. "This disappointment on top of our present poverty was a terrible blow," recalled Lansky. His father went into a state of depression from which he never recovered.

On the Lower East Side, poverty meant a lack of food and clothing. It meant freezing cold winters with no heat, and stifling, humid summers surrounded by concrete, garbage, and open sewers. Disease, especially tuberculosis and other respiratory ailments, was common. At night, rats the size of small dogs scurried through the streets while people rummaged in garbage bins for something to eat. The Lanskys were not among the poorest of the poor; every Sabbath they gathered together and ate *cholent*, a traditional meal of meat and potato stew. But the penny-pinching and anxiety over lack of money for rent, electricity, and running water were enough to crush the hardiest of pilgrims.

Little Meyer felt as though he had lost his father to the harsh realities of life, and he resolved never to let poverty overtake him. "Even as a little boy I remember swearing to myself that when I grew up, I'd be very rich," he said years later.

His last level of formal education was the eighth grade. The desire to create financial opportunities for himself and his family drove the boy out of the classroom he loved and into the streets of the Lower East Side. At the time, the neighborhood was teeming with immigrants living beside and on top of one another in what was the most densely populated piece of real estate in the United States.

In the streets, a kid had to be smart or tough, preferably both. Lansky was small for his age—"skinny as a matchstick," according to one neighborhood friend—but he knew that in the world beyond school, sooner or later a boy had to stand up and show what he was made of. For Meyer, that day came when he was walking home with a plate of food for his family and was stopped by a gang of Irish hooligans. One of them pulled a knife and demanded that Lansky take down his pants so they could see if he was circumcised. Acting on instinct, Lansky smashed the plate of food into the face of the gang's leader. He was set upon by the gang and beaten badly, but he defended himself valiantly. Lansky's willingness to show toughness on this and other occasions would eventually convince the Irish and Italian hoodlums in his neighborhood that he was no pushover.

Soon the little Jewish kid would come to be known more for his cunning than his physical fortitude. The activity that would stimulate Meyer's imagination and eventually prove to be his salvation was gambling.

From the beginning, Lansky understood that games of chance hit some men where they could not breathe. "Gambling pulls at the core of a man," he once famously uttered. Most of his life would be spent profiting from the truth of this maxim. It started on Delancey Street with crap games, which Meyer organized and controlled. The rules of the jungle were such that a percentage of all proceeds went to the neighborhood bosses—mostly Italians, and some Jews. The Irish were represented by the local cops, who also got their cut. Among the most prominent of underworld financiers was a prince among men who would become perhaps the only mentor Meyer Lansky ever had.

Arnold Rothstein was a Jew, like Lansky. He had established his reputation in and around the Lower East Side, where he seemed to be politically connected as well as popular among the gamblers and the kibitzers. He dressed like a star in custom-made wool suits, with monogrammed cuff links, polka-dot bow ties, shiny spats, and a felt fedora. Although Rothstein first made a name for himself in the political clubhouses and dance halls along the Bowery, he soon took his act uptown to Broadway. It was there that he cultivated a relationship with young Meyer Lansky and became the inspiration for a criminal career that would reach across the United States and all the way to Cuba.

Rothstein was smart, and he was smooth. He was variously known as "the Man Uptown," "the Brain," and "the Big Bankroll." The newspapers described him as "a sportsman," "a gambler," and "the man who fixed the 1919 World Series," but he was much more than that. A bootlegger, labor racketeer, shylock, and dope peddler, Rothstein virtually invented the process by which illegal profits found their way back into the system to generate more illegal profits. He was the underworld's central banking system, a man who financed the careers of numerous gangsters and received a return on investment ranging from 75 to 90 percent. He was a stock swindler and scam artist at the highest levels, but he was never convicted of committing a single crime.

Not only that, but Rothstein was a mythmaker. He understood the allure of the dark side for the average schnook. Having come from modest means on the Lower East Side, he knew that part of making the crime world irresistible—an arena to which young men would be drawn like moths to a flame—involved creating an environment, part reality, part fiction, that everyone wanted to be in. Rothstein hung out at Lindy's Restaurant in Times Square and schmoozed with reporters, song-and-dance men, and famous athletes. He knew the writer Damon Runyon and became the basis for the character Nathan Detroit in the Runyon-inspired Broadway musical, *Guys and Dolls*. F. Scott Fitzgerald is said to have used Rothstein as the basis for Meyer Wolfsheim, the sleek gangster immortalized in his masterpiece, *The Great Gatsby*. Rothstein was conversant with both gutter life and café society. He fostered the illusion that all of these universes—crime, entertainment, and a celebrity-filled nightlife—were part and parcel of the American underworld.

According to Lansky, he and Rothstein met initially at a bar mitzvah in Brooklyn. The attraction was instantaneous. The young aspiring bootlegger told the older, more experienced racketeer that he admired the way he had penetrated high society and operated as an equal among the city's most powerful businessmen and politicians. Rothstein listened, and in a notepad he wrote, "Meyer Lansky." He invited the young kid to dinner and told him that in Lansky's youthful ambition and "hunger" he saw something of himself. They became like father and son. Years later, when describing why Rothstein had become such an inspiration to him, Lansky could have been talking about himself:

> Like me he was a gambler from the cradle. It was in the blood with both of us. Rothstein seems to have had a gift with figures too, and he used to practice by asking his friends to fire off random numbers at him. He would multiply, divide, add, or subtract these numbers and produce the answers instantaneously. He had an ice-cold nerve when playing for the highest stakes; with hundreds of thousands of dollars at risk, he never lost his head.

From Rothstein, Lansky learned about diversification, the channeling of criminal proceeds into a vast array of rackets. Lansky would put this lesson into practice by parlaying his bootlegging money into the garment trade, jukeboxes, molasses, labor racketeering, real estate, and, most especially, every facet of the casino-gambling business. The most important lesson Lansky learned from the Brain, however, was the importance of bribing and cultivating powerful politicians. With Rothstein, it had been his financial investment in Tammany Hall, the political organization that spawned the mobster-friendly New York mayor Jimmy Walker. With Lansky, it would be his bribing and betting on Fulgencio Batista.

On November 4, 1928, Rothstein was found shot in the stomach following a high-stakes card game at the Park Central Hotel in midtown Manhattan. He died in a hospital shortly thereafter. Lansky was just twenty-six at the time; he had years to absorb the lessons learned from the Big Bankroll. For one thing, although he would always be a gambler, following Rothstein's death Meyer stopped being a bettor. He was rarely seen sitting in on a game of cards, spinning a wheel, or tossing dice. He was not going to be shot down like a dog following a high-stakes game like his mentor.

Another skill that Lansky would inherit, and in time further perfect, was Rothstein's criminal vision. The Man Uptown had been the most grandiose criminal financier of his day, but his reach did not stretch much beyond New York City. Meyer Lansky had bigger fish to fry.

IN LATE 1947 and on into 1948, in the wake of Lucky Luciano's highly publicized deportation from Cuba, Lansky did what he had always done following a major crisis: he retrenched and focused on rackets that were currently generating income. Under the tutelage of his brother Jake, Lansky's casinos in South Florida were doing better than ever. In Broward County, just across the city line from Miami Beach, Lansky fine-tuned the method by which he would later become known in Havana. In some quarters it was referred to as "the fix," in others "the share-out": a series of payoffs to high-ranking law enforcement officials and selected government legislators that made it possible for Lansky and his people to operate without undue harassment.

In Broward County, the fix was in. Each night, the Lansky brothers sat down in the counting room in one of three carpet joints—the Colonial Inn, the Plantation, and Club Bohème—and personally counted "the drop," i.e., that night's winnings, until they exceeded "the handle," the amount of cash necessary to meet daily expenses. Anything over the handle went into the pockets of Lansky and his partners, and much of that was used to finance the fix.

Lansky's casinos in South Florida were highly profitable. In the postwar years of the late 1940s, they became a major draw for the local elite and were also popular venues for top entertainers, singers and stand-up comedians alike. Lansky's notoriety grew along with his bank account. In later years, one biographer would place his annual earnings from the Colonial Inn alone at one to three million dollars. But the money from his Broward County carpet joints was not enough to satisfy Lansky. According to Bernard Frank, the local Miami Beach attorney who knew Lansky during these years, "He seemed restless."

Each night, with his brother, Lansky counted the stacks of cash and made the necessary payoffs, all the while keeping one eye on his dream for the future—Havana—just a stone's throw across the Straits of Florida on the northwestern shore of Cuba.

If Lansky was restless, it might have had as much to do with loneliness as anything else. His divorce had left him in a mood of self-recrimination. "Maybe it was my fault," he told his oldest son, Buddy, after his marriage fell apart.

Buddy was another problem. Handicapped from birth with what would later be diagnosed as cerebral palsy, he was confined to a wheelchair and often in physical pain. Lansky had a hard time dealing with his son's condition, which required constant and costly medical attention. He had another son, Paul, and also a ten-year-old daughter, Sandra, who had begun to exhibit behavioral problems. Lansky would become estranged from his children, leaving them mostly in the care of his sister in New York.

Unlike his pals Luciano and the late Bugsy Siegel, Lansky had never been much of a ladies' man. He was even more reserved with women than he was with his children, who later referred to him as "distant," or his business associates, who revered his brains and coolheadedness but would never look to Lansky for a swinging good time. He tended to be all business all the time. The word people used most often when describing Lansky was *gentleman*; some people interpreted this courteousness as a kind of standoffishness. The fact that much of his life was spent engaged in criminal activity may have had something to do with his general air of circumspection. Whatever the reasons for his temperament, Lansky was ill suited to intimate or even casual dalliances with the opposite sex—which is why, in the fall of 1948, those who knew the Little Man were pleasantly surprised when he fell wholeheartedly in love with a manicurist and divorcée named Thelma "Teddy" Schwartz.

It was a whirlwind courtship. Teddy was all personality, the perfect complement to Meyer's more austere nature. She was pert, brassy, and short—three inches shorter than Lansky. She had a teenage son from a previous marriage and rented an apartment in Hollywood, Florida. Originally from New York, where she had once been part owner of a failed nightclub, she was familiar with Lansky's reputation and smart enough not to ask too many questions.

In December 1948, just four months after they first met, Meyer and Teddy flew to Cuba to get married. The ceremony was a low-key affair; it took place at a lawyer's office in Vedado, Havana's central business district. There were few guests. One who did attend was Fulgencio Batista. Many years later, in an unpublished autobiography, Teddy Lansky wrote, "Batista, who was a senator at the time, came to the office to meet me, Meyer's wife. He seemed like a fine man."

The fact that Batista was there to honor Lansky was no accident. For fifteen years now, these two men had sought to curry favor with one another. Their relationship, which had been inaugurated with a cash bribe delivered to Batista by Lansky and his friend Doc Stacher, had languished through a sustained period of historical coitus interruptus. The original plan was for Lansky and Batista to spearhead the development of a major casino-gambling empire in Cuba. Then came a series of intrusions—political instability on the island, the Great Depression, and the Second World War. For more than a decade, Cuba's tourist prospects had lain dormant. But now the war was over and people had money to spend. The mobster conference at the Hotel Nacional was a signal to Batista and others that the American gangsters were looking to invest. The time had come for Lansky and Batista to reignite their underworld mambo.

It was a strange relationship. Over the years, the two men would rarely be seen together. Doc Stacher, Teddy Lansky, and others would attest to the fact that Meyer and Fulgencio knew and did business with one another, but the two power brokers were smart enough to leave no paper trail. There is no known photo of Lansky and Batista together, or any documents signed jointly by them. Their partnership seems to have existed on a near mystical plane, with each man knowing intuitively what the other required to manipulate the levers of power and create opportunities for personal remuneration. The two men would help make each other rich while hardly ever meeting face-to-face, and their enigmatic alliance would eventually form the core of the Havana Mob.

FULGENCIO BATISTA grew up in the shadow of the United Fruit Company. In the history of Latin America and the Caribbean, no U.S. corporation held a more dominant economic and political position than El Coloso, as the company was known in the six countries where it operated massive banana plantations. In Cuba the company had more or less given birth to the town where Batista was born and raised—Banes—located in Oriente Province on the eastern fringe of the island. By the time of Batista's birth in January 1901, United Fruit had decided to forgo banana production in the Banes region in favor of cultivating sugar, the island's main export. United Fruit constructed a huge sugar processing plant, and over the next few years it built a fence around its properties in Banes, imported managers from the United States, and created entire neighborhoods for its workers, with separate security, shops, and schools.

The east side of town was divided into several neighborhoods based on the social status of the residents. North American employees—identified in the company literature as "first-class Anglo-Saxon employees"— were provided free housing and maid services. There was a less prestigious neighborhood for lower-ranking Cuban managers and technicians, and an even worse neighborhood for workers. It was here that Batista was born of mixed-race (mestizo) parents and raised around the corner from a street called simply Callejón del Negro (the Black Man's Street).

Batista's father worked for United Fruit cutting sugarcane. It was backbreaking work. During the *zafra* (sugarcane harvest), typically from February to August, the workdays were long, usually ten or twelve hours. Batista's father was not employed directly by United Fruit but rather by a contractor hired by the company to organize and pay the work crews. The contractors were often free to exploit the workers by cheating them out of wages. To supplement the family income in the off-season, the Batistas grew bananas and sold them alongside their home. By the age of eight, young Fulgencio was forced to abandon his primary-school education and join his father as a cane cutter.

Batista's upbringing could not have been more humble—an irony given that he would one day be viewed as the protector of Cuba's landowning class and wealthy elite. Having spent an early existence in which nearly every aspect of daily life was controlled by a foreign conglomerate, Batista may have developed an inferiority complex in relation to the United States. At the very least he was inclined to see U.S. economic power on the island as an immutable force, to be harnessed and manipulated perhaps but never seriously challenged. Politically, Batista's attitudes and policies toward the United States ebbed and flowed, depending on the popular mood. Ultimately, however, he went where the money was, which brought him under the sway of companies such as United Fruit, IT&T (International Telephone & Telegraph), and General Motors, and led him to men like Meyer Lansky, a "tourism expert" who saw the wisdom of making sure gaming proceeds trickled upward all the way to the top.

Batista and Lansky had a few things in common: both were largely self-educated men forced to forgo formal education early in life because of economic hardship. Like Lansky, Batista professed to love books. Throughout his life, he told the story of how, at the age of thirteen, he used his savings to purchase a biography of Abraham Lincoln. Batista became a great collector of books and would eventually compile what was believed to be the island's largest private library.

Both Batista and Lansky may have been overcompensating for a lack of "breeding," which they eventually attempted to exhibit in a fawning and sometimes pretentious manner. Lansky's Achilles' heel his entire life was the desire to be viewed as a legitimate businessman; he resented the fact that men like Rockefeller, Joseph P. Kennedy, and Edgar Bronfman were viewed as brilliant titans of business while he was relegated to the criminal class. As for Batista, he at least attempted to maintain a symbolic connection to the "common man," though he exhibited a pronounced devotion to the trappings of social class and status based on race and family background.

Where Lansky and Batista differed most was in public appearance. While Lansky always looked impeccable in a respectable suit and tie (he maintained an impressive bow tie collection throughout his life), he could not change that face. Though not an unattractive man, he was no male model. With pinched features, a prominent proboscis, and oversized ears, his face certainly had character, but not the kind that made women swoon. He spoke with the gravelly voice of a Damon Runyon character, which lent him great credibility with other mobsters but would not go over big in a boardroom.

Batista, on the other hand, was a beautiful creation. In one of his early forms of employment as a railroad brakeman for the United Fruit Company railway line, he earned the nickname "El Mulato Lindo"—the pretty mulatto—from his fellow employees. Batista never liked the nickname, with its vaguely effeminate or even homosexual overtones. But it was true. With his smooth amber complexion, perfect teeth and hair, and exotic facial features, Batista had a somewhat androgynous beauty. Although he took pains to present to the public a masculine image, his looks suggested a Cuban Adonis, with a type of handsomeness that was the envy of both men and women.

It would have been a mistake to interpret Batista's physical beauty as weakness, however. He may have been El Mulato Lindo, but he was no pretty boy. At the age of twenty-one, he enlisted in the Cuban Army, the most manly of pursuits. Although he remained studious even in the military, where he trained to become a stenographer, he could drink and carouse with the best of them. In fact, a drunken brawl at a cabaret on the outskirts of Havana almost torpedoed his military career. An army investigator suspected Batista of taking part in the scuffle, and the young private's career was only spared when a colonel whom he had befriended stepped in and blocked the arrest. Among other things, Batista learned from this incident that in Cuba, as in most societies, justice takes a backseat to personal alliances—a truism best explained in the old Cuban adage *Sin padrino no se bautice* (Without a godfather there is no baptism).

Throughout his military career, Batista exhibited a steely reserve. He rose through the ranks and was assigned to a security detail guarding the president of Cuba. It was here that he developed his appreciation for the trappings of power. As a military stenographer, he sat in on many classified meetings and was privy to the inner machinations of governmental bureaucracy.

The military was the ultimate source of social control in Cuba. Elections were frequently determined by the elite of the officer corps, who vigorously supported one candidate over another through intimidation or outright election fraud. Much of the fleecing of public funds that had taken place during virtually every political administration since independence from Spain in 1898 was undertaken to buy off the officers. It was a version of the fix or buy-out as practiced by Meyer Lansky and the Mob. Fulgencio Batista's understanding of this process—his willingness to be both a recipient and a benefactor of graft during his long years as head of the military and also president—may explain why he and Lansky had such an intuitive understanding of each other.

By the time he was in his early thirties, Batista was a sergeant and well placed to benefit from one of the most tumultuous periods in Cuban history. As the brutal dictatorship of Gerardo Machado crumbled in 1933 and the president was forced into exile, there was a parallel revolt within the ranks of the military. Sergeant Batista had by then established himself as a skillful and charismatic orator. He had studied the writings of José Martí, the great leader of Cuban independence, and was able to make historical references that served as effective emotional flashpoints for most Cubans. He had emerged as a leader— handsome, well-spoken, and fiery. By the time the dust settled and the "Revolt of the Sergeants" played out, Batista, at the age of thirty-two, was the head of the military and the most powerful man in all of Cuba.

For the next seven years, presidents served at his pleasure, until Batista himself ran for and was elected president in 1940. Although the island continued to suffer under what was rightfully viewed as a repressive military dictatorship, Batista saw himself as benevolent—or, as he put it, a "democratic dictator." The historical consequences of colonization were such that there was always a more brutal leader of a former colony somewhere in the world. Batista had President Rafael Trujillo, who nearby in the Dominican Republic was engaged in a blood-soaked reign of terror that made the Cuban dictator look like a populist. The U.S. administration of President Franklin Roosevelt promoted and supported Batista. At Batista's behest, Roosevelt abrogated the Platt Amendment, a pernicious piece of legislation that allowed the United States to interfere in Cuban affairs whenever it felt like it. The Platt Amendment was replaced by the "Good Neighbor" policy, which guaranteed Batista U.S. financial support as long as he continued to help make it possible for corporations such as United Fruit to garner huge profits on the island.

Political violence and corruption continued to be the twin bridesmaids of the Cuban system. Batista had gotten where he was because of his skill at political hardball. The leaders of rival political parties were assassinated in the dead of night. The editor of a newsmagazine hostile to Batista was kidnapped by a group of unidentified men and forced to drink castor oil. Censorship was crudely enforced, and civil liberties were mere trinkets to be dispensed according to Batista's needs and whims. Student demonstrations and labor agitation were dealt with harshly, resulting in mass arrests and imprisonment. Violent repression fed into what had always been a fact of life in Cuba—revolutionary groups dedicated to the disruption of daily life through bombings and random acts of sabotage. A certain amount of civil strife was advantageous for Batista, who had been designated the man most capable of maintaining order in a society that often seemed to be perched on the brink of chaos.

The natural result of political violence engineered by the state is corruption. Batista himself was said to have made millions through kickbacks, graft, and fraudulent government contracts. Much of the money was flown off the island and deposited in overseas accounts. The national lottery, which Batista placed under the control of the military, was also a great source of graft, as was the daily *bolita*, the popular underground numbers racket. In Havana, Colonel José Eleuterio Pedrazo, who had been with Batista as far back as the Revolt of the Sergeants, received a piece of all illegal gambling activity—such as *bolita*, cockfighting, and sports betting—that was not directly connected to legal gaming, i.e., the casinos and the racetracks.

The fact that it appeared as though the general populace was tolerant of Batista's tendencies toward repression and corruption was a testament to his political acumen. He ruled through what R. Hart Phillips, a reporter for the *New York Times* who covered Cuba during its most turbulent periods of growth, called "a system of terror and reward." Batista implemented an ambitious rural education program designed to stamp out illiteracy. In 1939 he proposed a massive social reform agenda entitled "The Three-Year Plan." The program was optimistic to the point of absurdity (its detractors referred to it as "The Three-Hundred-Year Plan"), but that did not detract from its fundamental understanding of Cuba's social problems. While little of this program was ever implemented, its goals were similar to those instituted in "the new Cuba" by Fidel Castro many years later.

The achievement for which Batista would be most noted was his institution in 1940 of a legally binding sovereign constitution. To have a constitution had been the dream of most Cubans ever since liberation from the throne of Spain, but political instability and repression had made this impossible. Now women would have the right to vote, elections would be democratic, and military power would be defined within the bounds of civil power, not vice versa. It was a remarkable achievement accompanied by huge rallies in the streets and shouts of "*¡Viva la constitución! ¡Viva Cuba! ¡Viva el Presidente Batista!*"

Of all people, the pretty mulatto had emerged from a long apprenticeship as Cuba's preeminent strongman to deliver its greatest symbol of democratic achievement.

Having ruled the country as a military dictator, Batista's tenure as president seemed like an afterthought. His term was noteworthy mostly for his change in attire. Gone was his general's uniform, complete with enough medals and ribbons to paper a small building. In civilian khakis—mostly stylish white linen and cotton suits, well suited to the tropics—Batista looked like a matinee idol. In 1942 he visited the United States as a guest of President Roosevelt and was given the full foreign dignitary treatment, with a black-tie reception at the White House and many photo opportunities. For a humble cane cutter from Banes, it was a remarkable ride to the top, and Batista could be forgiven for believing that he had achieved his highest ambition and therefore did not need to run for reelection to a second term.

The decision to go into temporary retirement at the relatively young age of forty-four may have been more personal than professional. Although Lansky and his gangster friends believed that Batista remained the "puppet master" in Cuba, the truth was more complicated. Thinking perhaps that he could maintain control by proxy, Batista put forth a surrogate candidate for president in 1944. That candidate lost to Ramón Grau San Martín. Batista could have attempted to undermine the election, or contested the result, but he chose not to. Matters on the home front took precedence.

Although married for eighteen years, Batista had for some time been carrying on an affair with Marta Fernández Miranda, a twenty-year-old green-eyed beauty whom he had first met when his military motorcade almost ran her down as she rode her bicycle in the neighborhood of

Miramar in Havana. Batista set Marta up in a private home, and during the years of his presidency the relationship grew. It became apparent to Batista that he would have to choose between his illicit affair and his presidency. He chose the affair. While living in exile in Daytona Beach and New York City, Batista divorced his first wife and married Marta.

In New York, he lived in a suite at the Waldorf-Astoria, just a few floors removed from where Lansky, Luciano, and other mobsters had first made the decision to bribe Sergeant Batista fifteen years earlier. Most of Batista's time was spent with his new bride in Florida, where he liked to play golf and go fishing.

One afternoon, he was driving through South Florida with Edmund Chester, an American writer and friend (who would one day write an obsequious biography of him). Near the small town of Mount Dora, Batista became fascinated by the picturesque orange and grapefruit groves that lined the road. He pulled the car over and stopped, jumped out, and scurried over to the grove. After plucking a couple of oranges from a tree, he hurried back to the car and drove off. Chester asked Batista why he took the fruit—surely anyone in the area would have given him all the oranges he wanted.

"No," said Batista. "That would not have satisfied my needs. All my life I've wanted to steal an orange off the tree, and I've finally done it."

Mostly, while in exile, the former Cuban leader enjoyed a discreet existence. It wasn't until 1948 that his presence caused a stir, and that was because he had announced he was reentering the political fray. *Time* magazine, which had first put Batista's smiling visage on its cover back in 1937, reported the announcement in an article entitled "Senator from Daytona":

Batista was coming back. The tough ex-sergeant who bossed Cuba through clever years of "disciplined democracy" will run for Senator in the June 1 general elections . . . He has sat out a pleasant exile in some of the New World's toniest suites . . . Every morning, he is up at 7 for a brisk row in the nine-foot boat he keeps in the Halifax River. He plays tennis at the smart Daytona Beach Bath and Tennis Club, goes to the movies two or three times a week and occasionally speaks at Rotary Club luncheons.

Every fortnight, Batista drives off to Palm Beach, Orlando or Fort Pierce for secret meetings with aides who bring the political word from Cuba and take back his instructions. Only when the Cuban government discovers an arms cache and shouts "Batista plot" are Floridians reminded that their guest is dynamite.

Batista's decision to run for Senator (from Las Villas Province) is a hard-headed deal . . . it is a foot in the Cuban political door. Because most Cubans have forgotten his brutal police methods, [remembering] only that meat and butter were cheaper in his time, Batista is likely to win in a walk without so much as leaving Daytona Beach.

El Presidente in exile had his own reasons for wanting to reestablish himself as the boss of Cuba, but his decision to once again run for political office may have been influenced in part by Meyer Lansky. According to one source who frequented Lansky's Colonial Inn casino in Hallendale, Batista was an occasional presence there. "He showed up looking immaculate, usually in a white suit. He wasn't much of a gambler, but he liked to make his presence felt, walking through the place like a politician running for office. He seemed to know everyone by name."

For obvious reasons, Lansky needed Batista back in power in Cuba. The political administrations of Ramón Grau San Martín and his successor, Carlos Prío Socarrás, though as corrupt as previous Cuban presidencies, did not share Batista's visionary qualities when it came to casino gambling. Not only that, but Lansky had put his money on Batista long ago and had not yet received a commensurate return on his investment. Both Lansky and Batista were convinced that Cuba was about to enter a postwar boom in tourism potentially as profitable as anything since the Dance of the Millions in the 1920s. They wanted to be there when it happened.

By the time of Meyer and Teddy's Havana wedding in December

1948, Batista had been back in office for several months. Batista no doubt would have run for president, but he was prohibited from doing so by Cuban law. As a former president, he could not run for the top office until he had first served at least one term in a lower office. As senator from Las Villas, a rural province on the island's central coast, his duties were not taxing.

He put down roots at Kuquine, a palatial estate on the outskirts of Havana that would be his home for the next decade. The plan was to lie low for four years until he was eligible to run for president, at which time he would reclaim his rightful position as ruler of all Cuba and bring to fruition, once and for all, Lansky's scheme of turning Havana into the Monte Carlo of the Caribbean.

The years did not pass quietly. Once again, the problem was Cuba. Nothing had changed to alter the country's cycle of corruption, financial instability, and political violence and unrest. Only now a new element was added to the mix—what became commonly known as *gangsterismo* (gangsterism).

The 1940 constitution had diminished the ubiquitous power of the military, the result being that various political factions felt compelled to create their own individual gangs and goon squads. In a country where the army had once controlled everything, chaos set in. Cubans who lived through this era remember it as a time of random violence and paranoia.

Max Lesnick, who was a young student leader at the time and a founding member of the Cuban People's Party, or Ortodoxo, had a ringside seat. "It was a time when violence became a common part of the political process," he recalled. "The group with the most guns had the most influence."

Newspaper editors, student activists, and political operatives armed themselves with guns smuggled into the country or procured from the army. Gang warfare erupted throughout the island. Late-night assassinations were increasingly frequent, especially within the union movement and among the students. Carlos Prío, the newly elected president, even instituted a plan to combat *gangsterismo* by paying a government subsidy to gangster representatives at the University of Havana who agreed to turn in their arms. In other words, you could buy your way into the government through gangsterism. Prío's "gangster pact" touched off a firestorm of debate. One rich landowner suggested that the only practical solution was to round up all the gang members and transport them to his plantation, where he would then supply them with ammunition so that they could have a shoot-out and eliminate one another until there was only one man left standing.

Out of this violent political maelstrom a number of young Cuban males emerged as either feared gangsters or capable political leaders. One man who initially straddled both worlds was a young law student named Fidel Castro Ruz.

The twenty-two-year-old Castro burst onto the scene in June 1948 when he was accused of murder. A police sergeant at the University of Havana was shot in front of his house, and before dying he allegedly identified Castro as his assassin. An unnamed witness corroborated the claim. Castro had been accused of murder once before, just five months earlier. The allegation had been cooked up by a student rival at the university. Although Castro was arrested, he was never formally charged. This time, when Castro heard on the radio that he was once again being blamed for a political murder, he went into hiding. Eventually the witness recanted, telling newsmen that he had been bribed by the police to name Castro. The charges were thrown out.

Although not yet famous across the island, Fidel was well known at the University of Havana. Since the uprising against the presidency of Gerardo Machado in the early 1930s, the university had been a major source of political agitation and organized dissent. Castro had proved himself a dynamic orator and a future leader to be reckoned with, but he was also, according to some, overly enamored with the trappings of *gangsterismo*. He carried a fifteen-shot Browning pistol on his person at all times and was more than willing to engage rival gangs in confrontation. Despite his intellect and obvious leadership talents, he was thought to be somewhat reckless.

Tall and strapping, with curly black hair and a traditional, finely manicured Cuban mustache, Castro cut a dashing figure. He had been an exemplary student athlete and had a self-confidence that was attractive to women. He came from a prosperous family (his father owned land in Oriente Province) and married a young woman from a politically connected family. He borrowed money from his father so that he and his wife could honeymoon in New York City. They stayed at least one night at the Waldorf-Astoria, which had by then, at differing times in history, served as accommodation for nearly all the major players in the story of the Havana Mob.

By the latter months of 1948, having survived murder accusations and at least one assassination attempt, Castro was ready to settle down. He approached Max Lesnick, national director of the Youth Committee for the Ortodoxo Party, and declared that he would like to be a member of the twelve-person committee. Apparently Castro had begun to formulate the idea of entering politics and knew that he would have to be aligned with a formal party. Lesnick knew of Castro's talents as a leader, but he also knew that Fidel had been involved in various aspects of political *gangsterismo*.

"No member of the committee may be armed when he goes to the university," Lesnick told Castro, knowing that he always carried a pistol.

"Well, I won't carry it anymore," replied Fidel.

Through his association with Lesnick and the Ortodoxos, Fidel disowned his gangster past. In a dramatic speech before a gathering of administrators and students at the University of Havana, Castro proceeded to name all the gangsters, politicians, and student leaders profiting from President Prío's "gangster pact." Before the speech was over, automobiles filled with armed thugs had begun to materialize around the university. Castro finished his dramatic denunciation and was whisked away by Lesnick, who hid him because "he would be killed if he went out in the street." According to Lesnick, who would eventually leave Cuba and go into exile in Miami, it was Castro's first revolutionary act: "He made a courageous decision to take a stand against *gangsterismo*, and his position never wavered. From that point on, Cuba was changed forever."

One person who had watched Castro's emergence on the political stage with growing interest was Fulgencio Batista. Always on the lookout for young talent he could co-opt into supporting his personal agenda, Batista arranged a meeting with Fidel through Fidel's brother-in-law, who was an active supporter of Batista. Castro was brought to Kuquine, Batista's baronial estate outside Havana, and made to wait in a private office. In the office was a large painting of Batista from his days as a sergeant. There were other accoutrements of Batista's life and career: a bust of Abraham Lincoln and one of José Martí; a solid gold telephone that had been given to Batista by the president of IT&T; and a telescope used by Napoleon on Saint Helena.

Batista finally arrived. According to one account of this meeting, he kept the conversation away from politics and sought only to take full measure of this voluble new star on the scene. Another account has Castro telling the senator that if he were to stage a coup d'état against President Prío, Batista would have his support. Anyone who knew Fidel would have recognized this offer for what it was: the act of an agent provocateur who wanted to pit Batista against Prío and foster discord, or even rebellion, after which he, Castro, would emerge as a possible successor.

The meeting was congenial. Fidel left without Batista having offered any commentary or predictions on his political future.

To the senator from Daytona, there was no indication that the man he had just met would one day become his dreaded enemy and, by extension, the primary nemesis of the Havana Mob.

4

WELL-CHARACTERED PEOPLE

MEYER LANSKY FELT HE OWED HIS OLD FRIEND LUCKY Luciano a visit. It was the summer of 1949, more than two years since Luciano had been forced out of Cuba by the U.S. government. Lansky and his wife, Teddy, had not yet had a formal honeymoon, so why not Europe? They could charter a cruise across the Atlantic, travel leisurely through southern Italy, and meet up with Charlie Lucky in Rome. Among other things, Lansky could fill Luciano in on the latest developments with Batista in Cuba and reassure him that, in the hearts and minds of American mobsters everywhere, he was still Gangster Number One.

Luciano certainly could have used the companionship. Since being forced into exile, he had become isolated and bitter. Even though he was far away from New York and Havana, Harry Anslinger and the Narcotics Bureau continued to hound him. Just as Anslinger had used U.S. influence to force the hand of the Cuban government in deporting Luciano, so he kept up pressure on the Italian authorities to keep the Mob boss under constant surveillance.

Lansky knew that a visit to his old friend in Italy would attract law enforcement attention, but he wasn't concerned. The trip was for pleasure, not business. He booked passage on the *Italia*, a luxury liner scheduled to leave New York City on June 28.

Agents of the Narcotics Bureau kept a close watch on the passenger lists of ocean liners traveling to and from the United States, since it was believed that steamer trunks were a common mode for smuggling narcotics. The Bureau also believed that Luciano had used commercial ocean liners to transport heroin. When the name of Meyer Lansky—a known associate of Luciano—appeared on the manifest for the *Italia*, the Bureau took an interest. On Monday, June 27, the day before Lansky and his wife were scheduled to depart on their honeymoon, narcotics agents John H. Hanly and Crofton J. Hayes called Lansky on his home phone in Manhattan. They were surprised when he invited them up to his apartment across from the leafy splendor of Central Park at 40 Central Park South. The agents met Lansky in apartment 14C.

Meyer informed Hanly and Hayes that he was embarking on his European holiday "solely for pleasure." Yes, he would probably be seeing Charles Luciano while in Italy. Luciano was an old friend, said Lansky, but they had no current business relationship. Lansky explained that the bulk of his income these days came from gambling interests in Florida, where he was part owner of the Club Bohème and Greenacres casinos, both managed by his brother Jake. In New York, Lansky said, he kept his business "in his hat." This was a favorite expression of Lansky's to explain his mode of business, in which there were no central office, no accountants, and no record keeping of any kind.

When asked by the agents to characterize his current activities, Lansky replied, "Common gambler, I guess. I don't try to fool or impose on nobody. If I had met you casually, I would call myself a restaurant operator. If we warmed up to each other, I would tell you I was a common gambler. I don't sail under no false colors." As the agents continued to probe Lansky on his finances, he parried like a fleet-footed middleweight but always remained polite and civilized.

Eventually the conversation turned to Cuba. For the first time during the interview, Lansky stumbled a bit. The agents asked why his phone number in Hallendale had turned up repeatedly on Luciano's phone log while the Mob boss was living in Havana. Lansky suggested that the calls were between him and either Chester Simms or Connie Immerman, two former associates from his days running the casino at Oriental Park Racetrack. The two Americans had stayed on in Cuba and frequently called Lansky to compare notes on the credit of certain high rollers. Luciano may have come on the phone at some point, said Lansky, but his memory was vague on that.

Lansky's hesitation when talking about Cuba was understandable. His past involvements managing the casinos at Oriental Park Racetrack and the Hotel Nacional were entirely legal, but his relationship with Batista was not yet fully realized. Nor was it something the notoriously close-mouthed Lansky would have wanted to divulge to a couple of federal agents—no matter how polite he wanted to appear.

The conversation lasted more than an hour. The agents left and filed their report. The subject of Cuba aside, the report stands as an artifact of perhaps the most open dialogue Meyer Lansky ever had with American law enforcement.

Throughout his five-week trip to Europe, Lansky and his wife were followed by federal agents. Teddy was incensed at the invasion of their privacy, but Meyer tried not to let it bother him. At times he even engaged the agents:

> I used to recognize them and invite them to have a drink with me.
> They weren't even embarrassed—they used to accept my hospitality.
> They were trying to bug our hotel rooms, but they did it very incompetently, and I kidded them about their lack of professionalism.

The Lanskys traveled to Palermo in Sicily, Naples, and on to Rome, where Lansky had originally planned to meet with Luciano; however, Charlie called to say that, with the restrictions that had been placed on him by the Italian authorities, it was better that Meyer meet him in the Sicilian village of Taormina. Lansky and his wife therefore headed south again, where they finally met Meyer's old friend at the sun-drenched resort.

The last time Lansky and Luciano had seen one another was in the days and weeks following the Mob conference at the Hotel Nacional. Although Luciano was no longer the day-to-day boss of the Syndicate, he was still a kind of emeritus in exile. His ego required that he be treated as if his opinions still mattered, though his removal from Cuba had rendered him mostly powerless. Luciano listened as Lansky filled him in on the latest business developments with the Syndicate and also their updated plans for Havana. Recalled Luciano: "[Meyer] said things was goin' very good with all our gamblin'. He told me he was goin' to Switzerland to open up some new bank accounts for a few of the guys, like Joe Adonis and our good friend Batista."

After Lansky and his wife said good-bye to Luciano in Sicily, they continued traveling around Europe: the French Riviera, Paris, and Switzerland, where Lansky opened his first numbered bank account. When they returned to the United States, the world was turned upside down.

To begin with, Lansky's European trip garnered attention in the local press. By traveling overseas to meet with the notorious Luciano, Lansky had inadvertently elevated his underworld profile. The *New York Sun*, a newspaper that had made a name for itself through copious coverage of local gangsters, ran a photo of Lansky on the front page. It was the first time Lansky's picture had appeared in a major newspaper. The accompanying article identified him as "one of the nation's public enemies . . . once described by a police investigator's report as 'the brightest boy in the Combination.'"

Until then, Lansky's name had rarely appeared in the press. If it had, it was usually as an associate or "sidekick" of some more famous mobster, such as Luciano, Bugsy Siegel, or Frank Costello. Now Lansky had been outed as a major crime figure.

And there was more to come. The article in the *Sun* was the opening salvo in an investigation into the activities of Lansky and the nation's entire constellation of mobsters and gangsters. In the months ahead, this inquisition would move beyond the newspapers to the halls of various senate chambers throughout the United States. By the time the dust settled, not only were Lansky's plans for Cuba in serious jeopardy, but the entire Syndicate had taken a hit. Fortunes would be lost, indictments handed down, and, for the first and only time in his life, Meyer Lansky—the wiliest operator in the American underworld—would find himself pondering his future from behind the bars of a prison cell.

THE FEDERAL GOVERNMENT'S WAR on organized crime had been brewing for some time. Ever since Prohibition, the American Mob had been a perennial favorite in newspapers and on the radio, where commentators like Walter Winchell made a career out of gossipy, sensationalized crime reports. But until the early months of 1950, the Mob's activities were usually portrayed as those of isolated gangsters in major cities with little or no intercity affiliation. The theory that there existed a Commission or Syndicate of Mob leaders who coordinated underworld activity had been belittled by no less a personage than J. Edgar Hoover, director of the FBI. Hoover stated bluntly that there was no national crime syndicate and that the major threat to American values was not from organized crime but from a national Communist conspiracy.

Conversely, Harry Anslinger of the Narcotics Bureau had for years been pushing the national syndicate theory. His dream was to bring about the formation of a federal investigative committee headed by a like-minded U.S. senator, in which his agency would be prominently featured. Anslinger found his man in Senator Estes Kefauver from Tennessee.

The Kefauver Committee, as it would become known, was constituted on January 5, 1950. The purpose of the committee, according to the Senate resolution under which it was created, was to direct "a full and complete study and investigation of interstate gambling and racketeering activities and of the manner in which the facilities of interstate commerce are made a vehicle of organized crime." Unlike later organized crime committees based in Washington, D.C., the Senate Special

Committee to Investigate Crime in Interstate Commerce was designed to be a barnstorming tour, with subpoenas served and public and private sessions held in many major cities throughout the United States. In seeking to establish the existence of an underworld commission governed by mobsters in various jurisdictions, the committee wound up focusing heavily on organized gambling. Inevitably, the subject of Cuba would emerge as a titillating example of the Mob's far-reaching influence in the gaming trade.

The hearings kicked off in Chicago and then quickly moved on to St. Louis, San Francisco, New Orleans, Tampa, and other cities. From the beginning, Kefauver had an agenda. A plain-speaking politician with a rural pedigree, he had campaigned for senator wearing a coonskin cap and preaching "simple American values," though he was, in fact, a highly skilled attorney based in Chattanooga. With Kefauver as chairman, the hearings took on the trappings of a crusade. The members of the committee were primarily white Anglo-Saxon Protestants, while those subpoenaed to testify were mostly urban ethnics: Italian Americans, Irish Americans, and Jews.

Of the committee's many sessions spanning the next eighteen months, among the most explosive were those held in South Florida. On July 13, 1950, the operating director of the Miami Crime Commission was called to present a series of charts showing that no fewer than thirty-two illegal gambling establishments flourished on the Dade–Broward County line between 1946 and 1950. Of these, the most successful were those owned and operated by Meyer Lansky. Among the men named by the crime commissioner as having become part of the Lansky syndicate in South Florida were Vincent Alo, alias "Jimmy Blue Eyes," William Bischoff, alias "Lefty Clark," and Jake Lansky, all of whom would later become key players in Meyer's Havana operations.

The lengths to which the Lansky syndicate would go to buy off local officials was detailed for the committee by a former city assessor from Hollywood, Florida. The former assessor was part of a citizens' group that was trying to close down the illegal gambling clubs through an injunction. In open session, before the committee, the former assessor testified that one night there had been a knock at his front door. He answered and was greeted by an attorney who he knew represented gambling interests and gave free legal advice to Hollywood cops.

"There's someone in the car who would like to see you," said the lawyer.

The former assessor walked out to a black Cadillac sedan parked at the curb and opened the door. Inside, behind the wheel, sat burly Jake Lansky.

"This is Mr. Lansky," said the lawyer. "Mr. Jake Lansky."

Meyer Lansky's brother said to the former city official, "Let me ask you, don't you think you're taking on more than you can manage?"

"I don't know," said the man. "I'm doing the best I can."

"Would you be interested in twenty-five thousand dollars?" asked Jake.

The man turned and went back into the house. The car drove away.

Two or three nights later, another car drove up. A man came to the door and asked the former city official to come out to the car, there was something he wanted to show him. The former assessor complied. Two men were sitting in the rear of the car. One held a white shoe box.

"We have twenty-five thousand dollars here," said the man with the shoe box. "You know how these things end—either with a silver dollar or a silver bullet."

According to the city official, he walked back to the house and picked up a shotgun he kept near the door. "I told them, 'I'm going to count to five, and then I'm going to start shooting.'" The car drove off, but that wasn't the last of it. Weeks later, an anonymous letter was circulated in Hollywood accusing the man of accepting a ten-thousand-dollar bribe from gamblers.

Another person who testified at the South Florida hearing was Walter Clark, the longtime sheriff of Broward County. Sheriff Clark was a paunchy, gregarious good ol' boy who had presided over Broward since he was first elected in 1933. He liked to boast, "Broward has enjoyed the lowest crime-occurrence record of any resort county for its size." Of course, that record depended on whether or not you counted illegal gambling, of which there was plenty. In front of the Kefauver Committee, Clark feigned ignorance:

> COMMITTEE CHAIRMAN: You have never known that there was gambling in those places?
>
> SHERIFF CLARK: Rumors, but no actual evidence on it.
>
> CHAIRMAN: With all of the information around about those places, why didn't you close them up, and what is the problem?
>
> SHERIFF CLARK: I never had any kick on it. I never had any complaints that they were gambling.
>
> CHAIRMAN: As a matter of fact, it has always been your policy to operate on a liberal sort of basis, as you have told the committee.
>
> SHERIFF CLARK: Yes.
>
> CHAIRMAN: What do you mean by a liberal sort of basis?
>
> SHERIFF CLARK: Well, I am not going around snooping in private businesses and homes.

Clark had a problem: it was later shown to the committee that Jake and Meyer Lansky were major contributors to his reelection campaign. Also receiving checks totaling $750 from Jake Lansky were the Florida Sheriffs Association, Justice of the Peace and Constables Association, Police & Sheriff Association, and Peace Officers Association. These were the official contributions; payments under the table were probably much higher.

Everyone got a piece of the pie: a select corps of three cops from the Hallendale police was paid to supervise the parking of cars outside the Colonial Inn and other carpet joints. And at the end of the night's business, a call would be made and a posse of Sheriff Clark's uniformed deputies would arrive to escort the night's take to the bank. Sheriff Clark's brother, Robert, owned the armored truck company whose vehicles transported the money.

By the time the Kefauver Committee moved on after a long week of testimony, a system of payoffs to local police and judicial and political figures in Broward County had been thoroughly exposed. Sheriff Clark was disgraced and forced out of office, and Meyer Lansky's carpet joints in Broward County were raided, padlocked, and shut down for good.

As the Kefauver Committee arrived in New York City for the next round of hearings in the fall of 1950, awareness of its activities was simmering but nowhere near the heights it would reach in the following months. Until now, newspaper accounts of the testimony had tended to focus on issues of local interest, with little emphasis on what was supposed to be the committee's primary agenda: establishing the existence of a national crime syndicate. In New York, that all changed. For the first time, the full reach and star power of the Mob were put on display, and the Kefauver Committee was finally catapulted from a back-page story to a full-blown cultural event.

In the previous hearings, a name that had been a constant refrain was that of Meyer Lansky—not only in South Florida, where the Lansky name was a mantra, but also in New Orleans, where it was established that Lansky, along with Frank Costello and local interests, was co-owner of the Beverly Club, a popular nightclub-casino. Lansky appeared to be a key intermediary between mobsters in New Orleans, Detroit, Cleveland, Las Vegas, Los Angeles, and just about anywhere else that the forces of organized crime did business. Which is why the members of the committee were all in attendance when the Little Man himself, in answer to a subpoena, strolled into federal court in Manhattan to testify on October 11.

Given the buildup, the testimony was somewhat anticlimactic—which is probably just the way Lansky wanted it to be. Although the Mob boss was appearing without his attorney, he had been well coached as to his Fifth Amendment privilege—the right to remain silent on the grounds of self-incrimination—which, thanks to the Kefauver hearings, would enter into the lexicon of American discourse and become a lifesaver for criminals of all stripes. Under relentless questioning, Lansky rarely wavered:

COMMITTEE MEMBER: Have you ever been in the gambling business?

LANSKY: I decline to answer that on the grounds that it may incriminate me.

COMMITTEE MEMBER: Have you ever been in Saratoga Springs, New York?

LANSKY: I decline to answer on the grounds that it may incriminate me.

COMMITTEE MEMBER: Will the chairman please instruct the witness to answer?

CHAIRMAN: Mr. Lansky, you are instructed to answer these questions. Can we have an understanding that if, in the opinion of the chairman, any question counsel asks you is not a proper question, I will tell you not to answer it? Otherwise, you are instructed to answer every question that is asked of you.

LANSKY: Yes, sir.

CHAIRMAN: You understand that?

LANSKY: Yes, sir.

COMMITTEE MEMBER: Did you ever have an interest in the Flamingo Hotel in Las Vegas?

LANSKY: I decline to answer on the grounds that it may tend to incriminate me.

The following morning, with his attorney at his side, Lansky was more forthcoming. He answered questions when Moses Polakoff advised that it was all right for him to do so. Much of his testimony was used as an opportunity for grandstanding on the part of the committee members. In one revealing moment, Republican senator Charles Tobey, the committee's most self-righteous grand inquisitor, became outraged when he discovered that Polakoff had also represented Charles Luciano. Bristling with indignation, the senator asked Polakoff, "How did you become counsel for such a dirty rat as that? Aren't there some ethics in the legal profession?" adding later, "There are some men beyond the pale. [Luciano] is one of them."

Polakoff responded with a passionate defense of his profession, noting, "When the day comes that a person becomes beyond the pale of justice, that means our liberty is gone. Minorities and undesirables and persons with bad reputations are more entitled to the protection of the law than are so-called honorable people. I don't have to apologize to you or anyone else for whom I represent."

"I look upon you in amazement," said the senator.

"I look upon you in amazement," countered the attorney, "a senator of the United States, making such a statement."

The exchange went on a while longer, with Lansky sitting idly by, content that his time before the committee was being devoted to a rancorous debate about his old pal Charlie Lucky—who was living in Italy beyond the reach of the committee—and not about his own criminal activities.

Eventually Lansky faced the music. In testimony that stretched on for most of the morning, he admitted to acquaintance with a number of men who had been established before the committee as major underworld figures. Lansky could hardly deny his association with Luciano, Frank Costello, Bugsy Siegel, Albert Anastasia, and many others that he had been doing business with most of his adult life. On questions of substance relating to his business activities, or even whether or not he had set foot in certain cities where gambling was rampant, he religiously took the Fifth.

One subject Lansky was surprisingly loquacious about was Cuba. The committee knew nothing of Lansky's current relationship with Batista. Their questions about Cuba all related to the past. Lansky was aware that his activities in Havana were beyond the reach of the committee, which might be why he was willing to talk freely on the subject.

COMMITTEE MEMBER: What business did you have [in Havana]?

LANSKY: I had the racetrack, and a casino, Nacional.

COMMITTEE MEMBER: You operated all of the gambling, is that right? It is legal in Cuba?

LANSKY: Sure, it is legal; yes.

COMMITTEE MEMBER: Why did you go to Cuba?

LANSKY: Well . . . At that time, I was very much interested to try to get the Montmartre Club.

CHAIRMAN: Did you have the racetrack and the casino at the time Luciano was there?

LANSKY: No, no, we stopped when the war broke out. You see, because after that, there weren't any boats on the sea. And at that time you didn't have enough planes, and you couldn't live from the planes coming from Miami. You can't live from Cuban people themselves.

CHAIRMAN: May I ask, were these big operations, the racetrack and the casino at the Nacional Hotel?

LANSKY: Big operations?

CHAIRMAN: Yes.

LANSKY: Well, we took it when it was pretty well run-down.

CHAIRMAN: But it was a million-dollar operation?

LANSKY: No, nothing like that, senator. A leased proposition, and we tried to develop it. Unfortunately, the war broke out.

COMMITTEE MEMBER: Aside from the amount of money involved, the Nacional casino, it was a tremendous and beautiful place in Cuba?

LANSKY: Oh, sure it was.

COMMITTEE MEMBER: It has probably more floor space for gambling than any other place in the hemisphere, doesn't it?

LANSKY: Well, I guess it does.

COMMITTEE MEMBER: And it is a gorgeous, beautiful big building?

LANSKY: Oh, sure it was.

COMMITTEE MEMBER: With a tremendous, absolutely beautiful restaurant?

LANSKY: That's right.

COMMITTEE MEMBER: And another place for dancing?

LANSKY: Yes.

COMMITTEE MEMBER: It is quite a layout, in other words?

LANSKY: It is.

COMMITTEE MEMBER: And the track is a good-sized racetrack?

LANSKY: Yes, the track was a good-sized racetrack. I think it had one
of the most beautiful clubhouses in the country.

The committee stayed on the subject of Havana for a while, believing
perhaps that it was an opportunity to loosen Lansky's tongue—a transparent strategy that Meyer effectively undermined by noting, "I spent
four years in Havana, and about six months a year. I mean, to me, Havana used to become very tiring." He said no more on the subject and
finished his testimony.

Lansky made one more appearance before the committee five months
later, when Kefauver and his crew returned to New York in March 1951.
This final appearance was uneventful, and it was overshadowed by other
more sensational developments.

In early March, Willie Moretti was called to testify. An attendee of
the Havana conference, Moretti was the man who had initiated Frank
Sinatra into the universe of the American Mafia. In front of the committee, the balding, fifty-one-year-old New Jersey mobster talked inces-
santly, offering such pearls of wisdom as "They call anybody a mob who
makes six percent more on money" and, concerning his many gangster
acquaintances, "Well-charactered people don't need introductions." When
Moretti was thanked by Senator Tobey for his frankness, he answered,
"Thank you very much. Don't forget my house in Deal if you are down
on the shore. You are invited."

Moretti's testimony revealed nothing of any consequence, but his
prattling on nonetheless alarmed many in the Mob. On October 4,
while the Kefauver Committee was still ongoing, Moretti was having
breakfast at Joe's Restaurant in Cliffside Park, New Jersey, when unknown gunmen opened fire. He was hit multiple times and died in a
pool of his own blood. Someone had shut Moretti's mouth for good.

By far the most memorable moment of the Kefauver hearings—one
that would forever occupy a special place in the history of the Mob in
America—was the appearance of Frank Costello. By the time he was
called to testify, the Prime Minister of the Underworld was in no mood

to play ball. Costello refused to take the stand as long as television cameras were present in the hearing room. Television was a relatively new phenomenon—less than 20 percent of the American public had a set in their homes—but Costello and his attorney rightly surmised that having his face so strongly identified with a probe into the activities of organized crime would result in guilt by association. A compromise was worked out: cameras would be allowed in the hearing room, but they could not show Costello's face.

And so unfolded perhaps the first major event in television history. Costello's hands were shown, but his face was not. His disembodied voice—a raspy baritone that was the result of a youthful operation on his vocal cords—seemed to emanate from some mysterious place. The result was both sinister and mesmerizing. Millions of people in cities large and small became addicted to Costello's testimony, which on television consisted of a voice and hands. Store owners wanting to capitalize on the event placed television sets in their shop windows. People gathered on the sidewalks to watch, and the hearings became a national phenomenon.

By the time they were over, the Kefauver hearings had helped elevate the Mob into a new kind of American mythology. The names Luciano, Costello, and Lansky were now as well known as those of some movie stars. The results may have been succor to the egos of some mobsters, but the effect on their pocketbooks was devastating.

For Meyer Lansky, the results were akin to a hostile takeover. He expressed his bitterness directly to Senator Kefauver in a private backroom session before his final appearance. Lansky had heard through various sources that Kefauver liked to gamble, so he asked the senator, "What's so bad about gambling? You like it yourself. I know you've gambled a lot."

"That's quite right," answered Kefauver, "but I don't want you people to control it."

Lansky took this as a disparagement of his ethnicity. "I'm not a kneeling Jew who comes to sing songs in your ears," he snapped. "I'm not one of those Jewish hotel owners in Miami Beach who tell you all sorts of stories just to please you . . . I will not allow you to persecute me because I am a Jew."

Lansky's defense of his ethnic origins might have gone over well at the weekly meeting of the B'nai Brith, but in the halls of justice he was just another arrogant hoodlum—Jewish, Italian, Irish, or otherwise. By the time the Kefauver Committee wrapped up public hearings in early 1952, the Little Man was hurting. He was indicted on gambling charges in the state of Florida and faced similar charges in New York State as a result of his casino operations in Saratoga Springs. The future looked grim.

IT IS NOT KNOWN whether Fulgencio Batista watched the Kefauver hearings on television. Undoubtedly, he monitored them closely through the pages of the *New York Times* and also in the weekly newsmagazines. A devout observer of U.S. political and cultural events, the senator tended to view his former home and neighbor not as a separate country but as a fat, sometimes inattentive relative whose moods needed to be constantly monitored and massaged. The Mob, in particular, was a subject close to his heart. Through Lansky, Batista had a vested interest in the fortunes of the American underworld. From his estate outside Havana, he would have followed the Kefauver hearings the same way investors follow the fortunes of the New York Stock Exchange: with fingers crossed and an ear to the ground.

In the media, the hearings were presented as an unmitigated disaster for the Mob. The *New York Times* suggested that the Kefauver hearings were potentially "the biggest blow to organized crime since passage of the Twenty-first Amendment," which ended Prohibition. It was true that in the wake of the hearings, illegal casinos, bookmaking operations, wire-service syndicates, and narcotics routes were all shut down, but the senator from Daytona was astute enough to see beyond the headlines.

Having been born and raised in the shadow of the United Fruit

Company, Batista recognized a capitalist imperative when he saw one. Nothing had happened during the Kefauver hearings to change the central precept of American commerce: as with any business, the Mob needed to keep money in circulation to survive. Lansky, Luciano, Costello, and the others had committed themselves to a corporate strategy. As principles of operation, the generating and reinvesting of capital were the first and second commandments. Batista knew that the Mob still needed a place to hang its hat. Now, more than ever, it needed avenues of investment that were beyond the reach of hillbilly do-gooders like Estes Kefauver. In this regard, Havana never looked better.

The senator had one problem. If the argument were to be made that the time had arrived for the full-scale investing of dirty money in Havana, Batista was not yet in a position to reap the benefits. In March 1951, he took steps to remedy the problem. Around the same time that Lansky testified before the Kefauver Committee for the third time, Batista announced himself as a candidate for president in the June 1952 Cuban elections.

The announcement was met with a curious lack of enthusiasm. Most Cubans knew, of course, that Batista would be running. It was assumed that his reentry into local politics as senator from Las Villas was a prelude to larger ambitions. In some quarters, Batista was still popular, especially within the military. He also had followers in the rural provinces, where he was seen as a *guajiro* (peasant) at heart. But much had changed since Batista first went into self-imposed exile seven and a half years earlier. Cuba's decade-long experiment with constitutional democracy had opened the door to a rambunctious collection of competing factions. The Auténtico Party was backing a candidate handpicked by President Carlos Prío, who had decided not to run for reelection. The Ortodoxo Party had a strong following among the unions and the student groups at the University of Havana. And then there was the national Communist Party, a wild-card faction that Batista had manipulated effectively in the past.

Throughout the latter months of 1951, Batista campaigned around the island. A huge billboard was erected in the middle of a traffic circle in Havana. A gigantic depiction of the candidate, looking dapper in a linen suit and two-tone shoes, towered over his campaign slogan: "*Este es el hombre*"—This is the man. Batista was such a recognizable figure that it wasn't even necessary to show his name on the billboard. Even so, his campaign sputtered. In December, the weekly magazine *Bohemia* printed the results of a public opinion poll that showed Batista running a distant third in the race.

What happened next has been a source of debate in Cuba ever since the events occurred. In later accounts, Batista would claim that he was approached by a group of young military officers who said they had un-covered evidence that Carlos Prío was planning to stage a coup d'état and would call off the elections and hold on to the presidency through paramilitary force. Prío denied that any such conspiracy ever existed. In any event, Batista met secretly with many of his followers in the military throughout the early months of 1952. In March, while the country was preoccupied with the annual pre-Lent carnival that unfolded with music, dance, and street celebrations, Batista made his move.

In the early-morning hours of March 10, a convoy of vehicles arrived at Camp Columbia, Cuba's military headquarters outside Havana. Batista stepped out of one car and was joined by members of a military revolu-tionary junta that included many top officers. To the gathered men, he said, "We must be very careful that no news gets out until we have this matter properly adjusted. Have the radio stations been taken care of?"

Batista was informed that all the major radio stations were under military control, as were the newspapers and other sources of informa-tion. Satisfied, he gave the order for a formation of tanks and other combat vehicles to proceed to the presidential palace. Once the palace was surrounded, President Prío was given the option of vacating the of-fice of the presidency. He fled with little resistance, first to the Mexican embassy and then into exile in Miami. Batista took over.

The coup d'état went off without a hitch. There was only one fatality, a military officer who resisted. When the citizens of Cuba awoke that morning, they were informed via radio that Fulgencio Batista was once again their president. At 4 P.M., a manifesto to the people was issued by the new government:

> The military junta have acted to avoid the regime of blood and corruption which has destroyed institutions, created disorder and mockery in the state, aggravated by the sinister plans of the government, which intended to continue further beyond its constitutional terms, for which President Prío had placed himself in agreement with various military leaders, preparing a military *golpe* [coup] before the elections.

It was a crystalline example of the "big lie" theory in action. Batista was the one who had used the military to stage a coup. He immediately set about shutting down the levers of democracy: the constitution was suspended, the upcoming elections were called off, all political parties were dissolved, and strikes by labor unions were prohibited for forty-five days by executive decree. To the public, Batista announced, "The people and I are the dictators."

Initially, the reaction on the part of the Cuban populace was one of stunned acquiescence. Historian Hugh Thomas described Batista's coup as "an event comparable in the life of an individual to a nervous breakdown after years of chronic illness." In *Cuba: Pursuit of Freedom*, his comprehensive political history of the island, Thomas writes:

> The prostitutes of Virtue Street knew that the substitution of Batista for Prío in the National Palace would make little difference to them . . . The Cuban political system, such as it was, had already been tortured to death. The accumulated follies of fifty years were bearing their rotten fruit.

The U.S. government lined up behind its old friend Batista. A mere two weeks after he subverted Cuban democracy, the Truman administration recognized him as the legitimate president, and his government was accorded all diplomatic courtesies. The degree to which the United States was favorably disposed toward Batista's actions was further underscored by *Time* magazine, which put on its cover a smiling illustration of El Presidente with the Cuban flag as a near halo, accompanied by the blithe headline "Cuba's Batista: He Got Past Democracy's Sentries."

U.S. government support for and aggrandizement of a man who had stolen the presidency by force and pissed all over the Cuban constitution was an insult that some Cubans would never forget or forgive.

Not everyone took matters lying down. One person whose career ambitions had been directly thwarted by Batista's brazen actions was Fidel Castro.

As a candidate from the Ortodoxo Party, Castro had been running for congress and stood a good chance of winning when, just eighty days before the election, Batista called everything off. Three days later, in a mimeographed pamphlet that circulated in the streets of Havana, Castro offered a scathing denunciation:

> [Batista's military coup] is not a revolution but a brutal snatching of power! They are not patriots but destroyers of freedom, usurpers, adventurers thirsty for gold and power . . . And you, Batista, who basely escaped for four years and, for three, engaged in useless politicking, appear now with your tardy, unsettling, and poisonous remedy, making shreds of the Constitution . . . Once again the military boots; once again Camp Columbia dictating decrees, removing and appointing ministers; once again the tanks roaring threateningly in our streets; once again brute force ruling over human reason . . . There is nothing as bitter in the world as the spectacle of a people that goes to bed free and wakes up in slavery.

Castro's anger was a manifestation of the frustration and helplessness that many Cubans felt at the time. There had been *golpes* in Cuba before, but they were usually hard-fought affairs with much bloodshed and political positioning. This one had occurred in the dead of night, more like a surreptitious rape than a murder. Castro and others who saw themselves as part of a movement for social justice in Cuba were caught off-guard. Now, in the face of Batista's "brute force," there seemed to be nothing they could do. Secret meetings were held, proclamations issued, and the stockpiling of guns began, but it would be months before Castro or other enemies of Batista would be able to formulate a plan of action.

In the meantime, El Presidente held all the cards. Batista set about taking over all financial institutions in Cuba and devising a system by which he could plunder the country's resources for his personal gain.

Although few recognized it at the time, it was a major step forward in the evolving fortunes of the Havana Mob.

FAR AWAY IN NEW YORK CITY, in his apartment building over-looking Central Park, Meyer Lansky most likely read about the coup in the papers and watched the television news reports with more than a passing interest. At the same time Batista had made the decision to bug-ger Cuba, Lansky was in the midst of one of his most fallow periods as a professional mobster. The Kefauver Committee had left him with little to show for himself. In a matter of months, all of his once-lucrative gam-bling casinos had been shut down. He was facing criminal charges in two states. He had been identified in the final report of the Kefauver Committee as a common gangster and all-round bad citizen. To Lansky, Batista being back in power must have seemed like the one glimmer of hope in a world gone horribly wrong.

Over the following months the Jewish Mob boss dealt with his legal problems. He was able to get his IRS charges in Florida reduced to a three-thousand-dollar fine, but on September 10, he was formally in-dicted in New York State on charges of conspiracy, gambling, and for-gery. The forgery charge, which had to do with someone else's name being inserted on the liquor license at Lansky's Arrowhead Inn casino in Saratoga Springs, was eventually thrown out. The other charges were equally weak. Moses Polakoff wanted to go to trial. "We would have won the case," Lansky's lawyer said years later. "But [Lansky] didn't want it . . . He didn't want to risk trial."

In order to avoid the publicity that would result from open legal proceedings, Meyer was willing to plead guilty and do the time, if necessary.

Meanwhile, he kept his eye on events in Cuba and waited for Batista to call.

5

RAZZLE-DAZZLE

ON AN EVENING IN APRIL 1952—WITHIN WEEKS OF Batista's seizing power in Cuba—a Los Angeles attorney by the name of Dana C. Smith was gambling at the Sans Souci, one of Havana's better-known nightclub-casinos. Located in the suburb of Marianao, not far from Oriental Park Racetrack, the Sans Souci was famous for its fabulous floor shows under the stars—exotic extravaganzas advertised as "authentic voodoo rituals." Scantily clad black and mocha-skinned females danced alongside dark-skinned *batá* drummers, while a singer chanted in high-pitched Yoruba. To the tourists, it all came under the heading "wild jungle rhythms," and it often left them excited and ready for anything. After the show, many in the audience flooded into the casinos, which was the case with Dana Smith, who soon found himself hunched over a gaming table with a large crowd gathered around him.

The game Smith was playing was called cubolo, an eight-dice variation on craps that was popular with grifters and bunco artists in Havana gaming circles. Cubolo was a classic example of "razzle-dazzle," a catchall phrase used to describe the numerous local games that had been created to confuse and fleece the tourists. The game was nearly incomprehensible, or at least it was to Smith, but he was excitedly told by bystanders,

"You can't lose if you keep doubling your bet." So Smith kept rolling the dice and doubling down—and he kept losing—until he'd frittered away forty-two hundred dollars (more than forty thousand in today's terms).

The California lawyer wrote out a check to cover the damages, but he wasn't happy about it. He felt as though he'd been lured into the game and skinned under false pretenses. Not only that, but he later discovered that this game called cubolo was not sanctioned under Cuban law. It was classic razzle-dazzle, in which "steerers" and "shills" worked gullible tourists, leading them to the gaming tables, egging them on until they had no more money to bet, then splitting the take with the house.

Dana Smith was not your average tourist. He was a close financial adviser of vice-presidential contender Richard M. Nixon of California, and not a man to be taken lightly.

Within days of being scammed in Havana, Smith had called his bank, stopped payment on the check he'd written, and refused to make good on his debt.

A loser welshing on a gambling debt was not uncommon in Havana gaming circles. Often the house would be willing to take the loss. But this was a sizable amount of money. There was also the principle involved: the Sans Souci had ripped off Smith fair and square. For years, gambling establishments in Havana had been running crooked games. Those who allowed themselves to be taken were suckers—and what would gambling be without its fair share of suckers?

The contract for running the gaming at the Sans Souci that season was held by Norman Rothman, a well-known nightclub operator from Miami Beach. Rothman assigned the Beverly Credit Service of California to collect Dana Smith's forty-two hundred dollars. The credit service filed suit against Smith, who in turn telephoned his friend Senator Richard Nixon. As a courtesy, Nixon wrote a letter to the U.S. State Department, asking them to look into Smith's contention that he had been cheated by a fraudulent game of chance. The State Department contacted the U.S. embassy in Havana, which launched an investigation into claims by Smith and other American tourists that gambling in Havana was rife with scams and illegalities.

At the same time, as part of his legal defense strategy, Smith initiated an all-out publicity campaign against Havana gambling. Numerous allegations of American tourists being swindled were made public: a young couple honeymooning in Havana had lost their life savings to the razzle-dazzle; a mother of four had lost her husband's monthly salary. Later, these and other accusations were given added credence when Smith won his case in a California court.

As the 1952–53 winter season approached, rumors spread throughout Havana that because of the negative publicity, the government might have to halt gambling and shut down the casinos. In *Diario de la Marina*, an influential daily newspaper that was pro-Batista, columnist Reinaldo Ramírez-Rosell wrote that unless Cuba wanted to be viewed as a "paradise of vice and an apse in the temple of world corruption," immediate action was necessary. Under the headline "*El Razzle-dazzle, mala publicidad*"—Razzle-dazzle, bad publicity—Ramírez-Rosell called for a new strategy to clean up gambling in the casinos or the Cuban economy would suffer the consequences.

President Batista knew a potential scandal when he saw one. Normally he would have allowed the country's Institute of Tourism to handle the problem, but as anyone in Cuba knew, the tourism institute had been bought off by the casino operators. Batista needed to bypass his own corrupt tourism apparatus if he sincerely intended to save Havana's casino-gambling industry from itself. Luckily, El Presidente had an ace up his sleeve—and its name was Meyer Lansky.

The timing was perfect. Lansky was in New York licking his wounds, dealing with the fallout from the Senate crime hearings, when Batista extended the offer of a lifetime. Would Lansky be willing to come to Havana and serve as the Cuban government's "adviser on gambling reform" for an annual retainer of twenty-five thousand dollars? The answer was: "You bet."

Lansky made his triumphant return to Havana in mid-1952. He

rented an executive suite at the Hotel Nacional. It was no doubt tempting for the Mob boss to view his return as a prelude to the wholesale development and plunder of Cuba that he and Luciano had always dreamed about. But in truth, Lansky didn't have the luxury of focusing exclusively on the big picture. In the short term, he had work to do.

Although Havana's gaming industry was reaping the benefits of a vibrant postwar rise in tourism, the lack of regulation had been dangerously shortsighted. Perception was everything in the casino trade: if the public had the impression—either through firsthand experience or bad publicity—that the games in Havana were not on the up-and-up, they would look elsewhere. Countries such as the Bahamas, Puerto Rico, the Dominican Republic, and Haiti were all making efforts to break into the booming postwar gambling business in the Caribbean. Mexico had started offering cheap excursion packages to U.S. tourists, hoping to cut in on the quick-and-easy sun-and-sand market. Batista and Lansky knew that unless they salvaged Cuba's reputation for providing gambling that was fair, their longtime dream of a mobster's paradise in Havana might be irrevocably derailed.

The problem was that in the years Fulgencio had been away from the presidency, Havana's gaming industry had become something of a free-for-all. The city's nightclub owners were leasing out their gaming rooms—and sometimes even individual games and tables—to just about anyone with a bankroll. Some were serious professional operators; others had less experience and less bankroll, and to give themselves an edge, they turned to razzle-dazzle, which offered quick returns on a minimal investment.

At the Sans Souci, the razzle layout was under the control of a grifter from the States named Muscles Martin. Muscles purchased the right to run his racket at the Sans Souci from Sammy Mannarino, a Pittsburgh-based racketeer who owned a piece of the place along with a mobster from Chicago and one from Detroit. Pitching his razzle from the entrance to the casino, Muscles routinely skinned suckers for anywhere between ten thousand and thirty thousand dollars a night. This money was split fifty-fifty with the house.

Muscles Martin's razzle-dazzle scheme had been so successful that similar rackets sprang up at the Gran Casino Nacional, the Jockey Club, and even the casino at the Tropicana, Havana's most fabulous entertainment venue. It was said that one of the only places in Havana where you could be guaranteed not to be hassled by razzle operators was at the "louse ring," a private game under the grandstand at Oriental Park Racetrack. The louse ring was run by taxi drivers, waiters, laborers, and others of the lumpen proletariat, and razzle was strictly forbidden.

As the country's new adviser on gambling reform, it was Lansky's job to put the kibosh on razzle-dazzle. But the razzle wasn't his only problem. In the casinos, dealers, pit bosses, and floor managers had become sloppy. Standards were low. Blackjack dealers were allowed to deal cards not from a box—as was the practice throughout the United States and elsewhere where gambling was popular—but from a deck in their hand. Pit bosses were often nowhere to be seen. And floor managers made their rounds but had no way of knowing what was happening in different areas of the casino floor.

Lansky made changes. He insisted that card boxes be used on all blackjack tables. Floor managers became "ladder men," hoisted up to sit in little jockey seats, like referees at a tennis match. They were now able to survey the entire room and spot cheaters, and were also highly visible, which inspired confidence among players. The standards Lansky imposed were the same as those he had used for years in his U.S. casinos in Saratoga Springs, South Florida, and New Orleans. He knew that a well-run casino was a profitable casino and—most importantly—that the house did not need to cheat to have an edge. The odds were already overwhelmingly in favor of the house. The only reason for shoddy standards and cheating was pure, unadulterated greed.

As for razzle-dazzle, Lansky handled this problem with the kind of brilliance that had long made him one of America's most successful mobsters. Knowing that the various razzle racketeers were connected to U.S. gangsters such as Pittsburgh's Sammy Mannarino and others, he did not ride into town and immediately start putting the scam artists out of business. Mobsters were making money from razzle-dazzle. If Lansky were to immediately shut things down, it would create resentment, if not a response of outright violence. Instead, Meyer established a beachhead: he purchased a piece of the Montmartre Club, a venerable casino and show palace just blocks from the Hotel Nacional in the Vedado section of Havana. Meyer became a controlling owner of the club and took over management of the gambling tables.

The first thing he did was import table crews from his now-defunct Greenacres Club in Florida, people who were accustomed to handling high-stakes games and high rollers. It was Lansky's intention to set an example, to show the shady operators and scam artists in Havana that the most profitable casino in town would be the one that ran the cleanest, fairest operation.

The wisdom of Lansky's approach was borne out in spectacular fashion when in March 1953, near the end of his first season as Cuba's official gambling czar, the *Saturday Evening Post* published an exposé on gambling in Cuba. The article was entitled "Suckers in Paradise: How Americans Lose Their Shirts in Caribbean Gambling Joints." Written by journalist Lester Velie, the article named names, citing Sammy Mannarino and his Chicago mobster partner, Dave Yaras, as the muscle behind the Sans Souci. "Displaced American mobsters figure as partners or concessionaires in four of Havana's five casinos," the article stated. Lansky's Montmartre Club was cited as the only major casino in town that did not countenance razzle-dazzle.

The fallout from the article was immediate. Two days after it appeared, President Batista announced that Cuban military intelligence (Servicio de Inteligencia Militar, or SIM) was being used to arrest thirteen U.S.-born card dealers who were employees of the Sans Souci and Tropicana nightclubs. The event was reported in the *New York Times*: "Helmeted and bayonet-wielding Cuban troops marched into the gambling joints and ordered the [razzle-dazzle] games out. Gun [sic] in hand, they patrolled the casino entrances to keep the games banished."

The following day, all of the thirteen people arrested were deported to the United States. In the *Times,* a spokesperson for the Cuban government was quoted as saying: "The President of the Republic has given definitive instructions to the various police forces to intensify measures for foreign tourists."

It had been beautifully played by Batista's "adviser on gambling reform." Lansky did not have to kick out the mobster-sponsored card cheats and razzle artists. He let Cuban military intelligence do it for him, but only after the cheaters' actions had been exposed in the pages of a major U.S. magazine. This way their mobster sponsors could not object. Lansky had done his job. In a matter of months, he had cleared out the deadwood and reformed gambling in Havana, become co-owner of his own successful casino, and laid the foundation for what would soon become the most storied gambling empire in history. And he did it all without ruffling anyone's feathers.

It was Lansky's own version of the razzle-dazzle.

In terms of revenue, the tourist season was a good one in Havana that year. A potential crisis had been averted. Lansky was so pleased that on May 2, 1953, he had no hesitation in finally pleading guilty to gambling charges in upstate New York. He was fined twenty-five hundred dollars and sentenced to three months in jail. The judge offered him a few days to put his affairs in order before going into prison, but he declined the offer. He wanted to do his time and have it out of the way by the time the new tourist season in Cuba rolled around.

From the courthouse in Saratoga Springs, he drove directly to the county jail and began his sentence with two books under his arm—an English dictionary and a revised version of the King James Bible. His wife, Teddy, rented a room nearby and pledged to visit him every day of his brief incarceration.

The lone inmate to share a cellblock with Lansky was a local man also in on gambling charges. Of Lansky, years later the man said: "I liked him. He was a gentleman; a man of his word. If he told you anything, you felt you could believe it."

Lansky exercised every day in jail. Upon his release on July 2—one month early on account of good behavior—he was ready and rarin' to go.

THE FULL-SCALE REUNIFICATION of Batista and Lansky was a watershed event. As the people of Cuba struggled to deal with a sudden and ironfisted subversion of constitutional law and democracy on the island, mobsters everywhere recognized the Batista-Lansky alliance for what it was: a call to arms. Most of the mobsters who flooded into Havana over the next several seasons would come from differing parts of the United States, but some were already embedded in Cuban society. Many businessmen, bank presidents, and political operatives on the island had been waiting for this moment for years. Among those who stepped forward to become prominent members of the Havana Mob were:

Amadeo Barletta Barletta—A beefy, silver-haired Italo-Cubano with business links to the Mafia in Italy, Barletta was a formidable presence in Cuban business and financial circles. He was president of his own bank—Banco Atlántico—which would soon emerge as a conduit by which the American mobsters laundered money and diversified their gambling profits. Barletta had a famously shady past, which only added to his allure in Havana.

Born in Calabria, Italy, to a wealthy family, he first moved to the Caribbean in the 1920s. He opened the first automobile dealership in the region, in the Dominican Republic. At the same time, he served as Italian consul general in the capital city of Santo Domingo.

In May 1935, he was accused by the dictatorship of Rafael Trujillo of being involved in a plot to assassinate the president. Barletta was thrown in jail, and his holdings, which included a tobacco plantation, were confiscated by the Dominican government.

The Italian government of Benito Mussolini demanded Barletta's release. After paying a bail of fifty thousand dollars, Barletta was set free. He fled the island and settled in nearby Cuba, where he worked as a sales representative for General Motors.

In the early years of U.S. involvement in the Second World War, Barletta was accused by the FBI of being a double agent. He was apparently working as a spy for the U.S. government while at the same time serving as the "administrator of Mussolini's family in the United States." Barletta went on the lam and for the duration of the war hid out in Venezuela. When he returned to Cuba following the war, all was forgiven. He went back to work for General Motors and also became a sales agent for Cadillac, Chevrolet, Oldsmobile, and other major U.S. auto manufacturers in Cuba. In Havana, he constructed an eleven-story triangle-shaped building on Infanta Street and the Malecón known as Ambar Motors. He financed Channel 2 on Cuban television and was a controlling partner in *El Mundo,* a daily newspaper. With the backing of Cuban and U.S. financial institutions, he accrued a dizzying array of businesses, many of which served as fronts for various criminal rackets in Havana, including the trafficking of narcotics and precious gems.

Amletto Battisti y Lora—Like Amadeo Barletta, Battisti was an influential businessman in Havana who was known to work both sides of the law. As the owner of the Hotel Sevilla Biltmore—second only to the Hotel Nacional as Havana's most prestigious tourist address—Battisti was a powerful mover and shaker in the city. His restaurant-casino atop the Hotel Sevilla was popular with political functionaries from the presidential palace, located just a few short blocks away.

A Uruguayan of Italian ancestry who had resided in Cuba since the 1920s, Battisti was tall and lean, with a receding hairline and an impressive collection of linen suits. He presented himself as a dapper international businessman. To finance his many corporate dealings, he had his own bank, Banco de Créditos e Inversiones. Two of Battisti's side businesses were prostitution and narcotics. He sometimes bragged about how a fresh shipment of prostitutes arrived at his hotel on a weekly basis, to be hired out as high-priced escorts. As for narcotics, Battisti's Hotel Sevilla was the center of action in a city where cheap thrills and illicit pleasure were never more than a cab ride away.

According to a confidential memo from an undercover U.S. narcotics agent in Havana, shipments of cocaine arrived at the hotel from Madrid on a weekly basis aboard a commercial airliner. Cocaine and marijuana were sold from the Longchamps Restaurant in the Hotel Sevilla Arcade. The retail price was somewhere between fifteen and fifty dollars a gram, depending on availability. The coca was sold in tubes, or *pomos*. Larger drug deals were made with a Cuban on the premises known only as "El Guano." Harder drugs such as opium and heroin could also be purchased, but those usually involved a trip to one of the three or four nightclubs in the vicinity of the hotel.

Rolando Masferrer—In the two decades leading up to Fulgencio Batista's return to power, no political gangster on the island instilled fear more effectively than Masferrer. A legendary figure who began his career as a member of the Cuban Communist Party seeking to overthrow the dictatorship of Gerardo Machado, he also fought in the Spanish Civil War as a member of the Abraham Lincoln Brigade. Through his leadership of the notorious political club Movimiento Socialista Revolucionario (MSR), he established himself as an efficient hit man. During the heyday of *gangsterismo* at the University of Havana in the late 1940s, his primary rival was Fidel Castro. He twice tried to assassinate Castro, who returned the favor by sending a hit squad to kill Masferrer.

An attractive, dashing figure with a pencil-thin mustache à la Clark Gable, Masferrer liked to wear cowboy hats and sing country-and-western songs, affectations from having lived for a time in Texas. He was known to ride around like a potentate in a convertible Cadillac outfitted with military-issue machine guns, surrounded by bodyguards. He used gangsterism and outright murder as a form of social advancement, and by 1947 he was named to head the country's secret police. He was a firm believer in graft and was known to have amassed a fortune by enforcing his own private "tax" on commercial establishments. Later, he got himself elected to the Cuban senate as a representative of Oriente Province. He also owned and edited a magazine, *Tiempo en Cuba,* in which he published scathing diatribes against his political enemies.

Senator Masferrer liked to form alliances with other corrupt officials. Once, when he proposed a certain minister as a possible presidential candidate, a member of his own Auténtico Party objected. "But he's a gangster," the man said.

"Yes, *chico*," replied Masferrer, "but we're all gangsters. What do you expect? This isn't Europe."

In 1952 the gangster senator threw his weight wholeheartedly behind Batista, whom he recognized as a kindred spirit. Masferrer formed his own private army of approximately fifteen hundred men. In Oriente Province they commenced a campaign of robbing, killing, torturing, and extorting money. They called themselves *Los Tigres* (the Tigers) *de Masferrer*.

President Batista already had the army, the dreaded SIM, and a covert squad within the National Police to repress his enemies, but with Masferrer's Tigres he now had his own *pandilla*, or gang—a criminal extension of the state that was beholden to no one except Masferrer, Batista, and the rest of the Havana Mob.

The island's cadre of corrupt business and political figures was energized by what promised to be the opening of the floodgates in Havana. But even they knew that the criminal know-how and flow of capital would have to come from outsiders. For those who operated within the island's nexus of commerce, politics, and corruption, this was no problem. For nearly a century, Cuba's social elite had been intertwined with outside corporate interests, forming a ruling cartel that was a mix of U.S. industrialists, sugar barons, tourism magnates, and international financiers. President Batista made it clear where his loyalties resided by naming the retired sugar baron Marcial Facio as the head of a newly constituted Tourism Commission and placing its functions in the hands of his own handpicked team—one that included Meyer Lansky.

The U.S. mobsters arrived in stages. Some were men who had attended the Mob conference at the Hotel Nacional back in December 1946. It had always been understood that when the day came and the money began to flow, these men would get their piece of the pie. From

Cleveland came members of the old Mayfield Road Gang, with whom Lansky had formed the Molaska Corporation in the years following the repeal of Prohibition. Prominent among this group were Sam Tucker, Morris Kleinman, and Moe Dalitz, who had attended the Nacional conference and with whom Lansky would also do business in Las Vegas. Also present was Vincent "Jimmy Blue Eyes" Alo, who represented the interests of numerous mob outfits from New York to Chicago. Tall, slender, and balding, Alo would one day be immortalized in *The Godfather Part II*, where he was portrayed as a sinister character named Johnny Ola.

Mobster representatives from Buffalo, Kansas City, Pittsburgh, New Orleans, and the five families of New York also began making regular trips to the Pearl of the Antilles. In the well-shaded cabanas poolside at the Hotel Nacional, Lansky sometimes met with these men to eat sandwiches, discuss business, and play cards. The games were usually friendly, with small stakes, mostly for kibitzing rather than competition.

One man who was rarely seen fraternizing with Lansky poolside or anywhere else in Havana was Santo Trafficante. A green-eyed, bespectacled mafioso from Tampa, Florida, Trafficante had roots in Cuba that went back almost as far as Lansky's. People said Trafficante looked like a bank executive, or even a mild-mannered college professor, but in Tampa's Italian neighborhoods they knew better. A person who was told, "If you don't do the right thing, the man with the green eyes will come see you," often went into hiding. Santo Trafficante was not as harmless as he looked.

Although he was a generation younger than many of the gangsters who would come to make up the Havana Mob, Trafficante's contributions to the cause were monumental. He had been the youngest attendee of the 1946 conference at the Nacional and his contacts in Cuba were substantial. Maybe he did not have Batista in his pocket, as Lansky did, but unlike the New York Jew from the Lower East Side, Trafficante was a fluent Spanish speaker with a well-honed familiarity with Cuban culture. As the years passed and a hierarchy within the Havana Mob took shape, Trafficante would rate as the second most powerful mobster in town behind Lansky.

And therein lay the problem: from the beginning, Trafficante's relationship with Lansky was complicated and sometimes hostile. Jealousy, bigotry, and underworld competitiveness were all motivating factors for Santo. Lansky, after all, had usurped the patiently cultivated plans of Trafficante's father, Santo Trafficante Sr. As far back as the 1920s, the elder, Sicilian-born Trafficante had been establishing a domain in Cuba that he intended to bequeath to his son. The Trafficantes were supposed to be the Mafia bosses of Havana, until Lansky came along and reshuffled the deck.

Frank Ragano, who was Trafficante's lawyer for most of his life, once asked the mafioso about Lansky. "That dirty Jew bastard," said Santo. "If he tries to talk to you, don't have anything to do with him. My father had some experiences with him and you can't trust him."

Trafficante's connection to Cuba began before he had ever set foot on the island. In Tampa, the largest city on Florida's Gulf Coast (pop. 125,000 in the mid-1950s), Cubans were the dominant minority. As far back as the 1890s, the city's population was infused by Cuban immigrants fleeing the turmoil of their native island during the War of Independence. Ybor City, a neighborhood in east Tampa that was once its own city but was later incorporated into the city of Tampa, became a center of political activity for Cuban exiles. In the restaurants and *cafecitos* around Ybor Square, money was raised and guns stockpiled to be shipped to the *mambises*, or freedom fighters, in Cuba. The city was a popular rallying stop for revolutionaries, including José Martí. In 1893, while in the city to raise money and give a speech, Martí was the victim of a failed assassination attempt. Two Spanish agents attempted to poison the Cuban renegade, but the plot was foiled. Martí saved the two Spaniards from a lynching and forgave them. In gratitude, the two men joined the revolutionary movement and died alongside Martí in the 1895 skirmish at Dos Ríos in Cuba.

Along with the political activism in Ybor City, another favorite pastime of Tampa's immigrant community was a simple game of chance called bolita. In Spanish, the word *bolita* means "little ball." The game was played by placing a bunch of numbered balls into a sack and staging a public draw. Players bet on the number they felt would be the last to be drawn. The wagers were usually small—as little as a nickel or a dime—but everyone played, resulting in a substantial daily kitty. The payoff was guaranteed at 90 to 1.

Bolita had been hugely popular for generations back in Cuba (it was first brought to Florida by a bolita magnate named Manuel "El Gallego" Suarez) and in Tampa the game became the foundation for an entire criminal underworld. Gang wars were waged for control of the racket, and by the 1920s the man who emerged as the overlord of bolita in Tampa was the wily mafioso Santo Trafficante Sr. The elder Trafficante used his bolita bank to underwrite his involvement in rum-running. It was through this activity that Trafficante Sr. first met Lansky and Luciano, with whom he smuggled rum and molasses from Cuba into the United States.

With the repeal of Prohibition in 1933, Trafficante Sr. shifted his attention to narcotics. With his Cuban connections through the bolita racket, he traveled to Havana and began cultivating important contacts. Two men who formed a business relationship with Trafficante Sr. were Indalecio Pertierra, the influential congressman and operator of the Jockey Club inside Oriental Park Racetrack, and Senator Paco Prío, brother of the future president of Cuba.

In 1945, Pertierra was among the founders of Aerovías Q, an airline that initially operated out of military airports. The idea behind Aerovías Q was for the Mafia in Cuba to have its own airline and not be required to pass through local customs. According to Enrique Cirules, a Cuban author who has closely examined the roots of Mafia influence on the island:

From early on, Aerovías Q made a weekly flight: Havana—Camagüey—Barranquilla—Bogotá. A powerful laboratory in Medellín produced "powder" destined for Santo Trafficante Sr.; but everything indicates that this intrigue involved the participation of certain figures of the *Auténtico* party in Camagüey who were associated with pharmaceutical laboratories or drugstores. The Camagüey contacts were an essential link in the drug trade. The cocaine did not always reach the Cuban capital in a direct manner. Rather, the shipments were transferred at the Camagüey airport.

Trafficante Sr. was the boss, but when Charlie Luciano arrived in Havana in late 1946, things changed. Pertierra and Prío dropped Trafficante to go with the more powerful New York syndicate of Luciano and Lansky, which may explain why the Trafficantes forever after resented the Jew from New York named Lansky.

By 1950, Papa Trafficante was in semiretirement, due in part to deteriorating health, and his son stepped forward to assume full control of the bolita business, which continued to flourish in Ybor City. In fact, business was so good that it attracted the attention of the Kefauver Committee. In December 1950 the committee held hearings in the Tampa county courthouse. The Trafficantes had somehow avoided being subpoenaed, but one person who was called to testify was their longtime rival in the bolita business, a man named Charlie Wall.

Wall was an irascible old-timer who had survived numerous attempts by the Trafficantes to wipe him off the face of the earth. In the mid-1940s he had retired from the bolita business and moved to Miami, where he partnered with Lansky and others in a variety of rackets, including dog and horse racing. By the time Wall sat down in front of the Kefauver Committee, he was approaching seventy-one years of age and was slightly hard of hearing, but he still put on quite a show. He did not identify the Trafficantes by name, but he gave a thumbnail history of bolita in Tampa and described in detail several attempts on his life, including one would-be hit that was believed to have been engineered by Santo Jr.:

WALL: The first time it happened I came out of my garage.
COMMITTEE MEMBER: Yes.

WALL: And my wife was with me, and she was a little in front of me, and I came out on the sidewalk to my front gate, and some folks came by in an automobile, and a fellow began shooting with a pistol—I don't know whether it was a pistol or a revolver or what it was. But I didn't realize anybody was shooting until the thing hit me and then, of course—

COMMITTEE MEMBER [interrupting]: Hit you in the back?

WALL: Well, it kind of—as the Negro says—it glimpsed me.

COMMITTEE MEMBER: It glimpsed you?

WALL: Then, I fell down, and somebody shot a shotgun, but of course I was down when they shot the shotgun and the buckshot didn't hit me. Then the car drove away, and I think I was so scared I shot at it. I think maybe I had a pistol, too. And then I got in the house.

Wall's testimony riveted the committee and startled many in the Tampa underworld, who wondered if the old man had lost his mind. Although he had not named names, like Willie Moretti in New York he was far too loose with his tongue. Most felt it was only a matter of time before Charlie Wall paid the ultimate price.

Ironically, the old man struck first. In mid-1952, Wall began making moves as if he were trying to work his way back into the bolita rackets. A number of tit-for-tat Mob murders occurred in and around Tampa that harked back to the old days of the bolita wars. A key salvo in this skirmish took place on the evening of January 2, 1953. Santo Jr. and his wife had just come out of their house in Ybor City and were in the front seat of Trafficante's 1951 Mercury. Out of the corner of his eye, Santo saw a car approaching. Before he could even turn to look—*boom!*—a spray of 12-gauge buckshot pelted his arm. Another shot hit above the rear window, barely missing Trafficante and his wife. The gunmen sped away.

The attack was remarkably similar to the one Charlie Wall had described before the Kefauver Committee, right down to the buckshot and the fact that Trafficante was accompanied by his wife at the time.

Retaliation came quickly, in the Sicilian manner. Not long after the shotgun episode, Charlie Wall, the old-timer, was found by his wife in their home with his throat slit from ear to ear. Although the murder was never solved, all indicators pointed to the man with the green eyes.

The volley of gangland killings in Tampa made it a good time for Trafficante to hop on a plane to Havana. When he arrived there on a tourist visa in 1953, Lansky was in the process of straightening out the razzle-dazzle.

Trafficante did not need Lansky. Through his father, he owned an interest in the Comodoro hotel and casino, and he also had a narcotics-smuggling partnership with Amletto Battisti at the Hotel Sevilla Biltmore. Trafficante was a force in his own right. But it was also true that the momentum in Havana had shifted in favor of Lansky, who, through his connections to the Cuban government, was seen as the number one man in Havana gaming circles.

In October 1953, Trafficante purchased a controlling interest in the Sans Souci nightclub from the Pittsburgh-based duo of Sammy Mannarino and his brother, Kelly. This major transaction was most likely brokered by Lansky and perhaps even President Batista. The Sans Souci had been at the heart of the razzle scandal, and the moving aside of the Mannarino brothers was part of the cleanup.

It was a good deal for all involved. With Havana's gambling fortunes on the cusp of a boom, the Mannarinos most likely cashed out at a good price. The stain of razzle-dazzle was purged. And Santo Trafficante was now boss at one of the city's most prized nightclubs. He formed a company called International Amusements Corporation, which was in charge of booking entertainment at Cuba's various resorts and casinos. It was a lucrative side business for Santo. He gathered around him a group of men he could trust: Norman Rothman, who was allowed to stay on as gambling manager at the Sans Souci; Joe Silesi, alias Joe Rivers, who would become gambling manager at the Deauville Hotel; James Longo, Trafficante's Tampa-based bodyguard; and Joe Stassi, the former Manhattan bootlegger by way of New Jersey who served as a go-between for Trafficante, Lansky, and other important mobsters in Havana.

Traveling sometimes under the name Joe Santos, Trafficante shuttled back and forth between Havana, Tampa, and New York, where he maintained his father's old Mafia contacts. In Havana, he lived in a fabulous upper-floor apartment in the Vedado neighborhood, at Calle 12, No. 20.

Though married, Santo kept a Cuban mistress named Rita, a former showgirl who was twenty years his junior. He told Frank Ragano, his Tampa-based lawyer who visited him, "I've got a wonderful wife, but everybody in Cuba has a mistress, even Batista. You've got to have fun in this world."

THE CASINOS WERE in fine fettle and the Havana Mob was beginning to assert itself in the early months of 1953, but all was not right in the land of Christopher Columbus. Batista's *golpe* had created a mood of unrest that would not go away. A tradition of rebellion had been reawakened, though it was difficult to gauge the actual level of resistance. Censorship was rigorously enforced on the island. The regime enacted the Law of Public Order, which had as a subset Legislative Decree 997, a law that made it a criminal act to release any statement or information against the dictatorship. Through SIM, the government maintained a network of spies and paid informants who passed along information regarding "subversive activities." Newspapers were a common target, their offices trashed and editors threatened or imprisoned if they published anything even remotely contrary to the wishes of the government. In fact, anyone who disseminated anything perceived to be anti-Batista—pamphleteers, political activists, or rabble-rousers of any kind—was met with harassment, imprisonment, or death.

Another mollifying factor was that the entire country was occupied with the centennial anniversary of the birth of José Martí. In the years since Cuba had achieved its nominal independence, no single figure had galvanized the populace as much as the poet, journalist, exile, and *mambí* who died in battle at the age of forty-two. Batista himself had appropriated the image of Martí often in his career, calling him "the greatest inspiration in my life and the life of the Cuban people." Never mind that Martí preached a doctrine of freedom and liberation that was contrary to everything Batista had come to represent. El Presidente, much like Cubans of all ideological stripes, molded Martí's words and image to fit his needs.

On the night of January 27, a demonstration occurred that was supposed to be in honor of the Martí centennial. A huge phalanx of citizens that included university students, women's rights groups, high school students, labor groups, and others marched through the streets of Havana in a torchlight parade. On Calle 23, in Vedado, they passed the many nightclubs, casinos, bodegas, and bars overflowing with sailors and other tourists. The Cuban people and the tourists eyed each other warily, two ships passing in the night, players in a drama that had not yet begun to reveal its true nature.

Among the marchers was a well-organized contingent led by the young lawyer-activist Fidel Castro. Marching in military formation, the group chanted, "Revolution! . . . Revolution! . . . Revolution! . . ." The flaming torches they carried in their hands were outfitted with large, pointed iron nails at the top to be used as lethal weapons in the event of an attack by the riot police. Because of the large number of foreign visitors and international press at the parade, the police did not attack. The event went off with no disturbances.

The island had been remarkably quiet throughout the tourist season of 1952–53. Now that the season had passed and the hot summer months were approaching, many felt that, given the level of anger and resistance in the air, some sort of organized reaction was bound to occur.

In the early-morning hours of July 26, 1953, the other shoe finally dropped.

Shots rang out at the gate of the Moncada army barracks in the city of Santiago de Cuba in Oriente Province. It was an attack staged by a group of rebels disguised in Cuban Army uniforms. A corresponding attack also took place in the nearby town of Bayamo at another military barracks. Altogether, 160 rebels took part in the assault, which had been timed to correspond with a festival that had taken place the night before in Oriente. The thinking on the part of the attackers was that the soldiers would be stretched thin and inattentive at 5:30 A.M. on the morning following the festival. The plan was for the rebels to over- whelm the soldiers and capture the barracks. It was, in other words, a blatant act of armed insurrection against the military dictatorship of Batista, led by—among others—Fidel Castro and his younger brother, Raúl.

The attack went horribly wrong almost from the beginning. Al- though an initial group of rebels did in fact penetrate the barracks, they met strong resistance. Outside the barracks, Castro rammed a car into two soldiers armed with machine guns and tried to rally his troops. It quickly took on the quixotic appearance of a losing cause. The rebels were outnumbered by nearly ten to one, and they were poorly armed. Their entire armaments consisted of three U.S. Army rifles, six old Winchester rifles, one old machine gun, a large number of gaming rifles, small arms in the form of pistols, and some ammunition. The idea from the beginning was to overtake the barracks as quickly as possible and acquire more weapons from within, but that plan backfired when the rebels encountered fierce opposition. A volley of gunfire forced Castro and his men to retreat. Soldiers fired from the first floor of the barracks. The rebels ducked behind cars for cover. At this point, two of Castro's men had been killed and one was mortally wounded; the army had lost three officers and sixteen soldiers—a total of nineteen fatalities. Both sides had a large number of wounded. The battle had lasted about one hour.

The second attack at Bayamo had gone even worse. There, the battle had lasted fifteen minutes: six rebels were killed.

The surviving rebels tried to escape, but a military dragnet was quickly put into place. Within hours, 80 of the original 160 rebels were captured. Others, including Castro, were able to hide out in the nearby forest before being captured days later.

It would take some time for news of the attack to become known, at least officially. Rumors spread that many of the rebels taken into custody were being systematically tortured and killed by the army. The government announced that more than sixty rebels had been killed. On August 2, the magazine *Bohemia* printed photographs of bodies, many of them dressed up in fresh clothing to give the appearance that they had been killed while fighting rather than by being tortured and massacred, as the magazine suggested.

At the time of the attack, Batista was at his vacation home at Varadero Beach, a tourist resort 90 miles east of Havana. Six days later, he traveled to Santiago to commiserate with the surviving soldiers. He showed no great signs of concern. The failed attack had been quelled with a minimum of military casualties. Batista denied that there had been any kind of "massacre" of captured rebels; those who had survived and were in custody would be tried in a court according to Cuban law.

It seemed as though the Moncada attack was a minor affair—at least that was how it was portrayed by the government. *Bohemia* magazine aside, the government was virtually the sole official disseminator of information on the island. Unless you knew someone who was directly involved in the event, there was no way of finding out exactly what had taken place. The "fog of war" generated by the dictatorship had successfully obscured the event.

To the mobsters, casino owners, and businessmen who oversaw commercial activity in Havana, the incident was little more than a distant echo. After all, the Moncada attack and its aftermath had taken place in Oriente, on the extreme far end of the island from Havana. More importantly, it had occurred in July—during the off-season. In fact, given that the attack received little mention in the U.S. press, there was a good chance that Lansky, Trafficante, and other U.S. mobsters didn't even know it had taken place. From their home bases in New York, Miami, Tampa, and elsewhere, the mobsters had little way of knowing that the Moncada attack and the date of its occurrence—July 26—would go down in history as the opening salvo of an unprecedented revolution-ary campaign.

In the months and years ahead, they would be learning more than they ever wanted to know about the man who had organized the attack, a volatile, charismatic rebel leader whom everyone would come to know by his first name: Fidel.

6

THE GHOST OF JOSÉ MARTÍ

THERE WAS LITTLE IN THE CHILDHOOD OF FIDEL CASTRO Ruz to suggest that he would one day become the bête noire of the Havana Mob. Even by his own accounts, the budding revolutionary had lived a privileged youth. Born on August 13, 1926, into a world of automobiles, fine clothes, plentiful food, and later a private-school education, he was treated with deference by others in his town. Although his father had come from Spain in 1887 as a destitute orphan, by the time Fidel was born the Castros owned a *finca* near Birán, a village in the fertile agricultural region of Oriente. Birán was not far from where Fulgencio Batista had been born and raised. Like Batista, the Castros lived in the shadow of the United Fruit Company. Unlike Batista, whose father cut sugarcane to eke out a meager living, Castro's father was a *latifundista*, a Spanish-Cuban patriarch who made his fortune from the labor of others. As Fidel would one day tell an interviewer:

> All the circumstances surrounding my life and childhood, everything
> I saw, would have made it logical to suppose I would develop the hab-
> its, the ideas, the sentiments natural to the social class with certain
> privileges and selfish motives that make it indifferent to the problems

of others . . . I was the son of a landowner—there was a reason for me to be a reactionary. I was educated in religious schools that were attended by the sons of the rich—another reason for being reactionary. I lived in Cuba, in which all the films, publications and mass media were "made in the USA"—a third reason for being reactionary. I studied at a university in which, out of thousands of students, only thirty vere anti-imperialist and I was to become one of those. When I entered the university, it was as the son of a landowner and, to make matters worse, as a political illiterate.

It is an odd quirk of history that the two most powerful forces behind the Havana Mob—Batista and Lansky—were both born into harsh poverty, while Castro was weaned by the social elite. Having contributed to the flowering of lavish hotels, casinos, and cabarets in Havana, Batista and Lansky would devote their lives to the betterment of the bourgeoisie, while Castro, the son of privilege, would become an advocate for the poor and dispossessed. It was an inverse reality that would ultimately push the Havana Mob past the point of moral credibility and help Castro to destroy everything that Lansky and his associates had hoped to accomplish in Cuba.

For Fidel, the road to revolutionary fervor was partly the consequence of a rambunctious adolescence. Although in later years Castro would craft a biography in which his privileged youth was not particularly formative, his behavior suggested otherwise. Early photographs of Fidel show a well-fed, well-groomed child dressed up to look like exactly what he was: the son of a would-be aristocrat. An armchair psychiatrist might surmise that much of Castro's drive and ambition in his adolescence and young adulthood was a reaction against the aristocratic trappings of his youth. In school, his desire to prove himself played out in daring and even reckless behavior. He was physically assertive: hiking, swimming, and team sports were his favorite pastimes. He liked to challenge himself and others, even adults. In a rare biographical interview in 1959, he said of his grade school years in Oriente:

I spent most of my time being fresh . . . I remember that whenever I disagreed with something the teacher said to me, or whenever I got mad, I would swear at her and immediately leave school, running as fast as I could . . . One day, I had sworn at the teacher and was racing down the rear corridor. I took a leap and landed on a board from a guava-jelly box with a nail in it. As I fell, the nail stuck in my tongue. When I got home, my mother said to me: "God punished you for swearing at the teacher." I didn't have the slightest doubt that it was really true.

Castro was a good student, diligent and inquisitive, but he had a problem with authority. In his early adolescence, he attended a school run by the Christian Brothers, a Catholic order known for its strict discipline. Many times, Castro was on the receiving end of swats and slaps from the Christian Brothers, until one day he exploded. As Fidel remembered it:

We were playing ball one day. The kid who was at the head of the line always had the best position, and I was half arguing over first place with somebody else when the priest came up to me from behind and hit me on the head. This time I turned on him, right then and there, threw a piece of bread at his head and started to hit him with my fists and bite him. I don't think I hurt the priest much, but the daring outburst became a historic event in school.

Castro fared much better with the Jesuits. In 1941 he was accepted at Belén College, an exclusive Jesuit prep school in Havana. It was a big step, moving from the provinciality of Oriente to the urban maelstrom of Havana, but Fidel was ready. At the Catholic preparatory school, he maintained an interest in sports, excelling in basketball and baseball. He was a dynamic leader and showed great promise as an orator. Later he would credit the Jesuit priests for imbuing in him a thirst for knowledge and a sense of social justice that would change the direction of his life.

By the time he entered the University of Havana at the age of nineteen, Castro was mature for his years. He dressed conventionally in suit and tie, or a plain white guayabera, and grew a wispy, pencil-thin mustache in the Cuban style. He was politically active at a time when political activism at the university was a dangerous endeavor. He formed his own political "action group" and entered into the realm of *gangsterismo*. A U.S. intelligence report from around this time described Castro as "a typical example of a young Cuban of good background who, because of lack of parental education or real education, may soon become a fully fledged gangster."

In 1947 Fidel took part in the first of two major acts of political insurrection that would serve as precursors to his later attack on the army barracks at Moncada.

In the nearby Dominican Republic, the ugly dictatorship of Rafael Trujillo was engaged in one of its periodic purges of political dissent on the island, with the imprisonment and mass slaughter of large swathes of the population. Political groups throughout the world were in opposition—with the exception of the U.S. government, which tacitly supported the dictatorship. In Cuba, a group of Dominican exiles rallied support for a plan to overthrow the Trujillo dictatorship by force. A movement that crossed ideological lines and included a faction within the Cuban government backed the idea; they began to train for the invasion on a small islet off the coast of Camagüey Province known as Cayo Confites. Fidel Castro, age twenty, was among the force of twelve hundred men who, in blistering heat and under permanent mosquito assault, underwent armed guerrilla training on the islet for nearly two months.

At the eleventh hour, the mission was aborted. Some of the men at Cayo Confites decided to attack anyway and sailed for the Dominican Republic. Castro was among this group. Ironically, also on the small coastal freighter heading due east was Rolando Masferrer, Castro's primary rival among the political gangster squads at the university. This unlikely coalition was momentarily created by their desire to see Trujillo removed.

Not far from the coast of the Dominican Republic, the boat was intercepted by the Cuban Navy and everyone on board was arrested. As the failed expedition was being escorted back toward Cuba, Castro realized that he was now surrounded by his political enemies, that is, Masferrer and his cohorts, who, with the Dominican expedition now terminated, no longer had a compelling reason to view him as a comrade in arms.

Castro decided to jump overboard. Later he would claim: "I did not let myself be arrested, more than anything else, for a question of honor: It shamed me that this expedition ended by being arrested." A member of the expedition who served as an intermediary between Castro and Masferrer thought it had more to do with self-preservation: Castro jumped overboard because he was concerned that Masferrer and his men would try to kill him. The intermediary felt Fidel made the right move: "I could guarantee his life while he was in the camps but not after the invasion was aborted." Castro wound up swimming nine miles through shark-infested waters to reach the Cuban coast.

Political action was its own kind of narcotic: Fidel detested politicians and so-called activists who were all talk and no action. His next foray into the arena of armed insurrection occurred just seven months later, in April 1948. In Bogotá, Colombia, thousands gathered for what was to be a convention of Latin American activists. The purpose of the three-day conference was to put together and deliver a unified statement against U.S. imperialism. Castro and one other member of the law school had been chosen as delegates from the Federación Estudiantil Universitaria (FEU), or University Student Federation.

On the second day of his trip to Bogotá, Fidel set off to meet with a prominent politician who was popular with the progressive wing of the Colombian Liberal Party. Before he arrived for the scheduled meeting, Castro was informed that the politician had just been gunned down in the street. What followed was three days of explosive violence, a riot that would go down in history as the Bogotazo, the beginning of a sustained period of political violence in Colombia that continues to this day.

In later years, Castro's enemies would claim that he played a much larger role in the Bogotazo than he actually did. The fact that he was a witness to history in Colombia was mostly pure chance. He did, however, contribute to the upheaval. Police in Bogotá reported that the young Cuban law student was seen firing a tear-gas shotgun that had been stolen from a precinct. The situation was chaotic, so the cops were never able to ascertain what or whom Castro was firing at. Nonetheless, the police attempted to hunt down a group of students that included Fidel. After hiding out in Bogotá for a few days, Castro sought refuge at the Cuban embassy. He was flown home to Havana aboard a Cuban aircraft along with a shipment of bulls.

As Castro would note in later years, the violence he witnessed during the Bogotazo was horrendous. He vowed that no such explosion of anarchy would take place in Cuba, no matter how justified the action might be.

Mostly, the events in Bogotá—along with Castro's earlier involvement in the aborted invasion of the Dominican Republic—elevated his status among those in Cuba who felt that direct action was the noblest form of political expression.

Despite his adventurous nature, Castro settled down. He married, had a son, and graduated from law school in 1950. In Havana, he began his own legal practice, representing mostly the poor and indigent, often free of charge. Money was a constant problem, though in a pinch he could always borrow from his father. By the time Castro announced that he was going to run for political office, he seemed to have resigned himself to a middle-class existence: family, profession, politics—leftist politics, yes, but mainstream nonetheless. At this point, Fidel wasn't even a communist; he represented a party—Ortodoxo—that worked within the boundaries of the Cuban system.

Batista's *golpe* changed all that. Some would say that Fidel's strong reaction against Batista's actions was solely the product of his thwarted ambition. This is a myopic point of view. If nothing else, Castro's life up until this point had shown that he was a man willing to stand up for what he believed in. He had shown not only a willingness but also a strong desire to take action when the cause was right. In Fidel's view, violence was justified—even necessary—in the face of violent repression. Even as a kid, he had believed that the worst sin a person could commit was to submit to a perceived injustice. Of course, it was also true that he was sometimes rash and impulsive in his reactions, which may have been the case with the attack on the Moncada army barracks.

Although considerable thought and planning went into the attack, it is hard to believe that those involved could have placed much stock in their chances of success. One hundred and sixty men and women versus nearly two thousand well-armed soldiers does not make for good odds, even with a highly motivated squad of insurgents. After the fact, many of those involved in the Moncada attack—including Fidel—admitted that it was as much an act of frustration as of rebellion. Since taking over the government and suspending the constitution, Batista had successfully muzzled the opposition. The hope was that the Moncada attack would serve as a spark that would wake up the Cuban people and touch off an island-wide rebellion. In the weeks and months following the July 26 attack, whether or not it had achieved this goal still remained to be seen.

WITH THE 1953 – 54 tourist season fast approaching, President Batista wanted to deal with the Moncada prosecutions as quickly as possible. The last thing the Havana Mob needed was intimations of discord and revolution in the air as the planes and cruise ships arrived for another successful season of sun, gambling, and showgirls. Consequently, the trial of Fidel Castro and his *compañeros* was put on the fast track.

On September 21—just fifty-one days after the Moncada attack—122 defendants represented by 22 lawyers were dragged, bound and shackled, into the Santiago Palace of Justice. The tone of the proceedings was set not by the government but by Castro, who raised his manacled hands and addressed the chief judge: "I want to call your attention to this incredible fact . . . What guarantees can there be in this trial? Not even the worst criminals are held this way in a hall that calls itself a hall of justice . . . You cannot judge people who are handcuffed."

Fidel had fired the opening shot and the panel of judges backed him up. They declared a recess until the handcuffs were removed from all prisoners.

Castro and his followers were charged under Article 148 of the Social Defense Code, which provided for a prison sentence of between five and twenty years for "the leader of an attempt at organizing an uprising of armed persons against Constitutional Powers of the State." From the beginning, the rebels knew that they would be found guilty. Their legal strategy was not to contest the charge that they had taken part in the attack but to call into question the very legitimacy of the Batista regime. Castro posed the question: how could they be accused of violating the constitution if the government that was charging them was not a legitimate, constitutional government?

The other key component of the defendants' strategy was to expose the level of brutality on the part of the army following the attack. Within days of the trial getting started, it was revealed that seventy rebels were killed as a result of the July 26 attacks, but only sixteen of those had been killed in actual battle. Eyewitness testimony and forensic evidence showed that skulls had been crushed and bullets fired into the brains of prisoners at close range. During torture sessions, some rebels were castrated with straight razors and at least one had his eye gouged out with a knife. The government's attempts to cover up the wholesale murdering of suspects following the insurrection suggested that the country was drifting back to the bad old days of the Machado regime in the early 1930s, when torture, government-sponsored revenge killings, and the unexplained "disappearance" of political enemies was the law of the land.

Like a tropical depression, paranoia and the stench of death hung over the Santiago Palace of Justice. Although government-enforced censorship guaranteed that the trial would not receive coverage in the press, no government directive could stop *la bola en la calle* (the word in the street). Since the rebels were young people in their early twenties, it seemed as if the dictatorship was trying to wipe out the youth of Cuba. Castro, in particular, emerged as a leader with a strong sense of historical precedent. When asked who was the "intellectual author" of the attacks on Moncada, the young Galician answered firmly: "The only intellectual author of this revolution is José Martí, the apostle of our independence."

The Batista government knew a public relations disaster when it saw one. Just four days into the trial, it took the extraordinary step of moving Castro to a secret location and claiming that he could not continue to take part in the proceedings because he was suffering from a "nervous crisis." His supporters were certain that he would be assassinated. The military police, in fact, had tried to poison his food. In court, a rebel supporter produced a letter from Fidel, which he had succeeded in getting to his comrades even though he was locked away in solitary confinement. In the letter, Castro declared that he was not ill; he was being held against his will. Nonetheless, his case was severed from the others.

On October 16, after the other *fidelistas* had all been successfully prosecuted, Fidel was brought to a strange location, a tiny room inside a nursing school at a civilian hospital. Here, in near total secrecy, the leader of the Moncada attack was put on trial before a panel of three judges. The entire trial lasted four hours. Despite its brevity, the proceedings would go down as one of the most significant political events in Cuban history.

For seventy-six straight days, Castro had been held in solitary confinement, but he had used his time well, reading books on world history and political discourse. By the time he appeared at trial, he had absorbed a staggering amount of political philosophy, which he applied to his already established penchant for action. The result was a new level of political understanding and radicalism for Castro. Representing himself at trial, his entire defense consisted of a two-hour opening statement that, drawing on much of the reading he had done over the previous two months in prison, was a lacerating analysis of political and social inequities in Cuba. The speech instantly became known as "History Will Absolve Me" and remains to this day the philosophical blueprint for the Cuban Revolution, a kind of scripture of the rebel movement.

Castro delivered this speech wearing a heavy, dark-blue wool suit brought to him by a friend. He had lost so much weight in prison that the watch he wore kept slipping off his wrist. The speech began quietly, with a detailed condemnation of the illegalities surrounding the trial. Soon, he moved on to Batista, whom he referred to in Latin as *monstrum horrendum*. "Dante divided his hell into nine circles," intoned the young firebrand. "He put the criminals in the seventh, the thieves in the eighth, and the traitors in the ninth. What a hard dilemma the Devil will face when he must choose the circle adequate for the soul of Batista."

Quoting from a wide range of philosophical antecedents that included Saint Thomas Aquinas, Jean-Jacques Rousseau, Honoré de Balzac, Thomas Paine, and, of course, José Martí, Castro put forth an argument for revolution. Citing "the infinite misfortune of the Cuban people who are suffering the cruelest, the most inhuman oppression of their history," he addressed Cuban society's most glaring failures: land distribution, housing, education, unemployment, civic corruption, political repression, and the economic plundering of the island by outside forces.

Castro did not mention by name the Havana Mob, which was as yet an unknown and unquantifiable entity to the Cuban people, but he could well have been talking about Batista and his mobster friends when he said: "[This new regime] has brought with it a change of hands and a redistribution of the loot among a new group of friends, relatives, accomplices, and parasitic hangers-on that constitutes the political retinue of the Dictator. What great shame the people have been forced to endure so that a small group of egoists, altogether indifferent to the needs of the homeland, may find in public life an easy and comfortable modus vivendi."

Addressing his own predicament, Castro said: "I know that I shall be silenced for many years. I know they will try to conceal the truth by every possible means. I know there will be a conspiracy to force me into oblivion. But my voice will never be drowned; for it gathers strength within my breast when I feel most alone . . . I know that prison will be harder for me than it has ever been for anyone, filled with threats, with vileness, and cowardly cruelty. But I do not fear prison, as I do not fear the fury of the miserable tyrant who snuffed out the lives of seventy of my comrades. Condemn me. It does not matter. History will absolve me."

With these words, Castro concluded his summation. The three judges and the prosecutor whispered among themselves for a few minutes. Finally, the chief judge asked the accused to rise, and then said: "In accordance with the request of the prosecutor, the court has imposed on you a sentence of fifteen years in prison . . . This trial has been concluded." Fidel put out his hands to be handcuffed and was led away.

In the weeks that followed, Castro secretly transcribed his famous courtroom oratory word for word onto tiny pieces of paper that were smuggled out of the prison. The speech was reconstructed by his revolutionary followers and printed as a pamphlet entitled *"La historia me absolverá"* by Fidel Castro.

By the time busloads of tourists began arriving from the airport for the 1953–54 tourist season, Castro's booklet had begun to circulate among the Cuban people in Havana. At taxi stands, along the Malecón, or in city parks, everyday Cubans could be seen reading *"La historia me absolverá*," though they were careful to keep the book out of sight of the dreaded military police. To be seen reading Castro's booklet would have resulted in immediate arrest.

One place where Castro's manifesto was rarely seen was in the tourist hotels, cabarets, or casinos where revelers gambled, danced, drank, and screwed the night away, oblivious to the political climate around them. The fact that the Cuban people were being surreptitiously radicalized by the writings of a dynamic new political thinker while at the same time hedonism reigned in the domain of the mobsters was a harbinger of things to come. Life in Havana was now on two parallel tracks: that of Castro and the Revolution, and that of the Havana Mob. The huge gulf between these two diametrically opposed forces could not be reconciled; they were one day bound to collide.

MEYER LANSKY most likely never read *"La historia me absolverá."* For one thing, he didn't read Spanish, and in conversations with friends and associates he rarely exhibited much interest in Cuban sociopolitical affairs—except to the extent that they directly affected his business plans. Gnats like Fidel Castro were Batista's problem. Lansky had a casino to run and an economic empire to cultivate, and he was not about to get sidetracked by the intellectual ramblings of a spoiled rich kid turned revolutionary leader.

In November 1953, Lansky turned his attention to the Hotel Nacional. Ever since he'd first dreamed of setting up shop in Havana, Meyer had special plans for the Nacional. The Mob conference in December 1946 had established the place as legendary in the hearts and minds of American gangsters, whether they were at the conference or not. Lansky was determined to turn the place into a show palace for the Mob in Havana. His plans involved building an exclusive wing with luxury suites for high-stakes gamblers.

For years, Lansky had owned a piece of the place, but that ended when the Prío administration briefly nationalized the casinos in 1948.

Since then, the Nacional had been owned by the Cuban government. In recent years, the hotel had become a kind of expatriate club for foreign diplomats and the social elite. It wasn't until Batista came along for his second go as president that the Nacional was placed under new management. International Hotels, Inc., a subsidiary of Pan American, the principal air carrier from the United States to Havana, announced that they would be refurbishing the hotel, complete with a luxurious new complex of rooms, a restaurant, and a cabaret. It seemed as though International Hotels, Inc. and Meyer Lansky were on the same page.

As overall director at the Nacional, Lansky brought in an old acquaintance. Wilbur Clark was an experienced hotelier in his late fifties. He had built the famous Desert Inn hotel-casino in Las Vegas, with partial financing from Lansky and his Cleveland partners Dalitz, Kleinman, and Tucker. Clark was a master at promotion and knew how to get the most out of a dollar. His skills had even been admired by members of the Kefauver Committee. When Clark was subpoenaed to testify in Las Vegas, he was asked about his association with mobsters, particularly those who had floated him the money to finish the long-delayed Desert Inn:

COMMITTEE MEMBER: Before you got in bed with crooks to finish this proposition, didn't you look into these birds at all?

WILBUR CLARK: Not too much. No, sir.

COMMITTEE MEMBER: You have the most nebulous idea of your business I ever saw. You have a smile on your face but I don't know how the devil you do it.

WILBUR CLARK: I have done it all my life.

White-haired and avuncular, Wilbur Clark's forte was attracting topnotch entertainers and celebrities, but he had little experience in the day-to-day operations of a casino. For that, Lansky would need to look elsewhere. But he wouldn't need to look far.

There was nobody better to manage the gambling concession at the Nacional than Jake Lansky. Jake had been an associate of his older brother going all the way back to their days running crap games on the Lower East Side. Later, they fine-tuned their partnership in South Florida, until Kefauver came along and spoiled the show. Unlike Meyer, Jake spoke a little Spanish. He also had a personality that many described as the opposite of his brother's. Where Meyer was sometimes taciturn and cold, Jake was a joker and a backslapper. Jake was also taller than Meyer; he was beefy and imposing. The Cubans gave him a nickname, El Cejudo—"the Bushy Eyebrowed One"—a reference to the thick black eyebrows that were his most distinguishing physical characteristic.

Some questioned the depth of Jake's intellect. In *Little Man*, Robert Lacey's seminal biography of Meyer, a family friend is quoted as saying of Jake: "[He] had a way of chewing on his cigar. He would beetle up his eyebrows, so you thought there must be a lot going on inside there—when, actually, it was pretty dead."

Jake may have lacked Meyer's scholarly pretensions, but he was loyal. And he knew how to run a casino. He had the common touch, which made him especially popular with the dealers, croupiers, pit bosses, and floor managers who made up the casino's labor hierarchy. He was a highly visible figure, often taking a position atop the manager's perch, overlooking the floor. Even when Jake wasn't on the premises, there was no question who was in charge.

Once, a political official high up in the Batista regime was gambling in the casino at the Nacional. He lost all his chips and quickly ran out of cash. He asked the assistant manager to grant him a credit of twenty-five thousand pesos so he could continue playing. In the past, it was common for members of the political and military establishment to be granted this special privilege. This time, the assistant manager hesitated. He picked up the phone and called El Cejudo. Jake came down to the salon and, in front of everybody, denied the political official the credit he had requested.

Many native *cubanos* were surprised and impressed by the degree to which the Lanskys stood up to what had always been the privileged class. But this was very much in keeping with Meyer Lansky's approach to running a high-stakes gambling operation. And it is unlikely that Meyer or Jake would have enforced such a policy without the approval of President Batista.

The rules were simple: a substantial percentage of the "skim" from the casino was used to pay off military, police, and political officials. That was their cut, to trickle down through their various pecking orders as they saw fit. Any low-level military policeman or political party hack who came around looking for an extra privilege or piece of the action had stepped over the line. Maybe that had been permissible before Meyer and Jake arrived, when the casinos were haphazardly organized and wide open to extortion—but not now.

This policy on the part of the Lansky brothers became an operating principle of the Havana Mob. And Meyer rarely passed up an opportunity to show that he was beholden to no one except maybe the top guy: Batista. Once, Meyer was on his way to meet with Amletto Battisti. At precisely 9:00 P.M., Lansky arrived at Battisti's Sevilla Biltmore Hotel, located just blocks from the presidential palace on the outskirts of Old Havana. He stepped out of the car and entered the palatial Spanish-tiled lobby, where he came upon Santiago Rey Pernas, then minister of the interior. This high government official put out his hand to greet Lansky, who glanced dismissively at the man and kept on walking. The minister was left standing with his hand outstretched, while Lansky continued on to meet with his mobster associate.

Lansky may have had little time for military and government officials who were looking to feed off the Havana Mob, but he was downright solicitous of Cuban underworld figures he would need to bring his plans for Cuba to full fruition. The suave and debonair Amletto Battisti was one person Lansky met on a regular basis. Battisti's bank, Banco de Créditos e Inversiones, was located in an arcade on the basement level of the Sevilla Biltmore and would prove to be a vital conduit for laundering the casino skim. Another Lansky contact whose preestablished criminal history in Cuba was essential was Amadeo Barletta.

Barletta's bank, Banco Atlántico, had an even more dubious history than Battisti's. In the years leading up to Fulgencio Batista's *golpe* in March 1952, Banco Atlántico had been under investigation by the previous administration of Carlos Prío. The bank's executive council, which included Amadeo Barletta as president and his son, Amadeo Barletta Jr., as vice president, had claimed that, in accordance with Cuban law, Banco Atlántico had no financial relationship with "affiliated societies or companies." An investigator from Banco Nacional de Cuba (BNC), however, discovered that this was not the case. In a confidential report to the BNC, the chief of bank inspection wrote:

> Upon carrying out the inspection of [Banco Atlántico] in August 1951, it was determined that the company Santo Domingo Motor Corporation, constituted under the law of the Dominican Republic, represented in reality an affiliated holding company, possessor of more than 50 percent of the stock of Banco Atlántico. Credentials in the name of this company were not shown to the inspectors.

The BNC inspector went on to say in the report that there were no fewer than eighteen other companies with "unlicensed" links to Banco Atlántico—among them coffee distributors, sugar conglomerates, a department store, and Barletta's Compañía Editorial El Mundo, which published his newspaper. Amadeo Barletta had established a network of front companies financed by his bank, which was itself the recipient of under-the-table money from a number of sources, most notably the city's gambling casinos. Crooked banks with hidden links to a vast array of local shell companies—this was exactly the type of financial infrastructure that Lansky, Trafficante, and other U.S.-based mobsters would need if they were to expand their criminal empire in Cuba.

The BNC continued to investigate Banco Atlántico in the early 1950s, and other fraudulent practices were uncovered. When Batista took over the Cuban government, the investigations stopped. But Barletta still had a problem. There was an investigative paper trail on Banco Atlántico in the files of the BNC that was known to international banking investigators. The way to deal with this was simple: on March 1, 1954, Banco Atlántico announced its liquidation. Overnight, the bank disappeared from existence. Within weeks, a new financial entity—the Trust Company of Cuba—assumed the interests of the Barletta family.

Banks owned and controlled by Battisti, Barletta, and later one created by President Batista himself were crucial to the Mob in Havana. Already the money had begun to roll in from the hotels, casinos, cabarets, and other tourist-related businesses, but if all went according to plan, this would be only the beginning. For that plan to take shape, a number of key pieces still needed to fall into place.

One of those pieces materialized in August when the Batista government, by legal decree, created a financial institution known as BANDES (Banco de Desarrollo Económico y Social, or Bank for Economic and Social Development). BANDES was designed to be the ultimate national lending institution. Its objectives were officially explained as:

> To carry out a policy of economic and social development, of diversification of production, assuming for that purpose, among others, the functions of discounting and rediscounting public and private securities, issued with the purpose of increasing the money in circulation, as well as realizing many credit and banking operations as may be indispensable in the realization of such objectives, being authorized to subscribe, float, and endorse bonds of companies of economic and social development—whether state run, quasi state run, or privately run—to make loans to said companies and to issue their own securities.

Hidden within this dense legalese was a powerful reality: banks owned by Battisti, Barletta, and others would invest in BANDES, as would powerful U.S. companies looking to do business in Cuba. As a financial institution, BANDES was being given unparalleled power to finance any and all public works projects, to extend loans and securities, to virtually control the flow of money and social development in Cuba. It was to be, in other words, the economic high command of the Havana Mob; an institution that subsumed all the operations of Battisti, Barletta, Lansky, and the other mobsters into one, and then tied it into the economic and social development of Cuba itself, so that the fortunes of the Mob in Cuba were one and the same with the fortunes of the Cuban people. It was a political directive breathtaking in its corruption, an act of malfeasance that did something mobsters in the United States had rarely dared dream of: *officially* linking together the Mob and its financial operations with the development of the society in which it operated.

The financial infrastructure was now in place. The only thing missing was a piece of legislation that would provide an incentive to developers. Batista took care of this by passing a new law—Ley Hotelera (Hotel Law) 2074—which provided tax exemptions to any hotel providing tourist accommodation, and furthermore guaranteed government financing—via BANDES—for anyone willing to commit one million dollars or more toward hotel construction or two hundred thousand for the building of a nightclub. Hotel and nightclub investors were also guaranteed a casino-gambling license without having to be approved by a gaming commission, which, of course, did not exist in Cuba. U.S. investors with criminal records were not turned away. In fact, through Hotel Law 2074 they were encouraged to invest, as long as they were willing to pay the official license fee of twenty-five thousand pesos. The real fee, of course, also included a kickback to Batista amounting to somewhere around two hundred and fifty thousand pesos—equivalent to $1.6 million today. There was also an under-the-table monthly operating fee of two thousand pesos, plus a profit percentage paid directly to Batista or a member of his family.

The graft proved to be staggering. Once the benefits of Batista's new hotel law kicked in and rampant hotel-casino construction began in

Havana, the profits in kickback payments to Batista were estimated by some to total nearly ten million dollars a year.

Before the ink was dry on Batista's Hotel Law 2074, five new hotel-casino projects were announced, including the Havana Hilton, which would be the largest hotel to date in Havana; the Deauville, the first Mob-controlled hotel to open along the Malecón; and the Capri, which would go up in Vedado, just one block from the Hotel Nacional.

For years it was believed that Havana's tourism boom had been suffering from a dearth of top-flight hotel accommodation, but that was all about to change. With the passage of his new law, Batista was officially kicking off an unprecedented era of hotel and nightclub development in Havana. And of course, attached to each new hotel or nightclub would be a fully equipped, Mob-owned gambling casino. Let the games begin.

OF ALL THE U.S. gangsters poised to take advantage of Batista's new open-door policy toward investment in Cuba, few were as well placed as Santo Trafficante. But in the summer of 1954, as the tourist season approached in Havana, the Mob boss from Tampa was rocked by two events that threatened to knock him off his game. The first was the death of his father, Santo Trafficante Sr.

Having been diagnosed years earlier with stomach cancer, the elder Trafficante's passing on August 11 at the age of sixty-eight was no great surprise. Even so, it was a potentially disruptive event for Santo Jr., who had been methodically assuming control of his family's varied criminal businesses over the previous six or seven years.

Throughout the history of the Mafia in the United States, the passing of a titular leader had sometimes been an occasion for bloodletting and jockeying for power. Santo Jr. had reason to be concerned that his home base of Tampa might once again erupt in a violent war for control of the lucrative Gulf Coast bolita racket, but it never happened. Partly this was because Trafficante Sr. was such a revered figure in the city's Sicilian community, where he had long been viewed as a kind of founding father. His Mafia roots were well known. For many decades, he held court at the Nebraska Bar and Package Goods Store on Nebraska Avenue, an old-world social club where the dispensing of underworld favors and the counting of bolita proceeds were a regular afternoon occurrence. Trafficante Sr. was circumspect and soft-spoken. Although often identified by the local press as "patriarch of Tampa's most notorious underworld family," he was also a member of L'Unione Italiana Club and Elk's Lodge No. 708, two of the city's most influential fraternal organizations. Throughout his life, Trafficante Sr. was never convicted of a crime nor did he ever spend a day in jail.

The respect that had always been accorded "the Don" was readily apparent on the day of his burial. A crowd estimated at more than five hundred mourners gathered on a sweltering August day at the L'Unione Italiana Cemetery, an immaculate, well-cared-for burial ground built and maintained through the beneficences of Tampa's Sicilian immigrant population. The *Tampa Tribune* reported that "underworld faces were sprinkled throughout the crowd," including that of Santo Jr., who at age thirty-nine was now the undisputed Godfather of the Tampa Mafia, one of the most deeply entrenched and oldest Sicilian criminal fraternities in the country.

Santo Sr. was laid to rest in a solid-brass coffin with an inner glass sealer. His remains were placed in a marble crypt that, like others at the L'Unione Italiana Cemetery, was aboveground. The framed, oval-shaped black-and-white photo on Trafficante Sr.'s headstone is the only known photo of the secretive Mob boss. The *Tampa Tribune* reported that Santo Sr. left behind an estate of $36,300. Though that translates to nearly half a million dollars in today's terms, it was well below what most believed to be his true worth—which included a lifetime of contacts in Cuba that he had bequeathed to his son.

Santo Jr. mourned the passing of his papa and got on with his life. There were other issues that needed to be dealt with, including the fact that, even as the son witnessed his father's remains being sealed away in their final resting place, he was facing indictment on state gambling charges.

The arrests had gone down a few months earlier, in May. Trafficante, along with thirty-four others, had been arrested in a series of gambling raids throughout the Tampa area. Santo and his brother, Henry, were also accused of bribing a police officer to prevent further raids.

The crusade to eradicate bolita on the Gulf Coast had been building steam ever since the Kefauver hearings, which had blown through Tampa three and a half years earlier and led *Esquire* magazine to dub the town the "Hellhole of the Gulf Coast." As they had in other jurisdictions, the Kefauver hearings ushered in a mood of reform. It was estimated by the committee—and repeated often in the local press—that the Mafia in Tampa made an estimated five million dollars a year from bolita—a princely sum in the early 1950s. An ambitious local sheriff spent eighteen months building his case against the Trafficante organization. It would be the first time a Trafficante—senior or junior—faced a trial.

One of the lawyers handling Trafficante's defense was Frank Ragano, a young, relatively inexperienced criminal defense attorney who, like Santo, had Sicilian blood. Trafficante and Ragano struck up a close working relationship and friendship that would continue throughout the mobster's trial, his time in Cuba, and beyond.

Ragano was impressed with Trafficante, whom he described years later in *Mob Lawyer*, his published memoir, as being "a different species from the seedy bolita bankers I usually represented. They invariably dressed shabbily and spoke crudely; Trafficante could have passed for a bank executive or an Italian diplomat . . . His clothes had a custom-tailored look and he wore distinctive horn-rimmed glasses trimmed with gold. In those days, I didn't run across too many people dressed as elegantly and expensively as this man."

Trafficante liked to pay his lawyer's fees in cash, usually in untraceable bills stuffed into a brown envelope and delivered to Ragano under the table. The propriety of collecting huge fees in cash troubled the young lawyer. He spoke to a more senior member of his law firm about it; the man laughed and said, "These people always pay cash . . . They don't keep [checking] accounts and records of how much money they have."

"Is that how they pay you?" asked Ragano.

"Absolutely," answered the attorney. If Ragano was going to represent clients like Santo Trafficante—men who made their money from the underworld—he "better get used to it."

Ragano was well paid—better paid than he ever dreamed he would be back in his days at law school. His annual salary jumped from ten thousand to one hundred and forty thousand dollars, most of it from various defendants associated with the Trafficante organization that he would represent at trial. Santo and his brother were to be tried separately.

In the fall of 1954, most of the twenty-eight bolita defendants whom Ragano represented were acquitted or had their convictions overturned on appeal. Trafficante was pleased, but he told Ragano that if he had dreams of becoming a distinguished lawyer he would have to improve his overall appearance. "Stop buying suits and jackets off the racks in ordinary stores," he said. He recommended a tailor in Miami Beach, where he had his suits made; he also recommended a barber where Ragano could get a more stylish haircut, and also a professional manicurist.

At the trial of Santo and Henry Trafficante, Ragano was a spectator, watching from the sidelines as their case was handled by Pat Whitaker, a famous criminal defense attorney and lead counsel at Ragano's firm. The primary witness for the prosecution was a police sergeant detective who testified that Henry had tried to bribe him for protection against raids and that Henry and Santo were paying off high-level law enforcement officials in Saint Petersburg, the town on the other side of Tampa Bay. After a two-week trial, Santo and his brother were both found guilty of bribery, and Henry was convicted of operating an illegal lottery. But the conviction was quickly overturned because the prosecuting attorney made a bonehead mistake during his summation. By making an issue of the fact that neither Santo nor Henry had taken the stand to testify in their defense, the prosecutor violated criminal procedural law, which states that no negative motive can be imputed by a defendant's choice not to take the witness stand.

Ragano attended the post-trial celebration at Santo's favorite restaurant—the Columbia—in the Cuban-Sicilian neighborhood of Ybor City. It was there that Trafficante informed Ragano that he, not Pat Whitaker, would from now on be his personal lead counsel. Ragano was ecstatic. Only years later did it cross his mind that it was no fluke that Santo won his bolita trial on a technicality.

"It occurred to me," wrote Ragano in his memoir, "that Santo had somehow managed to bribe or influence the prosecutor into making the fatal mistake in his closing argument. There could be no other explanation."

Trafficante had dodged a bullet. He was a free man. Even so, his organization had been dragged into the light of day and exposed as never before. As with Meyer Lansky, the fallout from the Kefauver hearings had damaged Santo. His legal expenses were considerable, and there was a good chance that the bolita racket, which had sustained the Trafficante organization for generations, would be forced into a period of remission from which it might never recover.

On December 26, Santo returned to Cuba. The holiday season had arrived, and it was time for the Mafia boss to once again turn his attention to the best thing he had going: Havana, a place where gambling was legal, mobsters were welcome, and profits were virtually guaranteed by the government. Before Santo's trial, Cuba had seemed like a luxury, just one of many business opportunities that provided the Trafficantes with additional profits in an already thriving Mafia enterprise. But now the Pearl of the Antilles was looking like Santo's salvation. Just like Lansky before him, he'd been hit hard at home, suffering major losses, and was looking to heal his economic wounds in a land where "everybody . . . has a mistress," even the president.

Now, more than ever, Trafficante needed the Havana Mob, and the Havana Mob needed him.

7

GAMBLER'S PARADISE

NOTHING CLEANS UP THE IMAGE OF A FRAUDULENT GOVERN-
ment quite like a good old-fashioned election. Fulgencio Batista knew
this to be true. In the twenty years since he first rose to power in Cuba,
Batista had presided over many so-called democratic elections in which
the results were a foregone conclusion. The military controlled the elections in Cuba, and Batista controlled the military. With the notable
exception of the *golpe* of March 1952, there were few surprises come
election day. Batista's ability to maintain order and deliver uncontested
results at the polls had always been part of his appeal to his neighbor,
the great colossus to the north.

The United States was very much on Batista's mind in the autumn of
1953. A new U.S. ambassador—Arthur Gardner—had been appointed
by the newly elected Eisenhower administration. Gardner was an enthusiastic supporter of Batista, as had been virtually every U.S. government
representative who came into contact with El Mulato Lindo. Batista was
a friend to American corporations and investors, and he was, in keeping
with the tenor of 1950s Cold War politics, increasingly anti-Communist.
In case anyone had doubts about that, in November 1953 Batista outlawed
the Communist Party in Cuba and shut down its various newspapers

and publishing outlets. Ambassador Gardner registered his approval but also noted that for Batista to "legitimize his standing in the eyes of the world" he needed to bury the memory of his *golpe* with an "open election." Thus, in late 1953, it was announced to the Cuban people that a presidential election would take place one year later, on November 1, 1954.

From his prison cell on the Isle of Pines, Fidel Castro denounced the prospect of elections as a sham. In a series of letters to his supporters—some of which were published in underground newspapers—he now wrote less of replacing the existing government and more of Revolution, with a capital R. Cuba needed an entirely new system of government, Castro surmised, and a new kind of political leader. "The Revolution cannot mean the restoration to power of men who have been utterly discredited by history," he declared.

The problem for Castro was that he was locked away on a small island in the Caribbean Sea behind a stone wall and concertina wire, with a round-the-clock phalanx of armed guards. Another problem for the opposition was that, economically speaking, Cuba appeared to be doing quite well. The sugar crop that year was measured at 4.75 million tons, better than it had been in more than a decade. At an international economic summit in London, it was agreed that Cuba would supply more than half the world's sugar market—a return to the economic glory years of the Dance of the Millions. Cuba had a higher standard of living than anywhere else in the Caribbean and most of Latin America. Major construction projects were booming on the island, including one massive project: a tunnel that would pass under the Havana Bay canal and link the city with its easternmost neighborhoods. Under Batista, Havana was literally expanding, becoming a world-class metropolis. There was poverty, illiteracy, and social inequity, of course, but it was skillfully hidden behind a veneer of prosperity that made it appear as though all of Cuba was in the midst of good times.

It was in this atmosphere of rosy economic prognostication that the presidential election of November 1954 approached. Batista was given a major boost by his northern partner, the United States, when in May his most potent challenger, ex-president Carlos Prío, was indicted in Miami for violating the U.S. Neutrality Act. He stood accused of plotting to smuggle a cache of weapons to anti-Batista operatives in Cuba. Another potential challenger, ex-president Ramón Grau San Martín, pulled out of the election when it became clear that the voting process would be controlled not by a neutral organization but by the Cuban military. Batista stood uncontested on election day. Less than half the population voted, even though they were required to do so by law. For Batista's supporters in the Cuban and U.S. governments, his victory was a handy propaganda tool, but it did little to assuage those who felt his regime was and always would be unconstitutional and therefore illegitimate.

On Inauguration Day, February 1955, the sound of gunfire could be heard in the outskirts of the city. Havana police had tracked down an old enemy of Batista's—Orlando León Lemus, known to the public as El Colorado. León Lemus was a political gangster from the glory days of the MSR who was now considered sympathetic to former president Prío. At the end of a bloody gun battle that raged for hours, Cuba's public enemy number one was dead. A large stash of weapons was also uncovered. Police officers bragged that they had most likely foiled an assassination attempt on the president. Batista himself declared the death of El Colorado as a fitting first act of his new term, in which the city's premiere gangster had been eliminated.

For those in the know, the irony was palpable: Batista was taking credit for eliminating Cuban-born gangsters, while at the same time extending his relationships with professional mobsters from New York, Miami, Tampa, and elsewhere around the United States.

Having engineered an electoral victory, Batista was feeling emboldened. In keeping with his political philosophy of "repression and reward," he began to lessen some of the more egregious restrictions on civil liberties brought about by his *golpe*. Censorship was temporarily relaxed. Curfews were lifted. Organized labor activities—i.e., strikes—were now allowed under the law. Batista began to appear more readily in public,

especially at charity and ceremonial events, where he once again assumed the role of benevolent dictator that he had relished during his
earlier tenure as president.

One glittering event that Batista attended in early 1955 was a gala for
La liga contra el cáncer, Cuba's anticancer league. The president and his
wife, Marta, were the guests of honor at this prestigious charity gathering, attended by the top members of Batista's cabinet and the cream of
the social register. To anyone affiliated with the Havana Mob, the event
was significant not so much because of its purpose but because of where
it was held—the Tropicana nightclub. Although few could have recognized it as such at the time, this event marked the beginning of an
epoch in which the city's most famous nightclub became a dazzling
symbol for the Mob in Havana and the era it helped to create.

IF HAVANA IN THE 1950s was a soufflé of unbridled gambling,
extravagant showmanship, hot music, and brash sexuality, the Tropicana was the special ingredient that gave it its buoyancy. Located in the
midst of a tropical jungle on the outskirts of the city, the club had for
years been one of Havana's most innovative show palaces for dance,
music, and a particular brand of Cuban sensuality. The showgirls at the
Tropicana were renowned the world over for their voluptuousness, and
the cabaret showcased a kind of sequin-and-feather musical theater that
would be copied in Paris, New York, and Las Vegas. With the outdoor
floor shows ("Paradise Under the Stars") as a main draw and the club's
adjoining casino as a virtual license to print money, everyone who was
anyone wanted to be seen at the Tropicana. Amid the city's burgeoning
constellation of cabarets, hotel-casinos, and nightclubs, the Tropicana
was the North Star, a magnet for international celebrities, musicians,
beautiful women, and gangsters.

The club's connections to the underworld ran deep, and they began
with the owner, Martín Fox. Built like a longshoreman, with a thick
torso, leathery skin, and meat hooks for hands, Fox was the kind of man

who could handle himself around tough guys and mobsters. He resembled the actor Anthony Quinn and spoke with a kind of knowing, salt-of-the-earth Cuban slang that came from years of operating on the fringes of polite society. Fox was a skilled impresario, a man who knew how to conduct himself around movie stars, presidents, and kings, yet he often carried a .38-caliber Smith & Wesson tucked into the waistband of his well-tailored linen suits, a throwback to his days as an up-and-coming *bolitero*.

In *Tropicana Nights*, a picaresque history of the nightclub, cowritten by Rosa Lowinger and Ofelia Fox—longtime wife of Martín—Ofelia is quoted saying, "The defining feature of a Cuban is a person who will do just about anything for a minute of pleasure." Her husband, Martín, was a man who devoted himself to supplying those minutes, both to Cubans and to the tourists who flocked to the island. In doing so, he formed a partnership with the Havana Mob, though Ofelia Fox would deny the larger implications of this arrangement until her dying day. In her memoir, she describes being wined and dined by Frankie Carbo, a notorious mafioso affiliated with Lansky's New York crime syndicate: "People say and write a lot of things. I don't know about [Carbo] killing anyone, and if Martín did, he couldn't do anything about it, either. These men were part of the business world. Carbo treated us like royalty in New York."

There was a reason Martín Fox and his wife were treated like royalty by mobsters in faraway New York City; it was because Fox was an important business partner and conduit between the Cuban and U.S. underworld figures who came to make up the Havana Mob.

Like Batista, Castro, and almost every other Cuban who came of age in the early and mid-twentieth century, Fox was a child of the *zafra*. In Ciego de Avila, the midsized town in the middle of Cuba where he got his start, the harvest ruled all. As a young man in his early twenties, Martín worked in a sugar mill as a *tornero*, or lathe machinist. A minor industrial accident damaged his left hand and cost him his job. Young Martín needed to find a new way to make a living, so he turned to Cuba's other national pastime—gambling, or more specifically, *la bolita*.

Bolita had been a huge moneymaker for the Trafficantes among the Cuban émigré population in Tampa, and it would prove to be a wise career move for Fox. In Cuba, the game was played all over the island as a kind of black market alternative to the official national lottery. Fox made his living through *apuntando terminales,* or "the taking down of bets."

The game kept the young man busy. Part of the attraction of bolita was its so-called secret code, which, of course, everyone knew. Each day's winning number was based on the last three digits of the national lottery, which was published in the local newspaper. Anyone could bet on a number or number combination, but they usually did so by using an agreed-upon word that represented each number. Number one was *el caballo* (horse); number two, *la mariposa* (butterfly); eleven, *el gallo* (rooster); forty-eight, *la cucaracha* (cockroach), and so on, with different words representing different numbers all the way up to one hundred. Thus, when a bettor told Martín, "*Cinco a la cucaracha,*" he knew the person wanted to bet five centavos on number forty-eight.

Ostensibly, this system was devised so that if a policeman stopped a *listero* (numbers runner) and confiscated his list of bets, there was no way anyone could prove that this litany of colorful words had anything to do with illegal gambling. In truth, local police almost always received a piece of the action for allowing bolita to operate—an example of grassroots corruption that would prepare young Martín Fox for his days as a Batista-era cabaret owner.

Bolita was good to Fox, who rose through the *boliteros'* hierarchy, from *listero* to *banquero,* the one who financed the bets. Fox would now make the bulk of the profit, but he also assumed the largest risk. A number wagered on by many people—say, 8 for September 8, the date of the Feast of Charity, or 17 for December 17, the Feast of San Lazaro—could spell disaster for a *banquero.* Fox proved to be adept at spreading the risk of popular numbers, even if it meant giving up some of his profits. He also eventually consolidated most of the bolita operations in Ciego de Avila until he was the region's biggest *banquero.*

Like Lansky, Trafficante, and other professional gambling men he would come to know, Fox was not much of a bettor. He preferred to stack the odds in his favor. Gambling for Martín was a livelihood, but it was also an entrée into a broader social universe. His "bank" on Calle Independencia, the town's prime commercial street, was little more than a storefront with a kiosk in front. The kiosk sold cigarettes, cigars, sweets, and official lottery tickets, and was also where a person could place bolita bets. All kinds of men—rich and poor—came by Martín's kiosk to gamble, smoke, and gossip. Before long, Martín Fox was so popular he could have run for mayor. Instead, the former factory worker did what any young man with ambition might do—he headed out for the big city.

In Havana, Fox was known as El Guajiro, the country boy. Some might have taken it as a gibe, but not Martín, who was now operating in a crowded field where being known by any name was a help. In the early 1940s, the city's gambling underworld was thriving, though the city itself was about to enter the lean years of the Second World War. Fox's first operation was running bolita numbers in Central Havana. His *banco*, which he called La Buena, had no fixed location. As a new operator in the city, he needed to move around to avoid being busted.

Before long, Fox was presiding over a sizable underground network of card games, bolita, and casino-style gambling. This was an era in Havana before many of the large hotel-casinos had been constructed. The only major venues in town—the Gran Casino Nacional and the Jockey Club at Oriental Park Racetrack—were upscale establishments open only six months of the year. Common *cubanos* needed a place to indulge their habit year-round. Using many of the contacts he made as a bolita king, Martín offered private poker games out of the homes and apartments of friends. Eventually he expanded his operation to include roulette, baccarat, craps, and *monte de baraja*, a popular four-card game of Spanish origin.

By 1943, Fox was successful enough as an underground gambling czar to buy his way into the Tropicana. At the time, the club's casino operations were open to individual concessionaires. Fox rented two tables, one for monte and one for baccarat. With the Second World War under way, the club was not doing well, but that didn't matter to Fox. He now had an in at the city's largest club.

First opened on December 30, 1939, the Tropicana had always been a place with international pretensions. Constructed on a six-acre estate in Marianao, the club's setting was gorgeous. Surrounded by a natural jungle paradise, its main cabaret was outdoors and from the beginning showcased the largest orchestra in Cuba. In its first two years of operation, tourists from around the globe flocked to the Tropicana. After the war set in, tourism in Cuba plunged from 126,000 annual visitors in 1941 to a mere 12,500 in 1943. Nonetheless, Fox was able to maintain a decent trade at his two gaming tables because he had established a strong following among local gamblers.

The owner of the Tropicana was so frustrated by the club's dwindling fortunes that one afternoon, after a week of losses left him with insufficient funds to make his regular payoff to the military officers who provided "protection," he made a proposition to Fox: "Give me seven thousand [pesos] and the casino is yours." Martín jumped at the offer and purchased the club's casino concession. A few years later, in what amounted to a hostile takeover, he bought the estate on which the club had been built and squeezed out the other owners. It was only when Martín Fox became sole owner of the Tropicana in 1950 that the club began to develop the reputation for which it would become world-famous.

Although his background was as a gambling boss, Martín had always been most attracted to the club's possibilities as a cabaret. El Guajiro had a dream, and that dream involved a kind of showmanship and entertainment that could only exist in Havana, where dance was a national obsession, everyone was a natural musician, and the island's Afro-Cuban cultural heritage provided an exotic backdrop.

A key moment in the club's development occurred in March 1952, when Fox hired as his choreographer Roderico Neyra, known in Cuban dance and music circles simply as Rodney. Only weeks after Batista had staged his *golpe de estado*, inaugurating a period of tension, Martín's hiring of a new choreographer would be the beginning of a history that unfolded in near total obliviousness of the outside world. Fox cared little about politics. All that mattered was that he be able to fulfill his dream of making the Tropicana the most dazzling entertainment venue in Cuba.

Roderico Neyra was a fascinating character in his own right. Born a leper and raised in a leper colony outside Havana, he came of age in the streets. Even though his hands were gnarled by leprosy, he never let it get in the way of his ambition to become a famous song-and-dance man. Rodney achieved his dream, but as his physical incapacities became more apparent in his adulthood, he turned from performance to choreography. He was a short, light-skinned mulatto with a pencil-thin mustache. He had a wicked grin to go along with his lascivious sensibility—sort of a Cuban Bob Fosse, long before Fosse existed. He was also gay, which made it possible for him to work alongside some of the most desirable women in Havana without ever having to worry about succumbing to temptation.

One of Rodney's first regular gigs was at a burlesque theater called the Shanghai, on Zanja Street in Havana's Chinatown. The Shanghai was one of the city's most notorious strip clubs. It specialized in all-nude shows. In a guidebook published in 1953 entitled *Havana: The Portrait of a City*, American travel writer W. Adolphe Roberts described a show at the Shanghai most likely created by Rodney:

> The scene was a deserted city square at night, indicated by backdrops with street lamps painted in and the silhouettes of houses. There sauntered onstage a woman totally nude except for her hat and shoes, and swinging a handbag. Her implied calling was unmistakable. She produced a mirror from her bag and went through the motions of making up her face under a lamp. Presently she was joined by half a dozen other sisters of the pavement, all in a similar state of undress. They talked by means of grimaces and shrugs which established the

fact that business was poor indeed. Then appeared a tall and robust female, naked too except for a policeman's cap, brogans, and baton. The newcomer scowled at the harlots, menaced them with her night-stick, lined them up, and proceeded to search them for concealed weapons. The comedy of this last operation was broad. I need say no more.

Some viewed the burlesque at the Shanghai as lewd and seedy, but not Rodney. His acts were often a mix of sex, music, dance, and humor that would be a precursor to his more elaborate work at venues like the Tropicana.

By 1950, Rodney was working as head choreographer at the Sans Souci, located not far from the Tropicana. Managed by Norman Roth-man, the Sans Souci was the Tropicana's primary rival as an entertainment venue. Rothman's club was winning the battle, mostly because he staged lavish floor shows that were the envy of theater directors throughout Havana.

One of those shows was a production entitled *Sun Sun Babae*, which went up in 1952. The show incorporated many of the trappings of Afro-Cuban culture—*batá* drums, the ceremonial dress of Santería, and the rhythmic incantations of *bembé*, musical prayers devoted to the ori-shas (Afro-Cuban deities). Rodney was a devout *creyente*, or believer, in the Lucumí ritual, which he viewed as a meditative therapy to deal with his debilitating and often painful disease. But that didn't mean his religion was above the kind of irreverence and sense of fun he applied to all his work.

Sun Sun Babae was a kitschy, tropical burlesque. Onstage, a mulatto woman dressed in the traditional yellow garb of Ochun, goddess of love, danced rumba-style while encircled by a group of black Mandingo-like dancers. The woman moved suggestively to the sound of the drums; the faces of the men gleamed with perspiration. Suddenly, the men were drawn into the audience. As a spotlight followed, they descended from the stage and approached a table, where a blond female patron sat nursing a cocktail. The blonde was engrossed by the half-naked men who surrounded her but was also seemingly frightened. The men practically lifted her out of her seat and carried her to the stage, the spotlight following. Onstage, the woman became intoxicated by the drums and rhythmic chanting, which grew louder and more intense. The audience was both mesmerized and confused, not sure whether this was for real or part of the show.

Suddenly and without warning, the blonde ripped off her black cocktail dress and began dancing in black lace underwear and garter belt. The audience now realized this was all part of the act, and they tittered with laughter. The woman appeared as if she were hypnotized, her dancing more frenzied as she fell under the spell of the santos. The men tossed her around in their arms. Then, amid the heightening music and movement, the woman suddenly snapped out of her trance, let out an embarrassed scream, and grabbed her clothes. Still half-naked, she hurried off the stage, through the club, and out the back door of the cabaret. The audience applauded—stunned, amused, and aroused all at the same time.

Rodney, the choreographer, staged *Sun Sun Babae* for shock value and laughs, but behind the showmanship was a powerful theme. He was inviting the audience to be enticed by Afro-Cuban culture, to get up out of their seats and take part in the sensual pleasures of the island. In this and other shows he later staged at the Tropicana, Rodney was providing a seductive counterpoint to the mundane nature of life back home that would become one of the primary draws for the entire era. It was precisely the kind of entertainment that would give the Havana Mob its naughty, irresistible allure.

SCANTILY CLAD DANCERS and saucy floor shows were what made the Tropicana famous, but the economic engine that made everything possible was the club's casino operations. Martín Fox was smart. In early 1954, he converted a garage behind the cabaret into a smaller, simpler version of the main casino. The place became known as the Casino Popular, a refuge for taxi drivers and other less affluent *habaneros* who couldn't afford the prices at the main cabaret. Although Fox built his business on the backs of the rich and famous, he never lost the common touch. Not only did he tip the taxi drivers a peso each for every tourist they brought to the club, he also cut certain drivers in on a percentage of the house's profit each time their tourist lost in the casino. It was an ingenious move, giving the city's most basic workers a stake in the fortunes of the Havana Mob. And of course, with the Casino Popular open twenty-four hours a day, many taxi drivers gambled their profit share right back into the casino.

Many Cubans took a special pride in the Tropicana; it was promoted as the only major venue in town owned exclusively by Cubans. This was true, up to a point. Fox was a *guajiro*, and his administrative employees were mostly extended family members and friends from his lifetime in the gambling business. Also, the cabaret was the city's premiere showcase for Cuban-born talent—dancers, musicians, costume designers, set directors, etc. The club's casino, however, was a different story. Although there were more Cuban employees at the Tropicana than at most casinos, the gambling concession was coveted by the Havana Mob, who knew a profit-making venture when they saw one.

The initial overtures on the part of the Mob were subtle. On October 5, 1954, Ofelia Fox received a silver mink coat from Santo Trafficante. It was accompanied by a note, which read: "Wishing you a very happy second anniversary." At the time, Trafficante was in Tampa in the middle of his bolita trial, but he still had the presence of mind to send a lavish gift to the wife of his "friend" Martín Fox.

The sending of extravagant gifts to the wives and girlfriends of potential business associates was a common mobster technique. Lucky Luciano had done it back in 1946 when, having just arrived in Havana and looking to cultivate local contacts, he purchased a car from the United States and had it shipped to the wife of Senator Eduardo Suarez Rivas. In fact, during his time on the island, Luciano was known to bestow gold watches, diamond necklaces, and other expensive trinkets on politicians, club owners, and entertainers and their paramours on a regular basis. To those with a fanciful view of human nature, Luciano's largesse was touching. To others more firmly rooted in the corporeal world, it was a crude though time-tested attempt to buy the loyalty of men in power.

To Trafficante, the allure of the Tropicana was obvious: the club had become the proverbial icing on the cake. The mobster from Tampa owned the gambling concession at the Sans Souci, but by 1954 Rodney the showman had moved his act to the Tropicana. The celebrities and big-time gamblers followed. As a representative of the Havana Mob, Trafficante needed to establish a beachhead at the Tropicana to show that the Mob was the underwriter of all that prospered on their watch.

Back in the States, top mobsters routinely used intimidation or violence when they wanted to muscle in on a preexisting business. In Havana, this would not be necessary. Martín Fox understood the dictates of the underworld. If it were in his interest to form an alliance with Trafficante and the Havana Mob, he would do so. He just needed to be convinced.

Trafficante set out to seduce Martín, to kill him with kindness. He routinely called Fox at the club, identifying himself as El Solitario, the Solitary One. The nickname suggested to Fox that Trafficante was operating alone, which was hardly the case. But to someone like Fox, who ran a highly personalized operation, selling out to an individual partner was more agreeable than giving it all up to a budding conglomerate like the Havana Mob. Santo became a friend, his placid, inscrutable visage a recurring sight in numerous photographs taken at the owner's table, which Ofelia Fox collected and later published in her memoir.

Trafficante befriended Martín and his wife, but he also realized that he would never be fully welcome at the club unless he also won over the hired help. For this he used the same method he had employed to curry favor with the owner's wife: lavish gifts bestowed at the drop of a hat.

One person who experienced Trafficante's beneficence firsthand was

Felipe Dulzaides, the jazz pianist whose band, Los Armónicos, regularly played in the club's lounge. Dulzaides's band was a favorite of Santo, who often brought friends and business associates into the lounge for cocktails. Trafficante liked to reward his favorite employees. Dulzaides found this out one afternoon when the mobster made a big show of lining up the piano player and other members of the quartet. He handed Felipe a set of keys and said, "This is for you and the boys." Dulzaides was stunned when he stepped outside and laid his eyes on a brand-new Cadillac Seville parked in front of the Tropicana. Trafficante had given him the car seemingly with no strings attached.

The fact that the owner of a rival club was giving away big-ticket gifts to employees around the Tropicana might have been viewed as encroachment by some, but it was in keeping with the philosophy of the Havana Mob. Trafficante was making sure that everyone knew who was boss, and he encouraged others in his crew to do the same.

Norman Rothman was a Trafficante underling who operated the gambling concession at the rival Sans Souci, but he too was seen often at the Tropicana. Part of the reason was that Rothman's girlfriend, the stunning Olga Chaviano, was a showgirl under contract at the club. Rothman was an elegant older gentleman with a long career in the nightclub business going back to his days in Miami Beach. Many felt he had designs on the Tropicana. Again, a competitor having as his lover one of the cabaret's star attractions could be viewed as poaching, but it was tolerated and even encouraged. After all, what could be more in keeping with the image of the times than the pairing of a middle-aged Jewish nightclub owner and a luscious Cuban showgirl? The Havana Mob was in charge.

FOR THOSE WHO FOLLOWED Cuba's development as a tourist destination, the island seemed to be perched on the edge of a new Golden Age. Financiers, mobsters, investors, and sightseers liked what they saw. The number of foreign travelers spending money in Cuba grew by 35 percent between 1952 and 1955, with the prospect of even greater increases for years to come. Pan American airlines made it easier to get there by offering a thirty-nine-dollar round-trip flight from Miami, advertised in newspapers and magazines up and down the East Coast of the United States. Of course, the company had a vested interest: as owners of International Hotels, Inc., Pan American had a controlling interest in the Hotel Nacional and was therefore an investor in the Lansky brothers and the rest of the Havana Mob.

With Pan Am leading the way, other transportation companies jumped on board. Delta Airlines announced a year-round thirty-day excursion to various Caribbean destinations, culminating with a stop in Havana. A number of steamship lines reconfigured their schedules to connect New York, Miami, and New Orleans directly with Havana. An entity known as the West Indies Fruit and Steamship Company came up with a novel idea: they refurbished two of their largest passenger ferries so that they were equipped to transport automobiles. Tourists leaving from Florida could now drive their cars onto a ferry and disembark in the Port of Havana. The gimmick touched off a fascination with American cars in Havana. Fords, Chevrolets, Duesenbergs, and Cadillacs from the late 1940s and '50s flooded into Havana; it was the beginning of a vintage-car culture that exists in Havana to this day.

In the months leading up to the 1955 tourist season, a series of events signaled that it was likely to be the most lucrative season ever. First came the grand reopening of Oriental Park Racetrack, believed to be among the most attractive racetracks in the Americas. The occasion was chronicled in the *New York Times*, which described the new owners of the track as a "group of American and Cuban investors." Lansky, Trafficante, and a host of other mobsters were part of this group, and the action at the track promised to be fierce. A full schedule of races was slated for Thursdays, Saturdays, and Sundays. Purses were raised to a minimum of one thousand dollars, with a twenty-five-hundred-dollar handicap on weekdays and five thousand dollars on Sundays.

Those who did business with the new owners of Oriental Park

Racetrack got a taste of the company's Mob-style approach. An independent contractor named Joseph Lease attempted to install a totalizer—a mechanical apparatus that automatically updates the sums of money bet on a race. This new technology would eliminate the old-style hand-manipulated pari-mutual boards that had been a fixture at racetracks for generations. On the night of December 9—five days after the refurbished racetrack opened—two racketeers slipped into Havana, beat Lease over the head with blackjacks in his hotel room, and hopped on the next plane back to Miami. In an article in the *Havana Post*, police investigators speculated that the assailants wanted Lease to dismantle the newfangled betting equipment, which threatened their ability to manipulate the stateside bolita payoff—payoffs that were based on pari-mutual totals at the track.

A more sanguine event relating to the fortunes of the Havana Mob occurred later in December, when American entertainer Eartha Kitt performed at the grand opening of the Club Parisién, a lavish, newly renovated cabaret in the Hotel Nacional. Lansky underling Wilbur Clark was the entertainment director at the Nacional, and all major acts in Havana were contracted by Trafficante's International Amusements Corporation, so nary a show took place in the city in which the Mob did not get a piece of the action.

The Club Parisién had been renovated to attract major American talent. It did not have the size or ambitious floor shows common at the Montmartre, Sans Souci, or Tropicana, but it offered the same kind of intimacy that made clubs like the Copacabana and Stork Club so popular in New York City. With dark mood lighting, tropical flora and fauna, and cozy velour banquettes, the club was designed for lovers. No one personified the sleek glamour of the place better than Eartha Kitt.

Described by her former lover Orson Welles as "the most exciting woman in the world," Kitt was a sultry African-American actress, singer, and dancer with a trademark "purrrrrr." Her exotic, slightly Asiatic beauty and dancer's grace gave her a catlike quality that she would later parlay into her role as Catwoman in the popular 1960s TV series *Bat-*

man. In 1954 Kitt scored a major hit with a novelty song entitled "Santa Baby." The song was loaded with sexual innuendo. Onstage at the Parisién, Kitt caressed the microphone and slunk around like a jungle temptress. Dressed in a low-cut, tight-fitting black slip, she cooed, "Santa baby, just slip a sable under the tree, for me / Been an awful good girl, Santa Baby, / So hurry down the chimney tonight." To those who were there, Eartha Kitt's opening-night act at the Parisién would stand as one of the most alluring evenings of the entire era.

Another show that lit up the sky with star power was the arrival of Nat "King" Cole at the Tropicana. The suave Mr. Cole, who would later become the first African American to host a variety show on U.S. television, was then at the height of his popularity. His signature song, "Unforgettable," had been at the top of the charts for months, and his two-week engagement at the Tropicana was sold out weeks in advance.

Cole's lead-in act was an elaborate floor show entitled *Fantasia Mexicana,* with frolicking señoritas, conga drums, and a bikini-clad dancer whose headdress consisted of a four-foot-high stack of sombreros. Some were concerned that Cole's more intimate lounge style would not be able to compete with the elaborate lead-in act or the sheer size of the Tropicana's stage. Those worries were put to rest when Cole walked out on the proscenium in a white tuxedo, sat down at the piano, and began to sing in his milk-and-honey baritone. The audience was hooked. Said Ofelia Fox, wife of the owner, "No one loved the Tropicana shows more than me. But after hearing Nat King Cole sing, I didn't want to hear anything else."

Both Kitt and Cole were African American, as were Dorothy Dandridge, Sarah Vaughan, Ella Fitzgerald, Johnny Mathis, and many of the other entertainers who would headline Havana's nightclubs in the months and years ahead. The city's nightlife was a multiracial mix of blacks, whites, and Latinos, making it one of the hippest scenes in the world. Whereas the shows and casinos in Las Vegas were overwhelmingly populated by Caucasians, and nightclubs in New York City were still mostly segregated according to race, Havana provided entertainment venues that were an international swirl of race, language, and social class. You weren't cool unless you could speak a little *español*, dance the mambo, and drink a Cuba libre, daiquiri, *mojito*, or many of the other tropical cocktails that had been created for the tourists. The scene was sexy, percussive, and the envy of partygoers around the world.

Presiding over it all like a *guajiro* Wizard of Oz was El Presidente Batista. For the poor mestizo cane cutter from Banes, it must have seemed like the culmination of an impossible dream. Batista, who had once been turned down for membership at the Havana Yacht Club because of his race, was now the overseer of a fabulous mixed-race social scene. The president did not appear in the casinos and clubs very often, unless it was for a charity such as *La liga contra el cáncer*. But it was understood that he was the instigator and primary benefactor of the city's resurgence and, in time, the Tropicana, Club Parisién, Sans Souci, and other fabulous clubs of the era would come to be seen as the flowering of *Batistaismo*.

Things were going well in Havana—so well that some began to wonder if the island's political resistance, which had ebbed and flowed in the years since Batista's *golpe*, had finally been squelched. There was still the occasional pipe bomb, or other acts of sabotage against government facilities, but for the most part it appeared as though dissent had been drowned out by the inexorable flow of conga lines and popping of champagne corks. The common perception was that Cuba was now safe from rabble-rousers and revolutionaries. Batista himself had come to this conclusion earlier in the year when, in an unusual display of generosity, he issued a proclamation declaring that there would be a onetime amnesty for political prisoners. On the afternoon of May 15, twenty prisoners walked out of the Isle of Pines prison. Among them were twenty-nine-year-old Fidel Castro and his younger brother, Raúl.

Newsreel footage was shown in Havana movie theaters of Castro, in a gray suit, walking down the front steps of the prison, his arm raised defiantly in the air. Later, he issued a statement to the press: "As we leave the prison . . . we proclaim that we shall struggle for [our] ideas even at the price of our existence . . . Our freedom shall not be feast or rest, but battle and duty for a nation without despotism and misery." Contrary to the popular appearance of political acquiescence throughout the land, Fidel added, "There is a new faith, a new awakening in the national conscience. To try to drown it will provoke an unprecedented catastrophe . . . Despots vanish, peoples remain . . ."

The amnesty had been brewing for some time. President Batista was initially against the idea, feeling that to release Castro and his cohorts would make his administration appear weak. Public opinion was in favor of amnesty, however, especially after a group of Cuban mothers formed a group called the Relatives' Amnesty Committee for Political Prisoners. The mothers issued a manifesto entitled "Cuba, Freedom for Your Sons." Batista was also lobbied hard by the family of Castro's wife, which had connections high up in his administration.

The public message behind Batista's amnesty was simple. With the island's capital city booming economically and the Havana Mob coalescing as a behind-the-scenes force in Cuban affairs, El Presidente was dealing from a position of strength. Powerful financial institutions, casinos, cabarets, hotels, and a host of ancillary rackets were taking shape. Batista's grip on the populace appeared to be stronger than ever. Why not appease those who claimed to be enemies of the state by showing that he was not afraid of anyone or anything? What better way was there to demonstrate that the regime was above petty squabbles and was attuned to the demands of the people? Where others might seek to crush their enemies, by allowing Fidel Castro and his compatriots to walk out of prison Batista intended to show the world that he truly was a benevolent dictator after all.

It was a daring move by a man with a flair for the dramatic. It would prove to be the biggest mistake of his life.

Part Two

LA ENGAÑADORA
(THE DECEIVER)

8

ARRIVEDERCI, ROMA

FIDEL CASTRO DID NOT DANCE THE MAMBO. IN FACT, HE did not dance at all.

Although he had been a physically active person all his life, the young revolutionary viewed dancing and partying in general as a kind of useless frivolity. He associated the nightclubs and cabarets in Havana with the upper classes, which would lead him to denounce the sort of high life taking place in the country's capital city as the last refuge of the bourgeoisie. In a letter to a *compañero* on January 1, 1955, Castro found it hard to hide his contempt for the Cuban nightlife that was then attracting tourists from around the globe. "What do our homeland's pain and people's mourning matter to the rich and fatuous who fill the dance halls?" he wrote. "For them, we are unthinking young people, disturbers of the existing social paradise. There will be no lack of idiots who think we envy them and aspire to the same miserable idle and reptilian existence they enjoy today."

Out of prison, Castro immediately resumed his role as the country's preeminent political firebrand. While throngs danced the mambo and cha-cha-chá at the Tropicana and elsewhere, Fidel called for a unified resistance against the "fraudulent regime of the dictator." He soon found out that Cuba—and Havana in particular—had other ideas.

For one thing, in the nearly two years since Castro had launched his attack on the Moncada army barracks, the resistance movement had become factionalized. The most active group was the Directorio Revolucionario, commonly known as the Directorio, a radical student group founded by José Antonio Echevarría. There was also the Ortodoxo Party, with which Castro had been affiliated since he ran for congress years earlier. The official Communist Party was also an active underground organization, even though it had been outlawed by Batista. These groups were all interested in co-opting the regime but disagreed on strategy and tactics. Some were not yet ready to support Castro's call for removal of the Batista government through an armed insurgency.

On the radio and in left-leaning publications such as *La Calle* and *Bohemia,* Fidel denounced the regime. The government responded by banning his voice from the airwaves and forbidding *La Calle* from printing his articles. He was, in effect, silenced politically. Also, SIM and various groups within the secret police stepped up their periodic campaign of terror against opposition groups, with arrests, disappearances, and assassinations.

Somebody wanted Fidel dead. From the day he walked out of jail, agents of the secret police followed Castro everywhere he went and rumors of assassination plots abounded. The rebel leader moved from house to house, never sleeping anywhere for more than two nights in a row. Fidel and his followers came to believe that the amnesty had been a hoax. In prison, the government could not kill Fidel Castro without making it obvious that they had done the deed or allowed it to happen. Out on the street, he could be murdered and no one would be able to prove who was responsible.

It was in this atmosphere of repression and paranoia that Castro came to the conclusion that he could not function as an opposition leader in Cuba. In a message to his followers, he wrote:

I am leaving Cuba . . . Six weeks after leaving prison I am convinced more than ever of the dictatorship's intention to remain in power for twenty years masked in different ways, ruling as now by the use of terror and crime . . . As a follower of Martí, I believe the hour has come to take rights and not beg for them, to fight instead of pleading for them. I will reside somewhere in the Caribbean. From trips such as this, one does not return or else one returns with the tyranny beheaded at one's feet.

Much has been written about Castro's time in Mexico City, where he moved with his brother Raúl and a handful of other supporters who would eventually form the command structure of his 26th of July Movement, so named after the date of the Moncada attack. In Mexico, Castro divorced his wife of six years and entered into a protracted custody battle for his young son, Fidelito. He also met Ernesto "Che" Guevara, the Argentine doctor and intellectual with whom he would devise a strategy for dramatically returning to Cuba to wage war against Batista. After many late-night discussions with Guevara in Mexico City, Fidel began to evolve politically. He became a Marxist, though he realized that if he were to garner support and raise money for his cause it might be best to soft-peddle his more radical notions for the time being.

One of the most intriguing aspects of this period in Castro's life was his seven-week trip to the United States to raise money in support of his movement. Among the cities where Castro gave speeches, solicited funds, and sought to establish 26th of July Clubs were New York, Tampa, and Miami. In going to these three localities, Castro was following in the footsteps of his hero, Martí, who had lived for a time in New York and organized supporters in Tampa and Miami during Cuba's War of Independence. By traveling to these cities, Castro was also tapping into three capillaries that fed the main vein of the Havana Mob.

It is not clear how much Castro knew of the Mob's involvement in Havana at this point in history, but some facts were common knowledge. The Mob conference at the Hotel Nacional back in December 1946 had been a big enough event to become part of Havana folklore, not only in the halls of power but also in the street. Mafia involvement in Cuban political affairs was part of the public consciousness as far back as the 1920s, though few were privy to the details. With Batista's return to power, Meyer Lansky's hiring as a "tourism consultant" was certainly known and sometimes referred to in the press. In fact, early in his tenure with Batista, Lansky bought the services of a particularly influential Cuban columnist and radio personality who went by the name of Tendelera (his real name was Diego González). Tendelera was paid a retainer of sixty dollars a month to deliver only favorable stories about Lansky and his associates. Paying this kind of bribe to journalists was standard practice for the Mob going back to the days of Prohibition in New York, Chicago, and elsewhere.

Other mobsters in Havana had become well known: the duo of Amletto Battisti and Amadeo Barletta was notorious; they were the type of men Castro might have had in mind when he referred to "the accomplices and parasitic hangers-on that constitute the political retinue of the dictator." It was also part of the public discourse that a whole host of men associated with U.S. mobsters were being brought in to oversee management of the various hotels, casinos, and cabarets. Discerning *habaneros* would have known that these people were tied in with the Cuban government.

One manifestation of the mobster-Batista alliance that was self-evident was the link to Roberto Fernández Miranda, the president's brother-in-law. It was common knowledge that Fernández Miranda had been bequeathed control of the highly lucrative slot machine business in the city. The *traganíqueles*, as the one-armed bandits were called, were visible all over town. Not only were they in the casinos but also in the smaller cabarets, and in bars and corner bodegas. The machines were purchased in Chicago and imported into Havana, where Fernández Miranda rented them out; he and his partners were the only ones allowed to empty the machines. It was estimated that the *traganíqueles* generated profits of close to a million dollars a month, with Batista's brother-in-law guaranteed 50 percent of the take, courtesy of the Havana Mob.

Castro knew that U.S. gangsters were in bed with the Batista family, but he trod lightly in his direct linking of the regime to the mobsters. Lansky, Trafficante, and the others were investors not only in Batista but also in Cuba's future. Castro may have believed that he could appeal to these men as investors, use their money to finance his revolution, and then deal with them later. He revealed as much in a letter to a friend, when he wrote: "Martí once said, 'The great secret of success is knowing how to wait.' We must follow this same tactic . . . There will be plenty of time to crush all the cockroaches."

That October, Castro gave a rousing speech at Palm Garden Hall in Manhattan, where he announced for the first time, "I can inform you with complete reliability that in 1956 we will be free or we will be martyrs!" He later gave a similar speech in Miami on Flagler Street, just a few blocks from where Lansky had once headquartered his National Cuba Hotel, Inc. The following month, Castro was in Tampa, home of the Trafficantes.

He spoke at the Italian Club in Ybor City to an audience of college students and Cuban immigrants. At the end of this and other speeches in Tampa, he always passed around a *jipijapa,* an oversized Cuban farmer's hat, for sympathizers to give cash donations.

In general, Castro was well received in the United States. To the average American, the young firebrand was an unknown quantity; they would have had no strong opinion one way or the other. For obvious reasons, most Cuban Americans were sympathetic. They had been forced off the island or fled because of repression and turmoil. Anyone who presented himself as an alternative to the present regime and had a significant following would have been given a fair hearing by the exiles in America.

Fidel returned to Mexico City and continued to formulate his plans for revolution. The money raised in New York, Miami, and Tampa was used to purchase weapons. The 26th of July Movement recruited members and, through contacts all over Cuba, organized revolutionary cells on the island. In Mexico, Castro, Guevara, and a small army of insurgents engaged in intensive rebel training. Fidel continued to build toward his promise of a major revolutionary act in Cuba sometime in 1956, but events on the island proceeded according to their own timetable.

On October 28, 1956, an incident occurred that struck at the heart of the Havana Mob. Around 4:00 A.M. on a Sunday morning, Colonel Manuel Blanco Rico, chief of SIM, was leaving Lansky's Montmartre nightclub and casino with a group of associates. Onstage, the Italian opera singer and budding movie star Mario Lanza was singing an encore of his signature song, "Arrivederci, Roma." Blanco Rico and his people were in the foyer waiting for an elevator.

Two men entered the club and whipped out weapons—one a pistol, the other a submachine gun. They opened fire, sending the colonel, his entourage, and everyone else in the vicinity running for cover. Bullets sprayed the foyer of the club. Two of Blanco Rico's people, including the wife of an army colonel, accidentally ran headlong into a glass mirror. By the time the gunmen ran out of the club, the chief of military intelligence was dead and a dozen others injured amid shattered glass, screams for help, and much bloodshed.

It was a daring political assassination conducted in the lair of the Havana Mob. The shooters were clandestine members of the Directorio Revolucionario. They had come to kill Santiago Rey, Batista's minister of the interior, but when it was discovered that he was not there they settled on Blanco Rico as a target.

The killing touched off a wave of revenge violence on the part of the Batista regime. The very next day, a military squad stormed the Haitian embassy in Havana, where a number of Cubans had previously sought asylum. A violent gun battle took place. Ten people were killed, among them the head of the invading SWAT team, General Rafael Salas Cañizares, who died in the hospital from a gunshot wound. Although Batista was at the general's bedside when he passed on, according to those who knew him, the president did not view the death as a great tragedy, since it enabled him to get his hands on the general's gambling protection income—reputedly $730,000 a month.

The Mob hit back hard, via Batista. A series of government-sponsored killings followed, along with a renewed crackdown on subversive activity. Through Cuba's underground press, Fidel Castro issued a statement criticizing the government repression, but he also condemned the assassination at the Montmartre Club. "I do not know who carried out the assault on Blanco Rico," said Fidel in a newspaper interview, "but I believe that, from a political and revolutionary standpoint, the assassination was not justified, because Blanco Rico was not an executioner."

His condemnation of the killing surprised some, but it was in keeping with Castro's revolutionary philosophy, which eschewed indiscriminate acts of terrorism. Besides, he had his own ideas about how to topple the Batista government and its mobster acolytes. In fact, Castro's biggest concern with the assassination and violence that followed was how it might interfere with his own plans, which involved a dramatic invasion of the island that was supposed to take place before the end of the year.

THE BLOODY ASSASSINATION at the Montmartre startled the Havana Mob. Revolutionaries opening fire with machine guns inside a nightclub or casino was a realization of their worst fears. Finding and killing the perpetrators was Batista's job. Lansky had other concerns.

Not long after the shooting, the Montmartre closed down, a decision that was most likely made by Lansky and Batista together. The closure was announced as temporary, but in fact the club never reopened fulltime. The Montmartre Club would be the first casualty in the impending showdown between the Mob and the Revolution.

Lansky needed to make a big statement, both to show that the rampant development of Havana would proceed regardless of the political climate and to reassert his identity as the main cog in the machine. Though he was not a man normally driven by ego, Lansky's entire reputation was riding on developments in Havana. It was through his relationship with Batista that all things flowed; he was the one who had laid the groundwork for the new era of hotels, cabarets, and casinos. It was high time that Lansky initiated a project that he could call his own, one that would stand as a monument to his position as the designer and overseer of the Havana Mob.

In November 1956, Meyer founded a new company entitled La Compañía Hotelera Riviera de Cuba (the Riviera Hotel Company of Cuba). The purpose of this company was to preside over the financing, design, and construction of a new hotel-casino to be built near Calle Paseo, alongside the Malecón. The hotel would be called the Riviera and it would be the most lavish facility of its kind, with 21 floors, 440 rooms, 2 dining rooms, a casino, cabaret, swimming pool, cabaña club, park, gardens, and 2,600 square meters of arcade space for commercial use. The budget for this hotel was set at eleven million dollars, though it would eventually increase to fourteen million. Primary financing would be supplied by the Riviera Hotel Company, with all investments guaranteed by BANDES.

Lansky's name was nowhere to be seen on the list of directors for the company, though it was known by all who was the actual CEO of the enterprise. As president of the company, Lansky anointed Harry Smith, a Canadian-born millionaire who had owned a piece of the Jockey Club at Oriental Park Racetrack since Lansky's first tenure in Cuba back in the late 1930s. Secretary of the company was Senator Eduardo Suarez Rivas, former Luciano confidant and a jack-of-all-trades for the Havana Mob.

The Hotel Riviera would be Lansky's baby, from top to bottom. He would handpick the facility's designer and oversee all aspects of construction. In a way, this would be Meyer's opportunity to counteract any residual bad blood from the Bugsy Siegel–Flamingo Hotel fiasco. Lansky would show his Mob friends the right way to build a hotel-casino, with no outrageous cost overruns, no infighting, and no psychodrama of any kind. It would be the house that Lansky built, and it would be the pride of the Havana Mob.

In late November, ground was broken and construction began. Meanwhile, Lansky had realized that with all the casino construction currently under way in Havana, there was likely to be a serious shortage of experienced dealers unless something was done. Floor managers and upper-echelon employees could be imported from the States, but those working the floor would need to be culled mostly from the local population. A recruiting effort began, and in December Lansky created a stir by opening a dealer and croupier training school housed at the Ambar Motors building (owned by Amadeo Barletta), not far from the Hotel Nacional, on Calle 23, or La Rampa, as the main commercial street in Vedado was known. The school attracted many applicants and was staffed by dealers from around the United States.

Rafael "Ralph" Rubio was a young dealer working in Las Vegas at the time. One day he was approached by the assistant manager at El Rancho Vegas, the casino where he worked. The assistant manager had once been in the employ of Lansky at Ben Marden's Riviera, a casino in Fort Lee, New Jersey, that was owned by a consortium of East Coast mobsters loyal to Lansky. The man told Rubio, "I hear from Meyer Lansky's organization that things are opening up in Cuba. He's looking for dealers—especially bilingual dealers. You interested?"

Ralph was born in Tampa, the son of a Cuban-born immigrant father; he'd spoken Spanish and English all his life. He thought Havana might be an exotic alternative to the dry, nondescript Nevada desert. "Where do I sign up?" he answered.

With a wife and newborn son, Rubio headed to Havana. It was late November, a time when the temperatures are mild and the skies glisten in various shades of blue. Rubio originally settled with relatives in Vedado. It was understood that he would be employed at the Hotel Riviera's casino as a pit boss, which was an impressive position for a twenty-six-year-old. Still, the Riviera wasn't scheduled to be ready until the following year's tourist season. Rubio's services were presently needed at Lansky's dealer training school, where he would serve as one of eight to ten roving trainers.

Rubio first met Lansky at the school. Growing up in Tampa, he was familiar with the major players in the American underworld. In fact,

Ralph had a family connection. His uncle Evaristo "Tito" Rubio had been an associate of Charlie Wall, the bolita king of Tampa before he was moved aside by the Trafficante family. Tito Rubio had also been a co-owner of the Lincoln Club, one of the largest and most popular illegal gambling houses in Tampa. In March 1938, Tito was coming home after a night at his club. On the porch of his house in Ybor City he was ambushed by three gunmen. They opened fire with a shotgun, blowing away Tito Rubio. The murder occurred during the city's bloody bolita wars, and no one had any doubt who had arranged the hit—the Trafficantes.

Ralph Rubio was eight years old when his favorite uncle was taken out, gangland-style. He grew up with a deep hatred for the Trafficante name. Years later, Ralph remembered, "To me, Meyer Lansky was a competitor of Santo Trafficante. I chose to look at it that way. Working for Lansky was a way of getting even with the people who killed my uncle."

Lansky was, according to Rubio, a "brilliant man and a gentleman"; he treated his employees with respect. He told his trainers at the croupier school, "We need good, professional people working the tables. Be patient. Turn these Cuban kids into good dealers and we're all gonna profit."

The school was run by two of Lansky's most trusted associates, Giardino "Dino" Cellini and his brother, Eddie Cellini. The Cellini brothers were born of Italian immigrant parents in the steel-mill town of Steubenville, Ohio. As teenagers, they both got their start in the gambling trade as dealers at Rex's Cigar Store, which served as a front for bookies, numbers runners, and gamblers from throughout the Steubenville-Youngstown area. Both were established veterans of the casino-gambling business, with longtime Mob connections that were well known to the Narcotics Bureau, the FBI, and other U.S. law enforcement agencies.

Dino was an associate of Jake Lansky at the Nacional. At the croupier school, he was the boss. A courtly man who appeared older than his thirty-nine years (he was born in 1918), Dino was given to kissing ladies' hands. He was also a tough taskmaster. Ralph Rubio recalled, "I got along well with Eddie Cellini, but I had a personality conflict with Dino. He was stubborn and he wanted things his way all the time. But he was an absolute genius in the casino business."

The opening of the school was the talk of Havana. According to Rubio:

We had more students than we knew what to do with. We recruited mostly from the airlines because the employees there were bilingual. Their salary with the airlines was around ninety-five to a hundred dollars per month. We offered them fifty dollars a week to attend the training school, with full salaries if they were hired. The training sessions were a full day. We'd do three hours in the morning, break for lunch, then three hours in the afternoon. For those of us doing the training, it was exhausting.

The idea at the school was to re-create the actual conditions in the casino. In a room filled with gaming tables, the teachers would act as players and try to trip up the prospective employees.

The Cubans made excellent dealers at blackjack and roulette, but for some reason they were terrible at craps. They just could not get the hang of that game. It was a problem for us. We had to let many of them go and recruit our craps dealers from Vegas.

In later years, Lansky sometimes cited the training school as an example of his magnanimous approach to the Cuban people. "It was hard work because they were uneducated," he told a biographer. "It would have been easier to import Americans. But I ran it as a kind of social experiment." It is true that Lansky was providing jobs and opportunities for many young Cuban males (there were no female dealers in Havana), but according to those who worked both Vegas and Havana, the rates paid by Lansky in Cuba were lower than those in Las Vegas. The trade-off, of course, was that working in one of the casinos in Havana was a highly prestigious job. As the decade unfolded, croupiers, dealers, and floor managers associated with the Havana Mob were like royalty, virtual princes at the Court of Saint James's.

Also, the job had an added benefit. The Batista government made it possible for casino dealers to be classified as "technicians" and therefore be exempt from income tax, which made it especially attractive to experienced dealers like Ralph Rubio. Although his salary might have been less than it was at El Rancho Vegas, with his tax-free status he was likely to clear more than he ever had before.

From the beginning of his time in Cuba, Rubio revered Lansky and they developed a solid working relationship that would flower over the following three years. Lansky utilized Ralph's facility with both Spanish and English, and he often chose the young Cuban American as an emissary to various public functions, which Lansky hated to attend. He also sometimes used Ralph as a glorified errand runner. Once, he chose Rubio to deliver an expensive birthday gift to Marta Batista, the wife of the president:

It was a beautiful bracelet. I remember a car with armed soldiers came to pick me up. I was driven out to the Batista family estate near Camp Columbia, the main army base. With the revolutionary activity going on at the time, it was a little scary. The president was there at the house, but I didn't speak with him. I gave the gift to Batista's wife. She was very polite and friendly. We talked for a while; she even recommended a good school for my son.

It was an exciting time for anyone associated with the Havana Mob. Over the next year, at least three major hotel-casinos were scheduled to open. The city was seemingly alive with opportunities and activity. As would increasingly become the pattern, however, much of this activity was in counterresponse to an entirely different mood that was in the air. Beyond Havana, the winds of revolution were stirring once again.

The city of Havana, circa the 1920s. In the distance, the Hotel Nacional (with twin spires) towers over the Malecón, Havana's famous seafront drive. (© Getty Images)

Lucky Luciano (in overcoat) as he prepares to covertly leave Italy for his journey to Cuba. It was Luciano's plan to revive his role as boss of the Mob. He was later deported back to Italy by the Cuban government— under pressure from the U.S. government. (© Bettman/Corbis)

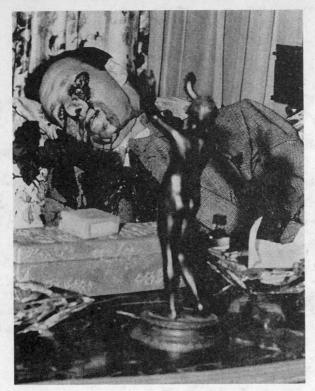

Benjamin "Bugsy" Siegel (LEFT), whose death was allegedly ordered at the December 1946 Mob conference at the Hotel Nacional. According to Luciano, it was Meyer Lansky (BELOW, CENTER) who made the decision to have Siegel whacked. Siegel was shot in the face and killed by assassins unknown. (© Bettman/Corbis)

Lucky Luciano (CENTER) is arrested in Havana. He is accompanied by Benito Herrera, head of the Cuban national police (LEFT), and Alfredo Pequeño, minister of the interior (RIGHT). Under pressure from the U.S. government, Cuban officials held the Mob boss in a detention center. In March 1947, he was deported back to Italy. (© *New York Daily News*)

Meyer Lansky, variously known as the financier of the underworld and, according to one early police report, "the brightest boy in the Combination." (© Library of Congress)

From 1933 to 1940, Fulgencio Batista ruled Cuba as the country's top military leader. Numerous presidents came and went, but Major General Batista always maintained control. (© Bettman/Corbis)

Batista returned to Cuba and ran for president in 1952. He was so well known that it wasn't even necessary to put his name on the campaign billboard, thus its slogan, *Este es el hombre* (This is the man)." (© Getty Images)

In 1955, Fidel Castro arrived in Tampa, Florida, to raise money for the Revolution. He spoke at the Italian Club in Ybor City, the center of Tampa's Cuban immigrant community. Note the U.S. and Cuban flags together in the background. (© *Tampa Tribune*)

Santo Trafficante (wearing fedora) stands next to his longtime bodyguard and driver, Jimmy Longo. In Havana, Longo was often at his boss's side. (© *Tampa Tribune*)

Frank Sinatra delivered money to Luciano in Cuba and, in February 1947, performed for a select group of mobsters at the Hotel Nacional. Later, he became an investor in the Havana Mob. (© Bettman/Corbis)

The original Mambo King: Pérez Prado (BELOW, CENTER), who created a musical style that underscored the era of the Havana Mob. (© Getty Images)

Fidel Castro and members of the revolutionary movement's first guerrilla unit as they reconnoitered in the mountainous region known as Sierra Maestra. This group of eight men would eventually multiply into thousands and become the bane of the Havana Mob. (© Bettman/Corbis)

President Batista vows to crush the rebels and maintain control. (© Bettman/Corbis)

Senator John F. Kennedy was one of numerous politicians who came to Havana looking for a good time. In December 1957, he was the recipient of an orgy provided gratis by Santo Trafficante. (© Getty Images)

There were nightclubs of all sizes in Havana. Here a rumba dancer named Zulema performs at Club Zombie. (© Getty Images)

At the Montmartre Club, the roulette wheel was especially popular with the ladies. (© Bettman/Corbis)

The dazzling Olga Chaviano: model, dancer at the Tropicana, and eventually trophy wife of Norman Rothman, gambling boss and arms smuggler. This publicity photo was taken circa 1955. (© Vicki Gold Levi Collection)

The luxurious Tropicana Nightclub operated within a fantasy world of its own creation until New Year's Day 1956, when a bomb exploded inside the club and the Revolution arrived. (© Rosa Lowinger Collection)

The Batista regime sought to violently crush any and all rebel activity, including an uprising at an army barracks in Matanzas in April 1956. Eleven rebels were killed. (© AP Photos)

Joe Stassi, the day-to-day manager of the Havana Mob. (© Richard Stratton Collection)

In 1957, mobster Albert Anastasia let it be known that he was dissatisfied with the division of spoils in Havana. (© AP Photos)

After making moves to cut in on Meyer Lansky's territory, Anastasia was gunned down in a famous midtown Manhattan hit that guaranteed his place in the gangster hall of fame. (© Getty Images)

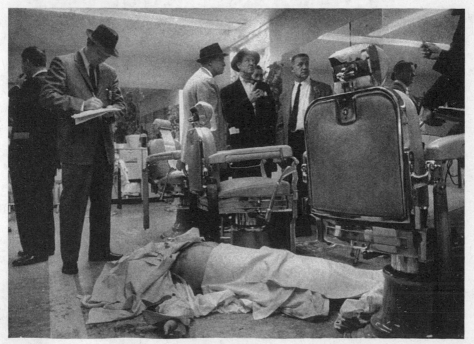

Jake Lansky, Meyer's brother, inside the Casino de Nacional. (© Getty Images)

Confidencial de Cuba, January 1958. (© Rosa Lowinger Collection)

A rare Havana photo of Meyer Lansky. He is seen here entering the Casino de Riviera with his wife, Teddy, who had no knowledge of Lansky's twenty-year-old Cuban mistress. (© Getty Images)

The Hotel Riviera opened in December 1957. Among its many attractions was the most glamorous casino in town, where the croupiers wore tuxedos and the women jewels and mink coats. (© Getty Images)

Havana's Oriental Park Racetrack had been "mobbed up" since at least the 1920s. The building to the right is the Jockey Club and casino. (© Getty Images)

George Raft at the blackjack table inside the Casino de Capri. (© Getty Images)

Mafioso Santo Trafficante (BELOW, FAR LEFT, WEARING GLASSES) was famous for courting associates. Here he hovers over Martín Fox, owner of the Tropicana, and Fox's sister (in white). Fox's wife, Ofelia, is seated to his left. (© Rosa Lowinger Collection)

The Mob had big plans for the Pearl of the Antilles. By 1958, many new hotels, casinos, cabarets, and high-rise apartment complexes were going up along the Malecón. Havana was supposed to become the Monte Carlo of the Caribbean. (© Getty Images)

The morning after: Following Batista's sudden departure from the country, many Cubans stormed into the casinos and trashed them. At the Plaza hotel-casino, people dragged gambling tables and equipment into the street and set them on fire. (© AP Photos)

1959: In the first few days of the new year, the rebels stormed the city and took charge. In the lobby of the Havana Hilton, they established their headquarters. Where there were once mobsters, now there were revolutionaries. (© Bettman/Corbis)

Fidel Castro savors the moment. (© Bettman/Corbis)

And from this point on, it would become harder and harder for the forces of the Havana Mob to look the other way.

AT THE SAME TIME that Lansky was attempting to make gambling professionals out of the youth of Havana, out in the Caribbean Sea a thirty-eight-foot yacht named *Granma* bobbed in turbulent waters. On board were Fidel Castro, his brother Raúl, Che Guevara, and seventy-nine others representing the vanguard of the 26th of July Movement. They too had a scheme that involved the youth of Cuba, one with a solitary goal: revolution.

Everything about Castro's latest undertaking made it look like another misguided enterprise, though the original plan was solid enough. The seventy-nine men and women had been culled from a highly trained squad of nearly one hundred and fifty rebels in Mexico. The rebels were in constant contact with rebel cells in Cuba, particularly a sizable group in Santiago led by a motivated young revolutionary leader named Frank País. The plan was for Castro and his group to sail ashore and attack military targets in Oriente Province, while at the same time in the capital city of Santiago, País would lead a rebellion. Eventually these two groups would come together, and the 26th of July Movement would control all of Oriente. The plan was then to build a unified rebel army that would work its way across the island, winning the hearts and minds of the people, before swarming Havana and unseating the Batista regime.

Problems began with the choice of boat. The *Granma* was a weathered vessel that Castro had bought from an American living in Mexico City. The yacht was equipped to hold a maximum of twenty-five people safely. Three years earlier, the boat had sunk during a hurricane, but Castro had had a number of people working on it to make it seaworthy. By late November the *Granma* still wasn't completely ready, but Fidel was determined to deliver on his promise to launch an attack by the end of the year. On November 25, the rebel contingent left Tuxpan, on Mexico's Gulf Coast, and headed out to sea singing the Cuban national anthem and the 26th of July march. Before long, they ran into strong winds and rough waters.

There were few experienced sailors on the ship, and almost instantly the rebels became violently ill. Che Guevara, the group's medic, searched frantically for seasickness pills, but none were to be found. In his *Reminiscences of the Cuban Revolutionary War*, Guevara wrote, "The entire boat took on an aspect both ridiculous and tragic: men with anguished faces holding their stomachs, some with their heads in buckets, others lying in the strangest positions, immobile, their clothing soiled with vomit." Another account described crew members "shitting in their pants."

At one point the boat began to take on water. It appeared as though there was a leak, so despite there being precious little food on board, the crew began throwing rations and supplies into the ocean to lighten the load. It was then discovered that what they thought was a leak was actually an open plumbing faucet that could easily be closed: the food had been thrown overboard unnecessarily.

The *Granma* listed off-course. The trip was supposed to take five days, but by the fifth day the boat was still far south of Cuba.

In Santiago, rebel leader Frank País had no way of knowing about the delays. On the morning of November 30, he launched an attack that was supposed to coincide with the arrival of the *Granma*. With a small force of twenty-eight men, País led an assault on the National Police and Maritime Police headquarters. Wearing olive-green uniforms with 26th of July red-and-black armbands, the rebels set fire to a police barracks and engaged in a gun battle with four hundred well-trained antiguerrilla troops. They were absurdly overmatched. Though Frank País escaped, most of the other rebels were killed in battle or later executed by the military police.

On board the *Granma*, Castro, Guevara, and others listened to radio reports of the slaughter in Santiago. "I wish I could fly," said Fidel.

The journey at sea continued for two more days. By the time the boat came ashore in Oriente at 4:20 A.M. on December 2, the men were famished and disoriented. Wrote Guevara: "This wasn't a landing, it was a shipwreck." In total darkness, the men waded through the mud of a mangrove swamp. They tried to salvage armaments and supplies, but it wasn't easy. They gathered on shore, conducted a head count, and headed toward high ground. They came upon a destitute and illiterate peasant living in a small shack cooking a meal on a charcoal burner. "Have no fear," Castro told the man. "I am Fidel Castro, and we have come to liberate the Cuban people." The man invited Castro and several of his men into his hut and shared food with them.

From the time of Frank País's attack on Santiago, Batista's army knew that Castro would be landing, though they didn't know exactly where. A Cuban coastguard vessel searching the shore spotted the *Granma* stuck in the mangrove swamp and immediately called in an air strike. Castro and his men heard the explosions and scurried up a hill into a wooded area, where they decamped and spent their first night in Cuba.

The next day the rebels began marching toward the Sierra Maestra, the series of rugged hills that encompasses many miles of land in Oriente Province. Castro's contingent knew that the hills were their only hope: with much brush cover and craggy, nearly impenetrable terrain, the Sierra Maestra would provide sanctuary. With a local peasant acting as guide, Castro and his people marched onward toward the mountains with only occasional stops for sustenance and rest over the following days. Early on the morning of December 5, they arrived, in a state of absolute exhaustion, at an area identified on a map as Alegría de Pío. The rebels set up camp, figuring they were safe for the time being.

The act of engaging in clandestine armed revolution required dedication and daring; it also put the insurgents at the mercy of the local population. Betrayal could be as disastrous as any bullet or bomb, as Castro's contingent soon found out. On the day of their arrival in Alegría de Pío, the rebels' peasant guide headed off to find provisions—or so he said. Instead, he sought out a garrison of the Rural Guard to report the rebels' presence in the area.

Starving and in need of energy, Castro's group had sucked on pieces of sugarcane as they marched, leaving behind a trail of husks that made it easy for the Rural Guard to trace their route.

At 4:30 P.M. the rebels were resting; many had removed their boots to wrap their bloodied feet in cloth. The ambush that followed caught them completely by surprise. Raúl Castro later described the event as a "hecatomb" and an "inferno." Gunfire rained down on the rebels from all sides and the men scattered like vermin. According to Che Guevara:

Fidel tried in vain to regroup his men in the nearby cane field . . . The surprise attack had been too massive, the bullets too abundant . . . Near me a comrade named Arbentosa was walking towards the plantation. A burst of gunfire hit both of us. I felt a terrible blow on the chest and another in the neck, and was sure I was dead. Arbentosa, spewing blood from his nose, mouth and an enormous wound from a .45 bullet, shouted something like, "They've killed me," and began to fire wildly . . .

Guevara was hit, but he was able to make his way to a tree for cover:

I immediately began to wonder what would be the best way to die, now that all seemed lost. I remembered an old story of Jack London's in which the hero, knowing that he is condemned to freeze to death in the icy reaches of Alaska, leans against a tree and decides to end his life with dignity. This is the only image I remember.

The Rural Guard set fire to the cane fields; what had been a metaphorical inferno became a literal one, with flames and black smoke blocking out the afternoon sun.

By the time the dust settled on the slaughter at Alegría de Pío, Castro's rebel army was seemingly destroyed. The carnage was complete: of the eighty-two men who landed with the *Granma*, a dozen were killed on the battlefield, others by the burning cane fields. Twenty-one others were known to have been executed within a day or two, twenty-two were caught and imprisoned, and nineteen simply vanished. A few made it out of the Sierra to return home and hide, or surrender, and some were never seen again. Only sixteen escaped, including the Castro brothers and Guevara, who survived his bullet wounds and disappeared into the Sierra Maestra.

To Batista and his government, the result was a smashing success. The military victory was announced on the radio and in the newspapers. In their excitement, the government's propaganda machine proclaimed that Fidel Castro himself had been killed. An army general said further that they had collected the bodies of the rebels and that, besides Fidel, the cadaver of Raúl Castro was also identified by documents in his pocket. Fidel was dead, Raúl was dead, the rebels were "literally pulverized." The Revolution had been strangled in its crib.

In Havana, news of Castro's demise wafted through the casinos and nightclubs at the height of the tourist season. Was he really dead? The U.S. media seemed to think so. The United Press bureau chief in Havana dutifully backed up the army's claims, reporting that Castro's body had been positively identified by the passport he carried in his pocket. Thanks to UPI, the information was disseminated around the globe. Ding-dong, the pesky rebel leader was dead. To anyone operating within the realm of the Havana Mob, it was welcome news.

Others had their doubts. Censorship and the manipulation of information had always been a key weapon in the arsenal of the regime. Aside from a spokesman for the army, no one was claiming to have actually seen Castro's dead body. The fact that it had not yet been exhibited publicly—in the manner of victorious regimes the world over—led the rebel faithful to conclude that it was all a lie. To them, Fidel was alive, hiding in the mountains, waiting to fight another day.

In truth, no one knew what to believe. Fidel was dead, or Fidel was alive. In Havana, it hardly seemed to matter. The blackjack and roulette tables spilled over with suckers and the showgirls worked their magic. Lansky, Trafficante, and the other mobsters were seemingly immune.

THROUGHOUT THE MONTH of December, the island seethed like a bitch with a low-grade fever. Outside of Havana, the arrival of Castro had unleashed a frenzy of activity. It didn't matter if he was dead or alive: the genie was out of the bottle. R. Hart Phillips of the *New York Times* captured the mood:

> Terrorism flared. Bombs exploded: trains were derailed; towns were blacked out by sabotage of power lines; incendiary fires were started by the young revolutionists. Molotov cocktails were hurled into trucks, government buildings, and warehouses, the exploding gas scattering fire in every direction.

Most of this activity took place in Oriente, where Frank País's aborted uprising had failed in its immediate goals but succeeded in destabilizing the populace. The resistance seemed to be scattered, unorganized, a spasm of rebellion that Castro had hoped to capitalize on with his invasion. Though far from coordinated, antigovernment activity on the island seemed designed to show the Batista regime that even if Castro had been captured or killed, it didn't matter. The spirit of revolution had been ignited.

In Havana, police and soldiers stood guard at public buildings and strategic points such as bridges, the harbor tunnel, and entrances to the city. Agents of SIM patrolled the streets day and night, and began a roundup of all revolutionary elements. Mostly the show of force was just that—a show. There were occasional bomb scares in Havana at movie theaters and in public squares, but it seemed more a game of cat and mouse than a coordinated guerrilla war.

It was a tradition in Havana that at 9:00 P.M. a cannon was fired at Fortaleza de San Carlos de la Cabaña, a colonial fortress located across the canal from Old Havana. The firing of the cannon was so precise that all of Havana could set clocks and watches in accordance with the familiar *boom*. Now, the revolutionaries timed their various explosions around the city to go off either shortly before or after the ceremonial sounding of the cannon. The result was an unsettling concordance of booms and crashes that made it, among other things, impossible to set the correct time. It was designed to contribute to a mood of chaos.

As New Year's Eve approached, the city's nightlife had never been more exciting. The bombs did not keep people away; in fact, there was something about explosions and rumors of revolution that made the music more heated, the dancing more sensual, and the sexual activity more urgent. The price for flights from Miami was lowered to thirty-six dollars, with regular advertisements in *Diario de la Marina* and U.S. newspapers proclaiming, "55 minutes of sheer pleasure, 5 swift flights daily."

At the Tropicana, the headline act during the Christmas season was Beny Moré, arguably the greatest Cuban entertainer of all time. Moré was as popular in Cuba as Nat King Cole and Frank Sinatra were in the United States. An accomplished composer and bandleader who first achieved acclaim with the Pérez Prado orchestra, Moré was as comfortable with a torrid mambo as he was with a tender bolero. His best-known song—the lush bolero *"Como Fue"*—was known to have facilitated the romantic process in Cuban nightclubs, hotel rooms, and *posadas* from Havana to Santiago. Moré could also be an effervescent entertainer in the manner of jazz great Dizzy Gillespie. He often wore a straw *guajiro's* hat and held a cane while dancing and mugging in front of the microphone.

The arrival at the Tropicana of El Bárbaro del Ritmo—as Moré was sometimes called—was cause for celebration. For years, Beny had been unofficially banned from the club. The problem was his drinking (Moré loved sweet Santiago rum) and his perceived unreliability. Other cabarets were willing to overlook Moré's tardiness because of his stature as the preeminent Afro-Cuban musician on the island. But at the Tropicana the standards were rigorous. The musical concept or theme of a show was the star, not any individual performer. Eventually, however, Moré convinced owner Martín Fox that he would be a good boy and he was hired for a two-week engagement.

El Bárbaro del Ritmo delivered on his promise. Not only did he draw huge crowds to the club, but he also arrived on time for every performance and completed his entire set without any displays of onstage drunkenness. Afterward he stayed late, carousing at Bajo las Estrellas, the club's bar, usually with a bevy of showgirls from his act.

The celebratory atmosphere brought about by Moré's long-awaited appearance at the Tropicana continued right up to New Year's Eve. The final night of the year was traditionally the busiest at any club. All the hotels in the city were full and the clubs were maxed out, with crowds that spilled into the parking areas. At the Tropicana, those gathered observed the usual New Year's Eve ritual: at midnight, twelve white doves were released into the sky above the stage. Everyone ate twelve green grapes for good luck. There were champagne toasts and kisses on the stroke of midnight. As the morning wore on, many gathered around the club's Bajo las Estrellas bar for more champagne and good cheer.

About an hour and a half into the New Year, the bar was rocked by an explosion that upended chairs and shattered glass. Pandemonium ensued. People grabbed their partners and began to run toward the car port and garden. Screams and shouts for help rang out in English and in Spanish. Fearing there might be another bomb somewhere on the premises, some fled the grounds entirely. The casino cleared out before the roulette wheel had stopped spinning. One young woman stumbled away from the bar with her arm severed near the shoulder.

It was a shocking event: coming just two months after the assassination of Colonel Blanco Rico at the Montmartre, it was beginning to appear as if the nightclubs and casinos were not immune after all. The revolution was spreading like a fungus, leaving chaos in its wake.

Martín Fox felt terrible about the bombing that took place at his club. The day after, he and his wife rushed to the hospital to visit the girl whose arm had been blown off. She was Megaly Martínez, a seventeen-year-old who was spending her first New Year's Eve at the Tropicana. When the club owner and his wife arrived, the girl was under heavy sedation, surrounded by weeping relatives. Fox insisted that he would pay all the hospital bills, and told the girl's family he would give her a yearly stipend for her education and also make sure she got the best prosthetic arm available in Cuba or the United States.

Back at the club, the destruction was considerable. Under the circumstances, it was a miracle that there were not more casualties or serious injuries to patrons. Police investigators surmised that the bomb had gone off before it was securely placed. It was a small, homemade explosive device, the same kind that was planted all over the city that New Year's Eve. The police had no specific clues as to who was responsible.

There were no further bombings at the Tropicana. In the days and weeks that followed, security was beefed up and government informants were allowed to infiltrate the club. These undercover operatives were referred to as "thirty-three" because they were paid exactly thirty-three pesos and thirty-three centavos a month to spy for the regime.

For a time, Martín Fox was obsessed with finding out who had planted the bomb. As the impresario of the most famous club in the city, he could not believe that anyone would want to attack him personally. He had no enemies. Why would anyone want to destroy his club? Only later did it occur to Fox that the bomber that night was most likely the very same girl who had lost her arm in the explosion. It made sense. Probably the bomb had gone off before the teenager was able to hide it in the club. She had paid a heavy price for her revolutionary sympathies.

Martín never seriously investigated his theory; he let it go. For a time, he continued to pay the girl's bills and send money to her family. Eventually communication ended and he never heard from the girl again.

THE YEAR HAD BEGUN with a bang. For a time it appeared as if the island would never be the same. Once again Batista unleashed his secret police. In Oriente, Rolando Masferrer's gang, Los Tigres, began to make their presence felt. In Santiago, four youths who had been suspected of revolutionary activity were arrested and then allegedly turned over to Masferrer and his gangsters. On January 2, 1957, the four boys were found tortured and killed in an empty building. One of the victims, William Soler, was fourteen years old.

The reaction was swift and poignant. Two days after the desecrated bodies were found, a massive gathering of five hundred women dressed in black moved through the streets of Santiago in a mostly silent procession. Some wore black veils while others held rosaries and prayed. Led by the mother of William Soler, they carried a banner that read "*Cesen los asesinatos de nuestros hijos*" (Stop the murder of our sons).

It was getting more difficult for the mobsters to pretend that all was peachy in the land of Christopher Columbus. Discontent was on the rise, and it was marching straight toward Havana.

9

A BULLET FOR
EL PRESIDENTE

MEYER LANSKY WAS WORRIED. ON SOME MORNINGS, BEFORE the city awakened, he asked his driver to pull over and stop along the Malecón. Lansky got out of the car near the large stone monument erected in honor of the sinking of the USS *Maine*. The sinking of the *Maine*, a U.S. battleship stationed in Havana harbor in 1898, was the event that had drawn the U.S. military into a war with Spain. That war took place on Cuban soil, and it led to the U.S. government's installing itself as the island's overlord. Lansky was not at war with Spain, but he was an American operating in Cuba, a stranger in a strange land. He never felt more isolated than on these early mornings when he stood facing the ocean, the waves lapping against the sea wall, and contemplated his future in a universe that was becoming increasingly complicated.

Lansky's driver waited in the car. The man's name was Armando Jaime Casielles and he had only recently been recruited by the boss of the Havana Mob as his valet and chauffeur. Until recently, Jaime had been living in Las Vegas, working as a croupier at the Flamingo hotel and casino. It was there that the young Cuban first met Lansky, who was in town on a business trip. Lansky had told Jaime, "You look like someone who can take care of himself. You should come work for me."

Jaime was born and raised in Havana's La Ceiba district, near Marianao. He was a smart kid, good in school, but he was also familiar with the more dangerous world of the streets. At the age of eighteen, Jaime got into a dispute with a hoodlum in the notorious Jesús María slum in Havana. He shot the man and was forced to flee the country. He did so by hiding in the trunk of a car aboard a ferry that made regular trips between Havana and Key West. In the United States, Jaime lived for a time with relatives and in 1949 enrolled at Northwestern University in suburban Chicago. Later, an acquaintance landed him the job in Las Vegas, first as a worker at the dealer training school at the Flamingo and eventually as a croupier in the casino. Jaime liked his job in Vegas; he harbored no immediate plans to return to Cuba. But then Lansky came along.

The Lansky name was legendary in Las Vegas, where Meyer was considered something of a founding father. The name was even more significant at the Flamingo, which had survived its shaky beginnings under the guidance of the late Bugsy Siegel to become one of the more prosperous enterprises on the Vegas Strip. Even though Lansky was famous in Vegas, Jaime did not recognize him when he first laid eyes on the short, unassuming Mob boss. It was another dealer at the Flamingo who said to him, "That's Meyer Lansky, financier of the Mafia."

Later, Jaime had an opportunity to speak with Lansky at the casino and also at a dinner party they both attended. It was at the dinner party that Lansky approached the young dealer with a proposition. "Look," he said, "I am an old friend of Fulgencio Batista. I do business with him in Havana. I have no need of recruiting nobody as a bodyguard because when I need one I just ask Batista and he sends me one. But I'm asking you to be my valet, my bodyguard, my driver."

From the moment they met, Jaime admired Lansky. To the young Cuban, the Jewish mobster was a physically unattractive man, but he had a kind of elegance that was borne of supreme confidence. When

Meyer Lansky spoke to you, he looked you in the eyes, as if he were assessing your true nature. Jaime had a feeling that—although he never talked about his past problems in Havana, with Lansky or anyone else—somehow Lansky knew or at least suspected that he had shot a man. This was most likely the reason why Lansky had chosen him as his chauffeur and bodyguard.

"Okay," Jaime told Meyer. "I would be honored to be your valet."

When the young Cuban arrived to work for Lansky in February 1957, Lansky was still living at the Hotel Nacional. Initially, Jaime was put up in a suite adjacent to Lansky's. The first time he entered Meyer's suite, the Mob boss began taking off his clothes. "Let's celebrate," he said. "Go down to the bar and get a bottle of Pernod."

"Pernod? What is that?" said Jaime.

"It's an exquisite drink. You've never tried it?"

"No," Jaime said.

He headed downstairs to the bar, picked up a bottle of Pernod, and returned to the room. When he got there, the Mob boss was in his underwear. "Go ahead and serve the Pernod," said Meyer. "There's ice and glasses over there. Pour one for me and one for yourself. You'll see how tasty it is and how good you'll feel afterward."

Lansky disappeared into the bathroom. "Could this guy be gay?" Jaime asked himself. He was walking around in his underwear, which was strange to Jaime. It made him think back to Lansky's initial overture, when he had told Jaime that he didn't need a bodyguard but wanted Jaime to drive him around anyway. Was the famous mobster coming on to him?

Lansky returned to the front room wearing a bathrobe. The two men sat and drank their Pernod. As they chatted amiably, Jaime's suspicions about Lansky's sexuality seemed more and more absurd. Years later, he remembered, "We talked about many things, then he [Lansky] went to the bathroom, took a shower, dressed himself, and that was all. Nothing unusual happened. But it made a big impression on me, Lansky walking around in his underwear like that."

Jaime was assigned various cars, including a 1957 Chevrolet Impala, a convertible, and a black Mercedes, which was used for special occasions. As Lansky's chauffeur, he drove the boss of the Havana Mob on his daily rounds, which mostly involved trips to the site of the Hotel Riviera, then under construction.

At first Jaime detected nothing amiss with Lansky, who was almost always gentlemanly and even-tempered. The only time Lansky chastised his valet was when he drove too fast along the Malecón. "*Despacio, Jaime, despacio*"—slow down—he would say in his remedial Spanish. It was only later that Jaime began to suspect that Lansky was distracted or worried about something. The pensive, early-morning stops along the Malecón were only part of it; Jaime noticed that Lansky was not finishing his meals at La Zaragozana, his favorite restaurant in Old Havana. And he was drinking—never in public, but sometimes in the privacy of his hotel suite he would down a half bottle of wine or a few stiff glasses of Pernod.

Jaime assumed it had something to do with the Revolution. Although the Batista regime stuck to its contention that Fidel Castro and his insurgents had been squashed like bugs in Oriente Province, rumors of Castro's survival persisted. Throughout the early weeks of 1957, bombings and acts of sabotage against the government continued, and there seemed to be an ominous shifting of public support, especially outside of Havana. Batista's repressive actions in response—which involved almost daily killings and disappearances of perceived enemies of the regime—only made matters worse.

Lansky had legitimate cause to be concerned about the political situation on the island. But as Jaime spent more time with his new boss, he began to realize that Lansky's worries had little to do with Castro and everything to do with the Mob back in the United States.

Among Jaime's duties was to drive Lansky to his weekly mobster summit meetings in Havana. These meetings took place on Thursday or Friday at the Miramar home of Joe Stassi, the gravelly-voiced mafioso from New Jersey.

"Hoboken Joe" Stassi and Lansky went way back. Born in 1906 on the Lower East Side of Manhattan, Stassi had known Lansky since the halcyon days of Prohibition. Stassi at the time was an underling of Longy Zwillman, the top bootlegger in New Jersey, who was also part of the Lansky-Luciano group. In his early twenties Stassi had been a feared hit man; he'd even played a role in organizing one of the most famous Mob hits ever—the murder of Dutch Schultz in Newark in 1936. Since then, Stassi had drifted toward the business side of organized crime, as advocated by Lansky. Both he and Lansky had been schooled by the Big Bankroll, Arnold Rothstein, and were now attempting to adapt Rothstein's philosophy—gangsters, showbiz types, and crooked politicians all together in one big stew—to the steamy realities of life in Havana.

Stassi's home was located on a winding, well-hidden road that ran parallel to the Almendares River, not far from the site of Lansky's highly anticipated Hotel Riviera. The house had a gate in front and a half-moon-shaped driveway. Lush tropical vegetation surrounded the house.

The weekly meetings usually took place in the late afternoon, with Stassi presiding as a kind of go-between for the various parties in attendance. Everyone gathered in the library and sometimes they spilled out onto the veranda. Along with Meyer, and sometimes his brother, Jake, the participants included Trafficante, the Cellini brothers, Norman Rothman, and Wilbur Clark. Others in attendance were a collection of men—most with experience in the casino-gambling business—who filled out the lower ranks of the Havana Mob, including:

Thomas "Blackjack" McGinty—Born and raised in Cleveland, McGinty was a former labor slugger, bootlegger, and proprietor of McGinty's Saloon, one of the more renowned Mob joints in that city's history. McGinty became an associate of Lansky through his connections to the old Mayfield Road Gang and since the 1930s had become involved in gambling operations in Youngstown, Ohio; Covington, Kentucky; and South Florida. He owned a piece of the Desert Inn in Las Vegas; in Havana, he was part owner of the gambling concession at the Hotel Nacional.

Charles "The Blade" Tourine, alias Charles White—In Havana, Tourine was known as Charles White. A former New Jersey nightclub owner who later moved to Miami, he had served for years as a link between the legitimate business world and the Mob. White was brought to Cuba to serve as manager of a nightclub at the Capri Hotel, then under construction in the Vedado neighborhood.

Nicholas "The Fat Butcher" di Costanzo—A mafioso with underworld connections from New Jersey to Miami, di Costanzo was known to have a volatile temper. He was summoned to Havana to serve as floor manager at the Capri's casino. At six feet seven inches tall and corpulent, di Costanzo was an imposing figure, and he quickly made enemies in town through his public berating of employees and fellow mobsters.

Joe Silesi, alias Joe Rivers—Rivers was a jack-of-all-trades for the Havana Mob. He was slated to serve in a managerial capacity at two new casinos, one at the Deauville Hotel and the other at the Hilton, both under construction. An associate of Trafficante, Rivers would become one of the most visible public faces of the Mob in Havana.

William Bischoff, alias Lefty Clark—Tall and silver-haired, Clark was a veteran casino manager with links to Florida and Las Vegas. He ran the casino at the Sans Souci and would later take over operations at the Tropicana, where he initiated many "giveaways" and other promotional gimmicks to draw players to his gambling enterprises. Clark worked for both Lansky and Trafficante in Havana.

Eddie Levinson—Brother of a famous gambler named Louis "Sleep Out" Levinson, Eddie ran gambling operations for the Mob in Covington, Kentucky, and also for the Lansky brothers in South Florida. He was a prominent member of what was sometimes referred to as "the Jewish Mafia," a collection of mostly New York and Florida businessmen associated with Meyer Lansky's gambling operations. Levinson arrived in Havana to serve as general manager of the casino at the Hotel Riviera.

At the regular meetings at Joe Stassi's place, there were no representatives from the Cuban government, nor Cuban-born mobsters like

Amadeo Barletta or Amletto Battisti. These were gatherings solely for U.S. mobsters and their businessmen acolytes. Often these meetings centered on business and Mob related developments back in the States that might affect operations in Havana, or vice versa.

Armando Jaime was not a participant at these meetings. As Lansky's driver, he usually stayed outside in the car or was allowed to run errands before returning to pick up his boss at a specified time. Sometimes others at the meetings reconvened in the backseat with Lansky to continue discussing issues important to the Havana Mob. While driving through the city, Jaime heard snippets of conversations between Lansky and the others. A specific name kept coming up: Anastasia.

Jaime was familiar with the name Albert Anastasia. He'd been a student at Northwestern University during the time of the televised Kefauver hearings, when Anastasia was identified as the leader of a murderous Brooklyn-based Mob crew known as Murder Inc. Among the constellation of mobsters and mafiosi exposed during the hearings, Anastasia had emerged as one of the most sinister and terrifying.

Through conversations Jaime overheard from the backseat of Lansky's car, he got the impression that Anastasia was somehow becoming a problem for the Havana Mob. Although he didn't know all the details, Jaime heard that it had something to do with Anastasia's dissatisfaction with the division of spoils in Havana. Anastasia didn't think he was getting his fair share and had apparently let his discontent be known. It was causing a ripple of concern among members of the Havana Mob.

The most worried of all was Lansky. Meyer had a history with Albert Anastasia going back to the beginnings of his involvement with organized crime. Of the numerous mafiosi who could cause problems for the Jewish Mob boss in the underworld, Anastasia was tops on the list. He was a volatile figure, a killer par excellence, and a veteran mobster who had attended every major Mob summit meeting, including the one at the Hotel Nacional in December 1946. Anastasia was stubborn and unpredictable. If anyone could throw a wrench into the plans of the Havana Mob and ruin things for everyone, it was Anastasia, the quick-tempered thug who was sometimes referred to by friend and foe alike as "the Mad Hatter."

SO FAR, LANSKY HAD had it relatively easy in Havana. Since taking over as Batista's gambling czar, he'd presided over a rapidly developing empire, dividing percentages and spreading the wealth with an eye toward peace and tranquillity within the ranks of the Mob. Representatives from New York, New Jersey, Miami, Tampa, Cleveland, Chicago, Pittsburgh, Detroit, and Las Vegas all received a piece of the action in Havana. Lansky was able to hold it all together and oversee the payouts with a minimum of discord—until Anastasia's name came up.

Anastasia was a tough, wide-shouldered man, 5 feet 8 inches tall and weighing 210 pounds. He had the face of an undertaker—cold—with deep-set eyes and thick, curly black hair. In all the public photos of Anastasia—most of which were taken when he was going to or coming from a legal proceeding of some type—he is never seen smiling. He appeared to be a man who was carrying a heavy burden, an unpleasant man who would just as soon unburden himself through violence or the dispensation of abuse as through the niceties of everyday conversation. His temperament was no doubt partly determined by his role in the Syndicate. He was the chief assassin, the man most responsible for making bodies disappear. As an investigator for the Kefauver Committee put it: "Mr. Albert Anastasia has a lot of skeletons in his closet."

For the most part, Anastasia was a loyalist, and he loved Charlie Luciano. He'd got his start in the Mob with Charlie Lucky and was believed to have been one of the gunmen—along with Vito Genovese—in the 1931 murder of Joe "the Boss" Masseria. That murder had helped pave the way for Luciano and Lansky to form the Commission, which launched a new era of organized crime in the United States. Anastasia rightly believed he was a founding father. He was rewarded by being allowed to control—along with his brother Anthony "Tough Tony" Anastasio—an underworld empire on the docks of Brooklyn that was highly lucrative, especially in the years before, during, and immediately after the Second World War.

The story of the Anastasia brothers is like a Mafia fairy tale, a classic up-by-the-bootstraps, Italy-to-Brooklyn mobster parable. Albert was born Umberto Anastasio in 1902 in Tropea, a fishing village in the province of Calabria. His father was a railroad worker who died sometime before the First World War. By the time the father passed on, the family had grown to include nine sons and three daughters. One son and two daughters died young. Another son emigrated to Australia. All the sons had to go to work at a young age on farms, the railroad, fishing boats, and freighters.

From the age of eleven or twelve, Umberto and his brother Tony shipped as deckhands on tramp steamers and knocked around some of the toughest ports in the world. In 1917 they jumped ship in Brooklyn and settled in a cold-water flat near the waterfront. Umberto Anastasio changed his name to Albert Anastasia, though Tony kept Anastasio as his appellation.

It didn't take Albert long to get into trouble. In 1921, at the age of nineteen, he was convicted along with another man for the murder of an Italian longshoreman. Anastasia was given the death penalty and sent to Sing Sing prison in Ossining, New York. After eighteen months on death row, he was awarded a new trial on a legal technicality. Meanwhile, two witnesses whose testimony had doomed Anastasia at the first trial wound up dead and another was frightened back to Italy. The charge that had taken Albert to within a few months of execution was now dropped. He was a free man.

Still in his early twenties, Anastasia returned to Brooklyn and picked up where he'd left off. He formed an alliance with Luciano, whom he viewed as a kind of Sicilian prince. Luciano returned the affection. "You know, Charlie," Albert once told Lucky, "I'll betcha I'm the only loud-mouthed bum you really like."

Anastasia had a hair-trigger temper and he didn't seem to mind killing. In fact, he seemed to like it. Albert would kill first and ask questions later. He jumped at the chance to serve Luciano by taking part in the all-important execution of Joe the Boss at Scarpato's Italian Restaurant on West 15th Street in Coney Island. Later, along with a Brooklyn Jew named Louis "Lepke" Buchalter, he became head of the enforcement arm of the Mob, which the press was later to name Murder Inc.

Nobody had heard of Murder Inc. or anything like it until 1940, when New York cops arrested Abe "Kid Twist" Reles on a homicide charge. A weaselly and talkative professional thug from Brooklyn, Reles began to spill the beans on a staggering number of murders carried out by a well-organized hit squad of Italian and Jewish killers. They met to plan their murders at Midnight Rose's, a candy store under the elevated subway tracks in Brownsville. This group, claimed Reles, had traveled around the United States during the dust-bowl years of the Great Depression—from New England to California, Minnesota to New Orleans and Miami—and carried out hundreds of contract murders. The leader of the group was Anastasia. As the Brooklyn D.A.'s office put it: "No Mob murder is committed in Brooklyn without Anastasia's permission and approval." Kid Twist Reles said of Anastasia: "He is the law."

Murder Inc. was something new: a murder squad that conducted out-of-town hits as well as local jobs. They used every technique imaginable: shooting, knifing, garroting, burying alive, bombing, poison, torture, and asphyxiation. The average price for a job was twenty-five thousand dollars, a substantial fee during the lean years of the Depression. The entire enterprise was highly secretive—the definition of an underworld operation—and would likely have continued to be were it not for the loose lips of Abe Reles.

In the lexicon of the Mob, Kid Twist was a "canary" who "sang like a bird." Before he was done singing to prosecutors, Reles had given details on some two hundred murders he had personally participated in or had intimate knowledge of, leading to forty-nine prosecutions. Several top killers went to the electric chair, including the murderous Louis Lepke.

By November 1941, Abe Reles was still giving information and building cases for the Brooklyn D.A.'s office. Next in line to be prosecuted was Albert Anastasia. The D.A.'s office announced that they were on the cusp of "the perfect case" against the feared boss of Murder Inc.

The most prized informer in the history of organized crime was being held in a room at the Half Moon Hotel, on the boardwalk in Coney Island. He was guarded round the clock by a contingent of six cops, proud members of New York's Finest. Somehow, Reles took the plunge. The cops said they didn't know how it happened. They were dozing off when Reles tried to escape and "fell" six stories to his death. Or maybe he tried to commit suicide. Forever after, some in the press and public believed that cops had been paid off and were part of the hit. Reles's demise led to one of the more famous epitaphs in Mob history: "He could sing but he couldn't fly."

Anastasia escaped prosecution. In 1943 he surprised prosecutors, cops, and even his friends by enlisting in the U.S. Army. According to Lansky loyalist Doc Stacher, it was Meyer's idea. Albert's enlistment in the army would increase his chances of obtaining U.S. citizenship and make it harder for investigators and the press to impugn his integrity down the road. Anastasia became a sergeant. His assignment was to train military longshoremen at a base in Indiantown Gap, Pennsylvania. In 1944 he was honorably discharged when it was discovered that he was overage.

By the time of the Kefauver hearings, Anastasia was a legend in his own time. He claimed to be a humble dress manufacturer. The fact that he'd recently moved into a massive home on a bluff in Palisades, New Jersey, with a spectacular view of the Hudson River, led many on the committee to question his employment history.

"Between 1919 and 1942, can you tell the committee of any occupation you had?" asked one senator.

"I don't remember," answered Anastasia.

"Well, did you have any legitimate business or occupation between 1919 and 1942?"

"I refuse to answer on the ground it might tend to incriminate me."

The committee pressed Anastasia on the subject; he dodged and parried in a manner that even had some on the committee chuckling. "In those years," offered Albert, "I went down to the racetrack, and I would make a little bet and get a winner now and then, and get a loser. That is the way I used to do."

The highly public nature of the Kefauver hearings led many mobsters to go into hiding or retrenchment, but not Anastasia. He seemed to revel in his increased notoriety. In 1951, while the hearings were still under way, an explosive book was published entitled *Murder Inc.: The Story of the Syndicate,* cowritten by Burton B. Turkus, a former assistant D.A. from Brooklyn who handled many of the Murder Inc. prosecutions. Turkus identified Anastasia as "the one who got away," writing, "this hard-mouthed, curly haired hoodlum has been close to some thirty assassinations with gun and ice pick and strangling rope, either in person or by direction . . . The killings claimed by the torpedoes of the troop he commanded ran well into three figures."

Anastasia had been outed as a major mobster, but it did not cramp his style. In fact, before the hearings were even finished, he started having people whacked. In April 1951, with *Murder Inc.* still on bookshelves everywhere, Albert arranged for the murders of Philip and Vincent Mangano, the brothers who headed the crime family of which he was a member. Anastasia had a long-running feud with Vincent Mangano, which had deteriorated to the point where they nearly came to blows on several occasions and had to be separated.

Philip Mangano was the first to go. He was shot symmetrically in each cheek and in the back of his head, his body found in the wetlands of Sheepshead Bay, Brooklyn, fully dressed except for his pants. Around the same time, Vincent Mangano was reported missing; his body was never found.

Anastasia never admitted to having anything to do with the Mangano murders, though he was quick to point out that Vincent Mangano had put out a contract on him before he disappeared. Apparently, the Mad Hatter had neglected to clear these killings with the Commission, which protocol required of all Mob bosses. Anastasia's actions created a hornet's nest of resentment and hostility that would have reverberations throughout the American underworld for the next eight years.

Meyer Lansky had always tried to keep his distance from Anastasia. There was a degree of hypocrisy in his aversion to the notorious Mafia thug. Many times in his career Lansky had benefited from the Mob's homicidal tendencies. From the murder of Joe the Boss onward, Anastasia had arranged for the elimination of many Lansky competitors, and he had provided the muscle that gave the Mob its fearsome reputation. In later years, Lansky often voiced the belief that he was as much a legitimate businessman as anybody else, but in truth he had achieved his stature in the world of high finance thanks in part to men like Albert Anastasia. The Mob's reputation for violence gave Lansky an edge in his business dealings. He reaped the rewards of fear instilled by the likes of Murder Inc.

By the early 1950s, Lansky liked to think that he had outgrown gangsters like Anastasia. Albert was everything that he was not: impulsive, hotheaded, crude, brazen. His audacity knew no bounds. The murder of the Mangano brothers had at least been business related, a consequence of underworld maneuverings for control, which was more than could be said for the murder of Arnold Schuster.

Schuster was an ordinary citizen, a person with no criminal record or attachment to the underworld in any way. One night in 1952, Anastasia was sitting in his mansion in New Jersey watching television when he saw an interview with Arnold Schuster, who described his experience as an eyewitness against famed bank robber Willie Sutton. Schuster was presented with a watch as a good citizen award. Anastasia became enraged, shouting at the TV, "I can't stand squealers. I want him dead." Albert didn't even know Willie Sutton, but he put together a hit team and arranged for the murder of Arnold Schuster.

On March 8, 1952, Schuster was shot dead on a Brooklyn street near his house. The murder touched off a firestorm in the press, with the public outraged at the brutal killing of this good citizen. The heat caused problems for Anastasia among his mobster associates, but he didn't seem to care. The Mad Hatter had his own way of dealing with such matters. When the gun used in the hit was traced to a hood named Freddie Tenuto—the man Anastasia had contracted to murder Schuster—Albert simply had Tenuto murdered. The body was never found.

The removal of human beings from the corporeal world was a way of life for Anastasia. Years later, Mafia turncoat Joseph Valachi remembered: "With [Anastasia] it was always kill, kill, kill. If somebody came up and told Albert something bad about somebody else, he would say, 'Hit him. Hit him!'"

Throughout the mid-1950s, while Lansky was down in Cuba building a gambling empire for the Mob, Anastasia was in his walled fortress in New Jersey plotting murders.

In November 1955, the U.S. Internal Revenue Service tried Albert on charges of income-tax evasion. A five-week trial ended in a hung jury; a second trial was scheduled for 1956. Charles Ferri, a sixty-eight-year-old plumbing contractor from Fort Lee, New Jersey, who had collected eighty-seven hundred dollars for work he performed on Anastasia's mansion, was expected to be a key witness. In May, about a month before the trial, Ferri and his wife disappeared from their home in a Miami suburb. According to an FBI report: "The Ferri residence in Miami was a shambles, with blood found on the living room, bedroom and bathroom floors, in addition to the hallway. There was also found a large pool of blood beside Mrs. Ferri's bed." The messy crime scene yielded no bodies and none were ever found. Not long after that, the body of Vincent Macri, an associate of Anastasia, was found shot up and stuffed in the trunk of a car in the Bronx. A few days later, Vincent's brother, Benedicto, turned up missing, his body supposedly dumped in the Passaic River. The murders of the two Ferris and two Macris were seen as part of a plot to eliminate all possible witnesses against Anastasia. The IRS case against him was in tatters. Albert entered a plea of guilty on two counts of tax evasion and wound up serving less than twelve months at a federal prison in Michigan.

Although he had succeeded in murdering, lying, and litigating his way to freedom, the legal costs for Anastasia were considerable. When he got out of prison, he needed to find new sources of revenue. This may have had something to do with his focusing on Havana. Another motivating factor may have been his close relationship with Luciano. According to an FBI report, Anastasia sneaked into Italy in May 1957 and met with Luciano and Joe Adonis, another mafioso who had been deported from the United States back to Italy. Luciano had become isolated and bitter in Italy. The exploitation of Cuba had been partly his idea, but he'd been forced to read about it from afar, with nary a word from his old pal Lansky. Luciano may have egged Anastasia on by encouraging him to persist in his demands for a fair share of the Cuban profits.

Soon after his secret trip to Italy, Anastasia requested a sit-down in New York City with the leaders of the Havana Mob. The meeting took place at the Warwick Hotel, a venerable edifice from the Prohibition era on West 54th Street in midtown Manhattan. Anthony "Cappy" Coppola, Anastasia's chauffeur and bodyguard, rented room 1009 for the occasion. According to an account printed months after the fact in the *New York World-Telegram & Sun*, the meeting was attended by "a half dozen American and Cuban hoods."

"Everybody's getting rich down there in Havana 'cept me," Anastasia said. When it was pointed out that Albert had a piece of the recently refurbished Oriental Park Racetrack, he answered, "Yeah, but what about the casinos? That's where the money is, and you know it."

Lansky and the others had already devised a plan. The details had been ironed out at the regular weekly meetings at Joe Stassi's house in Havana.

"The Hilton is yours," Lansky told Albert.

It was a seemingly substantial offer. The Havana Hilton had been under construction for almost two years and was scheduled to open in mid-1958. It would be the largest hotel in Havana—with a 660-room capacity—and a massive casino. Giving Anastasia a sizable share would cut into everyone else's profits, but it was worth it if it could head off a major confrontation with the Mad Hatter. The deal was agreed to by all the major players of the Havana Mob.

Anastasia seemed satisfied with the offer, but he said that he wanted to come down to Havana and see the operation for himself. He had not been to the island since December 1946, when he attended the big Mob conference at the Hotel Nacional. "The offer sounds good," said Albert. "I'll be down there in the next few months to check it out for myself."

Lansky left the Warwick Hotel thinking he had averted a major crisis. It was yet another example of his ability to resolve underworld contretemps in a dignified manner, without bloodshed. Anastasia had been bought off and brought into the fold.

All was right with Meyer, except for one thing: back in Cuba, events had taken a startling downturn for his partner and benefactor El Presidente Batista. The world of the Havana Mob was in the process of being turned on its head.

THE PROBLEM FOR THE BATISTA REGIME was that it had stuck its neck way out by proclaiming—with absolute certainty—that Fidel Castro was dead. In late February, Batista was made to look like a fool when the *New York Times* printed the first of a three-part series in which Castro was dramatically raised from the grave. Before, the so-called Revolution had been a scattershot affair. Now, with the news that Castro was alive and well and plotting in the Sierra Maestra, it was as if the opposition had lit the fuse of a 10-ton powder keg. Nothing would ever be the same.

The manner in which the story unfolded was as dramatic as the story itself. In early February, a fifty-eight-year-old *Times* reporter named Herbert L. Matthews was contacted by revolutionary operatives in Havana. Matthews was not the regular *Times* correspondent in Cuba, but he had written about the island before and had a good understanding of the local politics. When Matthews was informed by a member of the 26th of July underground that Castro was alive, he found it hard to believe. It was arranged for Matthews to trek deep into the Sierra Maestra, where he would see for himself and also conduct the exclusive interview of a lifetime.

The meeting was Castro's idea. In late January, he'd been hiding in his mountain camp, attempting to put together the beginnings of a communication network that would link his small band of surviving insurrectionists with revolutionary forces throughout the island. One day Castro asked a *campesino* who had just returned from the lowlands, "What do they say about me [in Havana]?"

"Well, actually, they say you are dead," the man answered.

"That I'm dead?"

"That's what they say."

Castro knew the history of Cuba's revolutionary struggle and understood how words could be powerful weapons. General Máximo Gómez, one of Cuba's heroes during the War of Independence, had said, "Without a press we shall get nowhere." Therefore, plans were made to smuggle a U.S. reporter into the mountains so that word could be spread to the world that the Revolution was still alive and kicking.

When Matthews arrived at Castro's mountain camp early on the morning of February 17, Fidel appeared through the dense *guaguasí* trees and underbrush like a spectral vision. El Comandante en Jefe wore fresh army fatigues and an olive-colored cap, and he carried a rifle with a sharpshooter's telescopic lens. "We can pick [soldiers] off at a thousand yards with these guns," he told the reporter.

The interview lasted three hours, with Castro doing almost all the talking. Matthews was no neophyte; he'd reported on Italian fascist Benito Mussolini's forays into North Africa and covered the Spanish Civil War for the *Times*. But the writer was obviously dazzled by Castro. "Taking him, as one would at first, by physique and personality, this was quite a man—a powerful six-footer, olive-skinned, full-faced, with a straggly beard," wrote Matthews in the first of his three articles.

Castro stage-managed the interview with consummate skill. Of the twenty or so men who made up Castro's revolutionary "army," he had ordered some to change their fatigues and strut around the camp, giving the impression that there were more soldiers than there actually were. He told Matthews, "I will not tell you how many soldiers we have, for obvious reasons. He [Batista] works in columns of 200; we work in groups of ten to 40, and we are winning. It is a battle against time, and time is on our side."

At the end of the interview, the two men smoked Cuban cigars together. Matthews asked Castro to sign his notepad, accompanied by the date, to prove that the two had actually met. Matthews then left the mountains and flew back to Havana, where he was staying at Amletto Battisti's Sevilla Biltmore Hotel. Days later, he returned to New York City and filed his story, which appeared with a photograph of Castro looking much as he had when Matthews found him, complete with fatigues and telescopic rifle. The article and photograph were prominently displayed on page one.

Under Batista's censorship laws, an individual censor was assigned to every newspaper circulated in Cuba. The censor responsible for the *Times* immediately ordered the article, along with Castro's photo, to be cut by hand out of each copy before it was distributed. But in this case there was no way to stop the flow of information. Tourists and businessmen traveling from the United States to Cuba brought copies of the paper with them, and within no time Matthews's scoop was the talk of the island.

The response by the Batista regime was another in a series of arrogant miscalculations that would eat away at the credibility of the dictatorship. Cuba's minister of defense issued a statement that read in part:

It is the opinion of this Government and, I am sure, of the Cuban public also, that the interview and the adventures described by Correspondent Matthews can be considered as a chapter in a fantastic novel . . . Mr. Matthews has not interviewed the pro-Communist insurgent, Fidel Castro, and the information came from certain opposition forces.

The statement went further, implying that the photo used by the *Times* was a fake.

It is noted that Matthews published a photograph saying that it was Castro. It seems strange that, having had such an interview, Matthews did not have a photograph taken of himself with the pro-Communist insurgent in order to provide proof of what he wrote.

Arrogant miscalculation number two: Matthews did have a photo of himself and Castro in the jungle. In the photo, the two men are seated together, Castro lighting his cigar, while the correspondent smoked a cigar and jotted down notes in a notepad. The *Times* printed the statement of Cuba's defense minister alongside the photograph, with a quote from Matthews: "The truth will always out, censorship or no censorship."

The Cuban government had shot itself in the foot: its insistence that Castro was dead when the world was being informed otherwise created a "Lazarus effect." In the eyes of the public, the mythology of Fidel Castro was born. The bearded ex-lawyer with a surviving army of fewer than twenty soldiers was now the most famous revolutionary in the Americas.

News of Castro's survival in the mountains touched off a flurry of activity. In Oriente, bombs went off every few hours and power lines were cut. In Havana, the Directorio Revolucionario hurried to carry out an audacious plot that had been in the pipeline for months.

On the afternoon of March 13—two weeks after the last part of Matthews's series appeared in the *Times*—Batista was in his second-story office at the presidential palace. He was reading a book—*The Day Lincoln Was Shot*—when he heard the sound of gunfire from outside and was informed that the palace was under attack. He slammed shut his book and, under armed guard, quickly made his way to a secret elevator that would take him to a higher floor.

The presidential palace was less than a block away from the Sevilla Biltmore Hotel, on the outskirts of Old Havana. A half-dozen narrow streets skirted the large stone structure with cascading concrete steps that led past marble pillars to the front door. The attackers arrived in delivery trucks and on foot. Dressed mostly in street clothes, the squad of fifty men crashed the front gate of the palace and, with pistols, machine guns, and grenades, fought their way into the building. Resistance was fierce; military guards fired back with rifles and revolvers. The shooting, sounds of shouting and explosions, and smoke from grenades engulfed the area.

At the same time rebels from the Directorio were attacking the palace, another armed group commandeered the broadcast studio of Radio Reloj, a popular radio station. This squad was led by José Antonio Echevarría, leader of the Directorio. The two attacks were coordinated to take place at approximately the same time, with the goal of assassinating the president, overthrowing the Batista government, and announcing it over the radio, all in one dramatic flourish.

It was something of a suicide mission. For one thing, Batista knew the attack was coming, though he had no idea of the precise date or time. Agents of SIM had infiltrated the Directorio. The president's security detail had been doubled in size. When the attack came, the army was ready.

Even so, the insurgents were able to penetrate the palace and—using submachine guns and grenades—shoot and bomb their way to Batista's second-floor office. By the time they burst into the office, he had narrowly escaped to the top floor and established a solid defense. The insurgents were forced to shoot it out with government soldiers in the marble lobby of the building. They were expecting backup from a second wave of attackers, but that group was unable to break through a perimeter of tanks and armored vehicles that had cordoned off the area once the attack began.

All in all, the attack on the palace was a bloody mess. Fifty people were killed—five soldiers and forty-five insurgents. Many more insurgents were injured or captured, and would later be tortured and used as an example by the regime.

Meanwhile, at the Radio Reloj studio, Echevarría and his crew of insurgents took over the station and announced over the airwaves: "People of Havana! The Revolution is in progress. The presidential palace has been taken by our forces and the dictator has been executed in his den!" After blowing up the station's control panel, Echevarría then headed out into the street, where he was immediately shot dead by police.

For a time, the audacious attack on the palace and radio station created a wave of sympathy for Batista. Business and financial leaders, the mainstream press, and foreign diplomats rallied to his support, denouncing the attacks as a threat to democracy. Batista, for his part, downplayed the severity of the attacks. Meanwhile, his secret police hunted down and murdered four students who were believed to have played a role in the attack. El Presidente could claim a major victory in his battle against political agitation, but his assessment of the larger picture on the island remained as delusional as ever.

One week after the attack, at the inauguration ceremony for a sparkling new twenty-five-million-dollar Shell Oil refinery in Cuba, Batista answered a question from a reporter by stating flat out: "There are no rebels in the Sierra Maestra." It was an astounding statement given what was now known about Castro and his burgeoning 26th of July Movement.

The Havana Mob were willing to accept Batista's assessment, though they did hedge their bets by developing a strategy of their own for winning over the Cuban public. Just as mobsters like Luciano, Trafficante, and Lansky had sought to endear themselves to key associates in Havana by showering their wives with cars, mink coats, and diamond bracelets, the Mob attempted to win over the populace through elaborate giveaways. At the Tropicana, where the gambling salon was now advertised in *Diario de la Marina* and the *Havana Post* as "Lefty Clark's Casino," a bingo game was instituted. Among the top prizes to be won were six brand-new 1957-model automobiles, a bonanza cosponsored by Cadillac, Oldsmobile, Buick, Mercedes-Benz, Pontiac, and Chevrolet.

In a country where the average monthly income was twelve dollars, giving away high-end American cars was a level of extravagance that rivaled the waning days of the Roman Empire.

If Batista could not capture the hearts and minds of the Cuban people, the Havana Mob and its corporate affiliates were prepared to do it their way. Giving away sleek new capitalist machines was a drop in the bucket for Lansky & Co., who never lost sight of the big prize: a gambling and racketeering empire that could not be denied, no matter how many bombs were set off or bullets fired by the expanding circle of Fidel Castro and his revolutionary *compañeros*.

10

CARNIVAL OF FLESH

SANTO TRAFFICANTE KNEW A GOOD THING WHEN HE SAW one. Although he was not the top man in Havana, as he was back in Tampa, he was sitting pretty in the spring of 1957. His new hotel—the Deauville—had opened along the Malecón. Built at a cost of $2.3 million, with a 140-room capacity, the 14-story hotel was nowhere near as lavish as Lansky's highly anticipated Riviera, but it was nonetheless a solid moneymaker for Santo. Along with bolita banker Evaristo Garcia Jr., he was a major investor in the hotel, and he owned the gambling concession outright. Havana Mob veteran Joe Rivers managed the casino for Trafficante.

Overall, business was going so well for the Mafia don from Tampa that on March 12 he applied for permanent residency in Cuba, the better to oversee his various assets. Included among those assets was not only the Deauville but also the Comodoro hotel and casino, the Sans Souci nightclub and casino, International Amusements, Inc., and a piece of the gambling concession at the Tropicana. He also had another major hotel-nightclub-casino—the Capri—scheduled to open within the next six months.

To run his many business enterprises in Cuba, Trafficante assembled a crew within the Havana Mob that was primarily loyal to him, not Lansky. His most visible partner was Jimmy Longo, his longtime body-guard and driver from the Tampa Mob. A key associate at the Deauville was John Martino, a Miami-based former loanshark and nightclub op-erator. Martino was also a specialist in electronic gaming machines, de-signed to increase the profits of casino owners. Another favored member of the crew was Ralph Reina, a former bolita partner of Trafficante's fa-ther who ran the Hotel Comodoro. Later, Reina would become Traffi-cante's bagman, with the all-important job of transporting suitcases filled with cash from the Havana casinos directly into Santo's private bank accounts in Florida.

In Cuba, Trafficante was legendary for not only taking good care of his crew but also extending that hospitality to their family and friends. He would sometimes set them up in suites, take them out to dinner, or get them prized seats for floor shows at the Sans Souci or Tropicana. Tampa born and raised Dr. Ferdie Pacheco, who would later acquire fame as boxing champion Mohammad Ali's cornerman, knew of Santo from his days in Ybor City. As a thirty-year-old doctor, Pacheco visited Havana, where Trafficante presided over his domain like a Sicilian prince. Remembered Pacheco: "If he knew you were from Tampa, every-thing you wanted in Cuba was on Santo."

With Santo's obsequious following and seemingly autonomous finan-cial base, speculation circulated within the Havana Mob about his po-tential side deals. The most heated topic of discussion within criminal circles—and also within the halls of U.S. law enforcement—was whether or not the Tampa Mob boss was using Cuba as a transshipment point for the smuggling of narcotics into the United States.

Ever since Lucky Luciano's time in Havana in 1946–47, the U.S. Nar-cotics Bureau had been obsessed with Cuba as a potential conduit for heroin and cocaine smuggling financed by the Mafia. From the time Trafficante arrived in Cuba, the Bureau had designated him as "a person of interest." Their focusing on the Tampa Mob boss was not without foundation. He was, after all, the son of Santo Trafficante Sr., who was believed to have used Cuba as a narcotics route as far back as the 1930s. One of Trafficante Sr.'s associates had been George "Saturday" Zarate, who at the time of Santo Jr.'s arrival in Cuba was still alive and kicking, and living in Havana.

Zarate was a classic Cuban-American gangster from the old school. He'd been born in Cuba in 1898 but moved in his teen years to Tampa, where he soon became both a user and trafficker of morphine. Zarate was one of the pioneers in establishing links between the Cuban and U.S. underworlds of the early and mid-twentieth century. In 1928 he was convicted in Florida on drug charges and served thirty-three months in prison. Upon his release, he returned to the Tampa underworld and staked his claim in the city's lucrative bolita racket. He was twice the victim of near-miss attempts on his life, one a shooting outside the El Dorado gambling club in Ybor City that left him with a shoulder and arm filled with buckshot. In 1941 he was tried in criminal court for running a bolita ring that the *Tampa Tribune* described as being financed by "the Cuban syndicate." He beat the rap, but the heat on Zarate was now so severe that he moved to New York City.

In New York, Zarate made many enemies. He opened a restaurant named La Fiesta on West 46th Street in the theater district and attempted to bully his way into local gambling rackets. He also became involved in narcotics trafficking. Zarate and a gang of Cubans smuggled shipments of Peruvian cocaine into the United States, via Cuba. On December 14, 1948, narcotics and customs agents raided Zarate's restaurant and uncovered $750,000 worth of pure Peruvian flake stashed on the premises. Zarate was arrested and charged as the principal defendant in a multicount narcotics-smuggling indictment. Rather than face trial, he skipped bond and fled to Havana.

By most accounts, Zarate lived in semiretirement in Cuba, but the U.S. Narcotics Bureau was interested to know if he maintained contact with old friends in Tampa. He was put under surveillance, and on October 8, 1953, according to a Narcotics Bureau report, he was "observed in the company of Santo Trafficante at the President Hotel [in Havana]. It was reported to us that Zarate was still engaged in narcotics traffic, acting as an intermediary between Peruvian sources of supply for illicit cocaine and American gangster customers such as Santo Trafficante."

The Bureau kept an open file on Santo. George Zarate, on the other hand, left their radar—and life on earth—when he suffered a fatal heart attack in Havana on August 22, 1955. He was buried at the massive Necrópolis de Colón, the city's famous cemetery and resting place for both rich and poor.

Most official commentary on Trafficante's time in Havana cites as a given his involvement in illicit narcotics trafficking, yet there is no hard evidence to substantiate the claim in law enforcement files, court documents, or among the few Trafficante family associates who talked to investigators or journalists over the years. Frank Ragano, who was Trafficante's attorney during the Havana years and for most of his adult life, wrote in his memoir:

> Although rumors abounded in Cuba that Santo was a drug kingpin, I never saw him use or sell drugs. He told me that the Cubans thought he was involved with drugs because his family name meant "trafficker" in Spanish. He made a joke out of it, dismissing the Cubans as gullible.

Ragano visited his client numerous times in Havana. He was not hesitant to divulge many of Trafficante's worst crimes in his book (which was published seven years after the Mafia don's death in 1987), but he reiterated many times, "I never saw any evidence that Santo was involved in narcotics."

On the other hand, there were drugs in Cuba, as noted by Santo himself and others. One night at the Sans Souci, Trafficante led Ragano through the nightclub's men's room to a back door, which he unlocked. He ushered Ragano into the room: in the rear was a wall filled with safety-deposit boxes. Inside the boxes, the rich Cubans kept their private stashes of cocaine. The Mob boss explained to his attorney that the Cuban elite used cocaine as a way to sustain their prodigious nightlife.

It was also known that Amletto Battisti, owner of the Sevilla Bilt-more Hotel, imported cocaine through a Peruvian source, as did Sena-tor Eduardo Suarez Rivas and other members of the Batista cabinet. These examples involved Cubans smuggling narcotics into Cuba for local consumption, with no known involvement by U.S.-born mobsters. In his book *La conexión cubana*, Colombian author Eduardo Saenz Rovner details numerous cocaine and heroin cases in Cuba from the 1950s, including one involving a group of Colombian nationals who were caught smuggling narcotics through Cuba into the United States in 1956. None of these cases involved members of the Havana Mob or their associates.

The obvious question is: *why*? If cocaine was indeed prevalent in Ha-vana, and Cuba was being used as a transshipment point by others, why would the Havana Mob not want their piece of the action?

The answer most likely lies somewhere in the psyche of Meyer Lan-sky. The Jewish Mob boss was well known for his aversion to narcotics trafficking, even before he set up shop in Havana. The argument against getting involved with drugs was compelling: in Cuba, especially, the risks outweighed the benefits. Through their connections to the Batista government, the Havana Mob had been given a virtual license to print money via casino gambling and related investments. U.S. law enforce-ment could not touch them. Why jeopardize what was shaping up to be the most lucrative epoch the Mob had experienced since Prohibition by getting involved with narcotics? This "no dope" edict was most likely passed down by Lansky to everyone connected with the Havana Mob, under threat of banishment or even death.

Trafficante did not need to smuggle drugs to make a living. He was doing quite well through his casinos, hotels, and other investments. Not only that, but Havana had become a showcase for Santo. With the city's hotel capacity doubling, even tripling, by the year, Havana was now a popular locale for business conventions and political junkets. High-stakes gamblers, businessmen, and American politicians who passed through town were given a taste of the Havana Mob's hospitality, with Trafficante serving as host and unofficial dispenser of comp rooms, free casino chips for gambling, tickets to floor shows and nightclubs, and other fringe benefits from the smorgasbord of entertainment that the city provided.

One American politician who passed through Havana in 1957 was Massachusetts senator John F. Kennedy. Kennedy's star was on the rise that year. He'd won a Pulitzer Prize for his best-selling book, *Profiles in Courage,* and he was already being discussed as a possible candidate in the next presidential election. At forty years of age, he was young and attractive, with a reckless penchant for womanizing that had brought him to the attention of—among others—the Federal Bureau of Investigation.

Late that year, Kennedy visited Cuba for the first of what would be numerous trips to the island over the next eighteen months. His companion on this trip was Florida senator George Smathers, whom Kennedy had befriended in the Senate. Ostensibly, the trip was to visit the recently appointed U.S. ambassador to Cuba, Earl E. T. Smith. Smith was a millionaire stockbroker who, like other recent ambassadors to Cuba, was an ardent Batista supporter. Kennedy was a good friend of Smith's wife, Florence, whom he had known since her days as Florence Pritchett, a blond model and photographer popular on the New York social scene. He'd been famously photographed with Pritchett in 1944 at the Stork Club in Manhattan and had over the years rendezvoused with the socialite in various far-flung locales around the world. They were believed to be carrying on a sporadic affair.

In Cuba, JFK was shown around Havana by Senator Smathers. "He [Kennedy] wasn't a great casino man," Smathers remembered years later, "but the Tropicana nightclub had a floor show you wouldn't believe." The senator from Florida was friendly with Trafficante and Lansky, who both later claimed to have met Kennedy in Havana. In fact, according to both men, they did more than just meet Kennedy. Trafficante told Frank Ragano that upon meeting the senator from Massachusetts "his instinct told him Kennedy had a yen for the ladies, and he and [Evaristo] Garcia offered to arrange a private sex party for him, a favor Santo thought might put the prominent Kennedy in his debt."

The orgy was set up in a special suite at Trafficante's Hotel Como-doro, a beachside hideaway in the upscale neighborhood of Miramar. The mobster arranged for Kennedy to spend an afternoon with "three gorgeous prostitutes." Unbeknownst to Kennedy, the suite was outfitted with a two-way mirror that allowed Trafficante and Garcia to watch Kennedy's tryst from another room.

For months afterward, the Kennedy orgy was a topic of conversation among members of the Havana Mob. Trafficante and Garcia were still amused by the incident when they told Ragano about it months after it happened. Both Santo and Lansky would later express disgust to friends and associates that a U.S. senator who preached law, order, and decency would accept sexual favors arranged by known mobsters like them.

Later, Trafficante kicked himself for not having secretly filmed Kennedy's dalliance at the Comodoro. It would have made terrific black-mail material.

THE DISTINGUISHED SENATOR FROM MASSACHUSETTS was neither the first nor the last person to fall under the spell of Eros in Ha-vana. Sex had been a commodity on the island almost since the time of Columbus. The Cuban *mulata*, lionized in verse and song as a skilled and compliant temptress, had been a centerpiece of the local tourist trade since at least the 1920s, when Havana was first marketed as a wild tropical playground catering to North American tastes. As for prostitu-tion, it was an institution in Cuba as old as the earliest Spanish settle-ments.

The era of the Havana Mob brought about a stratification of sex that was a culmination of everything that had come before. At the top of the pyramid were the showgirls from the most prestigious clubs, such as the Sans Souci or Tropicana. Magazines like *Cabaret* and *Show* presented the showgirls on their covers and in special features as *Diosas de Carne*, or Goddesses of Flesh. Although they were noted for their sequin-clad sexual attributes, some were also world-class dancers, choreographers, and singers. *Show*, a Spanish-language magazine published in Havana, featured dancers and models in a recurring section entitled *Ensalada de pollo*—chicken salad. Photos of *pollos electrizantes* (electrifying chicks) posing in bikinis, shorts, and garter belts were accompanied by titillating captions: "Monica Castell—with that anatomy one can never lose a battle"; "The sculptural Mitsuko Miguel—a splendid invitation to life"; "The sweet and spectacular Sarah Carona—few women in the world can offer the characteristic of a twenty-nine-inch waist and thirty-nine-inch hips . . . upon her graceful gait one can hear unanimous murmurs of exaltation among the public."

Most of these women were off-limits to the average Joe. A legendary showgirl like Olga Chaviano—a dazzling, raven-haired beauty—would make herself available to the likes of Norman Rothman, but weekend tourists need not apply. Showgirl lore at the Montmartre, Sans Souci, and Tropicana was filled with stories of dancers being swept off their feet by Parisian lords, Italian millionaires, and American mobsters. A number of these tales were most likely apocryphal. At some casinos, showgirls were asked to *fichar*, or sit at the gaming tables and pretend to gamble with chips provided by the house as a way to lure male customers to the table. Most of the women were smart enough to distinguish a high roller from a weekend tourist and adjust their availability accordingly.

A lower level of club existed, however, where an average guy's chances improved somewhat. For every high-end cabaret, there were five or six smaller nightclubs scattered in pockets around the city. The success of the cabarets created a spillover effect. The El Dorado was a popular club on the Prado, a good boulevard for people-watching. The Southland Club and the Sierra Club were also nearby in Central Havana. Across town in Vedado there were Club 21, Club 23, Mocambo, Johnny 88, Pigalle, Pico Blanco (Roof Garden) at the St. John's Hotel, and many others. In Miramar, there were Le Martinique, Mes Amis, Le Rêve, and Johnny's Dream, an after-hours club that stayed open until dawn. It was on the outskirts of the city that many of the most notorious venues were located, including Bambú (on Rancho Boyeros highway), the Ali Bar

(Beny Moré's favorite club), the Night and Day, Club 66, the Palette Club, the Topeka, the Alloy, and Las Vegas.

None of these clubs had a casino, but many had slot machines. Nearly all had a conjunto band that was a smaller version of the huge orchestras that played at the Tropicana and Sans Souci. Most of the clubs, even the smaller ones, had showgirls, or at least two or three shapely dancers who were hired to perform in front of the band. It was in these more intimate venues that the mambo, the cha-cha-chá, and Afro-Cuban jazz gave birth to a sweaty dance scene unlike anything ever seen before—in Havana or anywhere else. Prostitutes worked these clubs, but it was also possible that a man or woman might engage in a physical transaction that began on the dance floor, carried over to a hotel room, and wound up resembling something like true affection, love, or—at the very least—sweaty tropical lust, free of charge. In Havana, anything was possible.

A consumer's sexual options were highly varied. For instance, burlesque was a popular pastime in the 1950s, and Havana was a regular stop on the circuit, showcasing both Cuban- and U.S.-born talent. Betty Howard, who had been named among the world's top-ten erotic performers by none other than famed burlesque impresario Harold Minsky, appeared at the Campoamor and Martí theaters. *Cabaret Quarterly* noted that her "bumps to the bongo packed Havana theaters." Elvira Padovano was another erotic performer described in one men's magazine as "exciting and unpredictable as a tropical storm . . . A classic ballerina in her teens, she recently switched to a more torrid tempo and pirouetted into the [Havana] nightclub spotlight." *Pageant* magazine touted the talents of Tybee Afra as an "Afro-Cuban rhythm dancer . . . In Brazil they named a flower for her; in Havana her picture is shown even on matchboxes."

And who could forget the appearance in Havana of Bubbles Darlene?

An exotic dancer from Minnesota, Darlene (real name Virginia Lachinia) was in town to perform at the casino cabaret in the Sevilla Biltmore Hotel. One afternoon she decided to stroll along the tree-lined Prado wearing nothing but black panties and a transparent raincoat, carrying a parasol. Cars screeched to a halt and heads turned. Blond and topless, Bubbles Darlene sauntered with one hand on her hip and a sly smile on her face. She had wisely tipped off a photographer from *Cabaret* magazine to capture the moment on film. Supposedly, the entire stunt was inspired by a Cuban song, *"La Engañadora"*—The Deceiver—which tells the story of a woman who fools her boyfriend by wearing falsies.

Police arrived on the scene. An officer took the naked woman by the arm and asked, "What's wrong with you? Where are you from?"

"I do not want to deceive anyone," replied Bubbles. Then she tried to recite—in Spanish—the lyrics from *"La Engañadora."*

At the station, a cop asked her again, "Where are you from?"

"From everywhere," she answered. "Art has no boundaries."

Eventually she told the police that she was an exotic dancer who specialized in a striptease version of the mambo. Her explanation for walking the streets was reprinted in *Cabaret Yearbook:*

It was hot and I decided to get out of my hotel room for a walk. I was listening to the radio playing "The Deceiver." I knew that the lyrics of the song dealt with a girl who wore falsies in order to have a better figure. Well, I thought, I don't need falsies and I'm going to show the world the song is not true about all girls. So I went into the street like this. I did not think the Cubans would mind.

Bubbles was fined fifty dollars for indecent exposure and let go. Forever after, she billed herself as "The Dancer that Shocked Havana, Cuba!" Her walk through the streets without clothes was affectionately remembered as a symbol of the entire ribald era. In a time of fraudulent governments, secret police, clandestine political activity, and mobsters, Bubbles Darlene, at least, was no deceiver.

SEX IN HAVANA was for show, but it was also for commerce. With fabulous showgirls and burlesque dancers overheating the male populace, there were a lot of horny men stumbling around in the sultry neon night. Prostitution thrived, as it did in most Caribbean countries where European and North American men came looking for a type of sexual gratification they could not get back home. Legendary pianist Bebo Valdés told author Rosa Lowinger that he was frequently approached by American tourists at the Tropicana looking for prostitutes. For a five-peso tip, he sometimes led them to the notorious whorehouses in the barrio of Colón. "The Americans from the South wanted only black girls," remembered Valdés, who is of African ancestry.

Like everything else in the city's sexual underworld, the whorehouses were geared toward varied tastes and pocketbooks. Most of the upper-tier establishments belonged to a franchise owned and operated by a Spanish woman known as Doña Marina. Her chain of brothels serviced the city's luxury hotels. Casa Marina was a three-story house in Old Havana with special rooms, round beds, and antique artefacts. There was also El Templo de Marina next to the Sevilla Biltmore Hotel, on the corner of the Prado. Doña Marina had another brothel in a building on San Jose Street, and a chain of lingerie shops on the Prado.

Her establishments were so well known that she even made the pages of *Stag*, a U.S. men's magazine. Under the headline "Sin—With a Rumba Beat," Casa Marina was described as "one of the most luxurious houses of ill-fame in the Western hemisphere . . . Plush draperies and period furniture adorn her parlors. Refreshments are served to visitors by white-coated servants who graciously decline tips or payment. Marina's crowning service is rarely offered in Cuba or anywhere: two trained nurses stand by from dawn to dawn in a spotlessly clean 'clinic' to guard the health of customers and employee alike."

Not far from Casa Marina, on the other side of the Prado in Central Havana, was the barrio of Colón. Here, prostitution was more of a street-level affair. Along the narrow streets of Trocadero, Ánimas, and Virtudes (Virtue Street), women beckoned from doorways and windows. Sex in the barrio of Colón was a down-and-dirty exchange, as little as a dollar for an assignation that might last five minutes. The district was primarily for sailors, brutes, and the poverty-ridden.

There were other houses of prostitution around the city, including one out by the airport called the Mambo. A revolving-door establishment, the Mambo catered to arriving and departing tourists who wanted to have sex the minute they arrived or right before they left the island. At the Mambo, you could have sex with a so-called virgin for a flat fee of a hundred dollars.

With such a thriving prostitution trade in Cuba, it is sometimes assumed that the Havana Mob must have presided over the business. There is no evidence to support this claim. Throughout the century, law enforcement had long sought to link prostitution to organized crime or the Mafia. But aside from the case that famously put away Lucky Luciano, in the history of the Mob in America there have been few prostitution prosecutions. The trade never was as lucrative as narcotics or gambling—businesses that tended to metastasize and create other businesses. Where prostitution was valuable to a criminal organization was as a source of bribery, payoffs, or patronage.

In Havana, for instance, local and military police received a cut from the bordellos. Prostitution was their racket; it existed as a way to placate the lower rungs of the Havana Mob. As with narcotics and bolita, the sex trade in Cuba was left to the Cubans, while the U.S. mobsters concerned themselves with controlling the casinos, nightclubs, banks, political leaders, and gross national product of the island.

It is a fact of human nature that in a sexual universe as varied and sophisticated as that in Havana, there were likely to be those who tested the boundaries. Beyond the city's show palaces, burlesque theaters, and bordellos was a *mundo secreto*, a secret world. A highly varied homosexual scene existed, though this aspect of the city's nightlife was certainly less well known than the heterosexual strip clubs and whorehouses.

José "Pepe" Rodríguez was a male hustler who came to Havana from the town of Cienfuegos in mid-1957. Years later, Pepe, as he was known to his friends, remembered the era as a kind of glory period for homosexuality in Cuba: "It's true you could not be openly *maricón* in the daylight, but at night everything was different." In the shadow of every major cabaret, there were smaller clubs for homosexuals, with much overlap between the two worlds.

Pepe often worked the bar at the Tropicana, where some of the city's most distinguished citizens traversed both sides of the fence. "The one guy you had to watch out for was Papo Batista, the president's son. If he took a liking to you—¡*cuidado!* [watch out!]. You never knew where that might lead." Pepe also prowled many of the clubs near the Prado, especially Club 21, a small cabaret in Vedado across from the Hotel Capri, which opened for business in November 1957.

It was not commonly known that a gay shadow world existed alongside the Mob's most revered establishments, but given the city's taste for sex, it was not surprising. According to Pepe, the city's gay subculture was tolerated, and even encouraged, by Havana's economic overseers, including the mobsters.

Lesbians also had a role to play. At the Comodoro—the hotel where Senator Kennedy had his afternoon orgy—an exhibition was sometimes held for special guests. Attorney Frank Ragano remembered being taken there by Martín Fox, owner of the Tropicana. In a large suite at the hotel, a group of women danced and performed lesbian acts with one another, then offered to have sex with men in the audience. Fox told Ragano that, from his experience, many men found lesbian sex more stimulating than the heterosexual shows. This observation was revealing, coming from Fox, whose matrimonial bond to his attractive twenty-two-year-old wife, Ofelia, was one of convenience. Although few people knew it at the time, Ofelia Fox was a closet lesbian.

Of all the locales where kinky sex exhibitions were performed in Havana, the most notorious remained the Shanghai Theater. This venerable establishment, located in Havana's Barrio Chino, or China-town, had been around since the early 1930s. Originally designed as a legitimate theater for Oriental dramas, it changed hands and through the ages became known as a showcase for bump-and-grind. Tropicana choreographer Rodney Neyra got his start there in the 1940s as a producer of burlesque shows and nude theater. By the mid-1950s, its performances had become raunchier—they were described in *Cabaret* magazine as the "world's rawest burlesque show." Dirty movies were then added to the mix. Between acts, explicit 8-millimeter films were shown on a screen above the stage. But the primary draw was the theatrical skits themselves.

There were three shows a night, running from 9:30 P.M. to the wee hours of the morning. Prices ranged from 65 cents for a bench in the balcony to $1.25 for a chair in front of the stage. The place was surprisingly big, with seats for approximately five hundred on the main floor and three hundred in the balcony. A red velvet curtain was a holdover from the club's days as a legitimate theater.

A typical opening act featured the dance team of López and Romero. To a hot mambo rhythm, Alfred Romero and Conchita López negotiated an "apache dance," with Alfred stripping off pieces of Conchita's clothing as they went. Eventually the female would be dancing completely naked. Later came the main act, which usually involved some form of live sex. The headliner shows were better if you spoke Spanish because much of the dialogue involved vulgar street language and sexual innuendo.

One typical skit that played for weeks at the Shanghai depicted a man and woman at a restaurant. They are seated at a bare table. A waiter approaches with menus. The man asks the waiter, "Where is the tableware?" Without a word, the waiter produces forks, spoons, knives, and napkins from his pockets and sets the table. After some discussion of the menu, the woman says, "I'll have coffee." Out comes a cup and a pot, and black coffee is poured. Salt and pepper? "*Sí, señor*," right here in the hip pocket. Sugar? "*Claro*"—of course—in a bottle from the breast pocket. "Where, then, is the cream?" the woman asks. The waiter smiles, and then pulls out his penis. The woman fondles the waiter's *pinga* and proceeds with fellatio until, seemingly on cue, the waiter ejaculates into the coffee.

Of all the live sex acts at the Shanghai, by far the most memorable were those involving Superman, the name given to a famously well-endowed performer. Superman was a tall, lean Cuban of African descent who often came onstage wearing a cape. Various skits and scenarios were created to introduce what was the main attraction: Superman's 14-inch member. Sometimes Superman appeared onstage on a trapezelike swing high above the audience, his prodigious prod flapping in the wind. Other times he had sex onstage with two or three women consecutively. Decades after the fact, his act was immortalized in *The Godfather Part II,* in a scene where Don Michael Corleone, his brother Fredo, and a group of visiting American "dignitaries" take in a show at the Shanghai.

Like so many others who made their living in Havana during the era of the Mob, Superman was not what he appeared to be. According to the male hustler Pepe and others, this unassuming man, famous throughout Cuba for his heterosexual prowess, was, in fact, gay. "I know because he [Superman] many times had sex with a male friend of mine who worked at the theater," alleged Pepe.

Throughout the late 1950s, Superman's appearances at the Shanghai filled the theater with tourists. Ralph Rubio, who worked as a trainer at Lansky's croupier school and would later serve as his credit manager at the Riviera hotel-casino, saw Superman's act on numerous occasions. It was sometimes Rubio's job to serve as "entertainment director" and show high rollers, visiting political figures, and other important associates of Lansky a good time. Nearly everyone wanted to be taken to the infamous Shanghai Theater to see Superman.

On one occasion, Rubio accompanied a group that included Irving "Niggy" Devine, a gambling impresario, silent co-owner of the Fremont Hotel and Casino in Las Vegas, and a partner of Eddie Levinson, whom Lansky had imported to manage the casino at the Riviera. Devine could hardly contain himself when he saw Superman onstage. Part of the performer's act often involved audience participation: patrons were allowed to choose from among a group of women onstage which ones they wanted to see Superman penetrate with his enormous shaft. Remembered Rubio: "Nig Devine was a sexual degenerate. He put up three hundred dollars extra to see Superman have anal sex with a woman."

Devine handed over the cash to a representative of the theater; on-stage, Superman did his thing. As Rubio remembered it, he turned his head when the famous sex performer entered the woman from behind. Rubio couldn't watch. It was too painful.

THE SEXUAL DEGRADATION of Cuban citizens for the entertainment of North American and European tourists was the dirty little secret of the Havana Mob. Although U.S. mobsters were not the controlling force behind prostitution and pornography in Cuba (the Shanghai was owned by José Orozco García, an independent operator), commercial sex in all its many permutations was a major draw of the entire era. As Ralph Rubio put it, "Everything was geared towards sex." The cabarets with their goddesses of flesh were an extension of the casinos, which fueled everything in Havana. The whores and sex performers were the underbelly of the casinos and show palaces: it was all part and parcel of the same universe.

Fidel Castro and other members of the Revolution understood the true nature of Good Times in the capital city. It was not lost on the 26th of July Movement that at Havana's Martí Theater, named after the "spiritual architect" of the Revolution and Fidel's personal hero, burlesque star Betty Howard was shaking her posterior and twirling her bosoms at three shows a night. To the enemies of the Batista regime, a moral rot had taken hold in Havana that was a natural consequence of the president's unholy relationship with what Castro referred to as *desfalcadores* (embezzlers), his term of choice for those behind the economic plundering of the island.

By early 1957, the 26th of July Movement had begun to gather strength. In a number of initial skirmishes with the Rural Guard in the Sierra Maestra, Castro's rebels had acquitted themselves well, with no casualties and substantial gains in terms of arms and supplies. They kept moving and adapted to their surroundings. Remembered Fidel:

> We identified so completely with the natural surroundings of the mountains. We adapted so well that we felt as if we were in our natural habitat. It was not easy, but I think we identified with the forest as much as the wild animals that live there. We were constantly on the move. We always slept in the forest. At first, we slept on the ground. We had nothing with which to cover ourselves. Later, we had hammocks, and nylon . . . and we used plastic for covers to protect ourselves from the rain. We organized kitchen duty by teams. Each team would carry the cooking equipment and the food up the hill . . . We did not know the region well . . . We studied the terrain as we fought.

Until now, the movement had been dominated by urban intellectuals and students, but as the rebels were forced to live off the land in the most drastic of situations, priorities shifted. Castro's followers bonded with Cuba's most dispossessed people—a group that could not have been further removed from those in the capital city, who frolicked late into the night courtesy of the Havana Mob. As Castro put it:

> Batista was carrying on a fierce repressive campaign, and there were many houses burned, and many murdered peasants. We dealt with the peasants in a very different manner from the Batista soldiers, and we slowly gained the support of the rural population—until that support became absolute. Our soldiers came from that rural population.

Castro's second-in-command, Che Guevara, felt as though this convergence between rebel and peasant marked the true beginning of the Revolution:

> The guerrilla and the peasant became joined into a single mass, so that (and no one could say at which moment precisely of the long

march it occurred) we became part of the peasants . . . The idea of agrarian reform was born and that of communion with the people ceased to be a theory, being converted into a definite part of our being.

In May, the movement got another boost from the U.S. media when CBS aired a television documentary entitled *The Story of Cuba's Jungle Fighters*. Four weeks earlier, a CBS producer and cameraman had trekked into the Sierra Maestra to interview Castro and his followers—on camera. This time Fidel would be seen in the flesh, showing the interviewer around his rebel campsite. In clear, crisp English, Castro proclaimed, "Batista thinks he can obtain by lying what he cannot win with force of arms . . . When one of his soldiers is killed in battle, he says they died in an accident. Well, there have been a great deal of accidents here in Sierra Maestra in the last months."

The appearance on television was tremendous for public relations: Fidel solidified his status as a kind of tropical Robin Hood. Disgruntled Cubans flocked to the 26th of July Movement. By summer the *Ejército Rebelde*, or rebel army, had grown from its initial twelve surviving members to somewhere around three hundred. They divided up into columns and spread out around the mountains and surrounding *llano* (lowlands).

In July the movement released its first public statement of principles. The "Sierra Manifesto" was composed by Castro and two prominent opposition leaders from Havana, who met the rebel leader in the mountains. Among the principles set forth was the demand that, after Batista was overthrown and a revolutionary government was installed, gambling and corruption would be eradicated. For the first time, the movement declared on paper that it was an irrefutable enemy of the Havana Mob. From here on out, it would be war to the death.

PRESIDENT BATISTA BECAME agitated every time Castro's name was mentioned. His inner circle knew the symptoms: lack of focus, compulsive eating, a tendency toward self-pity. Most of all, Batista could not understand how, in a country that was experiencing its best economic climate in decades, there could be political unrest. His response to the news that Fidel was expanding his revolt in the countryside was to bomb indiscriminately. Repression and revenge became the rule of the day. When a contingent of the Cuban Navy attempted to capitalize on the general mood of discord and stage a mutiny at a base in Cienfuegos, they weren't just defeated, they were crushed. Many were killed in a shoot-out. Forty soldiers surrendered; they were taken out and summarily executed. All told, three hundred soldiers and civilians were killed during the siege at Cienfuegos.

In Oriente, much of the government-sanctioned terrorism was handled by Los Tigres de Masferrer. Senator Masferrer's gang adopted a new technique of displaying the bodies of their torture and murder victims. In July, four youths suspected of involvement in the civic resistance were killed, their bodies strung up on telephone poles outside of Santiago. The incident was eerily similar to the murder of William Soler and three other teenagers the previous January. For every four youths killed by the Batista regime, ten more joined the Revolution.

The secret police scored some successes. On July 30, twenty-three-year-old Frank País, the 26th of July Movement's popular leader in Oriente, was hunted down and assassinated by the government. A massive funeral procession was held for the fallen rebel and a crippling strike was organized by the labor unions. Cuba was now engulfed in a low-grade civil war.

All of this activity took place outside the capital city, and the Havana Mob remained blissfully unaware of the unrest around them. Though the attack on the presidential palace should have alerted the mobsters that their world was changing, they put their faith in the strong arm of the government. Besides, they had their own problems to deal with. As the 1957–58 tourist season approached, a dark cloud passed over the Mob's domain. It was a phenomenon that a meteorologist might have dubbed Hurricane Albert.

As promised, Albert Anastasia arrived in Havana to check on his investments. For five days in late September, he made the rounds, wearing a felt fedora as if he were still back in chilly New York. He appeared at many of the Mob's most noteworthy establishments, including Oriental Park Racetrack, where he owned a percentage of the take, the Sans Souci casino, and the Tropicana nightclub. At the Tropicana, he was given a special table and treated like a king by Martín Fox. Days later, Anastasia was seen at a business meeting at the Copacabana Hotel in Miramar. At the meeting and in the lobby of the hotel, Anastasia was loud; he made threats and gestures designed to intimidate others in attendance.

Lansky was not at this meeting. As his underling Ralph Rubio remembered: "We were warned about Anastasia. We were told to treat him with respect, but Mr. Lansky made it clear that, as far as he was concerned, Anastasia was not welcome in Havana."

The Lord High Executioner of the Mob had a beef with his associates in Cuba. His beef had to do with the Hilton Hotel. Anastasia learned that his piece of the hotel and casino was to be divided among no fewer than fifteen owners, including Cuba's hotel workers' union, the Sindicato Gastronómico. Money from the union's pension fund had been used to finance the building of the place, making the workers—at least symbolically—investors in the hotel. Anastasia didn't like the arrangement. Trafficante had his own establishments (the Comodoro, Deauville, and Capri) and Lansky had his (the Nacional and Riviera). Why should he, Albert Anastasia, have to share his piece of the action with a consortium of owners that included everyone from Cuban dishwashers to Kenneth Johnson, a junior senator from the state of Nevada?

After the Mad Hatter left Havana, there was an eerie calm. Lansky's driver, Jaime Casielles, noticed a palpable change in his boss. Anastasia was still a topic of discussion among the mobsters who gathered for the weekly meeting at Joe Stassi's house, but Lansky no longer seemed concerned to the point of distraction. The Anastasia contretemps had given way to a more deeply embedded principle.

"Lansky once told me," Jaime remembered, "the worst thing that could happen to a man was that he might lose his footing or be knocked off balance. If he had a philosophy, that was it: to always maintain balance in his life and business dealings."

Anastasia had destabilized things in Havana, but according to Jaime, his boss was proactive—he took the necessary steps to restore balance. "The impression in my mind was that he made up his mind what needed to be done. He consulted with his associates, and together they made a decision. And whatever that decision was, it gave Lansky a sentiment of determination, and it gave him a kind of peace."

Decisions can be liberating, or they can signify a point of no return. Lansky's decision was about to rock the American underworld to its core.

11

TROPICAL VENGEANCE

FOR SANTO TRAFFICANTE, THE HAVANA MOB'S PROBLEMS with Albert Anastasia represented an opening of sorts. The Tampa Mob boss knew that the syndicate in Cuba—as it had come together under himself, Lansky, Batista, and others—was not an autonomous operation: decisions made on the island created a ripple effect, with repercussions for a vast array of "families" who had a vested interest in the casinos and nightclubs. Given all the factions involved, it was perhaps inevitable that developments in Cuba would create layers of intrigue, which sometimes led to jealousies and misunderstandings. Like most high-level mafiosi, Trafficante recognized that rivalries within the underworld were often an opportunity for maneuvering and power plays; they brought out a mobster's Machiavellian spirit.

Less than two months after Anastasia's whirlwind visit to Havana, Trafficante caught a flight from Havana to Tampa, and then on to New York City. He traveled under the name B. Hill, an alias he frequently used. He landed at Newark airport, took a taxi into Manhattan, and checked himself into the Warwick Hotel at West 54th Street and 6th Avenue.

A few weeks earlier, he'd written a letter to Anastasia asking him to make arrangements for some Cuban business partners of his to stay at the Warwick. "Tell Cappy to take care of these people," wrote Santo. Cappy was the nickname for Tony Coppola, Anastasia's bodyguard and right-hand man, whom Trafficante had entertained in Havana on numerous occasions.

It was Trafficante's idea to gather together a group that included the Cubans and Anastasia to discuss plans for the casino at the Havana Hilton. Also present at the meeting would be Joe Rivers, a Havana Mob veteran, who flew up to New York because he was also a close personal friend of Anastasia.

The meeting took place in room 1009, Anastasia's suite on the tenth floor of the Warwick. Trafficante, Rivers, and Anastasia met with a group of four Cubans, which included Robert "Chiri" Mendoza. Sleek, black-haired, with a perennial tan, Chiri Mendoza was the well-connected contractor who was building the Havana Hilton and also a likely candidate to receive the sublease to operate the hotel's casino. A business partner of President Batista in several ventures, Mendoza was from an old and prominent Cuban family that owned the Almendares Alacranes (Scorpions), one of the island's most successful baseball franchises. In fact, it had been a dream of Mendoza's that he might entice the great Yankee center fielder Joe DiMaggio to serve as a meeter and greeter at the new Hilton casino.

Joe Rivers knew DiMaggio and helped set up a meeting. Out of respect, the Yankee baseball star met with this group at the Warwick Hotel. He told the men that he could not endorse liquor or gambling because of the adverse effect it would have "upon the youth of the nation."

After DiMaggio departed, the group reconvened at Chandler's, a restaurant nearby in midtown Manhattan. The discussion at the restaurant was about taking control of the casino concession at the Hilton. The price for the concession—to be paid to the Hilton Company—was $1 million, plus another $2 million under the table to Batista to close the deal ($2 million at that time was equivalent to $25 million today).

Trafficante was looking for Anastasia to contribute to the closing fees.

As an underworld veteran, Anastasia would have recognized the Trafficante offer for what it was: a way to bypass Lansky. Albert knew that Santo had his own partners in Havana, Cubans who had business dealings with the Trafficante family going all the way back to the days of booze smuggling. To Anastasia, Santo was an outsider from Tampa, as opposed to Lansky, whom Albert had known since they were young hoodlums together on the Lower East Side. But the underworld was full of partnerships of convenience, men who came together out of mutual interests and the realization of a common enemy. As far as these men were concerned, Lansky had a stranglehold on Havana; by meeting at a restaurant in Manhattan to discuss how they might better their positions, they were exercising their rights as players in the game.

What these men did not know was that there was another prominent member of the Havana Mob in town. A few days earlier, Joe Stassi, traveling under the name Joe Rogers, arrived in Manhattan and checked into the Park Sheraton Hotel, not far from the Warwick, at West 55th Street and 7th Avenue.

As day-to-day manager of the Mob in Havana, Stassi was considered to be friendly with all factions. When everyone met at his house near the Almendares River for their regular Thursday and Friday afternoon conferences to discuss developments on the island, there was a feeling they were on neutral ground. Stassi's tropical mansion was the closest thing the Havana Mob had to an official headquarters, and Hoboken Joe was thought to be an ideal mediator. In truth, Stassi was partial to Lansky.

The two men had known each other since childhood; Stassi would later refer to Lansky as "the smartest crook I ever knew." Though Stassi was Sicilian through and through, temperamentally he had more in common with his Jewish brethren from Stanton Street on the Lower East Side. As he put it to an interviewer when he was an old man: "The Jews made the Mafia. Without the Jews, the Italians wouldn't have gotten anywhere. The Jews were the ones that done the work."

To members of the Havana Mob, Stassi may have been a mediator, but his reputation for doing the dirty work went back decades. Stassi had killed for the Mafia on numerous occasions. One of his first killings was when he was in his mid-twenties and he was ordered by higher-ups in the New York Mafia to murder his best friend. He shot the man in the head at close range while sitting in a car. Stassi was not happy about having killed his best friend, nor did he particularly enjoy the other murders he committed for the Mob. As the years passed and he became more prominent in the organization, Stassi no longer did the dirty work himself. Like Albert Anastasia, he became more of an organizer of murders: he put together hit teams, devised plots, and arranged the getaways.

Stassi had the skills to pull off high-profile hits. That was part of what he did as a member of one of the world's oldest criminal fraternities.

Stassi was not in New York City to visit relatives or see the sights. He was in town because his professional services were required. He was in town to facilitate the long reach of the Havana Mob.

At Chandler's restaurant, Trafficante, Anastasia, and the Cubans broke bread and talked business. According to all, the meeting went well. Santo and Albert agreed to work out a payment arrangement regarding the Havana Hilton. Chiri Mendoza would be the point man. They all shook hands and said their good-byes.

Two days later—on the morning of October 25—Albert Anastasia went to get a haircut and walked right into the annals of gangland history.

HE NEVER KNEW what hit him. The fusillade of bullets came from behind—with no warning. Two assailants wearing handkerchiefs over their faces walked into the barbershop at the Park Sheraton Hotel, where one of the most feared mobsters in the underworld was sitting in a chair with a hot towel over his face. It was a professional hit, swift and brutal. *Bam, bam, bam, bam, bam, bam*—six shots, with one entering through Anastasia's back shoulder and continuing in a downward trajectory, piercing lung, kidney, and spleen. Two shots hit him in the hand, as he raised his right arm in a vain effort to protect himself. A shot grazed the back of his neck, and another hit him in the right hip. The last bullet struck him in the back of the head, shattered his skull, and lodged in the left hemisphere of his brain.

It was 10:20 A.M. Anastasia had come to the barbershop as part of a well-worn routine. He had thick, coarse Sicilian hair; if he didn't get a trim at least once a week, the hair went wild on him, as it had in a famous early mug shot taken when he was twenty-five years old, follicles askew, eyes cold and empty. By the time Anastasia got himself riddled with bullets at the Park Sheraton barbershop, the hair was speckled with gray and it had begun to thin a bit at the temples. To some, the fifty-five-year-old Mob boss had simply got old and careless. A younger hoodlum never would have left himself unguarded like that; Anastasia had come to believe that he was the king of the hill and therefore impregnable. He had authorized so many murders in his lifetime that he could be forgiven for believing that he was the one who meted out death in the underworld.

According to a witness, after being hit multiple times Albert bolted forward in his chair. One account had him lunging at his own reflection in the mirror, thinking it was the gunmen. The shooters kept their cool: they were dressed in long overcoats and wore black gloves and fedoras. Their bandanas made them look like bank robbers from the Old West.

The cacophony of gunfire and emanations of smoke from the .32-caliber Smith & Wesson and .38-caliber Colt revolver lasted less than a minute. Once Anastasia had slumped to the floor next to his barber chair, the gunmen turned to exit the same way they had come in. But the door on West 55th Street had locked behind them, so they left through another doorway, this one leading directly into the lobby of the Park Sheraton Hotel. They removed their masks and disappeared into the morning crowd without anyone realizing what had just happened.

There were plenty of witnesses in the barbershop: four barbers, three shoeshine boys, a manicurist, and three customers. One of those customers was Vincent Squillante, a Mob associate of Albert's, who was seated two chairs away when the shooting started. Squillante ducked behind a chair for cover. After the gunmen had taken care of business and fled, Squillante declared, "Let me out of here," and made for the door in a rush. The other witnesses were still there when the cops arrived.

A white sheet was thrown over Anastasia's body on the floor. Detectives on the scene began asking questions. The witnesses were able to describe the incident in detail, but as for motive, this was a question that would occupy the imaginations of higher gods.

The hit took place early enough in the day to make the afternoon papers: "Mobster Anastasia Murdered" screamed the New York *Daily News*; "Mob Hit Fells Boss of Murder Inc." read the *Daily Mirror*. In the annals of Mob assassinations, this was a doozy. Not since before the Commission was formed back in the early 1930s had there been a hit of this magnitude—a top boss taken out in broad daylight. Who had the *cojones* to kill Albert Anastasia? Such a person would have to be insane, or connected at the highest levels.

It didn't take long for detectives to uncover some promising leads. At the scene of the crime, they searched Anastasia's body and found a key for room 1009 at the nearby Warwick Hotel. They went to the hotel. They asked many probing questions. In no time the investigation into Anastasia's murder began to take on a pungent tropical aroma; it began to smell like Cuba.

EARLY ON THE MORNING of the Anastasia hit, Trafficante checked out of the Warwick Hotel. He flew from New York City directly to Havana's airport, where, coincidentally, he ran into Joe Rivers, who had also arrived back in Cuba on a separate flight.

"You hear the bad news?" Rivers asked Santo. "Albert's dead."

According to Trafficante, it was the first he'd heard about the murder at the barbershop.

In the days that followed, Trafficante's name was mentioned often in newspaper accounts of the hit. Detectives and reporters established that Trafficante, Rivers, and a group of Cubans had met with Anastasia not long before his murder. It was hinted in the press that perhaps Anastasia had been attempting to strong-arm Trafficante and the Cubans, to muscle in on the Mob's operations in Havana. For a time, detectives saw the two meetings at the Warwick Hotel and Chandler's restaurant as their most promising lead. They brought in for questioning one of the attendees at the meetings—Cappy Coppola, Anastasia's bodyguard. In particular, the cops wanted to know why Coppola was nowhere in sight on the morning his boss was murdered. Wasn't Coppola usually there when Albert got his haircut and shave? Wasn't it his job to make sure his boss was never left vulnerable to an attack? Coppola sealed his lips and said nothin'.

Meanwhile, Trafficante's attorney, Frank Ragano, saw a picture in the *Tampa Tribune* of Cappy Coppola being brought in for questioning by detectives in New York City. Ragano knew that Coppola and Trafficante were friends. On a couple of occasions, Ragano had traveled to New York City with Santo and they were always wined and dined there by Coppola, who seemed to revere Trafficante. That Coppola was brought in for questioning led to speculation that he and Trafficante were somehow involved with the murder of Anastasia—the theory being that Albert had made unreasonable demands regarding Cuba and got himself whacked.

Ragano met with Trafficante in Ybor City during one of Santo's regular shuttles back and forth between Tampa and Havana. They met at Trafficante's favorite restaurant, the Columbia, a classic old-world Spanish joint known for its exquisite paella.

"I suppose you've been reading all that nonsense about me," Trafficante said to his lawyer.

"Yes," answered Ragano. "The D.A. in New York is saying some pretty serious things about you—that you were in a showdown meeting with Anastasia and that he wanted to take over your casinos in Havana."

With contempt in his voice, Trafficante replied, "These people don't know what the hell they're talking about. Alberto was my *cumbate*."

Cumbate was a Tampa-Sicilian variation on the word *cumpari*, which in traditional Sicilian meant "baptismal godfather." Ragano was enough in touch with his Sicilian roots to know that the term was used to mean that two men had established the closest possible bond—a blood-brother relationship based on a deep sense of loyalty.

Trafficante explained to Ragano, "I went to New York to see Anastasia to get him to invest in a casino deal I'm trying to arrange in Havana. I couldn't swing the deal without him and wanted him in as a fifty-fifty partner . . . I told him the Hilton would be a gold mine."

As far as Ragano was concerned, Trafficante's explanation—and especially his use of the word *cumbate*, which was sacred to any Sicilian male—was enough to convince him that the Anastasia murder was not something his client had engineered.

The question remained: if Trafficante knew nothing about the murder of a man with whom he had met the previous night, then what sinister plot was in play?

One obvious mastermind was Lansky, but Trafficante said nothing to Ragano about the Jewish Mob boss who had become both his partner and his competitor in Havana. If Santo suspected Lansky, he kept it to himself.

In New York, Cuba, and elsewhere, Meyer Lansky was nowhere to be seen. In the days and weeks following the Anastasia murder, Meyer did what he was known for: he laid low and made himself inconspicuous. He had been nowhere near the murder scene on the day Anastasia received his final haircut. At the time, he was in Havana taking care of business. There would be no known evidence linking him to the hit. This was just the way Lansky liked it. He had been in on the decision-making process in high-profile Mob rubouts before, from Joe

"The Boss" Masseria to—perhaps—his pal Benny Siegel, and undoubtedly others. Lansky's ability to insulate himself from prosecution was legendary. He was an undeclared mobster whose criminal activities were often speculated about but rarely proved.

Back in Havana, Lansky's driver, Armando Jaime, found it curious that before Anastasia's death the famous mafioso had been a primary topic of conversation between Lansky and his associates, but afterward the subject rarely came up.

Joe Stassi returned to Havana and the weekly meetings resumed, free of rancor and distress.

Somehow, the Anastasia problem had disappeared.

THE MAD HATTER'S MURDER may have been verboten as a topic of discussion among Havana's mobsters, but it quickly became the talk of the town among Cuba's chattering classes. In the past, the subject of U.S. mafiosi operating in Havana had been largely absent from the media. Censorship in Cuba made it nearly impossible for journalists to investigate financial corruption since it was almost always linked to the government. On those occasions when Lansky, Trafficante, or other known gangsters were mentioned in the press, it was almost always as an "American businessman" or "casino operator."

The Anastasia murder altered the equation a bit. Since the hit seemed to have been designed for maximum exposure—or at least to deliver a message at the highest and broadest possible level—the result was a greater degree of public speculation. In Havana, the subject started popping up in society columns and casino-gambling reports. One magazine even plastered the story across its cover, under the headline, "¿Operan en nuestros cabarets gangsters americanos?"—Are American Gangsters Operating in Our Nightclubs?

Confidencial de Cuba was a scandal sheet sold at pharmacies, markets, the airport, and newsstands in Havana and Santiago. The magazine's slogan was "Todo lo vemos, todo lo oímos, y nada silenciamos"—Everything we see, everything we hear, and nothing left out. In truth, the magazine was little more than a collection of stories and gossip relating to Cuban high society, which inevitably involved personalities and events related to the nightclubs and casinos. Along with profiles and interviews, *Confidencial* often included full-page ads for the city's various Mob-controlled cabarets.

In the first issue to appear after the Anastasia hit, the magazine devoted numerous pages to the event. On the cover was a picture of Anastasia's prostrate body on the barbershop floor, alongside a photo of Trafficante with the caption "*Santo Traficanti o Traficante*," a play on Santo's name, which means "smuggler" in Spanish. There was also a photo of Anthony "Tough Tony" Anastasio, with a caption suggesting that he might be arriving in Havana to "avenge the death of his brother." Inside the magazine was a two-page spread with more photos and more provocative questions. The coverage was so inflammatory that Amletto Battisti felt compelled to take out an ad in the magazine, proclaiming, "Amletto Battisti never has, does not, nor will he ever, at any time, have business relations with gangsters."

The Anastasia hit stirred things up in Cuba, bringing an unprecedented level of awareness to the public of the mobsters in their midst, but this was nothing compared to the reaction within the Mob itself. The attention garnered by the killing brought about something that had not taken place in eleven years—a major sit-down by Mafia bosses from around the United States.

In Apalachin, a small town in upstate New York some 200 miles from Manhattan, sixty mobsters arrived on the morning of November 14—just two and a half weeks after the barbershop murder. The conference was to take place at the home of Joseph Barbara, a soldier in the upstate New York Magaddino crime family. Many Mafia heavyweights were in attendance, including Vito Genovese, Carlo Gambino, Joe Profaci, and Sam Giancana from Chicago. Also there was Santo Trafficante.

Trafficante had departed from Tampa under the alias B. Klein,

switched planes in Newark, New Jersey, and landed in the town of Bing-
hamton in upstate New York. He was then picked up and driven to
Barbara's 58-acre estate in nearby Apalachin. There, he joined a group
that included bosses and capos from New York to California.

The topics of discussion at the meeting were varied, but tops on everyone's list were the Anastasia murder and financial developments in
Cuba.

The fact that Meyer Lansky was not in attendance spoke volumes. In
recent months, a rift had developed between the Frank Costello and
Vito Genovese factions of the Mob in New York. Ever since the Havana
conference of 1946, Genovese had been vying to establish himself as
capo di tutti capi, boss of all bosses. Costello, who had been viewed by
many as the top man ever since Luciano was deported to Italy, was Genovese's primary competition. Five months before the gathering at
Apalachin, a Mob-hired assassin had taken a shot at Costello as he arrived home at his Manhattan apartment on Central Park West. The
bullet grazed Costello's head, wounding him slightly.

Lansky was strongly identified with Costello. Along with Luciano
and Ben Siegel, these four men were largely responsible for having created the Commission—the governing body for the Mob as it was constituted in the 1930s, '40s, and '50s. Lansky put out the word that he was
too sick to attend the Apalachin meeting. Costello was also a no-show.
The meeting was looking a lot like a gathering of mobsters who were
partial to Vito Genovese.

Trafficante's presence at this gathering suggested once again that he
was staking out a position contrary to Lansky. The two men did not like
each other, though they were inextricably bound together through their
mutual interests in Cuba.

The Apalachin meeting never got off the ground. As the dozens of
mobsters arrived by car in the tiny hamlet, a local state trooper became
suspicious. He set up a roadblock and then approached the house. The
mafiosi panicked. Nearly all of them had police records; some were out
on parole, the terms of which specified that they were not to consort

with known felons. The mobsters scattered, running into the woods surrounding Barbara's estate.

State trooper Fred Tiffany stopped Trafficante as he attempted to pass a roadblock behind Barbara's residence. Santo was apprehended along with Gambino family member Carmine Lombardozzi and Genovese family capo Mike Miranda, and they were brought to the local courthouse for booking. When he was questioned, Santo gave his name as Louis Santos.

All in all, fifty-eight men were detained that day. Of these, fifty had arrest records, thirty-five had convictions, and twenty-three had served prison sentences. All were Italian American.

The aborted gathering at Apalachin was a fiasco for those in attendance, though not for any immediate legal reasons. A number of the mobsters were brought up on minor charges, but most of these were later thrown out of court by a district judge. The real disaster was that for the first time in history, a major gathering of mafiosi from around the country had been busted and exposed as it was happening. Many in the press and U.S. law enforcement—including FBI director J. Edgar Hoover—had been claiming for years that there was no such thing as a national underworld commission. Even though the Kefauver hearings had established that organized crime did, in fact, exist, the Mafia was a different story. The FBI director and others continued to downplay the notion that there was an organized Mafia in the United States. In this regard, the busted meeting at Apalachin was a landmark. It established irrevocably for the first time that the American Mafia was, in fact, a national brotherhood.

In later years, it was suggested that someone tipped off local authorities that the meeting was to take place. Vito Genovese, organizer of the event, had been made to look like a fool, so whoever ratted out the meeting was most likely an enemy of the ambitious mafioso. One possible culprit was Lansky. It is curious that there were no members of Meyer's "Jewish Mafia" in attendance at Apalachin. And Lansky despised Genovese—for good reason. Genovese was behind the attempted assassination of Frank Costello. Also, Genovese had called the meeting partly to stir up resentment about the division of spoils in Cuba, giving Lansky another compelling motive for wanting to sabotage the event. In 1977 Doc Stacher—Meyer's lifelong friend and associate—confirmed to an interviewer that the Jewish Mob boss was the one who spilled the beans: "Nobody to this day knows that it was Meyer who arranged for Genovese's humiliation."

The ploy was effective: Genovese was ruined by the fiasco at Apalachin and later became enmeshed in a career-ending narcotics prosecution. Trafficante, Lansky's other sometime competitor, was put in his place; his efforts to form an alliance against Meyer were scuttled. The Mafia's desire to muscle in on the Havana Mob was derailed. Once again the Little Man was riding tall in the saddle.

BACK-TO-BACK, the Anastasia murder and the busted Mob meeting in upstate New York were a bonanza for the press. Not since the Kefauver hearings had the Mob been such a hot topic of speculation in newspapers and in radio and newsreel reports. Since Cuba figured prominently in both stories, the reputation of the island as "the Mob's playground" reached new heights. Murder and mafiosi were now part of the draw, along with gambling, fabulous entertainment, and the three Ss—sex, sun, and sand.

In Havana, the 1957–58 tourist season would prove to be the most popular ever. The city grew from a destination for gamblers, conventioneers, and sex tourists to a showcase for international celebrities.

The island had long been a vacation spot for movie stars and famous writers. Back in 1951, Frank Sinatra and Ava Gardner had come to Havana on their honeymoon; their visit was photographed and commented upon in the English-language *Havana Post*, where Walter Winchell had a column. "Word is The Voice has a special hankering for the Pearl of the Antilles," wrote Winchell. Sinatra, of course, had his own reasons for promoting Cuba as a destination. He was friendly with Lansky, Trafficante, and others in the Havana Mob and had expressed interest in investing in a casino-nightclub, as he later would in Las Vegas.

Sinatra blazed a trail. Later in the 1950s, he was followed by, among others, Marlon Brando. The brooding movie star and 1954 Academy Award winner for *On the Waterfront* was at the height of his fame when he came to Havana looking for a good time. An aficionado of Latin music, Brando made a point of checking out the band at the Tropicana. Led by Armando Romeu, the orchestra at the Tropicana was the biggest and most accomplished on the island. Brando was mesmerized. "Discovering Afro-Cuban music almost blew my mind," he wrote years later in his autobiography.

Brando was an amateur *conguero* (conga player). While in Havana, he went on a wild nocturnal hunt to find the perfect *tumbadora.* He offered to buy one from Romeu but was turned down. Brando left the club with two of the Tropicana's most beautiful *modelos* and headed out into the night. His guide in Havana was Sungo Carreras, the same ex-baseball player who had been valet for Charlie Luciano during his time in the city a decade earlier. Sungo took Brando to Club Choricera, where the actor was allowed to play conga alongside the great *timbalero* Silvano "El Chori" Echevarría. Later, Brando found and purchased a pair of congas. In an interview with *Carteles* magazine, he was quoted as saying, "I really like Havana . . . The sea is strange. It's like the sky. You can see the things you want to imagine."

The British writer Graham Greene was a regular in Cuba. On a trip to the island in 1957, he tried to secure an interview with Fidel Castro but was unable to make it happen. Instead, he stayed in Havana and put the finishing touches on a novel that would eventually be published in 1958 as *Our Man in Havana.* The novel mentioned many of Greene's favorite Havana haunts by name, including Doña Marina's bordello, where the writer indulged his longtime proclivity for prostitutes. Greene also liked to drink *añejo* and had the occasional taste for cocaine. He once bought a small packet of what was supposed to be coke from a

Havana taxi driver. When he tasted it, Greene discovered that it was mostly bicarbonate of soda. A few days later, the taxi driver he'd bought it from tracked Greene down to pay him back; he too had been fooled. The famous writer often told this story to friends to illustrate, as he put it, "the honesty of the Cuban people."

The actor Errol Flynn also blew through Havana in 1957. Flynn was known as an international playboy. He spent much of his time in the casino at the newly opened Hotel Capri and at the adjoining Salón Rojo nightclub. Flynn was fascinated by the Revolution and professed a desire to meet Fidel in the Sierra Maestra. He later bandied about a scarf inscribed with the insignia of the 26th of July Movement, which he claimed was given to him by Castro himself. Later, the famous movie star again visited Havana and announced his intention to produce a docudrama entitled *Cuban Rebel Girls,* which would trace the political education of a young peasant girl. The film was made, with financing by Flynn, starring his then-eighteen-year-old girlfriend, Beverly Aadland. Flynn played an American journalist covering the Revolution. Released in late 1959 at barely sixty-eight minutes in length, *Cuban Rebel Girls* stands as an odd, amateurish coda to the career of a major Hollywood star (Flynn died in October 1959; *Cuban Rebel Girls* was his last movie).

Of all the celebrities who came to be identified with Cuba in the 1950s, none was better known than Ernest Hemingway. The Pulitzer Prize–winning author had been coming to Cuba since the late 1920s. Fishing and drinking were his primary passions, though he also found time to write. He wrote most of *For Whom the Bell Tolls* in room 551 on the fifth floor of the Ambos Mundos Hotel, with a picturesque view of the Plaza de Armas in Old Havana. The writer discovered many sensual pleasures on the island, including lush tropical fruits, fragrant coffee, and world-famous tobacco—all of which he commented upon in a magazine article, "Marlin Off the Morro: A Cuban Letter," which was published in the debut issue of *Esquire* in 1933.

By the mid-1950s, Hemingway was a legend in Cuba. He'd published

The Old Man and the Sea (1952), which was set in the fishing village of Cojimar, outside Havana. When he won the Pulitzer Prize in 1953, he dedicated it to the people of Cojimar. Hemingway bought a home outside the city, and he frequently ventured into Havana to drink at El Floridita, an atmospheric restaurant-bar known as the birthplace of the daiquiri.

Hemingway's international celebrity status led to the creation of numerous myths about his time in Cuba, including the belief that he drank at another well-known Old Havana watering hole, La Bodeguita del Medio. This story was started by a Cuban gossip columnist named Fernando Campoamor, also known as "the Walter Winchell of Old Havana." Campoamor, who owned a piece of La Bodeguita, is believed to have been the one who scribbled on the wall, "I drink my daiquiris at El Floridita and my mojitos at Bodeguita," graffiti that was disingenuously attributed to Hemingway. In truth, the writer only visited the bar once at the behest of an underground tour guide named Bruno, who catered to rich Americans.

Hemingway was not an aficionado of the casinos and nightclubs, but that's where most of the celebrities spent their time. By the fall of 1957, the universe of the Havana Mob was the hottest entertainment scene on the planet. In a place where celebrities and movie stars merged, it was perhaps logical that the Mob would have as their mascot a person who embodied both traditions. That person was George Raft.

Raft was a character actor who was also a leading man. Suave and handsome, he was a tough guy who could walk the walk. Throughout the 1930s, '40s, and '50s, he'd made a career of playing hoodlums and gangsters alongside stars such as Jimmy Cagney and Humphrey Bogart. He was now so closely identified with his mobster roles that the FBI compiled a file on the actor that identified him as a "known associate" of the Mob. Raft's image as the epitome of gangster chic made him the perfect symbol for the Havana Mob.

In November, the actor was hired as a "meeter and greeter" at the Hotel Capri casino and nightclub. Raft didn't really have to do anything except hang out and be seen. He was paid to be George Raft, gangster movie star, the public face of the Havana Mob. It was a match made in heaven.

Born and raised in the rugged West Side Manhattan neighborhood of Hell's Kitchen, George Ranft (later changed to Raft) came from German and Italian stock. The oldest of ten children, George took to the streets at an early age to escape the stifling tenement apartment and rigid Catholicism of his parents. By the time he was in his early teens, Raft had fallen in with an infamous street gang known as the Gophers, so named because they liked to meet in tenement basements to hatch their criminal schemes.

In the early 1920s, with New York in the throes of Prohibition, Raft found work as a Broadway actor and dancer, while at the same time running booze for West Side racketeers. He became an active member of the Broadway set that included stars like Mae West, writers like Damon Runyon, and the gangsters Arnold Rothstein and Charlie Luciano. When the young hoodlum, hoofer, and thespian made the move to Hollywood in the 1930s, he was able to parlay his intimate knowledge of the gangster life into a thriving career. In movies such as *Hush Money, Each Dawn I Die, I Stole a Million, Loan Shark,* and many others, Raft perfected his image as a tough, urbane mobster. He was a sharp dresser, self-possessed to the point of cockiness, and a hit with the ladies—the perfect front man for American mobsters in Cuba.

With Raft presiding at the Casino de Capri, the celebrities flooded into town. Like Paris in the 1890s or Berlin in the 1930s, Havana was a nonstop party. Elizabeth Taylor, Eddie Fisher, Edith Piaf, Tyrone Power, Ava Gardner, Cesar Romero—many of the biggest stars of the day made the short flight "down Havana way." The island had arrived as the place to be.

THE STARS WERE A BIG DRAW for the tourists, but the big draw for the stars was something else. Marlon Brando wasn't the only celebrity with a yen for Latin music. Torrid and complex, sophisticated and primitive, Afro-Cuban music in the 1950s was the hottest thing since ragtime.

Music had always been part of Cuba's appeal. In the late 1920s—at the same time Capone, Lansky, Luciano, and other mobsters were first discovering the island—Cuba produced its first crossover hit with "*El Manisero*" (The Peanut Vendor). The song was so popular that it was lampooned by Groucho Marx in the movie *Duck Soup* (1933). By the time the mambo craze took hold in the late 1940s, Cuban-influenced music had entered the American mainstream through the Xavier Cugat orchestra, among others, and would be followed by the popular success of Desi Arnaz.

Arnaz was a Santiago-born musician and actor who came to the United States. He married comic actress Lucille Ball, and together they launched the wildly successful television sitcom *I Love Lucy*. The show introduced American audiences to the conga and bongo drum, which Arnaz played exuberantly on the show, and also to Babalú, the Santeria orisha, or god, of percussion whose name Arnaz frequently invoked. The popularity of *I Love Lucy* served as a bridge—albeit an incongruous one—for Americans who traveled to Cuba during the era of the Havana Mob.

Music and dance were the draw for a new generation of tourists who filled the hotels, casinos, and nightclubs. The mambo was reconfigured as the cha-cha-chá, a rhythmically simplified version of the music that was easier for North Americans to dance to. The rumba, a traditional music and dance culture that came from the Cuban countryside, was either languid or torrid, depending on the band. Singers such as Celia Cruz and Beny Moré rose out of the firmament to become major stars. Orchestras led by Pérez Prado, Arsenio Rodríguez, and Israel "Cachao" López became the home base for some of the best musicians in the world.

Of all the musical styles that became associated with the era of the Havana Mob, none was more representative of the underworld than

Afro-Cuban jazz, also known as cubop or, more commonly, Latin jazz. Jazz music was the classic American art form that had accompanied virtually every "glorious" era of mobsterism in the United States since the end of the nineteenth century. In Storyville, the legendary turn-of-the-century red-light district of New Orleans, ragtime gave way to a freer, more blues-influenced form of jazz as practiced by the likes of Buddy Bolden, Jelly Roll Morton, and Louis Armstrong. The music had its roots in the African-American experience; it was also the music of the bordello, the speakeasy, and Mob-owned nightclubs from Boston to Los Angeles. Jazz was race-mixing music, through which rich and poor alike came together out of a desire to skirt the placid white-bread veneer of American life (that is, until jazz itself was co-opted by white-bread America).

It is probable that jazz would have been born without the influence of the Mob, but it is unlikely the music would have grown and flourished as it did without the economic framework provided by organized crime. Particularly in the era of the Roaring Twenties (i.e., Prohibition), when jazz became an international obsession, money from bootlegging rackets made it possible for nightclubs to hire large orchestras. Jay McShann, Count Basie, and Duke Ellington all created world-renowned orchestras that were financed by Mob-controlled nightclubs. These orchestras spawned many legends of jazz who developed their talents and headlined in smaller clubs, some of which were also Mob owned.

In Chicago, Al Capone adored the music and fostered an entire generation of musicians. In Harlem, the Mob-owned Cotton Club had as its house band the sophisticated Duke Ellington Orchestra. Kansas City had an entire district of jazz clubs and after-hours joints that spawned their own version of the music known as "dirty jazz," a Delta blues–influenced sound that gave birth to McShann, Basie, and Charlie "Bird" Parker, among others. This flourishing jazz district in Kansas City—which existed from the early 1920s into the 1930s—was made possible by a corrupt political machine that served as a model for the Havana Mob as constructed by Lansky, Batista, et al.

It was in the late 1940s that jazz great Dizzy Gillespie first traveled to Havana on a musical expedition that would give birth to Latin jazz. The music was a cross-pollination of African rhythms as interpreted by the offspring of Cuban and American slaves. Gillespie discovered Chano Pozo, a legendary *conguero* with Afro-Cuban rhythmic patterns surging through his veins like ectoplasm. As a composer, Dizzy brought the percussive brilliance of Chano Pozo together with bebop, a challenging, virtuosic form of jazz pioneered by himself and Charlie Parker. The result was historic; among the many compositions that became cubop standards throughout the 1950s were "Manteca" and "Afro-Cuban Suite."

Jazz musicians from the United States flooded to Havana, and Cuban musicians headed north to play in the orchestras of Machito, Mario Bauza, and Tito Puente. The music they created was sultry, adventurous, lusty—the perfect sound track for an era marked by gambling, drinking, dancing, and fornicating into the tropical night. The music scene in Havana offered something a sterile, manufactured environment like Las Vegas could never hope to provide: an organic, exotic foreign culture mixed with the most adventurous aspects of Afro-Americana. Compared to Havana, Las Vegas was for squares—hillbillies, cowboys, and people "out west" who had lost touch with their ethnic roots.

The Mob did not consciously create this environment any more than it scripted or composed all the great music that grew out of the Jazz Age. But the gangster culture did undeniably foster its development—not only through the financial patronage that made the bands and clubs possible but also by understanding that jazz—in this case Afro-Cuban jazz—was the right sound at the right time. Latin jazz was the evolutionary music of two slave traditions—Caribbean and North American. It was something original. Unique. And it further elevated the era of the Havana Mob into the realm of mythology.

It is ironic that the mobsters and politicians who presided over this epoch were anything but hipsters. Lansky preferred *danzón*, a classical style of dance with its roots in French music that was romantic in a highly traditional way. Trafficante did have a taste for jazz, but he was by nature a reserved man who rarely took to the dance floor. Batista, who was a public figure most of his adult life, only danced when the music was a formal *contradanza*, a kind of Cuban waltz. The trappings of the era were peripheral to these men. Above all, they were businessmen.

Lansky, Trafficante, and Batista did not care what kind of music played as long as the revolutionaries were kept at bay and the money flowed from the casinos and nightclubs into their own private bank accounts. The sound of the conga drum was secondary to the sound of the casino counting room, where the daily drop made its own beautiful music.

12

A HANDMADE WOMAN

ON THE NIGHT OF DECEMBER 10, 1957, MEYER LANSKY surveyed his greatest creation—and it was good. The Riviera hotel and casino was officially open for business. It was the largest and most glamorous facility of its kind in Havana so far. Located off the Malecón, on the Vedado side of the Almendares River, the Riviera was chic and exciting. From the outside, the building was immaculately landscaped, with modern garden sculptures and an elegant green, gray, and black color motif that blended well with the sea and sky. Inside, the lobby was sleek and futuristic. Marble floors gave way to walls of turquoise mosaic and a speckled stucco ceiling. The building reminded some of Miami Beach with its art deco architecture, others of Las Vegas with its glitz, but what Lansky had in mind was something unique: an architecturally adventurous, spare-no-expense example of Havana at its best. On top of everything else, the hotel was the first major building in the city to have central air-conditioning as opposed to individual air-conditioning units. The building breathed cool air and shone like a jewel. It was Meyer Lansky's masterpiece.

Along with the hotel's luxurious rooms, huge pool, restaurants, and bars, there was the casino, a classy egg-shaped lair with deep carpets, a high ceiling, glass chandeliers, and gold-leaf walls with no windows. Across the lobby from the casino was the Copa Room, a performance space modeled after the Copacabana nightclub in New York.

The opening-night festivities were lavish. Headlining at the Copa Room was Ginger Rogers, the movie star and entertainer whose career had reached its peak when she starred in a series of wildly popular movies with Fred Astaire in the 1930s. Although past her prime as an ingénue and dancer (she was forty-six years old at the time), Rogers was a star from Hollywood's most starlit era. She may have been a top-flight entertainer, but her talents were not necessarily comprehensive enough to impress the inscrutable Lansky. After witnessing her opening act at the Copa Room, Meyer allegedly declared, "She can wiggle her ass, but she can't sing a goddamn note."

Lansky was the boss. Everyone knew the Riviera was his baby, though he preferred to maintain his reputation as a behind-the-scenes mastermind. There was no reason Meyer couldn't have listed his name as the owner of the Riviera—perhaps out of habit he chose to hide behind front men, in this case the Smith brothers, Harry and Ben, two Toronto hoteliers with whom Lansky had negotiated the management contract. The casino license was in the name of Lansky underling Eddie Levinson. The only place where Lansky's name appeared on the paperwork was as director of the hotel's kitchen.

The Riviera hotel and casino was an extension of Lansky's ego, but it was also conceived as a showcase for the Havana Mob. According to the plan, as concocted originally by Lansky and Luciano, Havana would one day resemble Monte Carlo, with a series of luxury hotels along the Malecón. The Riviera was the first to be overtly linked to the Havana Mob. As a show palace, it was state of the art, and its attributes would soon be beamed into living rooms everywhere via a major American television network.

On January 19, 1958—just five weeks after the hotel opened—the popular *Steve Allen Show* aired a one-hour special that showcased much of the facility. Elaborate dance numbers were staged in the lobby and pool area, and the show's host relentlessly promoted the Riviera. The entire program was one long advertisement for the hotel.

At the time, Allen's show was considered the hippest of the many variety shows on American television. Allen featured jazz musicians and cutting-edge comics that more staid shows, such as Lawrence Welk and Ed Sullivan, would not go near. His own material was sometimes gently political and he saw himself as a truth-teller in a satirical kind of way. The opening line of Steverino's monologue was as follows: "We are in Havana, home of the pineapple and Meyer Lansky. And we're happy to be here." The show had only just begun, and Allen was already tipping his cap to the boss of the Havana Mob.

The show went off without a hitch. Allen strolled through the casino surrounded by gamblers in evening wear. The seductive Tybee Afra danced, the camera following her out to the pool. Onstage in the Copa Room, ventriloquist Edgar Bergan scolded his dummy, Charlie Mc-Carthy, for gallivanting around Havana. "What were you doing out all night?" Bergan asked his talking dummy. "It's a long story—and a dirty one," answered Charlie. The audience laughed. Comic actor Lou Costello performed a skit entitled "The Dice Game," about a rube tourist· who is actually an expert practitioner of razzle-dazzle. The show was filled with wink-wink sexual innuendo and veiled references to gambling and mobsters.

The Allen show was a breakthrough for the Havana Mob. The best they had to offer was being beamed to millions around the United States and Canada, and it didn't seem to matter that notorious Mob figures were involved. In fact, it added to the allure.

Lansky was seemingly at the top of his game. From the day it opened, the Riviera was booked to capacity throughout the entire 1957–58 tourist season. And the hotel's casino quickly established itself as the home of the high roller. Tourists and pleasure-seekers scoured the city, but serious gamblers traveling the circuit from Monte Carlo to Vegas spent their evenings in the casino at the Riviera. "Lansky's reputation attracted the high rollers," remembered Ralph Rubio, credit manager at the casino.

"He didn't even have to show his face; the name of Meyer Lansky was enough to attract serious players from around the world."

Lansky's stature in Havana may have gone to his head and driven him to engage in behavior more representative of Luciano, Trafficante, and other gangsters. Sometime in late 1957 and on into 1958, the Jewish Mob boss embarked on an affair with a local Cuban woman. The affair was unusual for Meyer, and also risky. His wife, Teddy, was a frequent visitor to Havana, though she usually stayed separately from Meyer at the Focsa, a massive, newly constructed apartment complex not far from the Hotel Nacional. Lansky, of course, did not want his wife to know he had a paramour. Equally important, he did not want his business associates to know. Meyer had been critical of others who took unnecessary risks to maintain secret affairs. He felt that it projected an aura of weakness. To Lansky, appearances were everything.

The woman's name was Carmen. He met her at El Encanto department store. Lansky's driver, Armando Jaime Casielles, often dropped his boss off at the big house on Paseo del Prado where Carmen lived with her mother. She was around twenty years old, and Jaime thought she was one of the most beautiful women he had ever seen:

> [She] was olive-skinned, medium height, with curly black hair that fell down her back to her waist . . . She was a really pretty woman, with a graceful and pleasant stride, well mannered, soft-spoken, always keeping her voice down. She had the hands of a pianist, with fine long fingers and a well-shaped body. Her breasts were medium-sized and straight, didn't need a bra. She was completely covered with fine, fuzzy hair, barely visible, on her arms and her thighs—not too much, delicately scattered. Her knees and toes were adorable. She was a handmade woman, as we say in Cuba.

Jaime often found himself driving Lansky to and from the house on Paseo del Prado. One evening in particular, Lansky asked Jaime to come inside with him.

The apartment was located over a jewelry store. Jaime followed his boss up a flight of stairs. Lansky rang the doorbell and almost immediately the door opened, and there was the woman Jaime recognized from El Encanto department store. They entered the apartment.

"We'll have coffee," Meyer said to Carmen.

She nodded and headed off. Lansky then turned to Jaime and explained, "Nobody, absolutely nobody, can know that I'm here. Not Joe Stassi, not Trafficante, not Norman Rothman. I've told everyone that I'm going on a little trip to Caracas or Costa Rica. So nobody will think it's strange if they don't see me for a while. Nobody should bother you, but if anybody tries to ask questions where I am, tell them nothing. Understand?"

"Of course," said Jaime. For the first time, he realized that it was Lansky's intention to spend days, perhaps even a week or more, here in Carmen's apartment. Lansky had brought no bags or luggage; Jaime got the impression that everything his boss would need—a change of clothes, toiletries—had already been transferred to Carmen's place.

Lansky lowered his voice and spoke conspiratorially. He explained to his driver that a man was never more vulnerable than when he was having a clandestine affair. His enemies might use the opportunity to attack. Remembered Jaime:

I could see he was feeling a little paranoid, telling me things I already knew, like reminding me that when I went out to get the car I need to check the area closely. You have to check the lobby, he said, the gardens, the entrance to the hotel. And you have to do all this as if it weren't important at all, like something ordinary. And watch out, Jaime, if you see something strange, or something you think doesn't check out. And when you start the car and warm it up and come to pick me up, keep the engine running all the time until I arrive. Then take off right away.

Lansky explained to Jaime, "I want you to come here to visit me every other day. For the time being, it's probably best to leave the car and walk. Make sure you aren't followed. Don't stop to talk with anyone, not even someone asking you for a light. Above all, don't walk on side streets. Stay on the most crowded streets in Vedado. Under no circumstances should you get caught in deserted places, or dark places, or let any car drive up to you while you are walking."

Jaime listened carefully, taking in every word:

The last thing he made clear, with a gesture, a look, was that from now on the gun shouldn't be in the car's glove compartment. I had to carry it with me at all times, ready to use.

Carmen returned with a tray and two cups of coffee. She set the tray down and handed the cups to Lansky and his driver. Jaime was mesmerized by Carmen, but he didn't dare look too long or stare in case El Viejo—the old man—noticed. He found her beauty "unsettling." He said to his boss, "Okay, I'll come every other day. But what if you need me for something urgent, something right away?"

"I'll leave you a message, some word," answered Lansky. "You'll receive a signal, a clue, don't worry."

The two men drank their coffee. Lansky then told Carmen he wanted her to bring two drinks, a Campari on the rocks for him and a whiskey for Jaime. He wanted to make a toast. Carmen again headed into the kitchen and then returned with the drinks.

"Let's step out on the terrace," Lansky said to Jaime. They took their glasses and went to the balcony, which looked out over the tree-lined Prado, which was alive with activity even though it was near midnight. Jaime looked down the street toward the Sevilla Biltmore Hotel, with its famous Roof Garden, where Amletto Battisti ran his gambling room. Not far from the hotel was the presidential palace, also in view.

"I was foolish enough to make a remark," remembered Jaime years later, "in reference to those buildings; I think I said something like: 'So close, and nobody can imagine you're here.'

"Said Lansky, 'That's how it is, and that's how it should be, Jaime. Don't you think so?' I didn't answer, but I felt that in the darkness of the terrace his eyes tried to reach my mind. Then he put his glass on the small table and said: 'I want you to go see Don Amletto tomorrow.'

"'There,' I said, 'in El Sevilla?'

"'In his office.'

"'At what time?'

"'At night. Of course, at night.'

"'On your behalf?'

"'Yes, on my behalf.'

"'And what do I tell him?'

"'That nothing we agreed to stands.'

"'Just that?'

"'Just that. Nothing we agreed to stands. He'll know what it means.'"

Jaime nodded. The two men sat in silence for a while, the sounds of the Prado—laughter, singing, car horns, music—wafting up from the street. Jaime sensed that there was nothing more to be said. "I stood up, said goodnight, and left him there in the company of that beautiful woman." The next day he passed the cryptic message on to Don Amletto Battisti, one of many he relayed for Lansky in his time as valet. Upon receiving the message, the owner of the Sevilla Biltmore nodded his head and said nothing.

Several times Jaime visited El Viejo in his mistress's lair on the Prado. The Cuban did not think much of it; after all, for his entire life older men—Cubans, Americans, and Europeans—had been coming to Havana to have younger mistresses.

Jaime had only known Lansky for ten months; he did not yet realize how out of character it was for the Little Man to take a walk on the wild side.

IN THE ENTIRE ONE-HOUR airing of the *Steve Allen Show* live from the Riviera hotel, there was not one mention of Fidel Castro or the

Revolution. The Havana Mob lived in its own little world: starlets, gambling, drinking, whoring, killing—but no revolutionaries. *Fidelistas* were alive and well and living in the Sierra Maestra, but they might as well have been on the planet Uranus. The show must go on.

In the many decades since the Cuban Revolution, volumes have been written detailing the thinking behind Castro's guerrilla strategy. At the time, there was fierce debate within the movement about what was the best way to take down Batista and his friends. Many, including, most prominently, members of the Directorio, felt the best way was to cut off the head—i.e., assassinate the leader—as they had tried to do with the attack on the presidential palace the previous year. To take out Batista or someone else high up in his cabinet in one fell swoop might catapult the government into a state of chaos and bring the dictatorship to its knees.

Castro did not agree. Since setting up shop in the Sierra Maestra, Fidel—and to an even greater extent his intellectual partner, Che Guevara—had come to the conclusion that the Revolution should take place outside of Havana and move inexorably forward. To this end the 26th of July Movement spent the latter part of 1957 and the early months of 1958 establishing a "liberated zone" within the Sierra Maestra. Minifactories were constructed to produce shoes, repair weapons, and make bombs. There was also a butcher's shop, a *fábrica de tabaco* (cigar factory), and a hospital. A mimeograph machine was transported into the mountains, and the rebels produced a semiregular newspaper, *El Cubano Libre*. They also acquired a small radio transmitter and began to broadcast propaganda to the outlying areas.

Among those who heard Castro's voice on the radio was William Gálvez Rodríguez, a young activist from Holguín on the eastern side of the island. At the age of nineteen, Gálvez had been expelled from his local polytechnic institute for his "subversive" political activities. He later became a member of the *estudiantil*, made up mostly of college students who held secret meetings and engaged in anti-Batista agitation. In Santiago, Gálvez had been incarcerated and interrogated numerous times by agents of SIM. By his mid-twenties, he was a hardened member of the Revolution.

Hearing Castro changed Gálvez's life. "Fidel was putting into words things that we all felt," he remembered years later. "He was an inspiration to anyone who cared about *la patria* (the homeland)."

Gálvez became a clandestine member of the 26th of July Movement. He moved back to his home province of Holguín and became the underground leader of a *grupo de acción y sabotage* (Action and Sabotage Unit). By night, he was a secret member of the organization; by day, a postgraduate student. The Revolution gave new meaning to his life.

Eventually, Gálvez would be incorporated into the rebel army in the Sierra Maestra, where he would serve under Che Guevara and one of the Revolution's most effective leaders, Camilo Cienfuegos. Eventually he would rise to the rank of captain and became recognized as a *comandante*. "The fact that we were outnumbered so greatly by Batista's army did not deter us," remembered Gálvez. "Our morale was strong."

Young firebrands like Gálvez represented some of the most daring men of their generation: proud, brave, and dedicated to the cause of *fidelismo*.

By early 1958, Castro's revolutionary army consisted of approximately three hundred soldiers. Whereas the early months of the war had involved forming these rebel soldiers into a viable army, now the 26th of July Movement inaugurated a second phase, in which winning over world opinion was the primary goal.

In February, an article written by Castro appeared in *Coronet* magazine in New York. Under the headline "Why We Fight," El Comandante went to great lengths to assure American investors that the movement's "armed campaign on Cuban soil" was the surest path to a true liberal democracy in Cuba. Castro declared, "We have no plans for the expropriation or nationalization of foreign investment here." He acknowledged that a government takeover of U.S.-owned utilities "was a point of our earliest program, but we have currently suspended all planning on this matter." He also stated—in contradiction to the movement's own propaganda—that "we will support no land reform bill."

To those who opposed Castro, the *Coronet* article and a subsequent interview in *Look* magazine were examples of a grand deception. In *El Cubano Libre* and on Radio Rebelde, the movement advocated a sweeping political and social revolution based on Martí and Marx. For American consumption, Castro kept his cards close to the vest. "I know revolution sounds like bitter medicine to many businessmen," he was quoted as saying in *Look*. "But after the first shock, they will find it a boon—no more thieving tax collectors, no plundering army chieftains or bribe-hungry officials to bleed them white." As he had when he traveled to New York, Tampa, and Miami to raise money for *la lucha* (the struggle), Castro was working both sides of the fence.

In late February, Castro's followers staged one of their most dramatic public relations successes yet, this time in the front yard of the Havana Mob.

The Gran Premio Formula One auto race was a wildly popular event. It had been inaugurated the previous year by Roberto Fernández Miranda, Batista's brother-in-law and also the new director of the National Sports Commission. It was in his role as sports commissioner that Fernández Miranda was able to benefit from gambling: he controlled the national lottery, used the island's slot machines as his own personal slush fund, and was therefore a significant cog in the Havana Mob machine.

Fernández Miranda, along with the Cuban tourist board, had come to the conclusion that international sporting events were a better celebrity draw than the usual Afro-Cuban street festivals during carnival season. The Gran Premio de Cuba was modeled on the world-renowned Grand Prix held each year in Monte Carlo. The Cuban version involved premier Formula One drivers from around the world and would take place along the Malecón, with a full slate of drivers zooming past the Deauville, Nacional, Riviera, and other holdings of the Havana Mob.

Juan Manuel Fangio from Argentina was favored to win the race. At the age of forty-six, Fangio was greatly admired in Cuba. He had won the Gran Prix Monaco earlier in the decade, and he brought great prestige to the event in Havana. His car, a Maserati 450S, was seen zooming up and down the Malecón in the days before the race, as Fangio and his team attempted to iron out what they felt were inconsistencies in the handling of the vehicle.

On the night before the race, the famous driver was in the lobby of the Lincoln Hotel, in Central Havana. He and his team had finished a long day of trial runs and were deeply engrossed in a discussion about their Maserati when two men entered the lobby. They were both in their midtwenties and dressed casually. One of the men stood near the entrance to the hotel, while the other approached Fangio and his three crew members.

"Which one of you is Fangio?" asked the young man.

"I am. What do you want?" asked the driver.

The man pulled out a gun and pointed it at Fangio. "I am a member of the 26th of July Movement. I want you to come with me. Don't resist and you won't be hurt." The revolutionary stuck the gun in Fangio's rib cage and moved him toward the exit. At the entrance to the hotel, the kidnapper turned to the stunned people in the lobby and said, "Don't anyone leave the hotel until five minutes have passed. There are four men outside with machine guns pointed at the door." The rebels then whisked Fangio out of the hotel and pushed him into a waiting sedan. The car peeled away from the curb and drove off into the night.

Within minutes, telephones rang in every news agency in the city. Revolutionaries had kidnapped the champion racer and refused to say where he was being held. The next day, headlines blared the news to the world.

The police unleashed an intensive manhunt, searching all known rebel hideouts. There was little communication from the kidnappers. The race was delayed in the hope that Fangio would be released, but he was not.

The news only increased interest in the event: a hundred and fifty thousand spectators lined the Malecón to watch the race. The competition began, only to end in tragedy a half hour later when a Cuban driver skidded on a patch of oil that had leaked onto the racecourse from the burst oil line of another car. The driver's bright-yellow Ferrari spun out of control and hit one of the supports of a grandstand. Dozens of spectators came crashing down and spilled out onto the car and pavement. One of the other drivers ran over to help the people; he later told *Time* magazine, "I couldn't even see the Ferrari. The bodies were piled all over. I was wading in arms and legs." The crash killed four people and injured close to fifty. The race was over.

Government authorities charged sabotage, a deliberate act of murder by the rebels, but an investigation quickly determined that the crash was an unfortunate accident. Even so, happening as it did in the middle of a revolutionary campaign against the government, the event made it appear as though Cuba were cursed with death and destruction.

A few hours after the race was halted, Fangio was released. Calm and fresh-looking, he relayed the details of his captivity to the press. To avoid the police manhunt, he had been transferred to three different houses, all well-furnished homes. He was treated with respect and was well fed (steak and potatoes, chicken and rice). Faustino Perez, the 26th of July Movement's Havana commander, had made a personal appearance to apologize to Fangio for the inconvenience; he had explained the motive behind the abduction and the reasons for the Revolution.

Fangio had nothing but praise for his captors, whom he referred to as "my friends, the kidnappers." Given the tragedy that had taken place at the race, they may even have saved his life, he said. "If what the rebels did was in a good cause, then I, as an Argentine, accept it," he told the media.

The kidnapping and aborted race were major coups for the 26th of July Movement. Batista and his police force had been made to look vulnerable. Roberto Fernández Miranda looked incompetent for allowing spectators to so closely line the racecourse. Fangio had practically proposed a toast to the Revolution. And it had all taken place in the lap of the Havana Mob.

Castro seized the moment. In the days that followed it was announced on Radio Rebelde and in various underground newspapers that a new initiative was to commence. The rebels undertook one of their more controversial acts yet, as they began to torch sugar crops throughout the island.

Cultivation and processing of sugar constituted about one-third of the island's economy and employed two-fifths of the labor force. Hitting the sugar crop was going to affect everyone—including the Havana Mob. Castro acknowledged publicly that it was a "terrible decision," adding:

> I well know the heavy personal losses involved. My family has sizable holdings here in Oriente, and my instructions to our clandestine action groups state clearly that [my family's] crop must be the first one to burn, as an example to the rest of the nation. Only one thing can save the cane, and that is Batista's surrender.

In a matter of weeks, members of the movement's Action and Sabotage Units torched ten sugar mills around the perimeter of the Sierra Maestra. Closer to Havana, rebels set fire to 400,000 gallons of jet fuel at the Belot oil refinery owned by New Jersey–based Esso Standard. The fire, in a Havana suburb, burned for days, forcing the oil company to form an air brigade and fly in chemicals from the United States to put it out. It seemed as though the entire island were going up in flames.

In Santiago, the police murder of two seventh-grade students sparked an extended boycott by high school and college students. The 26th of July Movement and the Directorio organized the students, teachers, and administrators; by late February, they had shut down virtually all the public primary and secondary schools as well as colleges and universities across the country. The Revolution was growing so fast that it threatened to spin out of control. Bombs went off and acts of sabotage took place in virtually every province. Highways were shut down, hindering commercial traffic to and from Havana. The revolutionary army grew and split into separate "columns," one headed by Raúl Castro and another by Che Guevara, expanding their regions of control throughout the countryside.

Fidel and Guevara may have hoped to establish a rock-solid foundation for the Revolution outside of Havana first, but events were now taking on a momentum of their own. At the same time Havana was peaking as a playground for the Mafia, the Revolution began to exert itself within the city limits more forcefully than ever before. Just two days after the kidnapping of Fangio, a team of rebels raided the National Bank of Cuba, held employees at gunpoint, and set fire to the previous day's checks and bank drafts delivered from all over Havana. They took no money. The act was designed to demonstrate the inability of the Cuban state to manage the country's economic affairs.

Weeks later, a hit squad from the Directorio attempted to assassinate Raúl Menocal, a Batista minister. He miraculously escaped after being struck by half a dozen bullets. The night of March 16 became known as "The Night of One Hundred Bombs" because the underground resistance in Havana set off that many explosions across the city, from Old Havana to Miramar.

Rumors of multiple rebel arms shipments arriving on the island fueled the belief that Batista was in big trouble. His support in the island's business community and—more importantly—his heretofore steadfast relationship with the U.S. government began to erode. Things were moving fast now, spreading like wildfire, the Revolution looking more and more like a manifestation of the will of the people.

Castro sensed the growing momentum; he and others in the upper echelon of the movement engaged in intensive communications, trying to decide how best to capitalize on positive developments. The leadership in Havana strongly advocated for an all-out *huelga* (strike). By this, resistance leaders did not mean only a labor shutdown, though civic workers not showing up for their jobs on that day represented an essential aspect of the strategy. That was to be accompanied by further acts of industrial and agricultural sabotage, violence, selective assassinations of government officials, attacks against symbols of the regime, and generalized mayhem. The idea was to expose Batista's inability to maintain public and economic order and reveal to Washington, D.C., and the world that Cuba could not be governed by the current regime. It was announced publicly that there would be a strike; privately, the date was set for April 9.

This was it: the strike would shut down government offices, all commercial ventures, and, most pointedly, the casinos and nightclubs. Castro was going to hit Batista and his mobster cronies where they breathed.

DESPITE THE TURMOIL, for many, life in Havana went on as if nothing were amiss. Like a teething infant, the city clung to the maternal teat. The economic elite lived in their own little world, in which the good times continued, tourist dollars flowed, and President Batista ruled all with an iron fist. For members of the Havana Mob—and also families of U.S. businessmen, the diplomatic corps, the Cuban military, and members of Batista's administration—it was possible to believe that all was right with the world. The closer a person was to the mobsters and their associates within the system, the more likely they were to view what was happening in Cuba as nothing more than a grand adventure.

Such was certainly the case with Lansky's granddaughter, Cynthia Schwartz, who arrived in Havana in early 1958. Cynthia was the seven-year-old daughter of Richard Schwartz, Teddy Lansky's son from a previous marriage. Meyer had a chilly though cordial relationship with his stepson, who was nineteen years old at the time Lansky married Teddy back in 1948.

Richard was a silk-screener by trade. His business was not doing well in the late 1950s, so Teddy suggested to Meyer that maybe he could hire the young man to work in some capacity at the Riviera casino. Richard had been a frequent visitor to Lansky's various carpet joints in Broward County, including Club Bohème and the Plantation, where he often announced himself as "Meyer Lansky's son." Richard's penchant for dropping the Lansky name did not endear him with Meyer, though the Mob boss did agree to let his stepson work at the Riviera casino as a pit boss. Schwartz arrived in Havana in November 1957, a few weeks before the hotel-casino opened for business.

When young Cynthia and her two siblings joined their father and mother in Havana in January 1958, the city was bustling with activity. Little Cynthia knew nothing of the place. Years later, she remembered, "I knew I was in Havana, Cuba, but where it was on a map I couldn't have told you. I saw the ocean all around, so I knew it was an island, but not much more. I felt like the little girl in *Peter Pan*. I was on an adventure."

She joined her parents in an apartment at the Focsa, the prestigious apartment complex in central Vedado, also home to casino boss Norman Rothman. She was placed in a private primary school known as the Lafayette Academy, a school for Americans and the children of wealthy Cubans where only English was spoken. Her school uniform consisted of a tan shirt and brown pleated skirt with the Lafayette insignia.

Cynthia knew little of her grandfather's reputation, though it soon became apparent that Meyer Lansky was someone special in Havana. Each day, on her lunch break from school, she was picked up by her mother and brought to the Hotel Riviera, where her grandmother Teddy had a poolside cabaña. "We were treated like royalty at the Riviera," she remembers. "Every day at the cabaña I was given a turkey sandwich on rye bread with Russian dressing, which I loved. Then we went swimming in the pool. It was the only saltwater pool in all of Havana. I remember that because the water tasted like salt."

Occasionally Cynthia was taken to the casino to see and say hello to her father. Through the eyes of a child, the casino floor was especially exotic. Sometimes she got to spend time with her grandfather. Lansky would say, "Come on, Cindy girl, let's go for a walk." The Mob boss and his granddaughter would stroll through the casino and into the lobby, where the Great Lansky was treated like a king. To Cynthia, the experience was one of a kind: "I felt special when I was with my grandfather."

It was true that Lansky, the mobsters, and their extended families were treated like royalty in Havana, but such was not always the case back home in the United States. The high-profile Anastasia murder and busted Mafia convention at Apalachin had put the Mob front and center in the media. Press attention tended to attract the interest of ambitious law enforcement personnel looking to enhance their careers. Manhattan District Attorney Frank Hogan had put out the word that he was interested in talking with both Lansky and Trafficante following the Anastasia murder, though both had reason to believe that by early 1958 the heat had died down. Which is why on the afternoon of February 11, on a brief trip to Manhattan to see his personal physician, Lansky was surprised when he was "pinched." It happened on the corner of West 53rd Street and Broadway in midtown Manhattan as soon as Lansky stepped out of a taxi from the airport.

Meyer was in New York because he had recently begun to suffer from ulcers. It was cold and there was snow on the ground when detectives brought him into the precinct on West 54th Street. Though usually polite with cops, Lansky was annoyed at being brought in for no good reason. When a detective asked him what he knew about the Anastasia murder, Meyer snapped, "As much as an Eskimo in Alaska."

Another detective asked Lansky what he did for a living.

"Business," Meyer replied.

"What kind of business?"

"My business." Lansky declined to say anything further.

The detectives arrested Lansky on a charge of vagrancy, an obvious "fuck-you" charge sometimes used by police when they wanted to harass someone. Lansky called his attorney, but it was the following morning before Moses Polakoff made it to the precinct house with a bond of one thousand dollars to get his client out on bail. The charge of vagrancy was eventually dismissed by a judge.

A team of detectives continued to follow the Jewish Mob boss around while he was in New York. One afternoon Detective William Graff was seated in the lobby of the Hotel Novarro on Central Park South, where

Lansky was staying. Graff was part of the police surveillance team that was supposed to be operating unbeknownst to Lansky. On this particular snowy afternoon, Lansky entered the hotel and spotted the detective, who was acting as if he just happened to be there. Lansky walked over to him and sat down. Without bothering to introduce himself, the Mob boss began rubbing his stomach and complaining about his ulcers.

"I've got something on my mind," he said to Graff.

The detective sat forward expectantly. What if Lansky were about to divulge an important fact about his criminal life? He nodded for Lansky to continue.

"It's the chickens," said Meyer.

Huh? The detective had no idea what the mobster was talking about.

"The chickens," repeated Lansky. "You can't get good chickens in Havana."

Detective Graff listened, dumbfounded, as the famous Meyer Lansky gave him a treatise on how difficult it was to find fresh chickens in Havana. Beef—no problem. His hotel, the Riviera, had the best steaks in Cuba, he said. Nor was it hard to find lamb or seafood. But chickens—forget it. Cuban chickens were scrawny and malnourished. That was why he had come to New York—to arrange for a supply of decent chickens to be shipped by air to Havana.

The detective smiled politely and tried to steer the conversation in a more relevant direction, but Meyer could not be budged. All he would talk about were his worsening ulcers—and chickens. "He was playing with me," the detective told author Robert Lacey years later.

As had been the case periodically in his life, Lansky's notoriety was again causing him problems. In March, *Life* magazine published an article entitled "Mobsters Move in on Troubled Havana." Complete with photos of Meyer, Jake Lansky, Trafficante, Fernández Miranda, and Batista—a virtual who's who of the Havana Mob—the article suggested that the mobsters were swooping in to take advantage of political instability in Cuba. Of course, nothing could have been further from the truth. The mobsters had been there from the beginning. The article spelled out in greater detail than ever before the nature of financial arrangements between Lansky and Batista, describing Havana's gambling trade as "a private pension against the day the strongman is overthrown or the day his term expires, whichever comes first."

Lansky's arrest in New York and the article in *Life* created problems for U.S. diplomats in Cuba, who had taken an active interest in Batista's political future. Ever since the charismatic Fidel Castro appeared in the pages of the *New York Times* and on American television, public opinion in the United States had swayed in favor of "the tropical Robin Hood" and away from Batista. Now that El Presidente's business relationship with American mobsters was being laid bare, it reinforced Castro's claims that Batista was corrupt and an embezzler. Pressure was applied on the U.S. diplomatic corps to apply pressure on Batista. El Presidente was approached by U.S. ambassador Earl E. T. Smith, who inquired, "Isn't there anything you can do about the mobsters in your midst?" Smith made particular reference to Lansky, whose criminal charge of vagrancy was still pending at the time.

In mid-March, Batista announced publicly that Lansky would be banned from Cuba as long as he was facing criminal charges. Lansky knew better than to take the edict seriously. Years later, he told a biographer:

Batista played a little joke on me. He announced publicly that I wouldn't be allowed to return to Havana so long as these "serious charges" were outstanding against me. Naturally, [the charges] were dismissed. And when I returned to Cuba, Batista and I had a good laugh over the whole thing.

The Lansky-Batista relationship was at the center of the Havana Mob, but sightings of the two men together were almost as rare as sightings of Fidel Castro. The Mob boss and the dictator had constructed a financial universe that changed the course of Cuban history, but both men realized that the more successful their business ventures became, the more necessary it was to maintain the appearance of separation. Ralph Rubio, who as Lansky's credit manager at the Riviera interacted with his boss on an almost daily basis, never saw the two men together. Armando Jaime Casielles occasionally drove Lansky to meetings with Batista at the presidential palace, or at Kuquine, Batista's estate. One of the meetings at Kuquine took place on an afternoon in early 1958. Jaime waited in the car while Lansky met with the president in his library office—the same room where Batista had first met with a young Fidel Castro years earlier.

Lansky came out of the meeting obviously annoyed, which was rare for him. For a long time, as Jaime drove back into the city and along the Malecón, Meyer said nothing. Eventually he mumbled, almost to himself, "This guy every time wants more and more."

Jaime realized he was talking about Batista. "More of what?" he asked Lansky.

"*Pasta*, Jaime, *pasta*," said Lansky, using a colloquial Spanish word for money. "More and more. He's insatiable."

One person who did see Lansky and Batista together was a California attorney named Joe Varon. Varon had represented Lansky on a few minor matters and was in Havana to attend the formal opening of a hotel-casino. He was there with Lansky when Batista made a surprise appearance. In *Little Man*, Varon is quoted as saying, "They [Lansky and Batista] were very, very close. Like brothers." According to author Robert Lacey:

> Varon was impressed by how well Batista spoke English, and by the president's evident warmth towards Meyer. Batista kept hugging and embracing his little American friend in a most Latin fashion . . . Meyer seemed distinctly uncomfortable with this aspect of the relationship, wriggling unhappily in the bear hug of the nation's strongman. Such public fraternization was not the Lansky way.

Mostly, the two men were content to operate through middlemen. Every Monday at noon, a Lansky-appointed bagman was allowed into the presidential palace through a side door. He carried with him a satchel filled with cash, part of a monthly payment of $1.28 million that was to be delivered to the president. Batista himself never met the man; he always used a relative as an intermediary. This was the way Lansky and Batista liked it: there was no need to call attention to the fact that they were partners in a financial arrangement that was diverting millions from the casinos into their own pockets. Better to create the illusion of autonomy. Some things were more important than friendship.

13

THE SUN ALMOST RISES

THE MARCH 1958 GRAND OPENING FESTIVITIES FOR THE Havana Hilton hotel and casino were surprisingly subdued. There seemed to be as many members of the military police as there were dignitaries—the consequence of recent bombings and kidnappings. The establishment of the Hilton name along the Havana skyline was important to President Batista, who viewed the hotel as the biggest step yet in the city's attempts to present itself as the Monte Carlo of the Caribbean. Even so, Batista did not attend the event, though he did send his wife, Marta. Many viewed his absence as the result of security concerns, but there was another reason. In the weeks leading up to the grand opening, many Cuban businessmen had told U.S. ambassador Smith that Batista was so unpopular among his own people that they did not want to be seen in his company. Although most U.S. industrialists were still wholeheartedly behind the president, Cuban business leaders had begun to abandon what they viewed as a sinking ship.

For the Havana Mob, the opening of the Hilton was yet another plum in their basket. Located in Vedado not far from many of their other holdings, the hotel had a 660-room capacity, which made it even larger than the Riviera. The Hilton also included a large nightclub called El Caribe, a cabaret-lounge known as Turquino, and of course a massive gambling casino. With Albert Anastasia removed from the list of investors, ownership of the casino and nightclub was spread among fifteen different parties, including the Sindicato Gastronómico. The mortgage holder for the hotel was BANDES, the economic high command of the Havana Mob.

Lansky was not directly linked to the Hilton, but as with all major commercial developments in Havana, the business owed its existence to a climate of gambling and nightlife created by the mobsters.

The prestige of the Hilton name carried great weight throughout the hospitality industry, and the hotel's opening in Havana resonated as far away as Las Vegas.

Ever since the Cuban capital's gambling boom began in the early 1950s, Havana and Las Vegas had found themselves competing for the same entertainment dollars. For the most part, these two citadels of chance had coexisted peaceably. Many gambling investors, concessionaires, and mobsters owned stock in both cities. Since gambling in Havana was seasonal, dozens of casino employees bounced back and forth between the two biggest employers of gambling personnel in North America. Entertainers moved on from bookings at the big showrooms in Vegas to the cabarets in Havana and back again. The two cities revolved around the same axis of gambling and entertainment.

In recent years, Vegas had begun to stumble. In the early and mid-1950s, a building frenzy led to the rapid construction of no fewer than six major hotel-casinos and the creation of the Vegas Strip. The most recently opened hotels were all experiencing financial difficulties. The Nevada Gaming Commission came to the conclusion that the Havana Riviera, the Capri, the Nacional, and now the Havana Hilton were hurting business in their desert paradise. The action they decided to take would have profound consequences for the Havana Mob.

In April, just weeks after the opening of the Hilton, the gaming board in Vegas announced that anyone holding a Nevada gaming license who was also operating in Cuba would either have to give up their license or pull out of Havana. The commission specifically named nine men, including Moe Dalitz, Blackjack McGinty, Sam Tucker, Morris Kleinman, and Wilbur Clark, all leaseholders at the Hotel Nacional casino. Eddie Levinson of Las Vegas's Fremont Hotel was identified as a proprietor at the Riviera.

The announcement was a stunner for those involved. The men were being forced to make a choice between Havana and Las Vegas. They all hired attorneys and fought the decision, but in the end they were forced to safeguard their holdings in the United States. Within months of the announcement, they sold out their considerable interests in Havana. At the time, it must have looked like a financial tragedy. But as it turned out, the mobsters who were forced out of Havana by the commission would wind up looking like the luckiest gamblers in all of Cuba.

As the 1957–58 tourist season headed into its final weeks, Havana labored under a weird mix of good times and political paranoia. The problem was that relaxation and revolution were inherently incompatible. The city, which had always taken pride in having a wild side, now became even darker and more clandestine. Many years later, using the poetic imagery of history, some would say that these weeks and months in Havana resembled the last gasps of the Roman Empire.

Attorney Frank Ragano remembered coming to the city in 1958 to visit his client Trafficante. As he often did on his visits to Cuba, Ragano made the rounds with Santo, who loved to show off his "world." Trafficante escorted the lawyer to a number of casinos, including his favorite, the Sans Souci. Like Lansky, Santo never gambled. "Bartenders don't drink, because they see the consequences," he told Ragano. "I know the odds are stacked against the players. You can't beat the casinos."

Trafficante led his friend into the counting room at the Sans Souci. The room was small and stuffy, with armed guards at the door. At a table in the center of the room, two men —one wearing a head visor and the other making entries in a ledger—were seated surrounded by stacks and stacks of money. Explained Trafficante, "This is the most important room in any casino. We deal in cash and either you make it or lose it by what goes on in this room." Trafficante nodded toward the man with the ledger and an adding machine. "This is Henry. Henry is from Tampa and he watches that the count is right and that nothing gets lost. These people will steal you blind," he said, referring to the Cuban employees, "so I bring people from Tampa to watch the counting room."

Ragano was impressed with his client's holdings—hotels, casinos, nightclubs. He asked Trafficante, "Santo, you're making so much money through legitimate business here in Havana. Why not use the money to turn an honest dollar back home?"

Trafficante smiled. "Frank, a man who is blind in one eye has a great deal of vision among the blind." Ragano took Santo's statement to mean that corruption and loose standards made it possible for him to gain an edge in Cuba.

Ragano was no greenhorn. He had attended sex shows in Cuba and knew that the city had acquired a reputation for loose morality. He admired his client and saw that Havana gave him a kind of perverted confidence. He wanted to go along for the ride. As he wrote in *Mob Lawyer*:

I became a different man in Cuba. In Havana, my traditional values became less important, and Santo's became more honest and less hypocritical than those of most people. He extracted all the pleasure he could out of life without the slightest twinge of moral guilt and he was absolutely uncritical of himself. I wanted to fit into his life, emulate him, gain his respect.

Later, Ragano had his doubts:

I sometimes wondered if I had discarded my ethical standards in Havana. Then I would reflect on Santo's theme that Havana's lifestyle was created to be enjoyed, and since everyone else was savoring its delights, why should I be the exception?

The sexual depravity that had been the province of places like the Shanghai Theater now moved out into the community. Trafficante took his lawyer and friend to *las exhibiciones*, live sex shows that had become the talk of the town. "We don't want to go to the tourist traps," Santo told Ragano. "The first thing every secretary, schoolteacher, and nurse wants to see when they come here is *una exhibición*."

Trafficante had his valet drive Ragano and himself to a house in one of Havana's better neighborhoods. At the house, a hostess ushered them in and set them up in a room that had been converted into a cocktail lounge. "When you gentlemen are ready to see the show, let me know," the woman said. The two men had a drink. Trafficante explained to Ragano what was to take place. Normally, he said, the shows were presented to groups of six to eight people, but he had arranged for a private show.

"Across the hall," said Santo, "there is a room where they present three men and three women, and you select a pair who will be the performers. The charge is twenty-five dollars—pretty cheap when you consider the kind of show they put on."

The Mob boss and his lawyer carried their drinks into the other room. There, three men and three women wearing robes were presented for inspection. Trafficante did not wait for Ragano to make a choice. "We'll have El Toro and that girl over there," he told the hostess, pointing to the most well-endowed woman in the room.

The hostess nodded and asked Santo and Ragano to follow her into an adjoining room furnished with sofas and comfortable chairs. A crescent-shaped platform stage surrounded by mirrors had been set up in the middle of the room. On the walls were paintings of nude men and women.

The two men sipped their cocktails. The hostess clapped her hands and El Toro and the big-breasted woman entered the room and took the stage. They dropped their robes and proceeded to engage in sex, utilizing every position known to the human species, finishing off with oral sex.

Ragano was stunned by what he saw. Afterward, he asked Trafficante about El Toro.

"His cock is supposed to be fourteen inches long," explained Santo. "He's quite a guy. They also call him Superman."

Realizing this was the famous Superman who had become a legend in his own time in 1950s Havana, Ragano asked if he could use his Super-8-millimeter camera to film the show. Trafficante applied his influence to obtain permission. Using existing light, the lawyer captured Superman on film. The finished product is grainy and dark, but in a room surrounded by paintings of nudes, Superman's appendage is on display. He and the woman followed the same routine as before. It is the only known footage of Cuba's most renowned sex performer from the era of the Havana Mob.

"Incredible," concluded Ragano. "How can people do that for a living?" he asked Trafficante.

"Frank, you've got to remember, over here there's something for everybody. You want opera, they have opera. You want baseball, they have baseball. You want ballroom dancing, they have ballroom dancing. And if you want sex shows, they have live sex shows. That's what makes this place so great."

In the following days, Trafficante offered Ragano a chance to "buy in." Now that many of the Vegas mobsters had been forced to divest, there were openings for selected friends. A new casino was in the planning stages and shares were being sold privately at twenty-five thousand dollars for each 1 percent, or point, of the total investment. Ragano was tempted. He consulted his wife, Nancy, on the subject.

"Hasn't Santo heard about that revolutionary, Castro?" she asked her husband. "They say he's trying to take over the country."

Ragano mentioned Castro and his rebel insurrection to Trafficante, who sneered whenever the subject was brought up. As far as the Tampa Mob boss was concerned, the rebels were a joke. Besides, he figured that even if Castro were to achieve the impossible and take over the country, little would change.

"I'm sure Fidel will never amount to anything," said Santo. "But even if he does, they'll never close the casinos. There is so much damned money here for everybody."

BY THE SECOND WEEK OF APRIL, Trafficante had good reason to cast aspersions on Castro and his Revolution. The planned nationwide strike, which had been announced with great fanfare by Fidel, turned out to be a flop. The 26th of July Movement had envisioned a total shutdown, especially in Havana. Virtually everyone in the city was supposed to stay home from work, creating chaos and bringing the city to a standstill. It never happened. The casinos, nightclubs, bars, and *las exhibiciones* stayed open. The show went on as if nothing had changed.

The failed strike was a defeat for the Revolution. The reasons for the setback were varied. By announcing the strike publicly a month in advance, Castro had given the Batista regime plenty of time to react. The government didn't know the exact date, but they knew the strike was coming. In the weeks leading up to April 9, members of the secret police successfully hunted down and executed four of the movement's top leaders in Havana. Announcements were made by employers and by the government that those who took part in the strike would lose their jobs. Havana was the economic lifeblood of the island; employees in the city were privileged to have solid union jobs and did not want to lose them. This, in addition to poor organization by a depleted retinue of revolutionary leaders in the city, led to a bad result for the forces of revolution.

In the wake of the aborted strike, President Batista smelled victory; he let it be known that he was going all out in an effort to finally crush the rebels. The regime had scored few public relations victories against the Revolution in recent months; they saw the failed strike as an important strategic opening. Military leaders made plans to launch Operación Verano, a coordinated army and air force offensive against rebel columns in the Sierra Maestra. The bombing began in Oriente.

THE REVOLUTION WAS, in many ways, one big improvisation. Some of the movement's most significant events—the attack at Moncada, the landing of the *Granma*, the failed strike—had at first seemed like resounding defeats. But the 26th of July Movement had an uncanny knack for turning defeat into victory. Some of their most successful undertakings were born out of necessity or sheer desperation.

Such was certainly the case on the morning of June 26, when a column of guerrillas led by Raúl Castro decided to take matters into their own hands and kidnap a bunch of U.S. citizens.

Raúl and an armed brigade stormed the Moa Bay mining plant in eastern Oriente and rounded up the facility's employees, mostly Americans and a few Canadians. Elsewhere in Oriente—in a coordinated effort—a busload of U.S. military personnel were also kidnapped. Altogether, forty-eight hostages were taken into custody and held at a camp near Moa Bay.

The Moa Bay plant was one of two large U.S.-owned nickel-mining facilities in Cuba. For years, the island had been a major producer of nickel, which was extracted via an expensive ore-mining process that employed hundreds of Americans and also some Cubans. To the anger of many Cubans, the Batista government had given the Freeport Sulphur Company a virtually tax-free arrangement to operate the Moa Bay mine and another in nearby Nicaro. Together, these two plants supplied 11 percent of the world's nickel supply.

In the tradition of United Fruit—El Coloso—the Freeport Sulphur Company was a symbol of U.S. imperialism on the island. The company's board of directors was tight with the Batista regime, and it was said that American ambassador Smith owed his appointment to a cozy relationship with a former company chairman who was still a major

stockholder. To the rebels, the Freeport Sulphur Company was a symbol of the "unholy alliance" that existed between foreign capitalists
and the corrupt Batista regime—an arrangement, the thinking went,
that was contrary to the best interests of the Cuban people.

It would be a stretch to say that by targeting U.S. industrialists in
Cuba the movement was striking out against the Havana Mob, but in
some ways it is an accurate correlation. As the Revolution evolved, the
politics of the Castros, Guevara, William Gálvez, and others broadened
and deepened; the enemy was not only Batista, it was the historical tradition of exploitation and plundering in Cuba, the Caribbean, and Latin
America that went back to the time of Christopher Columbus. In this
sense, the U.S. companies that had been given sweetheart deals to own
and profit from Cuba's natural resources were indistinguishable from the
mobsters who owned and ran the casinos. They were all part and parcel
of the same occupying force.

The mass kidnapping at Moa Bay also served a strategic purpose.
One month earlier, Raúl Castro and his column had bivouacked in the
Sierra Cristal, mountains that surrounded the mining facility. Batista's
air force had located Raúl's column and begun a relentless bombing
campaign. The kidnapping of American citizens forced the Cuban Air
Force to halt all bombing while an American consul general negotiated
for their release.

The incident turned out to be yet another public relations coup for
the movement. Raúl used the opportunity to reveal to the press that the
nearby Guantánamo military base—owned under a lease arrangement
by the U.S. government since 1903—was being used by the Cuban Air
Force as a refueling depot. Bombs were being dropped on civilians in the
area. Raúl and the kidnappers took the hostages to towns that had been
bombed and showed them innocent civilian victims of napalm fire-
bombing. Overall, the hostages were treated with deference and care;
they were even given a 4th of July party during their captivity.

By the time the unharmed Americans were released under order from
El Comandante Fidel, public opinion in the United States necessitated

that Batista's air force no longer be allowed to use Guantánamo (i.e., U.S. property) to launch its bombing runs. Also, during the two-week period of negotiation for release of the hostages, the rebels were able to rest and replenish their forces. This proved to be a major break for the revolutionary army, who survived Batista's bombing campaign and came out of the ceasefire reinvigorated.

In the following months, there would be many stunning victories. At the Battle of Jigüe, one of the first major face-to-face confrontations of the war, a commanding officer and entire platoon of the Cuban Army surrendered to Castro's forces. The soldiers were treated with respect and then let go. Some soldiers left Batista's army and defected to the Revolution. It was the classic guerrilla strategy: win the hearts and minds, and their asses will follow.

Emboldened by successes in the field, the revolutionary army began preparations for a final push. By late summer, Column 2, a group that included Captain William Gálvez, was sent on a dangerous mission to cross the island, skirting Havana, and set up an encampment in the westernmost province of Pinar del Rio. In the province of Las Villas, Gálvez's column encountered resistance and was hit by an 81-millimeter mortar shell; the captain was knocked unconscious. When he awoke, he had been dragged to safety and was told he'd suffered only superficial shrapnel wounds.

Gálvez and his men continued on. Once they established an outpost in the west, the rebel army would have Havana surrounded and would thus attempt a final advance on the capital city.

Years later, Comandante Gálvez remembered this time with pride. "We could smell victory," he said.

AS THE NEW TOURIST SEASON approached, hotel bookings in Havana were down. For the first time, it became an undeniable fact that the war was having a negative effect on tourism. Las Vegas odds-makers placed Batista's chances for survival at less than two-to-one, a prognostication that even the Havana Mob could not ignore.

As a lifelong gambling impresario, Lansky knew how to play the odds. He still had the overwhelming majority of his chips on Batista, but what was to stop him from spreading his bet? Meyer had always planned on expanding his interests throughout the Caribbean and beyond. With Batista's forces crumbling on the battlefield and El Presidente suffering one public relations setback after another, the time was ripe for Lansky to explore other options.

In the summer and on into the fall of 1958, Meyer and other members of the Havana Mob undertook a series of trips around the islands. These trips included stops in Puerto Rico, the Bahamas, Jamaica, Barbados, and the Dominican Republic. Mostly, they were short trips of one to three days. The word among many in the Havana Mob was that International Hotels, Inc., the Pan Am subsidiary that owned the Hotel Nacional, had made it clear to Lansky and Trafficante that they were interested in expanding throughout the region. The Havana Mob would be given a sizable piece of the gambling concessions at hotels owned by the corporation. Thus, Lansky and Trafficante began to cultivate contacts and establish relationships throughout the Caribbean.

One particular trip to the Dominican Republic in July 1958 seemed more important than most. Armando Jaime accompanied Lansky on this trip, as he had on others. He did not ask where they were going; he simply drove Lansky to Rancho Boyeros airport, where they boarded a small Cessna along with Santo Trafficante and a man Jaime did not recognize.

The plane set out over the island, heading east. Lansky read a magazine and Jaime looked out the window as the landscape changed from flatlands to mountains and back to flatlands. Soon they were out over a huge sea, dark blue, almost black, and then they came upon a new tropical landscape. The flight lasted roughly two hours.

When the Cessna touched down at a commercial airport, a car was there on the tarmac to greet the arrivals before they had even disembarked from the plane. On the ground, Jaime stood by as Lansky and Trafficante were met by an American, who led them through the airport without having to pass through customs; everything had been arranged. It was in the airport terminal that Jaime saw a sign that read "Welcome to the Dominican Republic" and realized for the first time that Lansky and Trafficante had arrived as guests of the Dominican dictator, Rafael Trujillo.

The men were met in the airport parking area by a familiar face—Charles White, aka Charles "the Blade" Tourine. White was the Miami gambling expert and nightclub owner who had been brought to Havana to run the casino at the Capri. He would also be one of the most visible participants—a sort of public relations advance man—in efforts by the Havana Mob to establish a web of contacts throughout the Caribbean.

In a convoy of three cars, Lansky and Jaime, Trafficante, White, and others drove from the airport, through the city, and along a road to the outskirts of town. They stopped in front of a large wooden gate behind which stood a huge mansion. Armed guards met the cars at the gate and allowed them to pass into the courtyard area. The guards carried rifles and sawed-off double-barreled shotguns. In the courtyard, a group of men waited for the leaders of the Havana Mob. Armando Jaime remembered:

> The first surprise I had was that the estate, with all those impressive shotguns and rifles, seemed like a garrison. I have never seen so many armed characters. Never. People that I didn't know, that I had never seen before, neither in Havana nor Las Vegas. They were all there to greet Lansky—mostly white men, North Americans, elegantly dressed, between forty and forty-five years old. When the Old Man [Lansky] stepped out of the car, they came to greet him, one by one, with consummate respect, I would say with a little bit of emotion. And Lansky was offering them his hand, with a greeting, a phrase, some words that I couldn't hear from where I was.

As the group moved indoors, Jaime saw the familiar faces of Wilbur Clark, impresario of the Casino de Nacional, and Joe Stassi. It was then that he realized this was no quick routine trip around the islands but rather a major gathering of the brain trust.

If Jaime needed proof, it came less than thirty minutes after their arrival, when two black Cadillacs drove up to the gate. Trafficante received the call from the guardhouse; he authorized the two Cadillacs to enter the property. Out of the lead Cadillac stepped a tall, muscular black man dressed in a Dominican officer's uniform. He was an aide-de-camp representing the Trujillo government. The man greeted Trafficante at the door and he was led inside, where Lansky waited for them both in the library.

The men had a brief private meeting, lasting maybe ten minutes, and then the emissary from the Trujillo government left. Jaime got the impression that it was an official welcome of some sort, a recognition by all parties involved that whatever transpired in this gathering of businessmen and mobsters on the island, whatever deal was struck, it would take place courtesy of the Trujillo government, and would therefore be subject to the same sort of graft or "taxation" that the mobsters extended to Fulgencio Batista.

Jaime was introduced to the host of the gathering, an American who was the proprietor of the Dominican Goodrich Tire factory. The host had a group of servants lead Lansky, Trafficante, and Jaime up to their rooms. They convened in a room that was to be shared jointly by Lansky and Jaime. It was in that room, away from the other guests, that Jaime detected a change in mood. He remembered:

Santo gave me a .45 pistol with several cartridges and said, "This is to be used here—if necessary. But you cannot use it outside this house for any reason." It was the first time that I saw Trafficante armed. He was there with a pistol in his belt, and later a machine gun. He looked like a madman.

Back in Havana, Santo always showed himself to be very elegant, genteel, mellow, whether it was at the Sans Souci, the meetings at Joe Stassi's house, or the Hotel Nacional. But this Trafficante here at this house was a different man. He revealed himself such as he was.

Lansky entered the room, and Trafficante also handed him a .45-caliber pistol. Jaime was in for another surprise:

> It was the first time—and the only time—that I saw Lansky with a pistol. In a drawer at his suite in the Hotel Nacional there was a gun, but he never touched it. And I knew that there was also a pistol in an armoire in the living room of Carmen's house, but I never saw him touch that weapon either. Now, here was Lansky, who I had never seen touch a weapon before—not even the guns that were in the glove compartment of the cars; he took the pistol and checked the cartridges. Then he put the gun in his belt and the cartridges in the pockets of his jacket.

Clearly, something big was going down at this mansion in the Dominican Republic. "I had the feeling anything could happen," remembered Jaime.

The main guests began to arrive the following day. Jaime recognized these men as Sicilians, either native Italians with heavy accents or Sicilian Americans from places like New York, New Jersey, or Chicago. These men were also stopped and searched at the gate, which made many of them angry. Charles White was there to greet the new arrivals at the porch, with an apology for the search and seizure of all guns.

Inside, Lansky sat in a chair in the library and received the men, one by one. As on the day before, these men greeted Lansky with a respect bordering on reverence. Those who were not able to get through to the Little Man met with Trafficante, also in the library. Later, this entire crew of businessmen, mobsters, and mafiosi—perhaps forty or fifty men—reconvened in a room at the back of the house.

"Go for a ride, if you want," Lansky told Jaime. "Take one of the cars here, with Dominican license plates, and go familiarize yourself with the city. Stay out all night, if you want. You won't be needed again until tomorrow morning."

Jaime was given the keys to an Impala. He got behind the wheel, started the engine, and approached the gate. Magically, the gate opened, as though the guards had already been informed of his every move. He drove away from the mansion, through the capital city and beyond. He spent the night at a bordello in the town of Santiago de los Caballeros.

At 7 A.M. the following morning, Lansky's valet returned to the mansion. Again, the gates parted and shotgun-toting guards nodded as he entered the compound.

Inside the house, Jaime was surprised to hear the voices of the men in the back room. They had apparently been up all night. Some of the voices were loud, argumentative—speaking Italian or Italian-accented English. Jaime headed upstairs, undressed, and climbed into bed.

One hour later, Lansky abruptly entered the room and told him, "We're leaving." Just like that. He seemed annoyed. Jaime got up, dressed, and packed his clothes. Without saying good-bye to anyone, he, Lansky, and Trafficante went immediately to the airport. In the same Cessna they had arrived in, they left the Dominican Republic. Lansky and Trafficante did not say one word to each other during the entire two-hour flight.

Armando Jaime never did figure out what had gone wrong during that gathering of mobsters in Trujillo's front yard. There were other short trips in the Caribbean, even a few more to the Dominican Republic, though none as fraught with tension as that overnight stay at the mansion of the businessman from Dominican Goodrich.

Others in the Caribbean had been hearing stories about Lansky's plans for expansion, and some casino owners were worried. Joe Stassi Jr., the son of Joe Stassi and a dealer at the Sans Souci casino, had befriended a casino owner from the Dominican Republic who went by the name of Pat Slots. Joe Jr. arranged for a Havana sit-down between Pat Slots and Lansky. Slots was told by Lansky, "Don't worry. If you own a casino in the Dominican, nobody's gonna take it away from you." The casino owner was highly appreciative.

Stassi Jr. was one of a new generation with direct links to the Havana Mob. His father was an important player in Cuba, and Joe Jr.

could expect a commensurate level of deference in local gambling and even political circles on the island. This was partly because Stassi Jr. had married his way into the Batista regime.

The kid was sixteen when he first came to Havana in early 1957. Though he was the son of a reputed mafioso, Joe Jr. was not an aspiring mobster. He was a high-school student on vacation who came to stay with his father for a week and wound up spending close to three years on the island. He became one of the youngest dealers at the Sans Souci, hung out at the Tropicana, and quickly fell in love with a Cuban woman who happened to be the daughter of Senator Miguel Suárez Fernández, a notorious official from Batista's inner circle. In 1958 Joe Jr. got married, and he and his wife were soon parents.

The experience of Joe Stassi's son in Cuba was most likely a harbinger of things to come—that is, if things worked out for the Havana Mob. Lansky, Trafficante, Stassi, and others had put down roots on the island. Their commitment to plundering Cuba was a long-range project; it was supposed to carry on for generations to come.

OF ALL THE MOBSTERS rooted in Cuba, Santo Trafficante was the one who should have known better. Thanks to his Cuban friends and associates in Tampa, Santo had close access to the island's troubled history. Rebellion was nothing new. If Trafficante wanted to know, any of Ybor City's legion of Cuban exiles could have told him of the island's cycle of dictatorship, corruption, and political turmoil. This cycle had been recurring at least since the violent fall of Machado back in the early 1930s, when Trafficante's father was running booze and narcotics through the Pearl of the Antilles.

It was Trafficante's contention that whatever form of government followed Batista, it would still be dependent on the flow of capital that came from the casinos. In conversations with his lawyer Ragano, the Tampa Mob boss hinted that he had already begun covering his ass for the eventuality that Castro and his Revolution succeeded. Ragano took this to mean that Santo was secretly sending guns or money—or both—to the rebels in the Sierra Maestra.

There is no conclusive evidence linking Trafficante to gun smuggling, but it is a fact that certain characters in Havana associated with Santo's faction of the Mob were attempting to transport guns into the mountains.

Norman Rothman had been involved in gambling in Cuba even before Batista's coup of 1953; he was a partner of Trafficante at both the Sans Souci and Tropicana casinos. He had no particular allegiance to Batista; as a free-market capitalist in Cuba, Rothman would back whoever was in power, as long as that person was sympathetic to his gambling interests. If Castro were to take over—as it was beginning to appear he might—Rothman wanted to be in good standing; to this end, he established contact with the 26th of July Movement.

In August 1958, just weeks before the beginning of the new tourist season, Rothman met with José Aleman, a Cuban living in Miami who was actively involved in the anti-Batista resistance. The two men met at Rothman's off-season residence in Surfside, north of Miami. According to Aleman, who testified about the meeting years later before a U.S. congressional hearing, Rothman had in his possession several hundred Cuban pesos of various denominations. Rothman told Aleman that the pesos were counterfeit. He proposed that these pesos and others like them could be used to flood the market in Cuba, destabilize the local economy, and hasten the downfall of Batista.

Aleman examined the bills and then suggested that he would pass the idea along to the chief of the 26th of July Movement in Miami. Apparently the movement was suspicious of Rothman's motives. They turned him down flat.

The gambling boss was determined to put himself in good standing with the Revolution. For Rothman and others representing the Trafficante faction of the Havana Mob, the Revolution presented an opportunity. If they could establish back-channel ties with Castro—and Castro took over—they could use the relationship to minimize the power of

Lansky, who was closely identified with Batista. It was a dangerous game, but it made sense. The Trafficante and Lansky factions in Havana were uneasy partners, always on the lookout for ways to maneuver events to their advantage.

With this in mind, Rothman reached out to Sammy and Kelly Mannarino, the two brothers who had owned the gambling concession at the Sans Souci before Batista and Lansky took over in Havana. Rothman most likely suggested to the Mannarinos that by cuddling up to Castro they might work their way back into the Cuban gambling picture. It is unlikely that Rothman would have made such an offer to the Mannarinos without the backing of his underworld boss, Santo Trafficante.

On October 14, 317 weapons were stolen from a National Guard armory in Canton, Ohio. The Mannarinos contacted Rothman, who rented a plane for six thousand dollars to run the guns to Cuba. Rothman intended to pay for the guns via a Swiss bank account, using stolen securities as collateral for a loan. The weapons were in the process of being shipped when they were spotted on radar by the U.S. border patrol. The shipment was busted before leaving the United States, and most of the conspirators were indicted, including Rothman and the Mannarinos.

Rothman remained free on bail, and the Revolution continued. In fact, the 26th of July Movement was able to get its guns from other unlikely sources, including the U.S. Central Intelligence Agency (CIA).

At the same time the Trafficante faction of the Havana Mob was attempting to endear itself to the Revolution, a CIA case officer named Robert D. Weicha was arranging for a shipment of weapons to Raúl Castro's "Second Front." According to the late investigative journalist Tad Szulc, Weicha—who was in Cuba under the cover of the consulate general as a vice consul—had already made a series of payments totaling fifty thousand dollars to the 26th of July Movement in Santiago. Weicha's activities were top secret and have never been declassified. There is also evidence that the CIA was involved in smuggling shipments of weapons to the rebels. Since no one from the CIA has ever explained their thinking at the time, the reasons for financing and arming the movement cannot be easily explained. It is a sound assumption, however, that the agency wished to hedge its bets in Cuba and purchase goodwill among some members of the movement for future contingencies. This would have been consistent with CIA policy elsewhere in the world whenever local conflicts affected U.S. interests.

Cuba was becoming a cauldron of secret plots, double agents, and revolutionary conspiracies. And not all the weapons being sent to the island were destined for Castro. In March, the U.S. government had suspended all arms shipments to Batista on the grounds that the weapons were for self-defense against a foreign power and not to be used against fellow Cubans. This action on the part of the U.S. Congress came as a shock to Batista, who was now forced to arrange for guns to be shipped to his army via a third-party country. A major shipment arrived from the Dominican Republic; others were scheduled to arrive from Central America.

Multiple planeloads of guns flooded the island—some destined for the rebels and some for the Cuban Army. In the airspace over the island and surrounding waters, these planes most likely passed other planes that were leaving Havana with a different kind of precious cargo: money.

Nearly all the various factions of the Havana Mob had their own special bagmen, whose job it was to ferry cash and checks off the island into private bank accounts in the United States, Europe, or elsewhere in the Caribbean. Trafficante had Ralph Reina, the old-timer from Tampa who had been part of the Trafficante family operation going back to the 1930s. Lansky had Dan "Dusty" Peters, a lean, dapper character who had once been a host at the Colonial Inn and Meyer's other Florida gambling joints. At the Havana Riviera, where the high rollers thought nothing of writing a check for twenty or thirty thousand dollars to cover a gambling debt, it was dapper Dusty's job to take those checks on an early-morning flight to Miami, where they were express-cleared and deposited in a special account at the Bank of Miami Beach. Later, Lansky was also known to use Castle Bank in the Bahamas for large cash deposits.

Batista was believed to have various people for this duty, cabinet ministers and members of the secret police, whose job it was to transport suitcases full of cash and other valuables for deposit in private accounts in Switzerland.

At the Tropicana, owner Martín Fox had Lewis "Mack" McWillie, a fifty-year-old former blackjack dealer from Las Vegas who came to Havana in September 1958, ostensibly to work as a pit boss and later credit manager. McWillie was brawny and gruff, with thinning hair and an expanding belly. He was a knockaround guy originally from Dallas whom the FBI described as a murderer. McWillie had been around gangsters and gamblers most of his adult life. Years later, in front of the 1978 House Select Committee on Assassinations (investigating the assassination of John F. Kennedy), McWillie explained his role in Havana:

MCWILLIE: I managed the Tropicana some and then the government took it over and I was sent to the Hotel Capri by Martín, who said you could get a job there, so go there.

CHAIRMAN: Well, isn't it true that you made trips to Miami?

MCWILLIE: To take money for Fox.

CHAIRMAN: From Cuba, to deposit money?

MCWILLIE: Yes, sir.

CHAIRMAN: Explain that to us; tell us what you were doing.

MCWILLIE: They would ask me to go, if I would go to Miami and deposit some money for them, and I would do it.

CHAIRMAN: By what you were doing, you were sort of running for them, is that right?

MCWILLIE: Well, I was a casino manager, and if they wanted me to do that for them, I did it.

CHAIRMAN: The effect of what you were doing is they were getting their money out of Cuba into banks or deposit boxes here in the States, is that right?

McWILLIE: Well, the money I took over there was—I took it to a teller
and she put it in their account . . .

Lewis McWillie was typical of the kind of characters who descended
upon Havana for the 1958–59 tourist season. It was in newspapers all
over the world: Havana was teeming with revolutionary intrigue and
possibly on the verge of a major change. For underworld fringe players
like McWillie, the idea that a once all-powerful dictatorship might be
experiencing a major reshuffling of the deck was a golden opportunity. If
Havana were to fall, presumably gambling and other rackets once controlled by the Havana Mob would be broken wide open. The old guard
would be out on their asses and a whole new cast of characters would be
there like carrion, ready to pick over the corpse.

The promise of a new dawn approached, and a fresh set of hoodlums
arrived: hangers-on, mercenaries, spooks, leeches, and bottom-feeders.

Even so, Lansky, Trafficante, and other stalwarts of the mobster elite
believed they were still on solid ground. As long as the money flowed
from the casinos and nightclubs, they were able to cling to their illu-
sions. If the world beyond was changing, they would be the last to
know.

14

"GET THE MONEY"

THE MOST GRANDIOSE HOTEL-CASINO EVER CONSTRUCTED in Cuba was to be called the Monte Carlo de La Habana. On paper, it was breathtaking: a massive, all-encompassing resort complex with a marina, interior canals and berths for yachts, a landing pad for helicopters and hydroplanes, and a golf course, along with the usual casino, nightclub, piano lounge, restaurant, etc. The Monte Carlo would have a capacity of 656 rooms, and a modern design created by one of the world's best-known architects. Though the project had not yet been announced publicly, construction began in August 1958. The hotel and surrounding installations were projected to cost twenty million dollars, a new record for Havana. Financing would be assumed primarily by BANDES.

The Monte Carlo was to be the summation of everything that had come before, a hotel, leisure, and entertainment complex that was to be one in a series of similar hotel-casinos all along the Malecón. In this new phase of development in Havana, what had come before was a mere prelude—a pittance compared to what Lansky and the Havana Mob had in mind for the future.

"Havana will be a magical city," Meyer told his driver, Jaime, one afternoon while standing near the construction site for the Monte Carlo. "Hotels like jewels built right on top of the coral reef that supports the Malecón. Fabulous casinos, nightclubs, and bordellos as far as the eye can see. More people than you can imagine."

Lansky's driver listened; he could see the glint in Lansky's eyes but also the doubt. "Impossible," Meyer would say in a huff. Then he would take a deep breath of salty air and regain his optimism. "It could be, Jaimito. It could happen."

The Havana Mob's latest creation was to be run by a company called La Compañía Hotelera de Monte Carlo. The Monte Carlo Hotel Company had on its board of directors some of the most famous names in the world of business, politics, and entertainment. The most noteworthy stockholder was none other than "Chairman of the Board" Frank Sinatra.

Sinatra's interest in Havana went back at least as far as the 1946 Mob conference at the Hotel Nacional, when he allegedly transported a suitcase filled with cash to Charlie Luciano. After years of fraternizing with mobsters, Ol' Blue Eyes was ready to buy in. He had visited Havana numerous times but, surprisingly, had never officially performed there. If all went according to plan, that was about to change in a big way. Sinatra was not only listed as a stockholder and prospective board member for the Hotel Monte Carlo, but he also had plans to stage a weekly variety show from the hotel that would be televised live in the United States and—presumably—around the world. In a report to BANDES, lawyers representing the company explained Sinatra's intentions:

[Sinatra] wants to televise the hotel's properties from Cuba to the United States weekly, given that he is a producer and as an interested party in his programs intends to fulfill a double function: first, to put the hotel he manages in the spotlight; and second, to divert the profits produced by contracting the show in Cuba to a Cuban American company that will produce shows and movies from Cuba with panoramic vistas of the hotel serving as a backdrop.

Joining Sinatra in this venture were the singer and actor Tony Martin, a frequent performer in Havana, actor and dancer Donald O'Connor, who had recently been nominated for an Academy Award for his role in *Singin' in the Rain*, and New York restaurateur William Miller, who was also a producer of entertainment programs. Of Miller, the Monte Carlo lawyers were effusive in their praise:

> Mr. Miller is considered within the United States as the only person capable of what Americans call raising the dead. In other words, he has long experience staging shows that are huge tourist attractions in the United States, and he has contacts and connections with first-rate artistic businesses. As a guarantee, he has offered to bring to Cuba the 20 most important stars in the United States to promote international publicity in favor of the government directed by Major General Fulgencio Batista y Zaldívar.

Along with acting as a shill for the Batista dictatorship, the hotel's management was to have considerable political sway in the United States as well. Another of the proposed directors at the Monte Carlo was Walter Kirschner, who had lived in the White House for twelve years as a key adviser to President Franklin Roosevelt. It was noted in the lawyer's report that Kirschner had a personal relationship with the current occupant of the White House, Dwight Eisenhower, and he also had powerful connections in Vatican City, where he served as an envoy for the U.S. government. Kirschner knew the president and had a mainline to the Pope: what more could a Mob-affiliated dictatorship ask for?

The Monte Carlo was to be the epitome of all that the Mob had hoped for in Cuba—a mix of celebrities, powerful businessmen, well-connected politicos, and mobsters. The very name of the place—Monte Carlo— evoked everything that Lansky had dreamed about. The city had arrived: Havana was to be arguably the most glamorous vacation spot in the world, a veritable money machine whose proceeds from gambling and other leisure activities in Cuba would finance Mob ventures around the globe. The

Monte Carlo was the latest phase of a plan so ambitious that it was sure to awaken the ghosts of Jimmy Walker, Al Capone, Arnold "The Brain" Rothstein, and every other mobster or mobster acolyte who had hitched his wagon to the dream of a mobster's paradise in Cuba. It was all within grasp, so close that Lansky, Trafficante, Batista, and the others could taste it, hold it in their hands, savor the aroma of money, power, and sex that was the fulfillment of their wildest criminal fantasies.

So close and yet so far: for a dream that had evolved over decades of planning, manipulation, and repression, it was to have a relatively brief shelf life. The Monte Carlo may have been a "done deal" on paper, but in reality the project never got off the ground. The Cuban people had other ideas.

IT WAS HARD FOR ANYONE to tell whether the Revolution was a pipe dream or a foregone conclusion. Censorship made it difficult to know. Articles about the war in *Diario de la Marina* were based on army press releases, with the emphasis invariably on surrender: "Five outlaws were arrested yesterday after surrendering near Trinidad and saying they were sorry they ever went to the mountains." On one occasion, it was alleged that eight surrendered, saying, "They were sorry they had been fighting with the rebels." Sometimes there were reports of an actual battle: "40 Rebels, 5 Soldiers Die, Army Reports." Or "180 Casualties Reported in Oriente." Rebel casualties were always high, army deaths always low. If you read only the mainstream press in Cuba, you might have thought the government was holding its own.

By December, Los Nortes swept down from the Gulf and waves began to pound the seawall along the Malecón, as they sometimes did with the onset of winter. Even with the press blackout, the city was rife with rumors that Batista could not last much longer. Communications with the rest of the island had been shut off because the rebels had severed telephone wires and bombed electrical installations. Highways leading to the city were blockaded by revolutionary militias, hindering supplies of food. Many of Havana's best restaurants were forced to drastically reduce their hours of operation or shut down completely because they had no produce, meat, or dairy. On an island where sugarcane was more common than grass, there was a sugar shortage as a result of rebel sabotage; the sugar that survived was used for export.

Havana had never been more isolated. The hotels, casinos, and cabarets still functioned but with greatly reduced profits. To believe things were going well required that a person spend twenty-four hours a day in a casino, where there were no rebels, no broadcasts of Radio Rebelde, and no clocks, calendars, or windows. At night, the only vehicles that moved freely on the streets were blue-and-white police cars, the olive-green Oldsmobiles of the SIM, and the battered old autos carrying the men of Los Tigres. In recent weeks, senator Rolando Masferrer's gang had moved from Santiago to Havana in anticipation of the showdown between the regime and the rebels that seemed likely to occur.

In his office at the presidential palace, Fulgencio Batista conducted the country's business from behind windows that had been outfitted with steel plates to block out sniper attacks. The president rarely attended public functions, where his mere appearance might touch off an act of civil disobedience, a riot, or, worst of all, an assassination attempt. Outside of an occasional proclamation over the radio, Batista had removed himself from the public discourse. Most of his time was spent at Kuquine, his palatial estate thirty minutes outside the city. He had lately begun to engage in strange behavior. He would eat huge meals that lasted for hours, then disappear into his back garden, where he stuck his finger down his throat and vomited in violent bursts. He would then return to the table, wipe his mouth with a white linen handkerchief, and resume eating. Was it vanity or a compulsive behavior disorder? Either way, El Mulato Lindo had begun to exhibit tendencies that were well known to the average Havana showgirl, a type of behavior commonly known as bulimia.

At night, Batista liked to watch movies in his private screening room. There, in the darkness, he was able to lose himself in a world of fantasy and pat resolutions. His favorites were American horror flicks, especially Dracula movies and anything starring Boris Karloff. On Sunday nights, the president invited his dwindling circle of friends over to play canasta for relatively small stakes (ten to fifty dollars a game). Few realized that Batista cheated. Using a system of codes and secret signs, he had aides who doubled as waiters tip him off to the cards other players were holding.

Among historians, there is a difference of opinion about how fully Batista understood the gravity of the situation in Cuba. Perhaps he had deluded himself into believing he could somehow manage the crisis. In November, his administration had staged an election in which a puppet candidate was elected president. Batista had already announced that in late February 1959, when his term was over, he would be retiring from public life. Although the elections had been denounced as fraudulent by the 26th of July Movement, and even the U.S. State Department would not commit itself to officially recognizing Batista's handpicked successor, it is possible that the president believed he could maneuver his way through the remaining few months of his term. Perhaps he had come to believe his own propaganda. After all, as long as he had the loyalty of high-ranking officers in the Cuban military, how could he possibly be deposed?

Batista's faith in the ubiquitous power of the army was rattled to the core when, in early December, he was approached by the head of SIM and told that upper-echelon members of the army were plotting his overthrow. Batista might have dismissed the plot, except that the conspiracy allegedly involved General Martín Díaz Tamayo. The general was one of Batista's most trusted confidants. He was the man who had backed Batista during the coup of 1952, making possible his reascension to the throne. Being betrayed by Díaz Tamayo was like being stabbed in the back by his own brother. Batista had Díaz Tamayo arrested and successfully quashed the military conspiracy, but it was clear that a mood of sedition had crept into the president's last true bastion of support—the officer corps.

Worries about dissension at the top were made worse for Batista by the reality of events on the ground. It seemed as though each day a new town fell to the rebels. The most startling thing was that most of these take-overs occurred without much bloodshed; military brigades and towns-people were simply acquiescing to the rebels without a fight. Batista usually received news of the encroaching Revolution with a blank look on his face. He was like a Cheshire cat, his countenance without emotion. When he was asked a question by aides or American diplomats, he in-variably began by saying, "You know, last night while I lay in bed reading *The Day Lincoln Was Shot,* I got to thinking . . ." It was an opening line that personified the president—detached, disconnected, living in his own world as the government crumbled around him.

On the afternoon of December 17, things changed. Batista was ap-proached by U.S. ambassador Smith at his Kuquine estate. The meeting had been requested by the ambassador. In recent weeks, the U.S. gov-ernment had been putting pressure on Batista to step down. They had proposed numerous scenarios, including a transition bartered by the Catholic Church, or a government run by a military junta, or govern-ment by a committee to be determined by all interested parties, includ-ing the 26th of July Movement. Batista rebuffed all suggestions that he step aside. He remained on friendly terms with the Eisenhower adminis-tration, but it was clear that he had no intention of willingly turning over the reins to any junta or consortium that included representatives of the enemy.

At the meeting on December 17, Smith detected a change in the president's attitude. Batista was noticeably subdued. The ambassador had always liked and supported Batista; in fact, he had advocated strongly on the president's behalf within the U.S. government. But oth-ers in the State Department had come to believe that Batista's tenure was doomed. They wanted the dictator out, and as ambassador, Smith was the man who had to deliver the news. As he sat in the library at Batista's estate, he reminded the president of the long, cooperative relationship that had existed between him and the U.S. government. It was "like applying the Vaseline before inserting the stick," Smith remembered years later.

The problem for Batista was that his lifelong benefactor, the U.S. government, not only wanted him to leave the presidency, they also wanted him to leave the island. When Batista heard this news, Smith detected a slight irregularity in his breathing, as if the Cuban dictator had been kicked in the testicles. There was worse news to come. When Batista asked if he would be allowed to enter the United States and live in his home in Daytona Beach, Smith answered, "I'm afraid not." The U.S. government felt it would be better if he tried some other country, such as Spain or the Dominican Republic. Maybe later, after the dust settled and Uncle Sam was able to broker an orderly transition of power in Cuba, Batista would be allowed to take refuge in his former home state of Florida.

For a man who had served as a vassal of American political and business interests during a world war and through numerous U.S. presidential administrations, it was a cruel blow. El Mulato Lindo had outlived his usefulness.

Batista spoke up in his own defense, but by the time the two-and-a-half-hour meeting was over, Smith knew his friend had finally faced reality. The fact that he was asking about safe passage to Daytona Beach for himself and his family was evidence enough that Batista knew the end was near. Somewhere in the back of his mind he had accepted defeat.

Even so, the president said nothing. In the following days and weeks, he told no one of his change of heart. Through back channels, Batista arranged visas for his wife and children. Publicly, he continued to act as if the rebels would be crushed and he would survive. Maybe earlier he had been living in denial, or been delusional or unaware of the full extent of the Revolution, but now he had willingly chosen to mislead his followers. He had become something else: La Engañadora, the Deceiver. The song so provocative it had inspired Bubbles Darlene to stroll topless through the streets of Havana, "La Engañadora" told the story of a grand deception. Batista fit the bill; he had gone from being a benevolent dictator to an outright fake—a gangster whose own survival was more important than the fate of the nation.

El Presidente did not tell his advisers or, more importantly, his friends in the Havana Mob that he intended to cash in his chips. Lansky, Trafficante, and the others would be left to fend for themselves.

EVEN WITH THE GATHERING tropical depression, Havana remained festive during the holiday season. El Encanto department store advertised authentic Christmas trees—"Nordic pines just unloaded from freezing ships"—at 85 cents a foot. Another store boasted a window display complete with Lionel trains, selling "at Miami prices." Christmas lights were everywhere, and numerous Santa Clauses rang bells and collected centavos on behalf of the U.S. Salvation Army. Temperatures were mild and the idea of snow nothing more than a Hollywood fantasy, but the spirit was real. Christmas in Havana was a time of good cheer.

The holiday atmosphere continued through to New Year's Eve, which was traditionally the biggest bash of the year in a city that had earned its reputation as one of the great party towns in the world. Bookings were down, but there were still droves of tourists at the hotels and in the casinos.

Early on the night of New Year's Eve, the city was calm. News of rebel successes throughout the previous week had led many to believe that the end was near for Batista, but there had been no unusual announcements. At Lansky's Riviera, the rooms were near total occupancy and the hotel restaurant booked to capacity. All seemed normal, except for a few telltale signs.

Ralph Rubio ate with his family in the hotel restaurant that evening. As was often the case, Lt. Col. Esteban Ventura entered with his two daughters and a bevy of bodyguards. Ventura—dressed in his usual white linen suit—was chief of the island's anti-Communist and antisubversion squad. He was one of the most feared and hated police officials in all of Cuba. His squad was run out of the Fifth Precinct and later the Ninth Precinct, a virtual chamber of horrors where revolutionary collaborators were interrogated, tortured, and sometimes murdered.

Rubio was used to seeing Ventura take his seat at a table surrounded by bodyguards. But tonight he saw something different: the lieutenant colonel's bodyguards took their .45-caliber pistols out of their holsters and either put them on the table or held them in their laps, covered by a napkin. The guns were conspicuous and ready for immediate use.

The official word at the hotel was that Mr. Lansky's ulcers were bothering him; he would be spending most of the evening in his room on the twentieth floor. According to Lansky's driver, Armando Jaime, this was a ruse. Even though Teddy, his wife, was in town, Lansky had chosen to spend New Year's Eve with his mistress, Carmen. Teddy was left in the company of Eduardo Suarez Rivas, longtime associate of the Havana Mob and the Riviera's attorney. Mrs. Lansky would dance in the New Year in the Copa Room, while her secretive husband cavorted elsewhere.

Around 9:00 P.M., Lansky was just finishing up a meeting at Joe Stassi's house when he said to his driver, "Let's go pick up the women. We'll have dinner at the Plaza Hotel." By women, Lansky meant Carmen and Jaime's girlfriend, Yolanda Brito. Jaime proceeded to drive the open-air convertible by Yolanda's home in Vedado and then on to Carmen's apartment building near the Prado. Around 10:00 P.M., all four settled into a booth in the Plaza Hotel's modest café, near Parque Central in Old Havana.

Built in 1909, the Plaza was an elegant hotel, one of the city's oldest and most revered. Only recently had a casino been opened there. Its gambling concession was jointly owned by Joe Stassi and his son, Joe Jr. The Stassis had another partner at the Plaza: Angelo Bruno, a Mafia boss from Philadelphia who had recently bought into the Havana syndicate.

Though it was one of the Havana Mob's chosen spots, the Plaza was not as established as the Riviera, Capri, Tropicana, and other locations.

By choosing to spend the evening at the Plaza, Lansky was deliberately hoping to avoid the large crowds that would be gathering elsewhere; he preferred something more discreet and less popular with the high-end tourists and his high-ranking associates in the Mob.

According to Jaime, there was an ominous mood in the air that night. Throughout the week there had been rumors and reports of rebel advancements. Che Guevara and his troops had penetrated the province of Las Villas, on the central highway, and seemed poised to make a move toward the capital city.

"That night," noted Jaime, "it seemed as though something was happening, something was going on. Everything was tense and disquieting."

Jaime remembered a conversation he'd had earlier in the week with Lansky. "The *barbudos* (the bearded ones) are close to winning the war," Lansky told Jaime. The driver was surprised; his boss did not usually volunteer opinions about Cuban politics. Obviously, he was worried. He told Jaime that although he was familiar with the political inclinations of the *barbudos*, he didn't know what the top leadership was going to do. Most importantly, he was uncertain what their position would be on the casinos, whether they would keep them open or immediately shut them down.

Even though Lansky had reason to be on edge, Jaime was struck by how calm he remained. All through dinner, "He was subdued, lost in his thoughts, with the occasional courtesy or compliment for the beautiful Carmen. It was as if he knew everything or foresaw what was going to occur." The subdued atmosphere at Lansky's table was in stark contrast to the New Year's Eve revelry going on around them.

At midnight, everyone counted down the New Year and drank champagne. The louder and drunker the gathering became, the more reserved was Lansky. Jaime was on the dance floor with his girlfriend when, around 1:30 A.M., he saw Charles White enter the bar, scan the room, and then walk quickly over to Lansky's booth. White leaned down and whispered something in Lansky's ear.

Jaime knew White to be an important member of the Havana Mob. On trips to the Dominican Republic, White had been the man out front. As manager of the Casino de Capri and other Mob-connected gambling facilities, he was a key player. When the man spoke, Lansky listened.

Whatever White whispered into Lansky's ear, the Mob boss received the news "with absolute tranquillity." Lansky stood, then he and White left the table and made for the exit.

"Stay here with Carmen," Jaime told Yolanda. "I'll be right back."

He left Yolanda with Lansky's mistress; the two women were now sitting with the manager of the Plaza casino. Jaime followed Lansky and White out into the lobby. Lansky motioned for Jaime to keep his distance, as he often did when he wanted to converse privately with an associate.

The two Americans stepped outside and talked quietly, standing in the shadows between two columns of the portico along Neptuno Street. Jaime watched from the front entrance of the hotel. After a few moments, the two men parted, with White hurrying off to find his car. Lansky walked back to Jaime. "He's gone. The *barbudos* have won the war."

The Mob boss need say no more; Jaime knew that "he" was President Batista. The bastard had waited until the entire nation was occupied with the New Year's celebration and then fled under cover of darkness.

Jaime was startled by Lansky's reaction: "He remained so unflappable, more unflappable than ever, more than was usual for him. I never before saw him quite that way, not even in the best of circumstances."

Lansky said to his valet: "We better send the women home to Carmen's place. Right now, me and you, we got a lot of work to do."

Carmen's apartment was only three minutes away. The four of them—Lansky, Jaime, Carmen, and Yolanda—piled into a taxi. After they had been dropped off, Lansky and Jaime made sure the women were safe inside, then headed back toward the hotel on foot. "We better get moving," Lansky told Jaime. "We have to make the most of what's left of the evening."

When they reached the Plaza, Lansky went straight to the casino and spoke to the manager. "Batista has abandoned the country," he told him. Lansky ordered the man, "Take all of the U.S. money on the premises—safe-deposit boxes, cash reserves, money on the floor—and separate it from the Cuban money. After securing both currencies in something safe, bring it immediately to Joe Stassi's house." The manager nodded and did what he was told. Lansky then turned his attention to Jaime. "Get the car," he said. "Not the convertible, that's too dangerous. One of the other cars."

Jaime knew that the Havana Mob kept a number of vehicles in the garages of many of their hotel-casinos. He retrieved a car from the garage and picked up Lansky in front of the Plaza. "Fast," said Lansky, once in the car, "before the people take to the streets. We need to make the rounds to all the casinos and secure the money. First stop is the Sans Souci."

It was 3:00 A.M. when Jaime and Lansky sped down 51st Avenue in the direction of the Sans Souci nightclub and casino. The streets were eerily deserted—no cars, no pedestrians, no police. Nothing. Jaime pressed down on the gas pedal and reached speeds of over 100 kph. They were at the Sans Souci in no time. Both Lansky and his valet entered the casino. They headed toward Trafficante's booth. The Tampa Mob boss, seeing Lansky's arrival, had risen to meet them.

Apparently no one at the Sans Souci had yet heard the news. Jaime saw Trafficante flinch when Lansky told him that Batista was gone. Lansky repeated what he had been told, that the rebels had taken over Las Villas and could be advancing on the city as early as the following day. In a calm tone, he told Santo, "Make the rounds at all of your casinos. Get the money. All of it. Even the cash and checks in reserve. Take it to Stassi's house for safekeeping."

Lansky added: "The best thing now is to pull back, to be absolutely invisible. Close the casinos—and fast. Because at dawn the crowds will take to the streets and nothing and nobody will be able to stop them."

Trafficante nodded and motioned to someone in the distance. Lansky turned to Jaime. "Let's go," he said. "Swing by the Nacional and then on to the Riviera." The two men left the Sans Souci in a hurry.

Unfortunately for the Havana Mob, neither the manager at the Plaza nor Trafficante fully understood the urgency of Lansky's instructions. They secured the cash but were slow about closing their establishments. Within the next few hours, both casinos would be trashed.

THE CUBAN PEOPLE DID NOT wait till dawn to take to the streets. By 4:00 A.M., news of Batista's departure had begun to spread. At first, people merely left their homes and gathered spontaneously in the streets; there was much cheering and singing. People honked their car horns and, as in any good Cuban celebration, buckets, sticks, and cymbals were used as impromptu percussion instruments. As the minutes wore on and the magnitude of what had happened began to sink in, the mood turned angrier. There were sporadic clashes between police and rebel militia, who came out of hiding to begin the process of taking over the city now that Batista was gone. In Parque Central, across from the Plaza Hotel, a wild shoot-out ensued between the rebels and members of Los Tigres. The *Masferristas* were in a building on Manzana de Gómez Street and the rebels were firing at them, hitting balconies and windows on the second and third floors. People in the street ran for cover.

The years of frustration were bubbling over now, anger mounting and being directed at anything and everything that symbolized the Batista regime. Among the first things to go were the parking meters.

The meters were associated with Batista's brother-in-law, Roberto Fernández Miranda. Along with the ubiquitous slot machines, Fernández Miranda's other profitable patronage plum was the meters that soaked up the centavos of the Cuban people. It was common knowledge that this money went directly into the pockets of Batista's brother-in-law. With hammers, lead pipes, and baseball bats, the Cuban rabble went after them, whacking them until they were separated from the metal poles that held them aloft. Some sought to crack open the meters and steal the coins, but this was, for the most part, not an act of robbery; it was an act of revenge against one of the city's most obvious symbols of corruption.

Next came the slot machines. People stormed into the corner bodegas, cafés, and bars, uprooted the machines, and dragged them into the street. They were beaten with clubs and sledgehammers. Most of the slot machines were in the casinos, and so the crowd separated into smaller groups and each made its way by car or on foot toward the greatest symbols of all, the hotel-casinos that had sustained the Batista dictatorship for all these years.

Movie star George Raft was on duty at the Capri. That night he had circulated in the casino greeting people, as he was hired to do. Accompanied by a girl who had recently won the Miss Cuba contest, he was in the casino until the New Year's Eve festivities seemed to be winding down. He gave his date the key to his suite and told her he'd be there shortly.

By the time Raft returned to his room, Miss Cuba was ready and waiting. According to the movie star:

There she was, asleep in my bed, but I noticed how she opened one eye when I came in the room. Now she's half awake and amorous. "*Feliz año nuevo,*" I said as I got between my silk sheets, alongside this fantastic girl. In the middle of this beautiful scene—suddenly—machine-gun fire! And what sounds like cannons! I phoned down to the desk. "This is Mr. Raft," I said. "What's going on down there?" The operator answered, but I could hardly hear her—there was so much commotion. Finally, I made out what she was saying. "Mr. Raft, the Revolution is here. Fidel Castro has taken over everything. He's in Havana! Batista has left the country!"

Raft bolted out of bed and left his Cuban honey. Down in the lobby, it seemed as though all hell had broken loose:

Everybody working the hotel is yelling and screaming, "Bandits are coming! Hide everything!" It was mass confusion. People running back and forth. I realize no one's in charge at this time except maybe me, since people are asking me what to do. Then I remembered the old gag about how to be a weatherman—first look out the window. Which is what I do—to see the people running, soldiers shooting in the streets. I actually saw people being killed! But along with this— there are all these civilian kids—mostly teenagers, throwing rocks and bottles through store windows and houses. Then some of them began to aim at the hotel.

A group of revolutionaries charged the Capri. According to Raft, there were more than a hundred hoodlums yelling and screaming in Spanish. They began to demolish the casino. One of the rebels sprayed the bar with machine-gun fire, shattering bottles and sending splinters of wood and shards of glass flying everywhere.

I wasn't sure what to do . . . so I got on this table—in the middle of all this mayhem—and began to shout something like "Calm down! For chrissake, calm down!" . . . The leader of these armed hoods, this girl, pointed and yelled in English, "It's George Raft, the movie star!" Now I had their attention, but I didn't really know what the hell to say. I had no script, no lines, but I managed some kind of speech about how I was an American citizen and neutral. That if they cooperated they could have food and things like that. It worked! They calmed down, did some lightweight looting, then most of them left . . . But we [still] couldn't get out of the hotel. It was dangerous to go into the streets . . . So while the shooting and all that continued in the streets, the Capri was saved, at least for the moment.

Other holdings of the Havana Mob were not so fortunate. The casino that suffered the worst vandalism was the Plaza, the very place where Lansky had dined earlier that night with his mistress and driver. The raging gun battle across the street from the hotel in Parque Central continued into the wee hours. Slot machines and gambling equipment were dragged out of the Plaza casino and into the street, where they were tossed atop smoldering bonfires. A similar scene took place at the Sans Souci, with parts of the casino doused with kerosene and torched. At the Deauville, the front windows of the hotel were shattered as the crowd tried to penetrate the casino with bad intentions. At the Sevilla Biltmore, the casino was destroyed. Amletto Battisti, the owner, immediately sought refuge at the Uruguayan embassy, where, as at most embassies in Havana, armed soldiers nervously stood guard.

The greatest indignity of all was saved for the Riviera. In an act of revolutionary audacity, campesinos brought into the city a truckload of pigs and set them loose in the lobby of the hotel and casino, squealing, tracking mud across the floors, shitting and peeing all over Lansky's pride and joy, one of the most famous mobster gambling emporiums in all the world.

For some, the rage against the casinos came as a surprise. Batista might have been hated by many, but not everyone made the link between the so-called president and the city's gambling empire. They preferred to live in a dream world, where commercial development in Havana was separate from the repression and social inequality that festered elsewhere on the island. But as the Revolution progressed, this disparity created an internal pressure that built up like the insides of an active volcano. There were many reasons to dislike Batista—his shameless coup, violent repression, censorship, corruption, obsequious relationship with gangsters and embezzlers—but in the end the hotel-casinos came to symbolize all of the above. Emotionally, the revolutionaries and ultimately the Cuban people had come to identify the Havana Mob with everything they despised about the Batista regime. And so they attacked the fruits of their rule in Cuba with a kind of savagery usually reserved for bullies, wife-beaters, and child molesters. *Death to Batista! Death to the collaborators! Death to the American gangsters!*

THERE WERE GUNS ALL OVER the room, on tabletops, on the floor, in shoulder holsters, and tucked into the waistbands of the well-fed

American mobsters and their bodyguards. Armando Jaime kept his .45-caliber pistol tucked in the small of his back, for easy access.

It was 9:00 P.M. on the evening of January 1. After a day of destruction around the city, the crowds had become more organized. There was no more shooting and looting, but the demonstrations were, if anything, more formidable. Huge waves of people marched through the streets, many carrying the black-and-red flags of the 26th of July Movement. Cars filled with armed revolutionaries motored around the city to signify that they were in charge now. Anyone associated with the Batista regime retreated behind closed doors and went into hiding. Soon there would be a mass exodus of *Batistianos* and tourists from the island.

The mobsters gathered at Joe Stassi's mansion in Miramar, surrounded by palm trees and with a view overlooking the Almendares River. Stassi was there, as were Lansky, Trafficante, Norman Rothman, and Charles White. Others also came and went. Jaime, along with other bodyguards and helpers of the Havana Mob, stood in the background as the mobsters plotted strategy.

There were mounds of cash in the living room of Stassi's estate. Money was being divided into equal denominations and distributed among the mobsters. Jaime had no idea how much cash was there, but he figured it had to be in the millions.

Joe Stassi was dressed in a short-sleeved shirt. He seemed nervous and was sweating profusely even though the temperature was, if anything, on the cool side. Lansky, as always, was calm. He had brought along a small suitcase, which he now filled with neat stacks of one-thousand-dollar bills. Jaime watched but did not even try to count the money; it was too much. Days later, while Jaime was driving his boss to the Rancho Boyeros airport to leave the country, Lansky told him that there were "several millions of dollars" in the suitcase.

Through the first week of January, the revolutionaries celebrated and the mobsters tried to figure out what was going to happen. For the time being, the casinos were closed, though some of the nightclubs stayed open. Fidel Castro had not yet arrived in the city. He was traveling in a caravan across the island, stopping in cities and small towns in a kind of victory march. Meanwhile, American government personnel, tourists, and others flooded to the airports and cruise ships in an attempt to get off the island.

Wayne S. Smith was a young U.S. consular officer who had arrived in Havana earlier that summer. Smith and others in the consulate spent the week trying to help American tourists and well-connected Cubans get off the island. "It was hectic," Smith remembered years later. "There were more people wanting to leave than there were seats on the planes and boats. Obviously, if you were in any way connected to the Batista government, there was a sense of urgency about wanting to get off the island."

Cynthia Schwartz, Lansky's eight-year-old granddaughter, was able to leave with a group that included her grandmother Teddy, Meyer's wife. Leaving the Focsa building where she had lived, Cynthia saw armed soldiers in green khaki uniforms. Many people were leaving and there was a great deal of turmoil. Cynthia had been told by her grandmother that they couldn't take much with them. "We had been warned," remembered Lansky's granddaughter. "It was time to go."

Ralph Rubio had only recently moved with his wife and kids to Playa Estes, a beautiful spot near the beach in East Havana. With great reluctance, he packed up as much as he could on short notice and got his family out of Cuba. Many other casino employees did the same, feeling that as visible benefactors of the Batista regime their lives were in danger.

Those closest to the president had been tipped off. Interior Minister Santiago Rey—described by Armando Jaime as "Batista's lapdog"—had escaped the night before with the president. Eduardo Suarez Rivas, whose connections to the mobsters in Cuba went all the way back to the days of Luciano, escaped on a private flight, though he had to leave behind $780,000 in a bank account that would be seized by the new government. The home of Lt. Col. Esteban Ventura was vandalized by an angry mob, but he was also able to escape by plane. Rolando Masferrer was not given the courtesy of being tipped off by Batista's inner circle; he was forced to hide out in Cuba for a few days before finally securing passage by boat to Miami.

Meyer Lansky did not immediately leave the island. Out of curiosity, he waited until Castro entered the city on January 8. Castro had given many interviews during his celebratory march across the island, and Lansky most likely examined El Comandante's words closely to determine what the new revolutionary government's position on the casinos would be. Fidel equivocated on the subject, preferring instead to reassure the Cuban people that the 26th of July Movement was in charge now and Cuba would be entering a new era of peace and prosperity. Lansky, Trafficante, and the other gangsters were convinced that, no matter what Castro said, he would have to allow the casinos to stay open if he hoped to keep the island's economy afloat.

When Fidel and his entourage finally arrived in Havana, the crowds along the Malecón were staggering. To the throng, Fidel announced: "The people won this war. I say that just in case some individual believes he won it, or some troops believe that they won it. Before anything, there is the people." Later, Fidel appeared at Camp Columbia, seat of the country's military power, to reassure the army that he had never considered them the enemy. It was there that a famous moment of political theater took place: as Fidel stood on a platform before another throng of celebrants, two white doves were let loose by a member of the 26th of July Movement. One of the "peace doves" fluttered about and then landed on Castro's shoulder as he spoke. The crowd was stunned by the symbolism. Fidel had gone from being a tropical Robin Hood and revolutionary leader to a full-blown Christ figure.

It did not take long for the mood to change; Fidel's new saintly persona did not embrace the concept of unconditional forgiveness. The executions began almost immediately, mostly of men who were deemed to deserve it: the worst torturers and assassins of the Batista regime, betrayers of the Revolution, or anyone who had engaged in "counterrevolutionary activity." They were put up against a wall at La Cabaña fortress and gunned down by firing squad.

The executions without trial brought criticism from the United States and other quarters. Wasn't the 26th of July Movement now engaged in the same kind of blood vengeance that typified the previous regime?

Castro not only defended "the people's right" to exact revenge on their enemies and oppressors, he became agitated whenever the question came up. Standing in the massive lobby of the Hilton Hotel, which the revolutionary leadership had commandeered as their new headquarters in Havana, Castro was asked by a reporter if he was worried that the United States might intervene. He responded by saying that if the U.S. Army attempted to invade the island, there would be "two hundred thousand dead gringos" in the streets of Cuba's cities. Castro later apologized for the intemperate remark, but the damage was done.

For anyone even remotely connected to the deposed regime, a mood of paranoia set in. Few had a better reason to be concerned than the American mobsters who operated the casinos. In a quote that was widely circulated in Cuba and the United States, when asked about the casino owners Castro declared, "We are not only disposed to deport the gangsters, but to shoot them."

Initially, the mobsters dismissed Castro's statements as mere bravado. Lansky, Trafficante, and the others wanted it known that they had not fled Cuba in fear, as was reported in some newspapers. "The gamblers took their cue from their benefactor and protector, President Fulgencio Batista, and fled the country in three chartered planes," the New York Daily News had reported. A Lansky spokesperson immediately telephoned the U.S. embassy in Havana to say that the casino boss had not run away from Cuba. He was at the Hotel Riviera, "taking care of personnel there, even though he is very sick and should be in the hospital."

Nor was Santo Trafficante inclined to flee. In a phone conversation with his attorney, he declared, "Castro is a complete nut! He's not going to be in power or office for long. Either Batista will return or someone else will replace this guy because there's no way the economy can continue without tourists, and this guy is closing all the hotels and casinos. This is a temporary storm. It'll blow over."

Castro had indeed shut down the casinos, canceled the national lottery, and declared in one of his first decrees that cleaning up "vice, corruption, and gambling" was among the highest priorities of the new government. Nonetheless, it was only a matter of weeks before Fidel relented. The Sindicato Gastronómico complained to Castro that his edict was costing their membership some six hundred jobs. Economic advisers gave Fidel the bad news that the economy would collapse unless he reopened the casinos.

As his governmental liaison with the casino industry Castro appointed Frank Sturgis, better known to the 26th of July Movement as Frank Fiorini. At thirty-four years of age, Sturgis was a U.S.-born Second World War veteran and former nightclub manager from Virginia Beach who had become a soldier of fortune. In late 1957 and on into 1958, he aided the 26th of July Movement by smuggling arms to the Sierra Maestra from the United States, Mexico, and elsewhere around South America. On July 30, 1958, Sturgis was arrested on illegal gun possession charges in the United States but was released for lack of evidence. For his role as an important arms supplier for the movement, Sturgis was named chief inspector of the gambling casinos. Sturgis knew nothing about the casino business and admitted as much to Lansky, Trafficante, and anyone else who would listen.

The casinos were reopened, but the uncertain, vengeful, paranoid environment that existed in Havana made it impossible for tourist-related businesses to flourish. Though the rebels finally moved out of the Havana Hilton (soon to be renamed the Havana Libre), the hotel was operating at less than half of its capacity. At the Riviera, operating losses for the period from December 1958 to April 1959 were listed by accountants at $750,000. Within months, all the major hotel-casinos were awash with debt.

To Castro and his new government, the failure of the casinos was a point of contention. A Cuban bank—part of the system now overseen by the new minister of finance, Che Guevara—accused the casinos of skimming revenues and assumed responsibility for counting the casino take. *Rebels in the counting rooms*! It was too much for the mobsters to bear. When the casinos continued to bleed money, the government added insult to injury by rounding up many of the casino operators and placing them under arrest.

Among the most prominent mobsters incarcerated by Castro was Santo Trafficante. The Mob boss from Tampa had consistently underestimated the wrath of the Revolution, and in the months after Batista's fall and the entrance of Fidel, he tried to operate as if nothing had changed. Years later, Santo recalled this period in testimony before the 1978 House Committee on Assassinations:

COMMITTEE CHAIRMAN: When Fidel Castro took over, how soon did he order the casinos to be closed?

TRAFFICANTE: Well, even before he reached Havana, because he didn't come down from the mountains until after Batista had left. He had a walkathon, you could call it, from the mountains to Havana. And they kept interviewing him and he kept saying that the casinos would close. Everything was in turmoil. There were people all over the streets, breaking into homes. There was complete enmity, and the only thing at that time was to try and stay alive.

CHAIRMAN: Did a time come when you were detained or imprisoned in Cuba?

TRAFFICANTE: Yes.

CHAIRMAN: Can you tell us when that was?

TRAFFICANTE: I cannot tell you the exact date . . . I got news that Cuban officials were looking for me to put me in jail because one of the things was that I was a Batista collaborator. They raided my apartment. They were looking for money. They tore up all the furniture. They used to come and get me at nighttime, take me out in the woods, trying [to get me] to tell where I had my money, this and

that, until I finally went into hiding. And they kept on . . . I mean,
these were a bunch of—most of them were fifteen, sixteen, seventeen years old. They had weapons; it was a bad time to be around.

Santo was arrested at his Vedado apartment on June 8 and incarcerated at Triscornia detention camp—the same facility where Charlie
Luciano had been held while awaiting deportation twelve years earlier.
The Havana Mob had come full circle: from being outcasts to being the
ultimate insiders to being outcasts again. The world had shifted on its
axis.

Trafficante was not alone at Triscornia. The Cuban government had
come to the conclusion that if the mobsters could not generate profits in
the casinos, then what were they good for? They were rounded up. Trafficante, Jake Lansky, Dino Cellini, and John Martino, gambling manager at the Deauville, were all incarcerated for being "undesirable aliens."
Meyer Lansky and Norman Rothman were out of the country by then,
or they too would most likely have been arrested.

Joe Stassi was in Havana. On the night Trafficante, Jake Lansky, and
the others were incarcerated, Stassi called the Capri. "Joe," he was told
by the casino manager, "don't come down here. They just pinched everybody." Stassi had been arrested numerous times since Castro took over,
but he was always let go. The fact that Santo and Jake had been collared
was enough for Stassi to realize that this time the authorities were serious. He went into hiding and eventually left Cuba in late 1959.

Stassi's son, Joe Jr., was not so lucky. Because Stassi Jr. had married
into a family strongly associated with the Batista regime, he was constantly being arrested. He was determined to stay in Havana with his
wife and newborn child and make it in the casino-gambling business, but
the new government had other ideas. He wound up spending a total of
112 days in jail before he eventually gave up and left the island in 1961.

Trafficante had it the worst of all. The day of his arrest, his attorney
Frank Ragano got a call at his Tampa office. It was Santo, informing
him that this time it looked as if the Cuban government was not going

to let him go. "It's not exactly a jail," said Trafficante of his cell at Triscornia. "It's a big house across the bay from the Malecón and I've been ordered to stay here until a decision on my case is made."

"Are you all right?" asked Ragano.

"I can hear them shooting Batista people down the road. But I'll be okay."

Trafficante's biggest concern was that he had scheduled his oldest daughter's wedding to take place at the Hilton Hotel on Father's Day, June 21. His daughter was determined to have the wedding as planned, with her father in attendance. As the date approached, it was uncertain whether the government would allow Trafficante to view his daughter's wedding vows. Somehow, Santo's wife, Josephine, was able to get a personal message through to Castro and he authorized a brief furlough for the Mob boss to participate in the ceremony.

Ragano flew in for the wedding, which Trafficante presided over wearing a white dinner jacket and black bow tie. There were about two hundred guests in the reception room at the Hilton, with more than a dozen armed soldiers standing on the perimeter of the festivities. Immediately afterward, Trafficante was taken into custody and returned to Triscornia.

During his stay in Havana, Ragano noticed the stark difference from when he was last in town. "A happy-go-lucky atmosphere had been replaced by a grim military barracks lifestyle. Bearded sentries, barely out of their teens, patrolled the streets on foot or screeched about in armored cars. I stayed at Lansky's Riviera, a virtual ghost hotel, and could hear the echoes of my footsteps on the marble floor of the vacant lobby."

By early August, Jake Lansky and Dino Cellini had been released from incarceration and had left the country. Lewis McWillie moved up the ladder from pit boss to casino manager at the Tropicana, and later at the Capri.

Trafficante was still being held. In fact, in a state of panic he called his attorney to say, "They're going to execute me! I'm on the damn list!"

He implored his attorney to get on a plane, fly to Havana, and try to negotiate for his freedom. Ragano flew back to the island and began a torturous negotiation process with bureaucrats of the revolutionary government. He was told: "In the first place, [Trafficante] was a Batista supporter and Batista made life miserable for the Cuban people, except for the rich. Furthermore, Mr. Trafficante is a drug trafficker and there is no room for drug traffickers under the new government."

Asked Ragano, "What evidence is there that he's a drug trafficker?"

"Because of the name he uses—Trafficante. One who traffics in illegal drugs—that's what the name means in Spanish."

Ragano explained that Trafficante was Santo's real name and that he had never been charged with drug trafficking in the United States or anywhere else. "If you're going to judge him by his name," continued Ragano, "then he's a saint, since Santo, in Italian, means saint."

Eventually Trafficante was brought to meet with Raúl Castro, who was now defense minister. Afterward, the former casino kingpin was released from custody. In subsequent conversations with Ragano, Santo was cryptic about how he convinced Raúl to let him go, but the lawyer was certain there had to have been a bribe. "Either Santo used his own money that he had hidden in Cuba," said Ragano, "or he had one of his wealthy Cuban friends reach someone in Castro's government." The amount Trafficante was rumored to have paid for his freedom was one hundred thousand dollars.

Many years later, Santo denied under oath that there was ever such a payment. He did admit, however, that Raúl Castro played a role in his release. "I think he helped," Trafficante told the 1978 House Committee on Assassinations. When asked if he ever encountered Raúl after he got out of prison, the Mob boss recalled:

I met Raúl Castro one time at the Hilton Hotel. I happened to be there and [a friend] told me that if you want to thank him, he is upstairs in some kind of place, some kind of room, like a public bar or something. So I went up there and he was going down the stairs. So this fellow called to [Raúl] and he stopped. I went there and thanked him. He said, "Well, just behave yourself and don't give nothing to nobody, don't let nobody shake you down or nothing like that. Just behave and you'll be all right. You don't have to leave. You don't have to go no place."

By October of 1959, Santo had left the island, never to return.

MEYER LANSKY MADE ONE last trip to Havana. He arrived in March and stayed in his favorite suite at the Hotel Nacional. Mostly he was there to see if he could deal with the Castro regime and salvage his hotel-casino business; he was also there to try to find his mistress, Carmen. His plan was to help her leave the island and resettle in Miami or New York. But the Jewish Mob boss could not locate his clandestine paramour; she had moved out of the apartment on the Prado and maybe even left Cuba. No one seemed to know for sure.

It didn't take Lansky long to realize that business prospects for the mobsters in Cuba were dead. At that time, political executions at La Cabaña fortress took place at a rate of two or three a day (there would be an estimated three hundred executions in the first two months of Castro's leadership). Meyer recognized Cuba's new government as the same sort of totalitarian regime as had forced his family out of Russia early in the century. He offered his opinions to Armando Jaime Casielles, who he was surprised to hear had decided to stay in Cuba under the Castro government. Recalled Jaime:

When he invited me to go out of the country, he said that this revolution was a communist revolution. I said that it wasn't a communist revolution, that this was *fidelista* revolution. "I am in this revolution because it is *fidelista*," I said.

Lansky had a hard time accepting that Jaime wanted to stay; he seemed to take it as a personal rejection. Meyer, after all, had for most of

his adult life been in the thrall of the bourgeoisie; he dressed and be-
haved in a manner that was supposed to connote class and breeding,
though he and his other mobster associates mostly came from the lower
rungs of society. As the top man in the Havana Mob, Lansky catered to
the well dressed and well fed. His entire existence was based on creating
the illusion that life was one big party, with champagne, music, and exquisite women all around. It was a vision shared by his most powerful
partner—President Batista. The revolutionaries—Castro and his ilk—
were something else entirely. Bearded, unwashed, intellectual, and doc-
trinaire in a way that Lansky could never understand, they were an
affront to the Havana Mob. They smelled bad, and they tracked mud
across the carpets at the Hilton, Tropicana, Riviera, and other treasures
of the Mob in Havana. It was a clash of cultures that could never be
reconciled.

"The problem," said Lansky to his driver, "is that you don't really
know who I am." They were sitting on a bench in the garden of the Hotel Nacional, surrounded by palm trees and bougainvillea.

"I know you are Meyer Lansky," said Jaime, "my boss, my teacher, and
an American citizen."

"No. I am not American. I am from a small town that has been dis-
puted over the years between Poland and Russia. I am more than anything a Jew, a Russian Jew, and I left Russia with a revolution going on
when I was twelve and a half years old, when the communist revolution
triumphed. I know a communist revolution when I see one, and this is a
communist revolution."

"Well, if it is as you say, then it is for the benefit of the people."

"Yes, but what about your source of income, your livelihood? If they
close down the casinos for good, you will be out of work."

Jaime shrugged. "You've been more than a boss to me. You've been a
mentor. But I am staying here in Cuba." The two men said their good-
byes; they never saw each other again.

Lansky remained in Havana less than a month. He flew back to Miami, then to New York, monitoring the situation in Cuba from afar.

Technically, he was still the owner of the Riviera. His Compañía Hotelera la Riviera was still the primary shareholder, though Meyer, as before, was down on paper as the "kitchen manager." The hotel's owners stayed afloat by borrowing money from various financial institutions on the island until they, like most of the other hotel-casino entities in Havana, were operating under a mountain of debt.

When, in October 1960, the *Gaceta Oficial de la República de Cuba* announced the confiscation and nationalization of the Havana Riviera, it was the final nail in the coffin. The gazette announced the same fate for other hotel-casinos, as well as 165 other U.S. enterprises, including franchises of Texaco, Goodyear, Kodak, and General Motors.

The Castro government had simply confiscated all U.S. holdings on the island: the legacy of the United Fruit Company, the foreign-owned sugar mills, the huge U.S. mining corporations, and all holdings of the Havana Mob were now the official property of the Cuban government.

It was the most audacious in a series of hostile economic maneuvers between the U.S. government and Castro that had begun the moment the 26th of July Movement took power. The new administration of John F. Kennedy pressured Castro to hold elections and continue to give U.S. companies the kinds of tax breaks they had received under previous regimes. In numerous interviews on American television, Fidel continued to promise democracy. He promised elections and denied that he had any interest in officially holding office in Cuba. Soon, however, Castro revealed himself to be the latest version of La Engañadora. Elections kept getting delayed until it was apparent there would be no elections. The tenor of government in Cuba became more and more totalitarian, as Fidel became the sole decision-maker in all matters of state. Many who had played major roles in the Revolution became disenchanted and spoke out—they were either shot or given decades-long prison sentences, or fled into exile. Eventually Fidel proclaimed proudly that he was a Marxist, and the new slogan of the government became "*Socialismo o muerte*"—socialism or death.

Ninety miles to the north, Castro's young American counterpart needed to show that he was tough; Kennedy had made it an issue during his election campaign that his opponent, Richard M. Nixon, was soft on Cuba. Consequently, the American president who had once enjoyed the gift of an orgy from the Havana Mob established an economic blockade against Cuba—an embargo that remains in effect half a century later.

Kennedy continued to flex his muscles vis-à-vis Cuba, but for Lansky, Trafficante, and others of the Havana Mob the damage was done. They were big losers in Cuba. Certainly none were as lucky as the ex-president, who, in the weeks before he fled, was able to ship suitcases full of cash from the island into private Swiss bank accounts and elsewhere. It is estimated that Batista plundered Cuba to the tune of three hundred million dollars. One indication of his bounty was that he was able to leave close to three million dollars in a safe in his office in the presidential palace. A brigade of revolutionaries found the cash and showed it off to the press. Apparently, Batista didn't need the money; perhaps he left it behind as a tip.

Even more telling was the Cuban bank account in Batista's name, the balance of which he'd been unable to transfer before it was seized. The balance—which would be used to help stabilize the new government—was a cool twenty million.

Lansky and his friends certainly could have used that kind of bread. Given the fluid nature of casino bookkeeping and the proclivity of mobsters to hide their profits, it is impossible to calculate exactly how much they lost, but the figures had to be staggering. The Hotel Riviera alone had cost fourteen million dollars to build and equip, according to official records, or eighteen million by an estimate that Lansky himself later gave to friends. Of that investment, six million was provided by the Batista government under the provisions of Hotel Law 2074. A fair estimate of the Havana Mob's personal investment in the hotel would be eight to twelve million.

According to the hotel's own records, gambling at the Riviera before Castro arrived showed a profit of three million dollars annually—and that was without factoring in the skim, which was undoubtedly in the millions. And that was only one casino in one hotel; the Hilton, Capri, Deauville, Comodoro, Sans Souci, Tropicana, Nacional, Plaza, St. John's, Presidente, and other holdings of the Havana Mob had all been highly profitable.

The money was only part of what the mobsters lost in Cuba. Men like Luciano, Lansky, Trafficante, Anastasia, and others with financial interests in Havana were among the founding fathers of organized crime in America. In many ways what they created in Cuba was the most grandiose achievement ever for the Mob—a dream come true. They had infiltrated a sovereign nation and taken control of financial institutions and the levers of power from the top to the bottom. In the underworld, it was sometimes said in an exaggerated way that mobsters "ran" a town or city; in Havana, the Mob actually did run the place. There had never been anything like it before.

The level of attainment for the mobsters guaranteed that the fall would be big—and it was. In the end, Cuba was the Mob's most costly defeat. They had positioned themselves as legitimate businessmen in Cuba. They had placed all their faith in the brute power of American capitalism. The more Castro's incipient Revolution gained traction, the more the mobsters invested, in the belief that they could drown out the will of the people through a massive infusion of capital. Rampant development would trump Revolution—or at least that was how it was supposed to go. In the end, the Cuban people made their own choice, and the mobsters were chased out of town.

Santo Trafficante never would say how much he lost in Cuba, but the word back in Tampa was that he was flat broke. The others—Rothman, the Clarks Lefty and Wilbur, Blackjack McGinty, Charley the Blade, Dino Cellini, et al.—scattered far and wide, most of them maintaining some connection to the casino-gambling business in Las Vegas, Reno, the Bahamas, or Europe. Joe Stassi was so broke that he was forced into the heroin-smuggling business, something he had never done before in his long life as a gangster. He was eventually incarcerated on narcotics charges and spent the better part of his remaining years behind bars. In 1999 Stassi did an interview with writer/filmmaker Richard Stratton in which he said, "I haven't had an erection in forty years"—placing his last protuberance right around the time he was forced out of Havana.

As for Lansky, his hopes of expanding his gambling interests to the Dominican Republic were dashed for good in 1961 when dictator Rafael Trujillo was assassinated. (Four years later, the U.S. government— fearing another Castro-like uprising in the Americas—staged a military invasion of the island.) For Meyer, it was probably a blessing in disguise. He opened a couple of big casinos in the Bahamas and in England, but they were nothing compared with what he had in Havana. Over the years, he would sometimes think back ruefully on what he had gained—and lost—in the Pearl of the Antilles. He told friends he had to leave behind seventeen million dollars in cash, which just missed being shipped out and distributed to his various partners via Switzerland. But seventeen million was nothing compared to the dream deferred— the dream of a mobster paradise in Cuba and beyond.

The Little Man had gambled everything—and come up empty. Years later, with the wisdom of age, he could have been speaking for the entire Havana Mob when he said of his time in Cuba: "I crapped out."

Along the Malecón, the winds still sweep down from the north and the ocean sometimes pounds the shoreline. Where there were once mobsters, there are now revolutionaries. *¡Viva Fidel! ¡Viva la patria! ¡Socialismo o muerte!*

EPILOGUE

ON APRIL 15, 1961, ALMOST TWO AND A HALF YEARS after Castro took power in Cuba, a small army of Cuban exiles attempted to invade the island and seize control. The event is known as the Bay of Pigs invasion, after the area in Matanzas Province where the insurgents first came ashore. The attack was a disaster for the invaders: from an army of nearly 1,500 men, 115 were killed and the rest captured and jailed in Cuba. Some were later executed for treason.

The event is remembered as a fiasco for the anti-Castro movement and also for the U.S. government, which had first hatched the plot in the waning days of the Eisenhower administration. Both Eisenhower's State Department and the CIA had come to the conclusion that the Castro government must be toppled and/or Castro assassinated. The mandate to remove Fidel became one of the worst-kept secrets in the Americas and inspired numerous schemes and plots to take him out. One of the first was allegedly put forth by Meyer Lansky, who offered a contract of one million dollars to have Castro whacked.

The man who was contacted about devising a plot to murder Fidel was Frank Sturgis, the former 26th of July gunrunner who had become Castro's minister of games of chance. The new Cuban government didn't know it yet, but Sturgis had turned against Castro and begun an under-cover dialogue with both the Havana Mob and the CIA. Many years later, in 1975, Sturgis would testify under oath before a U.S. government commission that he was approached by casino boss Charles White and offered one million dollars to help the Mob kill Castro. Meyer Lansky was the financier, said White. Sturgis was ready and willing, but he could not get "the go-ahead from his contacts in the American embassy."

Of his involvement in a plot to assassinate Castro, Lansky told his biographers:

> A number of people came to me with a number of ideas and of course
> I had my own suggestions to make. It was no secret that I was well
> known in Havana and did have influence. But I don't think I should
> go into the details of what was said.

Lansky's one-million-dollar offer remained on the table throughout 1959, an open invitation to anyone with the means or inclination to take out Fidel.

By the onset of the new decade, Lansky was gone from Cuba, but the efforts to remove the Bearded One from power were just getting started. The Mob's reasons for wanting Castro dead merged with the desires of the Cuban exile community and the U.S. government. The April 1961 failure at the Bay of Pigs was not an impediment; in fact, following that disaster the newly elected Kennedy administration inaugurated a clandestine initiative known as the Cuba Project, which included as a subset the CIA-sponsored Operation Mongoose.

With Operation Mongoose, the CIA took over the role of eliminating Castro. To achieve their goal, they turned to a group that was identified in confidential CIA memos as "the gambling syndicate"—their name for the Havana Mob.

The CIA-Mob partnership that grew out of the Cuba Project and Operation Mongoose has been chronicled in many books and documentaries. In the mid-1970s the American public was shocked when it was revealed for the first time—through a series of congressional hearings—that the CIA had reached out to the Mob in an effort to assassinate Castro. Many law-abiding citizens found it hard to believe that the U.S. government would work hand-in-hand with the forces of organized crime. Of course, this was nothing new. U.S. naval intelligence had made similar overtures to Lucky Luciano and Meyer Lansky back in the early 1940s at the onset of the Second World War. Luciano's top secret partnership with the U.S. Navy made it possible for him to get out of prison and laid the foundation for the entire era of the Mob in Cuba.

It is hardly surprising that the person who became the CIA's point man in the Castro assassination plots was none other than Santo Trafficante. Of all the mobsters who lost big in Cuba, few had suffered as ignominiously as the man with the green eyes. Along with losing all his financial holdings to Castro's communist government, Trafficante had languished for months at Triscornia detention center, been on an execution list, and was most likely forced to pay a substantial cash bribe to see another day. Trafficante had the motive, the CIA had the will: it was a marriage of convenience.

The intermediaries were fellow mafiosi Johnny Roselli and Sam Giancana, both investors and occasional guests of the Havana Mob in the 1950s. The CIA first contacted Roselli, who led them to Trafficante— much as Lansky had once led the U.S. Navy to Luciano. A series of meetings took place, the most important of which occurred at the Fontainebleau Hotel in Miami Beach. There, a CIA station chief passed along lethal pills that were to be used to poison Fidel. Contaminated cigars and exploding seashells were also discussed as possible assassination methods. A payment of approximately twenty-five thousand dollars cash was also delivered to the mobsters, down payment on the full fee of a hundred and fifty thousand.

Castro, of course, was never assassinated. The Cuban missile crisis of October 1962 led to the disbanding of Kennedy's "Get Castro" squad.

Both Lansky and Trafficante also gave up on any direct involvement in plots to murder the Cuban leader, but efforts to bring about Castro's removal continued to metastasize. Many people associated with the Havana Mob were involved. Casino veterans Norman Rothman, Dino Cellini, John Martino, and Lewis McWillie all took part in arms-smuggling schemes, assassination plots, and counterrevolutionary coup attempts. Some gave their lives for the cause.

Rolando Masferrer had survived some of the most violent periods in Cuban history. Ever since the late 1940s, when he emerged at the University of Havana as a formidable student gangster and enemy of Fidel Castro, he cast a dark cloud over Cuban politics. His role as the leader of Los Tigres and associate of the Havana Mob continued well after the fall of Batista. In 1960, before the Bay of Pigs invasion, Masferrer was involved in a plan to invade Cuba from the Dominican Republic. The plot also involved Chiri Mendoza, former owner of the Havana Hilton, and ex-senator Eduardo Suarez Rivas. It was to be partially financed by Fulgencio Batista, who anted up two million dollars of his own money—possibly cash left over from the casino skim. The plan was aborted when four members of the plot were arrested in Cuba.

Masferrer devoted the remainder of his life to Castro assassination plots and dreams of recapturing all that had been lost in Havana. He arranged gun shipments with former Havana casino mobsters Rothman, Martino, and McWillie. He cofounded a paramilitary group known as Alpha 66, which devoted itself to carrying out bombings, assassinations, and other acts of terror in support of the burgeoning anti-Castro underground in Miami. As he had in Cuba, he founded a newspaper, *Libertad*, which was devoted to attacking his enemies. Masferrer was an effective writer and, according to those who knew him, an intelligent man, but he never shook off the stench of *gangsterismo*.

In October 1975, in an editorial in his newspaper, Masferrer advocated bombings as a legitimate political tool. One week later—on Halloween—he was blown to pieces in his car, which had been wired with C-4 explosives. Masferrer died as he had lived—violently. FBI investigators in Miami had no shortage of suspects but no cooperating witnesses. The murder of Rolando Masferrer remains unsolved to this day.

Compared with the former leader of Los Tigres, other prominent players in this drama passed through their later years in one piece. Their fates were as follows:

Fulgencio Batista—After fleeing Cuba, Batista lived for a time in the Dominican Republic but soon moved on to Portugal. On the island of Madeira, off the coast of Lisbon, the former major general lived at a resort hotel under constant armed guard. A British journalist reporting for the *Miami Herald* was allowed to interview Batista in late 1959. On the third floor of the hotel, the journalist was led into a small anteroom. "The door was draped with a Cuban flag," he wrote. "Two tough-looking men looked up as I entered. One, who was chewing gum, went back to studying the South American football results. The other, puffing on a seven-inch Havana cigar, strolled to the doorway, leaned against it, and eyed me suspiciously. Both looked as if they had read too many Raymond Chandler novels."

Batista lived in constant fear of an assassin's bullet. "Yes," said the ex-president, "Castro's men may seek me out even here. But if I thought about that all my life I would never be at peace . . . Castro is a sick man. How do you say it? He is sick in the head."

In the years that followed, Batista wrote a number of self-justifying books that even supporters acknowledged were filled with half-truths and lies. He denied having absconded with tens of millions of dollars, comparing reports of his wealth to the Arabian folk tale *One Thousand and One Nights*. "Every time a new story, every time a new figure," he said of those who variously placed his personal fortune at thirty-nine million, eighty million, one hundred million dollars, and above.

Batista lived his golden years in Spain. He had no known contact with his former associates in the Havana Mob. On August 6, 1973— fourteen years after being chased out of Cuba—he died of a heart attack in the town of Mirabel. He was seventy-two years old.

Santo Trafficante—By early 1963, Trafficante had given up his attempts to assassinate Castro and turned his attention to JFK. Kennedy had angered two powerful underworld constituencies—the anti-Castro Cuban exiles, who felt he had betrayed them by withholding crucial air support during the Bay of Pigs invasion, and the Mob, who were on the receiving end of a relentless judicial assault engineered by the president's brother Attorney General Robert Kennedy. Trafficante was uniquely positioned as an influential player in both of these worlds: the anti-Castro underground and the Mob. According to many subsequent histories of the JFK assassination, Trafficante played a key role in the conspiracy to kill the president, along with New Orleans mafioso Carlos Marcello, who had also been an attendee at the Hotel Nacional Mob conference back in December 1946.

In his memoir, attorney Frank Ragano contends that Trafficante virtually confessed his role in the Kennedy assassination. "We shouldn't have killed Giovanni (John); we should have killed Bobby," said Trafficante to Ragano many years after the fact.

Trafficante's relationship with his attorney ebbed and flowed. Ragano's son, Chris—who was born the year the mobsters were chased out of Cuba—got to know Trafficante in his later years. Santo had never fathered a son and he became obsessed with Chris as an adolescent and young man, lavishing him with attention and expensive gifts. The attention made Chris uncomfortable. Eventually Trafficante tried to endear himself to Nancy, Frank Ragano's wife, telling her that she should leave Frank, she and Chris could start a new life with him. Mrs. Ragano declined.

In the mid-1980s, Trafficante became embroiled in two major criminal trials, one stemming from his attempts to bilk millions from the health and pension fund of a labor union, the other for racketeering and conspiracy. Trafficante sought the services of Ragano, with whom he had had a falling out years earlier. Ragano declined to represent his former client, but Trafficante insisted that Ragano take the case or something might happen to his son. According to Chris Ragano: "My father never told me about [the blackmail]. I learned about it from my mother after he passed away."

Of Trafficante, Chris remembered, "You could never forget his eyes. You looked into his eyes and you knew you were looking straight into the face of evil."

Santo Trafficante died of heart failure on March 17, 1987, at the age of seventy-two. He was buried alongside his father at the L'Unione Sicilione Cemetery in Tampa.

Meyer Lansky—The final two decades of Lansky's life brought a level of notoriety that outstripped anything from his pre-Cuba years. In 1969 the *Wall Street Journal* profiled the sixty-eight-year-old mobster, noting, "of the group that in the 1930s formed the giant conglomerate that is organized crime today, Lansky alone survives and wields power." His worth was estimated to be near three hundred million dollars, an epic number that elevated his status in business circles around the world. Then came *The Godfather Part II*. For the first time in his life, Lansky became a cultural icon—a Jewish wizard who was given most of the credit for the corporatization of organized crime in America.

To Lansky, notoriety was a whore to be kept at arm's length. It would prove to be his undoing. The federal government designated Lansky as Gangster Number One. He was beleaguered with tax charges, a bogus narcotics charge for carrying prescription drugs through an airport, and threats of deportation. The FBI placed a bug in the Las Vegas office of Eddie Levinson, Meyer's former casino manager at the Hotel Riviera in Havana. Agents followed Lansky and his wife virtually everywhere they went—including on overseas trips. The feds had little in the way of evidence and they never did mount a serious case against Lansky. The idea was to prosecute the mobster legend outside the courtroom, to make his life miserable.

Scrutinized by prosecutors and under constant surveillance by federal agents, Lansky sought an escape. He became a modern-day version of the Wandering Jew. He was not allowed to live in England or the Dominican Republic because of his criminal record. The ultimate insult came when he tried to settle in Israel under the Law of Return. He was rejected by an Israeli high court and sent packing. Lansky spent his later years in Miami Beach. He was often seen walking his dog along Collins Avenue, usually with two FBI agents watching from a sedan somewhere nearby. On January 15, 1983, after a protracted battle with cancer, Lansky died in a Miami hospital with Teddy at his side. He was eighty-two years old.

Stories of Lansky's wealth persisted. In his waning years, the aging Mob boss told associates and his lawyers that the losses in Cuba had been enormous. In response they would often give him a wry smile. Lansky was the wiliest of all mobsters—"the smartest boy in the Combination." How could the great Lansky, former boss of the Havana Mob, die with nothing to show for himself?

Teddy Lansky's granddaughter Cynthia (Schwartz) Duncan was part of a group of family members who gathered for the reading of the Lansky will. In the chambers of a Dade County judge, the family members' jaws dropped when they were told that Meyer Lansky's entire estate amounted to fifty-seven thousand dollars cash. Remembered Lansky's granddaughter, "Everybody at the reading knew there was no three hundred million, but we thought there would be at least five million . . . Afterwards, we all went to a nearby bar and had a strong drink."

In the following years, exhaustive efforts were made to track down Lansky's millions, but the money simply did not exist. Lansky meant what he said—he and the Mob had lost a fortune in Havana.

Fidel Castro—The era of the Havana Mob lived on in the person of El Comandante. Chasing the mobsters out of Cuba became a source of great pride within Castro's revolutionary government and to the Cuban people. As the years passed, evoking the era became a kind of party trick; slipping a reference to the time of "*la mafia en la habana*" into a speech or official statement was good politics. As recently as December 22, 2005, when the head of the U.S. diplomatic mission in Havana criticized the Cuban government for its checkered human rights record,

Castro publicly denounced the man as "a little gangster." In a speech to the Cuban National Assembly, Castro said he did not know who was worse, the man who currently held the job or the one who came before, whom he called "the previous gangster."

The term was not used lightly. By referring to U.S. government representatives in Cuba as gangsters, Castro was deliberately evoking memories of the Havana Mob. To the Cuban government, American officials on the island came from a long line of gangsters going back to the days when the hoodlums, corporate businessmen, diplomats, and politicians all fed at the same trough.

As various U.S. presidencies came and went, Castro's greatest achievement was that he remained in power and aboveground. He survived invasion attempts, internal coup attempts, and assassination plots too numerous to mention. He partnered with the Soviet Union, became a pawn in the Cold War, and attempted to export the Revolution. He was crippled by the perennial financial crisis back home. The U.S. embargo against Cuba succeeded in isolating Castro, but it also turned him into a hero among the world's downtrodden.

In Miami, those who fled the island after Castro took over formed into a powerful voting bloc. Fidel routinely referred to these exiles as "the Miami mafia." American politicians—both Democrats and Republicans—pandered to this group, especially during presidential elections. The most hard-line of the exiles skillfully brokered and safeguarded the U.S. government's myopic policies on Cuba. In July 2006, when Castro mysteriously disappeared from public view and turned over the reins of government to his brother Raúl, the Miami Cubans danced in the streets. The celebration evoked the early days of 1959, when Cubans reveled over the fall of Batista. The following months revealed that Castro had undergone a series of major gastrointestinal operations and was slowly recuperating. His revival did little to dampen the spirits of the exiles, who continued to dream of the day when they would return to Cuba and reclaim all they had lost in the Pearl of the Antilles.

In August 2007 the rumors persisted: the dictator is dying. He is dead. Our moment of triumph is near.

As of this writing, Fidel has survived them all.

THE PASSAGE OF TIME does not heal all wounds. Like a cheap jail-house tattoo, the loss of Cuba left an indelible mark on members of the Havana Mob. For Lansky, Trafficante, and many others, there was the humiliation of defeat and there were also the financial consequences that shaped their lives for decades to come. Some became immersed in the never-ending quest to assassinate the Bearded One and reestablish themselves as major players in a post-Castro Havana. In time, the CIA would replace the mafia as the spiritual enemy of the Revolution.

Organized crime as concocted by Luciano, Lansky, Costello, and company never fully recovered. The Mob survived into the new century, but it was not the same enterprise that had dared to infiltrate a foreign country and establish an offshore empire—which it then intended to use as a base for further criminal explorations. By the dawn of the twenty-first century, the Mob no longer had the reach or influence to shape world events; it no longer represented the kind of vision advocated by people like Luciano, Lansky, Stassi, and Trafficante. Those men dreamed of a vast criminal state with the power to elect presidents and shape the global economy. In their day, there was seemingly no limit to what the Mob could achieve. That was what Cuba had come to represent: political control, fabulous corruption, and the ability to put on a hell of a show. Owning the place and then losing it to the will of the Cuban people was cruel justice.

The dream was that Havana would be a party that never ended. Instead, it turned out to be one of the great hangovers of all time.

ACKNOWLEDGMENTS

As most authors know, the birthing of a book is a strange adventure, with many epiphanies, setbacks, surprises, and long stretches of isolation. This book in particular was for me a leap of faith. From the start, I knew there was a dramatic story to be told. Whether I could unearth the facts and bring that story to life in all its many facets was a daunting challenge. The task took on an added sense of urgency given that the generation of people who lived this story—both Americans and Cubans—are entering the final chapters of their lives. Some of the people I interviewed passed away before the book had been published. I was driven by the knowledge that this was perhaps a last chance to tell the story utilizing sources who actually lived through the events, as opposed to relying solely on archival research or previously published material.

To make it happen, I depended on the kindness of strangers. I could not have made the necessary connections or discovered key sources without the generosity of many people in Havana, Miami, New York, Tampa, Los Angeles, Washington, D.C., and elsewhere. Most people, I believe, cooperated with me for one simple reason: they wanted to see this story finally told, free of cant, propaganda, and misinterpretation. I hope I have fulfilled that expectation.

First and foremost, I would like to thank Rosa Lowinger, an esteemed author in her own right, who led me to many important sources in Havana and Miami. Rosa also welcomed me into her Los Angeles home, which is a miniarchive of books, magazines, art, and erotica relating to Cuba in the 1950s.

I made numerous trips to Havana, each one filled with work-related revelations and tempting diversions. Raquel Carrera and her family were my initial contacts, and I thank them for making me feel at home. Aquiles Jacas was an essential *socio* and assistant who helped me in ways too numerous to mention. I am also grateful to Aquiles's father, Manuel Jacas Tornés, a distinguished veteran of the Cuban Revolution, doctor, and writer, who took an interest in my project. Special thanks also to documentary filmmaker Estela Bravo, journalist Marta Rojas, musicologist Helio Orovio, historian Estela Rivas at the Hotel Nacional, and Chef Gilberto Smith Duquesne, president of the Federación de Asociaciones Culinarias de la República de Cuba, who shared his personal memories of Meyer Lansky. Special thanks to Comandante William Gálvez Rodríguez for agreeing to talk with me. And I am also indebted to the indomitable José "Pepe" Rodríguez and his five cats and three dogs.

For logistical and other kinds of support in Havana I would like to thank the lovely Yuri Moreno and her band at Café Sophia on Calle 23 in Vedado; José Alberto Figueroa; Orlando Brolla; Casa de Moisés Quiñones and Zoraya Lobet on Calle 21 in Vedado; the staff at the Biblioteca Nacional José Martí; and Deysi, secretary at the Conjunto Folklórico Nacional.

In Miami, I was aided greatly by Cynthia (Schwartz) Duncan, granddaughter of Meyer Lansky, who shared her thoughts and memories to the point where we thought Lansky's spirit was present with us in the house. She is now the proprietor of a website devoted to the preservation of memorabilia related to her late grandfather. Cuban-born Bernardo Benes is a legend in Miami for his efforts to improve relations between the governments of Cuba and the United States; his willingness to help me out was a great inspiration. Benes led me to Max Lesnick, a veteran of Cuba's political wars of the 1940s and '50s and now the voice of Radio Miami. I also must thank Judge Bernard Frank, another legendary Miami figure whose knowledge of South Florida mobsters, entertainers, cops, and politicians goes all the way back to the early 1940s. Special thanks also to Delio Valdes, Gordon Winslow of the Cuban Information Archive, Ed Sherry of the South Florida Research Group, and Zoe Blanco Roca, archivist at the University of Miami Library (Cuban Heritage Collection).

Another important stop along the Cuban exile circuit was Tampa. Special thanks to Scott M. Deitche, who has written two books on the history of organized crime in Tampa. Scott shared his knowledge, time, and files with me. Also thanks to Chris Ragano, the son of Frank Ragano, longtime attorney for mafioso Santo Trafficante. Among other things, Chris showed me 8-millimeter home movies made by his father in Havana in the 1950s. I also want to thank Henry Beltran, Cookie Garcia, and, most especially, Ralph Rubio, who was an excellent source on all matters relating to Lansky's Riviera hotel and casino.

In Washington, D.C., my thanks go out to Fred Romanski and Bill Davis of the U.S. National Archive, at both the Washington, D.C., and College Park, Maryland, facilities. Also thanks to Wayne S. Smith, a former diplomat at the U.S. consulate in Havana and a knowledgeable source on Cuba past and present.

Some of my most important work took place at my home base in New York City. First, special thanks to Franklin Díaz, who served as translator of documents, Spanish instructor, and all-round *compañero*. I owe a special debt of gratitude to Richard Stratton and Marc Levin, who screened for me their impressive documentary on mobster Joe Stassi while it was still a work in progress. They also led me to Joe Stassi Jr., to whom I am grateful for agreeing to be interviewed. Special thanks to the El Taller Spanish Workshop in upper Manhattan, where I was able to improve my Spanish language skills. The director of this fine school is Bernardo Palombo, and one *maestra* and friend to whom I owe special thanks is Libia Gil.

Thanks also go out to Carl Ginsberg, who took a keen interest in this project; culinary author Beverly Cox, who shared with me knowledge and contacts from her travels in Havana; author Michele Wucker, who offered support at an early stage; Howie Sann, who shared memories of his father, the great crime writer Paul Sann, and his experiences trying to write a book with Meyer Lansky; Vicki Gold Levi, who helped with photos; and author Ned Sublette, whose knowledge of Cuba is vast and willingness to share a beer or two at the Wakamba Cocktail Lounge was an important respite from the computer screen. I also want to offer thanks to the following friends and family for support along the way: my sister Margi English, Joel Millman, Yuri Osorio, in Mexico, Ashley Davis, Ryan Schafer, and, as always, the incandescent Sandra Maria English.

Finally, there are the people who ushered this book through the publication process. My agents Nat Sobel and Judith Weber were enthusiastic from the start and went above and beyond the call of duty in their efforts to help out in any way they could. Adia Wright at SobelWeber Associates also deserves special mention for her contributions.

Judith Regan, formerly of Regan Books, was one of the first people to recognize the value in doing this book, and she deserves credit for getting the ball rolling. Cal Morgan guided the book from Regan Books to William Morrow with a steady hand. And I was lucky for the second time in my career to have the services of Anna Bliss as an editor; her attention to detail and feel for the full dimensions of this story helped to turn a rough manuscript into the finished product you now hold in your hands.

Attendees of the Havana Conference at the Hotel Nacional, week of December 22, 1946:

Anthony Accardo, age forty
Joe Adonis, forty-four
Albert Anastasia, forty-three
Joseph Bonnano, forty-one
Anthony Carfano, forty-seven
Frank Costello, fifty-five
Moe Dalitz, forty-eight
Charles Fischetti, forty-five
Rocco Fischetti, forty-three
Vito Genovese, forty-nine
Phil Kastel, fifty-two
Meyer Lansky, forty-four
Thomas Lucchese, forty-six
Charles "Lucky" Luciano, forty-nine
Stephano Magaddino, fifty-five
Giuseppe Magliocco, forty-eight

Carlos Marcello, thirty-six
Mike Miranda, fifty
Willie Moretti, fifty-two
Giuseppe Profaci, fifty
Joseph "Doc" Stacher, forty-six
Santo Trafficante, thirty-three

NOTES

INTRODUCTION

xiv **U.S. business investments in Cuba**: *Gente de la Semana*, American Edition, January 5, 1958.

xvi **The mambo craze:** There are many good books on the history and cultural significance of Afro-Cuban music, the best being *Cuba and Its Music* by Ned Sublette. Of Dámaso Pérez Prado, Sublette writes: "His unique sense of showmanship, combined with a taste for nervous, aggressive dissonance . . . branded the mambo for all time."

xviii **"It would not be accurate to say":** Author interview, William Gálvez Rodríguez, Havana, March 8, 2007. As well as being a seventy-five-year-old veteran of the revolutionary 26th of July Movement, Gálvez is a writer, historian, and author of many books, including the novel *Otro jinete apocalíptico*, a fictional musing on the mobster infiltration of Cuba from the 1920s to 1959.

xix **Salón de la Historia, Hotel Nacional:** The room is not only a veritable museum in honor of the mobsters and celebrities who have stayed at the hotel, it's also a bar and lounge open to the public.

1. FEELING LUCKY

3 **Pearl of the Antilles:** The term can be traced to the earliest expeditions of Christopher Columbus, who first landed on the island in 1492. Though the

term originally described Cuba, it has since been appropriated by other Caribbean islands, including Haiti, Martinique, and Antigua.

3   **Luciano's arrival in Havana:** There are differing accounts of the route Luciano took to enter Havana. In Gosch and Hammer, *The Last Testament of Lucky Luciano,* the mobster is described as having left Naples via freighter for Caracas and then flown to Mexico City before continuing on to Cuba. In Cirules, *The Mafia in Havana* (I), the author states that Luciano traveled from Italy directly to Rio de Janeiro, though he does not footnote his source. Cirules was the first to establish—presumably through Cuban visa records—that Luciano landed at the airport at Camagüey. A Federal Bureau of Narcotics (FBN) record group (RG) 170, confidential report, March 21, 1947, states that Luciano entered Cuba via Caracas.

4   **Luciano and Lansky at Grand Hotel:** Cirules (I), p. 36.

5   **"Lucky Luciano Walks":** *New York Daily Mirror,* March 12, 1946.

6   **Luciano's arrival at Hotel Nacional:** Author interview, Estela Rivas (official historian of Hotel Nacional), Havana, August 15 and 17, 2006; Gosch and Hammer, p. 305; Cirules (I), pp. 36–37.

6   **"When I got to the room":** Gosch and Hammer, p. 305.

7   **Luciano's mansion in Miramar:** FBN RG-170, confidential report, March 21, 1947; Gosch and Hammer, pp. 306–7; Cirules (I), p. 37. Luciano's mansion and the Miramar neighborhood were viewed by the author on March 5, 2007.

7   **"I took it easy":** Gosch and Hammer, p. 306.

7   **Senator Eduardo Suarez Rivas:** The Cuban senator being at Luciano's going-away party aboard the SS *Laura Keene* is cited in FBN RG-170, confidential report, March 21, 1947; Suarez Rivas's narcotics connections are cited in the same FBN report and are further detailed in Eduardo Saenz Rovner's *La conexión cubano.*

7   **Luciano–Suarez Rivas relationship:** Gosh and Hammer, p. 306; Luciano at the pool with the senator and his family, and also Luciano's attempts to import a car as a gift for Suarez Rivas's wife are in FBN RG-170, confidential report, March 21, 1947.

8   **"Charlie liked pussy":** Author interview, confidential source, 2006.

8   **Luciano and prostitutes, Hotel Nacional:** Author interview, Estela Rivas; Cirules (I), p. 36; Lucky's taste for whores is also cited in Feder and Joesten, *The Luciano Story*; Powell, *Lucky Luciano*; Lacey, *Little Man*; and Summers, *Sinatra: The Life.*

9   **Bernard Frank anecdote:** Author interview, Bernard Frank, Miami, May 15, 2006. Ninety-three-year-old Bernard Frank is known to many in Miami as "the Judge" because he served for five years as a municipal court judge. Before that, he was a criminal defense attorney and also the house lawyer for the Fontainebleau Hotel in Miami Beach.

10   **Prohibition era**: There are many fine books on the interplay between Prohibition and organized crime, including John Kobler's *Ardent Spirits* and Herbert Asbury's *The Great Illusion*, and countless mobster biographies and histories that summarize the era.

11   **Early Mob forays in Cuba:** William Gálvez Rodríguez, *Otro jinete apocalíptico*, pp. 26–120; Messick, *Syndicate in the Sun* (I), p. 5; Fox, *Blood and Power*, p. 33; Deitche, *Cigar City Mafia* (I), pp. 11–14; Lacey, p. 231; Eisenberg, Dan, and Landau, *Meyer Lansky*, p. 12; Gosch and Hammer, p. 300.

11   **Al Capone in Havana**: *Havana Post*, March 25, 1930; Schwartz, *Pleasure Island*, p. 70; Capone's stay at the Sevilla Biltmore Hotel is today memorialized with framed photos in the lobby of the hotel.

12   **Cuba in the 1920s:** Thomas, *Cuba: The Pursuit of Freedom*, pp. 328–56; Sublette, pp. 347–78; Phillips, *Cuba: Island of Paradox*, pp. 1–34; Argote-Freyre, *Fulgencio Batista*, pp. 23–52.

12   **Dance of the Millions:** As author Rosa Lowinger notes in *Tropicana Nights*, p. 27, the term comes from the title of a 1916 musical by Cubans Jorge Anckermann and Federico Villoch.

12   **"Beautiful young whores everywhere":** Stratton, "The Man Who Killed Dutch Schultz," in GQ, September 2001.

12   **Creation of "pleasure trust":** Schwartz, pp. 56–62.

13   **Mayor Jimmy Walker in Havana**: *Havana Post*, January 29 and 31, 1927; Schwartz, pp. 56–57. For a biographical profile of Jimmy Walker with an emphasis on his relationship to the underworld, see T. J. English, *Paddy Whacked*, pp. 127, 205–8.

14   **Castellammarese War and early New York Mob history:** Bonanno, *A Man of Honor*, pp. 42–126; Peterson, *The Mob*, pp. 363–66; Fox, pp. 113–15; Gosch and Hammer, p. 129; Raab, *Five Families*, p. 89; Lacey, pp. 62–65; Maas, *The Valachi Papers*, pp. 57–75.

14   **Luciano taken for a ride:** Gosch and Hammer, pp. 117–19; Peterson, pp. 245–46; Feder and Joesten, p. 29; Powell, p. 18.

14   **Origin of Luciano nickname:** Feder and Joesten, p. 19; Powell, p. 11; Gosch and Hammer, p. 119.

15   **Night of the Sicilian Vespers:** There is some difference of opinion about whether the Night of the Sicilian Vespers is underworld fact or legend. The theory was first put forth in early Mob histories and reinforced by Joe Valachi during his congressional testimony of 1963. More recent Mob histories suggest that there is little evidence to back up the claim of multiple murders carried out across the United States.

15   **Lansky approach to Fulgencio Batista:** Lacey, pp. 108–9; Eisenberg, Dan, and Landau, pp. 173–74; Gosch and Hammer, pp. 233–34.

15   **Luciano meeting at Waldorf Towers:** Gosch and Hammer, p. 169.

16   **"It was like droppin' a bomb":** Gosch and Hammer, p. 169.

16   **"Lansky and I flew to Havana":** Eisenberg, Dan, and Landau, pp. 173–74.

17   **Cuban tourism revenues:** Schwartz, p. 117.

17   ***Thomas Dewey* v *Luciano* prostitution trial:** Powell, entire book; Feder and Joesten, pp. 145–71; Peterson, pp. 201–15; Fox, pp. 89–99; Gosch and Hammer, pp. 193–223.

19   **Lansky early forays in casino gambling:** Lacey, pp. 97–111; Messick, *Lansky* (II), pp. 129–31.

19   **Molaska Corporation:** Messick (II), pp. 67–69; Eisenberg, Dan, and Landau, pp. 159–69; Lacey, pp. 79–81.

19   **Cuba National and National Cuba Hotel Corporation:** Russo, *Supermob*, pp. 94–95.

20   **Lansky in Havana, 1937–40:** Lacey, pp. 108–9; Messick (II), p. 98; Eisenberg, Dan, and Landau, pp. 173–74; Schwartz, pp. 100–1.

21   **Luciano-Lansky alliance with navy intelligence (Operation Underworld):** Campbell, *The Luciano Project*, entire book; Gosch and Hammer, pp. 263–77; Lacey, pp. 116–27.

23   **"He had obviously been well briefed":** Eisenberg, Dan, and Landau, p. 189.

24   **"[Charlie] could hardly believe his eyes":** Ibid., p. 191.

26   **Party on the SS *Laura Keene*:** This incident is another that has entered the annals of Mob lore but the veracity of which is debatable. In Gosch and Hammer's *The Last Testament of Lucky Luciano* and other books, the gathering is presented as a lavish party, complete with music and prostitutes. Lacey debunks the story in *Little Man*, citing lack of documentary evidence. All sources agree that there was some kind of gathering; the question is how large and how festive. Attendance by Senator Eduardo Suarez Rivas is cited in FBN RG-170, confidential report, March 3, 1947.

26   **Vito Genovese at 1946 Mob conference in Havana:** Gosch and Hammer, pp. 308–14; Cirules (I), p. 39; Eisenberg, Dan, and Landau, pp. 232–34.

27   **"It was a couple days before":** Gosch and Hammer, p. 308.

28   **"Let me tell you what I think":** Ibid., p. 310.

28   **"That guinea son of a bitch!":** Ibid., pp. 310–11.

2. THE MOB'S PLAYGROUND

30   ***The Godfather Part II:*** (Paramount, 1974) Director: Francis Ford Coppola; screenplay: Mario Puzo and Francis Ford Coppola; "*El padrino y las relaciones entre la tiranía de Batista y la mafia*," *Granma,* October 21, 1975.

31   **Labor strike at Hotel Nacional:** "*En Cuba*," *Bohemia* magazine, December 8, 1946; Cirules, *The Mafia in Havana* (I), pp. 37–38.

32   **Mob conference at the Hotel Nacional:** Author interview, Estela Rivas, Havana, August 15 and 17, 2006. The conference is described in detail in Gosch and Hammer, *The Last Testament of Lucky Luciano*; Eisenberg, Dan, and Landau, *Meyer Lansky*; and Cirules (I). Additional details, as well as references to those in attendance, are included in Bonnano, *A Man of Honor*; Summers, *Sinatra* (I); Demaris, *The Last Mafioso*; and Deitche, *The Silent Don*.

33   **Banquet menu:** Cirules (I), p. 38.

34   **"I must have talked for an hour":** Gosch and Hammer, pp. 314–15.

35   **Having Ben Siegel murdered:** The circumstances surrounding the hit on Siegel are explored in detail by Gosch and Hammer, and Eisenberg, Dan, and Landau, along with Jennings, *We Only Kill Each Other*, and many other Mob histories. All present some version of Siegel being killed because of cost overruns on the Flamingo Hotel in Las Vegas. However, in the documentary film *O.G.: Joe Stassi, Original Gangster*, mafioso Joe Stassi contends that Siegel was not whacked by the Mob. Stassi says he investigated the murder on behalf of his friend Meyer Lansky and came to the conclusion that Siegel had been murdered by the brother of Virginia Hill. The motive, according to Stassi, was that Siegel had physically abused Hill, angering her brother. Stassi convincingly makes the point that the hit—which was done from a distance, with a high-powered scope rifle—did not follow the Mafia's modus operandi. If the Mob had wanted Siegel killed, the thinking goes, they would have done it in their usual manner: up close and personal, with the act being carried out by someone close to Bugsy.

39   **Lansky divorce:** Lacey, pp. 136–38; author interview, Bernard Frank, Miami, April 15, 2006.

39   **Sinatra at Mob conference:** The most convincing account of Sinatra's appearance at the conference comes from Jorge Miguel Jorge Fernandez, a former employee at the Nacional. Jorge Jorge is interviewed in two documentaries: *La Habana en los años 50s* and *La mafia en La Habana* (both produced by Marakka 2000). See also Summers (I), pp. 129–40; Gosch and Hammer, p. 312, 318; Kelley, *His Way*, pp. 134–35.

39   **Sinatra-Mob partnership:** Summers and Swan's *Sinatra* (I) deals extensively with Sinatra's Mob connections; also Kelley; Mortimer, "Frank Sinatra Confidential," *New American Mercury*, August 1951; Gosch and Hammer, pp. 312, 318, 375.

41   **Sinatra-Luciano orgy at Hotel Nacional:** FBN RG-170, general file, box no. 2; Summers and Swan (I), pp. 130–39; also Sondern, *Brotherhood of Evil*. Sondern describes the incident in detail, leaving out Sinatra's name; the details coincide exactly with the FBN confidential report, which does name Sinatra.

41   **Robert Ruark:** Summers and Swan (I), pp. 13–34.

43   **FBN surveillance of Luciano:** Details drawn from FBN RG-170, along with various confidential reports filed by Agent J. Ray Olivera and others, 1946–47.

44   **Luciano connections in Cuba:** Luciano's relationship to Indalecio Pertierra, Paco Prío, and other powerful people in Cuba is detailed in FBN RG-170; also Cirules (I), pp. 32–53; Fuentes, "Mafia in Cuba," *Cuba International,* August 1979; Saenz Rovner, *La conexión cubana,* pp. 19–20.

44   **Assassination attempt on Luciano:** FBN RG-170, confidential report, March 21, 1947.

45   **Clemente "Sungo" Carreras:** After having been both a player and coach for the Almendares Blues (later the Tigers) in the Cuban League, Sungo Carreras played three years with the New York Cubans in the U.S. Negro League. It was while playing second base for the New York team that he learned to speak English. Sungo's boss with the New York Cubans was owner Alejandro "Alex" Pompez, a Cuban-born former numbers runner who, in the early 1930s, operated a lucrative policy bank in Harlem. Pompez's numbers business was eventually taken over by mobster Dutch Schultz; it is likely Pompez had dealings with both Luciano and Lansky during his time as a New York racketeer.
        I am indebted to Roberto González Echevarría, author of *The Pride of Havana: A History of Cuban Baseball,* for information on Pompez: author interview, Roberto González Echevarría, May 21, 2007.

46   **Deportation of Luciano:** FBN RG-170, plus various confidential reports; "U.S. Ends Narcotics Sales to Cuba While Luciano Is Resident There," *New York Times,* February 22, 1947; Gosch and Hammer, pp. 26–32; Feder and Joesten, *The Luciano Story,* pp. 119–25; Cirules (I), pp. 47–53; Eisenberg, Dan, and Landau, pp. 231–39.

48   **"[Triscornia] is the Cuban version":** Gosch and Hammer, pp. 325–26.

3. EL JUDIO MARAVILLOSO
(THE MARVELOUS JEW)

51   **Lansky early biography:** Lacey, *Little Man,* is the most scholarly biography of Lansky. Eisenberg, Dan, and Landau, *Meyer Lansky: Mogul of the Mob,* has value in that it quotes directly from Lansky and Doc Stacher. Messick, *Lansky* (II), was the first biography of Lansky and is unfortunately sensationalized and almost entirely without notated sources. Also with biographical detail on Meyer: Cohen, *Tough Jews;* Russo, *Supermob;* Fried, *The Rise and Fall of the Jewish Gangster in America.*

53   **Lansky-Rothstein relationship:** Lacey, pp. 48–61; Eisenberg, Dan, and Landau, pp. 78–95; Katcher, *The Big Bankroll,* p. 352; Cohen, pp. 46–67.

55   "Like me he was a gambler": Eisenberg, Dan, and Landau, p. 103.

56   Lansky, South Florida casinos: Lacey, pp. 97–111; Messick, *Syndicate in the Sun* (I), pp. 12–25, 31–33.

57   "He seemed restless": Author interview, Bernard Frank, Miami, May 3, 2006.

58   Thelma "Teddy" Schwartz: Author interview, Cynthia (Schwartz) Duncan (granddaughter of Teddy), Miami, May 4, 2006; Lacey, pp. 160–61.

58   Meyer-Teddy wedding: Lacey, pp. 164–65; author interview, Cynthia (Schwartz) Duncan; Cohen, "The Lost Journals of Meyer Lansky," *Ocean Drive*, January 2005.

58   "Batista, who was a senator": Cohen, "Lost Journals."

59   Fulgencio Batista, early biography: Much detail was drawn from Argote-Freyre, *Fulgencio Batista*. Also Chester, *A Sergeant Named Batista*; Thomas, *Cuba: The Pursuit of Freedom*; Phillips, *Cuba: Island of Paradox*.

60   Batista in power: In addition to the books mentioned above, see Gellman, *Roosevelt and Batista*, entire book; Whitney, "The Architect of the Cuban State," *Journal of Latin American Studies*, 2000.

66   Batista in exile: Chester, pp. 85–89.

66   Batista stealing oranges: Chester, pp. 88–89.

66   "Batista was coming back": *Time*, April 12, 1948.

67   "He showed up": Author interview, confidential source, 2006.

68   Rise of *gangsterismo*: Author interview, Max Lesnick, Miami, May 4, 2006; author interview, Bernardo Benes, Miami, May 3, 2006; Thomas, pp. 466–68; Bardach, *Cuba Confidential*, pp. 239–40; Geyer, *Guerilla Prince*, pp. 145–55; Szulc, *Fidel*, pp. 143–47; Farber, "The Political Gangster," in Chomsky and Smorkaloff, *The Cuba Reader*, pp. 287–89.

69   Castro bursts on the scene: Author interview, Max Lesnick; Szulc, pp. 148–67; Geyer, pp. 112–25; Bonachea and Valdes, eds., *Revolutionary Struggle 1947–1958*, pp. 129–36; Thomas, pp. 523–34; Sublette, *Cuba and Its Music*, p. 514.

71   Batista-Castro meeting at Kuquine: Szulc, pp. 212–13; Thomas, p. 529.

4.   WELL-CHARACTERED PEOPLE

73   Lansky FBN interview: FBN, Strike Force 18, confidential report, Agent John H. Hanly, June 28, 1949; Lacey, *Little Man*, pp. 173–76; Eisenberg, Dan, and Landau, *Meyer Lansky*, pp. 243–44, though the investigative agency is misidentified as the FBI.

74   "I used to recognize them": Eisenberg, Dan, and Landau, p. 113.

74   Lansky meeting with Luciano: Gosch and Hammer, *The Last Testament of*

Lucky Luciano, pp. 347–48; Messick, *Lansky* (II), pp. 168–69. Note: Luciano describes the meetings with Lansky in detail as having taken place in Sicily; Lansky, in his Kefauver testimony, says the meetings took place in Rome.

75   **Lansky makes headlines:** Johnson, "Lansky Sails in Luxury for Italy," *New York Sun,* June 28, 1949.

76   **Kefauver hearings:** Moore, *The Kefauver Committee and the Politics of Crime, 1950–1952,* entire book; Kefauver, *Crime in America,* entire book; Kefauver Committee Transcripts, U.S. National Archives, Washington, D.C.; Bernstein, *The Greatest Menace,* pp. 35–51; Eisenberg, Dan, and Landau, pp. 303–8; Lacey, pp. 190–207; Peterson, *The Mob,* pp. 263–77; Wolf and DiMona, *Frank Costello,* pp. 181–99.

78   **Jake Lansky incident:** Messick, *Syndicate in the Sun* (I), pp. 161–62.

79   **Sheriff Walter Clark testimony:** Kefauver Transcripts, U.S. National Archive, Washington, D.C.

81   **Lansky testimony:** Ibid.

85   **Lansky-Kefauver backroom exchange:** Lacey, pp. 197–98; Eisenberg, Dan, and Landau, pp. 306.

87   **Batista to run for president:** Thomas, *Cuba: The Pursuit of Freedom,* p. 477; Chester, *A Sergeant Named Batista,* pp. 125–27.

88   **Batista, coup d'état:** Author interview, Max Lesnick, Miami, May 4, 2006; author interview, Bernardo Benes, Miami, May 3, 2006; Bonachea and Valdes, *Revolutionary Struggle,* pp. 31–34, 145–48; Thomas, pp. 493–500; Szulc, *Fidel,* pp. 213–35; Geyer, *Guerilla Prince,* pp. 125–29; Phillips, *Cuba: Island of Paradox,* p. 244; Ameringer, "The Auténtico Party," *Hispanic American Historical Review* (1985); "Batista at Work," *Newsweek,* March 24, 1952.

89   **"The military junta have acted":** Thomas, p. 498.

90   *Time* **magazine cover:** March 14, 1952.

90   **"[Batista's military coup]":** Bonachea and Valdes, pp. 147–49.

92   **"We would have won the case":** Ibid.

92   **Lansky pleads guilty:** Lacey, pp. 208–9.

5. RAZZLE-DAZZLE

93   **Dana C. Smith incident:** Lacey, *Little Man,* pp. 224–25; Lowinger and Fox, *Tropicana Nights,* pp. 229–30; Schwartz, *Pleasure Island,* pp. 143–44; Velie, "Suckers in Paradise," *Saturday Evening Post,* March 28, 1953.

95   **"El Razzle-dazzle, mala publicidad":** Ramírez-Rosell, *Diario de la Marina,* April 12, 1953.

95   **Lansky return to Havana:** Schwartz, pp. 145–47; Lacey, pp. 226–29; Lowinger and Fox, p. 151; Eisenberg, Dan, and Landau, *Meyer Lansky,* pp. 253–55; Velie,

"Suckers"; Reiss, "The Batista–Lansky Alliance," *Cigar Aficionado*, May/June 2001.

96   **Muscles Martin and. Sammy Mannarino:** Velie, "Suckers"; Schwartz, pp. 144–45.

99   **Casino dealers deported:** "Cuba Ousts 13 US Gamblers," *New York Times*, March 31, 1953.

99   **Lansky pleads guilty and does time:** Lacey, pp. 208–9.

99   **"I liked him":** Ibid., p. 209.

100   **Amadeo Barletta Barletta:** "Caribbean Tyranny," *Time*, May 13, 27, 1935; "Lese Majeste," *Time*, May 27, 1935; Cirules, *The Mafia in Havana* (I), pp. 16–17, 89–98; Cirules, *La vida secreta de Meyer Lansky en La Habana* (II), pp. 13, 24–25, 39; Gálvez, *Otro jinete apocalíptico*, pp. 27–41; U.S. Treasury Department memo, Dade County, Organized Crime Bureau file #1–139, September 1961; Pardon, "Amadeo Barletta," *Granma*, March 30, 1971.

101   **Amletto Battisti y Lora:** FBN RG-170, Box 154, #0660 (foreign countries), no date; FBN RG-170, confidential memo, Agent Olivera, March 21, 1947; Cirules (I), pp. 16, 33–34; Cirules (II), pp. 117, 155–56; official history, Hotel Sevilla, http://www.hotelsevillacuba.com, November 1, 1995.

102   **Rolando Masferrer and Los Tigres:** Author interview, Max Lesnick, Miami, May 4, 2006; Thomas, *Cuba: The Pursuit of Freedom*, pp. 466–68, 578; Szulc, *Fidel*, pp. 143–44; Phillips, *Cuba: Island of Paradox*, pp. 318–19; Cirules (I), p. 54; Farber, "The Political Gangster," in Chomsky and Smorkaloff, *The Cuba Reader*, p. 289.

103   **"Yes, chico":** Thomas, p. 488.

104   **Lansky kibitzing poolside at Nacional:** Lacey, p. 232.

105   **"That dirty Jew bastard":** Ragano and Raab, *Mob Lawyer*, p. 43.

105   **Tampa–Ybor City history:** Deitche, *Cigar City Mafia* (I), entire book; Deitche, *The Silent Don* (II), pp. 23–25, 28–30; Ragano and Raab, pp. 11–13, 15–19.

105   **Martí in Tampa:** Martí, *Selected Writings*, introduction.

106   **Bolita in Tampa:** Ragano and Raab, pp. 9–13, 15–19, 21–25, 64–68; Deitche (I), pp. 19–85; Deitche (II), pp. 21–24, 34–36, 50–63.

106   **Santo Trafficante Sr. and Cuba:** Ragano and Raab, pp. 15–18, 23–25, 78–79; Deitche (I), pp. 66–68; Deitche (II), pp. 24–26, 35–36; Saenz Rovner, *La conexión cubano*, pp. 21–23; Cirules (I), pp. 16–17, 33; Gálvez, pp. 124, 148.

106   **Origins of Aerovías Q:** FBN RG-170, confidential memo, March 21, 1947; Cirules (I), p. 33; Gálvez, p. 94.

107   **Charlie Wall background:** Deitche (I), pp. 15–18; Atkins, *White Shadow*. Atkins's fictionalized account of Charlie Wall and the Tampa–Ybor City underworld of the 1950s is well researched and evocative.

107   **Wall testimony at Kefauver hearings:** Kefauver Committee Transcripts, U.S. National Archives, Washington, D.C.

108   **Attempted assassination of Trafficante:** Ragano and Raab, p. 18; Deitche (I), p. 91; Deitche (II), p. 46.

109   **Charlie Wall murder:** Ragano and Raab, pp. 16–18; Deitche (I), pp. 68–70; Atkins, pp. 7–13. Atkins's entire novel deals with the residue of the Wall murder.

109   **Trafficante takes over Sans Souci:** U.S. Treasury Department memo, Dade County, OCB file #1–139, September 1961; Findings of the House Select Committee on Assassinations, Vol. 5, testimony of Santo Trafficante, September 28, 1978; Lowinger and Fox, pp. 180–84; Deitche (I), pp. 99–100; Havermann, "Mobsters Move in on Troubled Havana," *Life,* March 10, 1958.

109   **International Amusements Corporation:** Deitche (I), p. 99; Deitche (II), p. 69.

110   **"I've got a wonderful wife":** Ragano and Raab, p. 40.

110   **Law of Public Order (Legislative Decree 997):** Mencia, *The Fertile Prison,* p. 76. Effects of Batista-era censorship also discussed in Thomas, *Cuba: The Pursuit of Freedom;* Sublette, *Cuba and Its Music;* Phillips. Additional insights from author interview, Delio Valdes, Miami, October 17, 2006. Valdes was a journalist in Havana in the 1950s.

110   **Martí centennial:** *Diario de la Marina,* extensive coverage, January 28, 1953.

110   **Batista appropriation of Martí:** Thomas, pp. 387, 392, 435; Argote-Freyre, *Fulgencio Batista,* p. 340.

111   **Moncada attack:** The circumstances surrounding the attack on the Moncada army barracks are detailed in Franqui, *Diary of the Cuban Revolution;* Castro, *La historia me absolverá;* Castro, *My Early Years;* Thomas; Szulc; Geyer, *Guerilla Prince;* Phillips; Bonachea and Valdez, *Revolutionary Struggle 1947–1958;* Chester, *A Sergeant Named Batista;* DePalma, *The Man Who Invented Fidel;* Mencia.

6. THE GHOST OF JOSÉ MARTÍ

115   **Castro early biography:** Castro, *My Early Years* (II), entire book; Szulc, *Fidel,* pp. 83–221; Geyer, *Guerilla Prince,* pp. 5–35; Thomas, *Cuba: The Pursuit of Freedom,* pp. 516–20; Phillips, *Cuba: Island of Paradox,* pp. 292–93; *American Experience: Fidel Castro,* PBS documentary.

115   **"All of the circumstances":** Franqui, *Diary of the Cuban Revolution,* pp. 1, 2.

117   **"I spent most of my time":** Ibid., p. 2.

117   **"We were playing ball one day":** Ibid., p. 4.

118   **Castro university years:** Castro (II), pp. 83–109; author interview, Max Les-

nick, Miami, May 4, 2006; Szulc, pp. 177–90; Geyer, pp. 145, 61; Thomas, pp. 522–28; Bonachea and Valdes, *Revolutionary Struggle 1947–1958*, pp. 129–36; *American Experience: Fidel Castro.*

118   **U.S. intelligence report:** Matthews, *The Cuban Story*, p. 140.

118   **Cayo Confites conspiracy:** Castro's involvement in the planned invasion of the Dominican Republic and overthrow of the dictator Rafael Trujillo is detailed in Szulc, pp. 157–60; Geyer, pp. 136–38; Thomas, pp. 475–76, 525.

119   **"I did not let myself be arrested":** Szulc, p. 160.

119   **"I could guarantee his life":** Ibid.

120   **Fidel and Bogotazo:** Castro (II), pp. 110–48; Szulc, pp. 183–88; Geyer, pp. 154–63; Thomas, pp. 526–28; Sublette, *Cuba and Its Music*, pp. 521–23. In *American Spy*, former CIA agent E. Howard Hunt gives the official U.S. intelligence community view that Castro was involved in an all-out insurrection in Bogotá, though there has never been much evidence to support that view.

121   **Moncada prosecutions:** The show trial of Fidel Castro and others involved in the Moncada attack is dealt with in detail in Castro, *La historia me absolverá* (I), which came about because of the trial; Szulc, pp. 306–22; Geyer, pp. 198–205; Thomas, pp. 547–50; Phillips, pp. 267–69; Bonachea and Valdes, pp. 161–220; Mencia, *The Fertile Prison*, pp. 12–86.

126   **Lansky plans for Hotel Nacional:** Author interview, Estela Rivas (official historian of Hotel Nacional), Havana, August 15 and 17, 2006.

127   **International Hotels, Inc. (subsidiary of Pan Am):** Lacey, *Little Man*, p. 229.

127   **Wilbur Clark:** Russo, *Supermob*, p. 205; Lacey, pp. 232, 256; Schwartz, *Pleasure Island*, pp. 153, 156, 163; Lowinger and Fox, *Tropicana Nights*, pp. 180, 256; Cirules, *The Mafia in Havana* (I), p. 152 (though he is misidentified as Walter and Willberg); Cirules, *La vida secreta de Meyer Lansky en La Habana* (II). Clark's significance to the Havana Mob is noted throughout. Clark was so famous in professional gambling circles that his face and name appeared on the gambling chips at the Nacional.

127   **Clark testimony:** Kefauver Committee Transcripts, U.S. National Archives, Washington, D.C.

128   **Jake Lansky at Casino de Nacional:** Author interview, Estela Rivas; author interview, Armando Jaime Casielles, January 24 and 26, 2007; Lacey, pp. 229–30, 232, 253–63; Cirules (I), p. 120; Cirules (II), pp. 112, 125–27; Lowinger and Fox, pp. 88, 329; Eisenberg, Dan, and Landau, *Meyer Lansky*, pp. 255, 257–58; Havermann, "Mobsters Move in on Troubled Havana," *Life*, March 10, 1958.

128   **"[He] had a way of chewing":** Lacey, p. 52.

128   **Jake denying credit to Batista official:** "Lansky 'El Cejudo' no hace caso," *Granma*, August 29, 1988; Cirules (I), p. 113; author interview, Armando Jaime Casielles.

129   **Lansky refusing handshake:** Cirules (I), pp. 113–14; author interview, Armando Jaime Casielles.

129   **Banco de Créditos e Inversiones:** FBN RG-170, confidential memo, undated; Cirules (I), p. 16.

130   **Banco Atlántico:** Cirules (I), pp. 17, 89–95.

130   **"Upon carrying out the inspection":** Ibid., p. 90.

131   **Formation of BANDES:** Schwartz, pp. 154–58, 163; Cirules (I), pp. 107–110; Fuentes, "Mafia in Cuba," *Cuba International,* August 1979; Pardon, "Amadeo Barletta," *Granma,* March 30, 1971.

132   **Ley Hotelera (Hotel Law) 2074:** Lowinger and Fox, pp. 255–56; Lacey, pp. 231, 257; Schwartz, p. 152; Reiss, "The Batista-Lansky Alliance," *Cigar Aficionado,* May/June 2001; Lahey, "Gamblers Find Cuban Paradise," *Washington Post,* January 9, 1958; Havermann, "Mobsters."

132   **Batista graft:** Thomas, pp. 428, 461, 687, 722; Lowinger and Fox, pp. 256, 310–13; Cirules (I), pp. 127–47; Phillips, p. 283; Bardach, *Cuba Confidential,* pp. 244–45; Dorschner and Fabricio, *The Winds of December,* pp. 63–64, 66, 455.

132   **Hotel-casino boom:** Schwartz, pp. 147–63; Cirules (I), pp. 148–55; Batista, *The Growth and Decline of the Cuban Republic,* pp. 89–93.

133   **Death of Trafficante Sr:** "S. Trafficante, Underworld Family Head, Dies of Cancer," *Tampa Tribune,* August 12, 1954; "Over 500 See Trafficante Buried in Costly Coffin," *Tampa Tribune,* August 13, 1954; "$36,000 Estate Reported Left by S. Trafficante, Sr," *Tampa Tribune,* September 20, 1954; author interview, Scott M. Deitche, Tampa, July 7, 2006; Ragano and Raab, *Mob Lawyer,* p. 18; Deitche, *Cigar City Mafia,* pp. 89–90; Deitche, *The Silent Don* (II), pp. 55–56.

135   **Frank Ragano introduction to Trafficante:** Author interview, Chris Ragano, Tampa, July 18, 2006, and March 1, 2007; Ragano and Raab, pp. 5–25.

135   **"A different species":** Ragano and Raab, p. 12.

136   **"These people always pay cash":** Ragano and Raab, p. 13.

136   **Trafficante bolita trial:** "Deputies Pick Up Trafficante and Bodyguard 'On sight,'" *Tampa Tribune,* January 23, 1954; author interview, Scott M. Deitche, Deitche (II), pp. 47–53; Ragano and Raab, pp. 9–27.

7. GAMBLER'S PARADISE

140   **Ambassador Gardner urges elections:** Thomas, *Cuba: The Pursuit of Freedom,* pp. 629–30; Smith, *The Fourth Floor,* p. 20.

140   **"The Revolution cannot mean":** Franqui, *Diary of the Cuban Revolution,* p. 80.

140   **Economic upswing in Cuba:** Thomas, pp. 562–63; Schwartz, *Pleasure Island,*

pp. 147–54; "Havana's New Tunnel," "New Public Works Projects of the Batista Regime," and "Havana Crossroads of the World," *Gente de la Semana*, January 5, 1958.

141   **Ex-president Carlos Prío indicted:** Jacobs, "Prío Spent Most of His Career Fighting Cuban Dictatorships," *Miami Herald*, August 6, 1977; Schwartz, p. 149.

141   **Killing of Orlando León Lemus (El Colorado):** Thomas, pp. 481, 483; Schwartz, p. 150; Bonachea and Valdez, *Revolutionary Struggle 1947–1958*, p. 298.

142   **La liga contra el cáncer:** Lowinger and Fox, *Tropicana Nights*, p. 263.

142   **Tropicana background:** Much detail comes from Lowinger and Fox. Also, "Tropicana Is Most Beautiful" and "Guide to After-Dark Havana," *Cabaret Yearbook* 1, winter Resort No. (1956); "Cabaret Guide to Havana," *Cabaret Quarterly* 5, special Resort No. (1956); Mallin, "Havana Night Life," unpublished article, 1956–57; Sargent, "Cuba's Tin Pan Alley," *Life*, October 6, 1947.

143   **Martín Fox early biography:** Lowinger and Fox, entire book.

146   **Roderico "Rodney" Neyra early biography:** Lowinger and Fox, pp. 116–26; Cruz, *Celia: My Life*, p. 42; Sublette, *Cuba and Its Music*, pp. 476, 574, 576; "Tropicana Is Most Beautiful."

147   **"The scene was a deserted city":** Roberts, *Havana*, pp. 227–28. Roberts does not identify the Shanghai Theater by name but leaves little doubt when he writes: "On the edge of the Chinese quarter a theater of this sort [strip club] has existed for a long time. I shall not name it, but identification by a visitor is not difficult since it advertises discreetly and every bartender and taxi driver knows about it."

148   *Sun Sun Babae:* Mallin, "Cuba's Carefree Cabaret," *Cabaret*, April 1957; Lowinger and Fox, pp. 124–26, 189–92. There is also a detailed description of *Sun Sun Babae* in Cruz, pp. 42–44.

150   **Trafficante gift to Ofelia Fox:** Lowinger and Fox, pp. 22, 182–83.

151   **Trafficante befriends M. Fox:** Lowinger and Fox, pp. 180–84, 206; Deitche, *The Silent Don* (II), p. 67.

152   **Trafficante gift to Felipe Dulzaides:** Author interview, confidential source, 2006.

152   **Rothman-Chaviano relationship:** Lowinger and Fox, pp. 205, 207; Cirules, *The Mafia in Havana* (I), p. 122. Rothman and Chaviano were eventually married in Havana and had a son. Chaviano was renowned for her exotic beauty and, according to Cirules, also known for having affairs when Rothman was out of town.

153   **Travel to Havana (Pan Am, Delta, West Indies Fruit and Steamship Co.):** Schwartz, pp. 66–67, 107–8, 123; Lowinger and Fox, pp. 256, 337.

153   **Reopening of Oriental Park Racetrack:** Phillips, "Cuba Is Betting on Her New Gambling Casinos," *New York Times*, November 6, 1955; Schwartz, pp. 123–24.

154   **Beating of Joseph Lease:** *Havana Post*, December 11, 1955; Schwartz, p. 124.

154   **Eartha Kitt at Club Parisién:** Author interview, Estela Rivas, Havana, August 15 and 17, 2006; Acosta, *Cubano Be, Cubano Bop*, p. 124; Lacey, *Little Man*, p. 229; Thomas, p. 570. Curiously, Kitt makes no mention of her famous Havana appearance in her autobiography, *Confessions of a Sex Kitten*.

155   **Nat King Cole in Havana:** Epstein, *Nat King Cole*, p. 153. Epstein describes Cole being disturbed by the sight of conspicuously armed soldiers at his show; Lowinger and Fox, pp. 278–81, 296–300; Schwartz, p. 125; Depestre Catoney, "Nat 'King' Cole at Tropicana," http://www.CubaNow.com, undated.

155   **Interracial entertainment scene in Havana:** There is a difference of opinion about how interracial the scene truly was. According to Delio Valdes, a journalist in Havana at the time, who is of African descent, there were racist policies at some of the large high-end clubs, especially at the Sans Souci and Montmartre. Dark-skinned Afro-Cubans were not welcome—not even as hired help. "Tropicana was not as bad as the others," said Valdes. "The smaller clubs is where most of the race mixing took place." Author interview, Delio Valdes, Miami, October 17, 2006.

156   **Castro amnesty:** The circumstances surrounding Castro's release from prison are drawn from Szulc, *Fidel*; Geyer, *Guerilla Prince*; Thomas; Bonachea and Valdes; Franqui; Mencia, *The Fertile Prison*; *American Experience: Fidel Castro*, PBS documentary.

156   **"As we leave the prison":** Szulc, p. 346.

157   **Relatives' Amnesty Committee:** Ibid., pp. 343–45.

8.   ARRIVEDERCI, ROMA

161   **Fidel Castro did not dance:** Neither did his fellow comandante, Ernesto "Che" Guevara.

161   **"What do our homeland's pain":** Mencia, *The Fertile Prison*, p. 59.

161   **Castro out of prison:** Castro's first months in Havana after being released from prison are chronicled in: Szulc, *Fidel*; Geyer, *Guerilla Prince*; Franqui, *Diary of the Cuban Revolution*; Thomas, *Cuba: The Pursuit of Freedom*.

162   **"I am leaving Cuba":** Franqui, p. 90; Szulc, p. 346.

163   **Castro in Mexico City:** For a detailed presentation of Castro's time in exile, see Szulc; Geyer; Franqui; Anderson, *Che Guevara*; Casteñeda, *Compañero*.

164   **Lansky payments to Tendelera:** Lacey, *Little Man*, p. 247; Cirules, *The Mafia in Havana* (I), p. 112.

164   **Control of slot machines by Roberto Fernández Miranda:** Lowinger and Fox, *Tropicana Nights*, pp. 253–54, 316–17; Schwartz, *Pleasure Island*, p. 184; Havermann, "Mobsters Move in on Troubled Havana," *Life*, March 10, 1958; Reiss, "The Batista–Lansky Alliance," *Cigar Aficionado*, May/June 2001.

165   **"Martí once said":** Mencia, p. 116.

165   **Castro fund-raising in United States:** Szulc, pp. 369–72; Bonachea and Valdes, *Revolutionary Struggle 1947–1958*, pp. 281–87; Mormino, "Rallying for the Revolution," *Tampa Tribune*, February 19, 2006.

165   **"I can inform you":** Bonachea and Valdes, p. 285.

165   **Castro in Tampa/Ybor City:** Mormino, "Rallying"; author interview, Cookie Garcia, Tampa, July 7, 2006; author interview, Henry Beltran, Tampa, July 7, 2006. Cuban immigrant Henry Beltran remembers attending Castro's speech at the Italian Club in Ybor City in 1955. He even gave five dollars to the cause, of which he now says, "Fidel Castro owes me five dollars."

166   **Assassination of Blanco Rico:** Author interview, Delio Valdes, Miami, October 17, 2006. Valdes provided the detail that Mario Lanza was singing "*Arrivederci, Roma*" when the shooting began. Also Bonachea and Valdes, pp. 85–86; Franqui, p. 176; Cirules (I), p. 120; Thomas, pp. 582–83.

166   **Death of General Rafael Salas Cañizares:** Thomas, p. 583.

167   **"I do not know who carried out":** Bonachea and Valdes, p. 86.

168   **Creation of La Compañía Hotelera Riviera de Cuba (the Riviera Hotel Company of Cuba):** Lacey, pp. 233–37; Messick, *Lansky* (II), pp. 194–98; Cirules (I), pp. 148–55; Schwartz, pp. 156–59.

169   **Creation of dealer training schools:** The school in the Ambar Motors building on La Rampa and Calle Infanta was one of numerous schools opened by the Havana Mob over a two-year period. Author interview, Armando Jaime Casielles, January 24 and 26, 2007; author interview, Ralph Rubio, September 16 and October 24, 2006; Lowinger and Fox, p. 181.

169   **Rafael "Ralph" Rubio:** Rubio worked closely with Lansky over a two-year period as a dealer and eventually credit manager at the Hotel Riviera casino. Author interview, Ralph Rubio.

170   **Evaristo "Tito" Rubio background and murder:** Author interview, Ralph Rubio; Deitche, *Cigar City Mafia* (I), pp. 30–34.

170   **The Cellini brothers (Dino and Eddie):** Messick, *Syndicate in the Sun* (I), pp. 196, 217, 229, 233, 237.

171   **"I got along well with Eddie":** Author interview, Ralph Rubio.

171   **"We had more students":** Ibid.

171   **"The Cubans made excellent dealers":** Ibid.

171   **"It was hard work":** Eisenberg, Dan, and Landau, *Meyer Lansky*, p. 255.

172   **"It was a beautiful bracelet":** Author interview, Ralph Rubio.

173   **Granma expedition:** Like the attack on the Moncada army barracks, the

landing of the *Granma* is one of the seminal events of the Cuban Revolution and is dealt with at length in Guevara, *Reminiscences of the Cuban Revolutionary War*; Franqui; Thomas; Szulc; Geyer; Anderson; Casteñeda; Matthews, *The Cuban Story*; Phillips, *Cuba: Island of Paradox.*

174   **"The entire boat took on":** Guevara, p. 40.

174   **"I wish I could fly":** Szulc, p. 408.

175   **"This wasn't a landing":** Szulc, p. 409; Anderson, p. 367.

175   **Slaughter at Alegría de Pío:** Guevara, pp. 42–55; Szulc, pp. 14–21; Thomas, pp. 589–90; Casteñeda, pp. 99–101.

176   **"Fidel tried in vain":** Guevara, p. 44.

176   **"I immediately began to wonder":** Ibid., pp. 44–45.

177   **Fidel and Raúl Castro announced dead:** Szulc, pp. 411–12; Thomas, pp. 591–94.

178   **"Terrorism flared":** Phillips, pp. 291–92.

179   **Bombings coincide with firing of cannon:** Author interview, Delio Valdes.

179   **Ad in *Diario de la Marina*:** The ads also appeared in U.S. newspapers, especially in New York and Miami.

179   **Beny Moré (El Bárbaro del Ritmo):** Author interview, Helio Orovio, Havana, August 24, 2006; Orovio, *Diccionario de la musica cubano*, pp. 111–12; Acosta, *Cubano Be, Cubano Bop*, pp. 114–28; 138–40; Sublette, *Cuba and Its Music*, pp. 547–49, 560–61.

179   **Moré at Tropicana:** Lowinger and Fox, pp. 257–59.

180   **New Year's bombing at Tropicana:** Ibid., pp. 286–87, 291–93, 304–5.

182   **Murder of four teenagers:** Thomas, pp. 600–1; Phillips, "Cuba Suppresses Youths," *New York Times*, March 14, 1957; *American Experience: Fidel Castro*, PBS documentary.

9.   A BULLET FOR *EL PRESIDENTE*

183   **Lansky at the Malecón:** Author interview, Armando Jamie Casielles, January 24 and 26, 2007; also Armando Jaime interview, *La mafia en La Habana*, documentary.

183   **Armando Jaime background:** Author interview, Armando Jamie Casielles; Cirules, *La vida secreta de Meyer Lansky en La Habana* (II), pp. 23–31; González, "El mafioso que se fue con Castro," *Crónica*, October 23, 2005; "Yo fui guardaespalda de Meyer Lansky," *Juventude Rebelde*, February 6, 2005.

183   **Lansky and Jaime meet in Vegas:** Author interview, Armando Jaime Casielles; Cirules (II), pp. 66–74; "Yo fui guardaespalda"; *La mafia en La Habana.*

185   **Lansky and Jaime at Hotel Nacional:** Author interview, Armando Jaime Casielles; *La mafia en La Habana.*

187   **Joe Stassi background:** Stratton, "The Man Who Killed Dutch Schultz," GQ, September 2001; O.G.: *Joe Stassi, Original Gangster,* documentary.

187   **Stassi house and meetings:** Author interview, Armando Jaime Casielles; Cirules, *The Mafia in Havana* (I), p. 115; Cirules (II), pp. 93, 174–75. Location of Stassi house was viewed by the author in March 2007. The house had been converted into a precinct for the Cuban military police, and it was forbidden by law to take photos.

187   **Thomas "Blackjack" McGinty:** U.S. Treasury Department memo, Dade County, OCB file #1–139, September 1961; Lacey, *Little Man,* pp. 99, 232, 256; Fox, *Blood and Power,* p. 89; Havermann, "Mobsters Move into Troubled Havana," *Life,* October 10, 1958.

188   **Charles "the Blade" Tourine, alias Charles White:** Cirules (II), pp. 156–60; *Time,* January 20, 1958; Havermann, "Mobsters"; U.S. Treasury Department memo, Dade County OCB file #1–139, September 1961.

188   **Nicholas di Costanza:** Cirules (I), pp. 119–20; Cirules (II), pp. 111, 145, 202; U.S. Treasury Department memo, Dade County, OCB file #1–139, September 1961.

188   **Joe Silesi, alias Joe Rivers:** U.S. Treasury Department memo, Dade County OCB file #1–139, September 1961; Cirules (I), p. 121; Lacey, pp. 244–45; "Anastasia Case Holds '150 Angles,'" *New York Herald Tribune,* October 30, 1957; Havermann, "Mobsters"; Lahey, "Gamblers Find Cuba Paradise," *Washington Post,* January 9, 1958.

188   **William Bischoff, alias Lefty Clark:** Lowinger and Fox, *Tropicana Nights,* pp. 22, 181, 280, 286, 323, 326; Schwartz, *Pleasure Island,* pp. 139, 142, 177; Lahey, "Gamblers"; U.S. Treasury Department memo, Dade County, OCB file #1–139, September 1961.

189   **Eddie Levinson:** Lacey, pp. 232, 234; Eisenberg, Dan, and Landau, *Meyer Lansky,* pp. 256, 274, 279; Cirules (I), p. 153; U.S. Treasury Department memo, Dade County, OCB file #1–139, September 1961.

188   **Concerns about Anastasia:** Author interview, Armando Jaime Casielles; author interview, Ralph Rubio, September 16, 2006, and October 24, 2006; Cirules (I), pp. 7, 14–15; Cirules (II), pp. 103–23; "¿Operan en nuestros cabarets gangsters americanos?" *Confidencial de Cuba,* January/February 1958.

190   **Albert Anastasia biography:** Anastasia's personal and criminal history and role in the formation of the U.S. underworld are covered in Turkus and Feder, *Murder Inc.*; Bernstein, *The Greatest Menace*; Bonnano, *A Man of Honor*; Fox, *Blood and Power*; Maas, *The Valachi Papers*; Nelli, *The Business of Crime*; Peterson, *The Mob*; Raab, *Five Families.* Also details drawn from FBI File #62–98011, Subject: Albert Anastasia (FOIA).

193   **Murder of Abe "Kid Twist" Reles:** Covered in all the above Mob histories, most notably *Murder Inc.*

193   **Anastasia testimony:** Kefauver Committee Transcripts, U.S. National Archives, Washington, D.C.

194,   **Mangano, Ferri, and Macri murders:** All are detailed extensively in FBI file
196   #62–98011, Subject: Albert Anastasia (FOIA).

195   **Arnold Schuster murder:** An interesting and detailed examination of this murder can be found in Willie Sutton with Edward Linn, *Where the Money Was* (New York: Broadway Books, 1976, reprint edition), chapter entitled "Who Killed Arnold Schuster?," pp. 319–35.

197   **Sit-down at Warwick Hotel:** Meskill, "Yen for Cuba Cash Doomed Anastasia," *New York World-Telegram and Sun*, January 9, 1958; Ragano and Raab, *Mob Lawyer*, pp. 33–34; Lacey, p. 239–45; Deitche, *The Silent Don* (II), pp. 77–78; "Anastasia Case Holds."

198   **Castro reemergence:** DePalma, *The Man Who Invented Fidel*, entire book; Matthews, *The Cuban Story*, entire book; Szulc, pp. 442–52; Thomas, pp. 598–608; Matthews, "Cuban Rebel Is Visited in Hideont," *New York Times*, February 24, 1957; "Rebel Strength Gaining in Cuba, but Batista Has the Upper Hand," *New York Times*, February, 25, 1957; "Old Order in Cuba Is Threatened by Forces of an Internal Revolt," *New York Times*, February 26, 1957.

200   **Reaction to and fallout from Matthews's articles:** DePalma, pp. 102–3, 107–9; Szulc, pp. 452–54; Thomas, pp. 608–12.

201   **Attack on the presidential palace:** Thomas, pp. 613–19; Szulc, pp. 456–59; Franqui, pp. 147–69; Smith, *The Fourth Floor*, pp. 41–42; *La Habana en los años 50s*, documentary.

203   **"There are no rebels in the Sierra Maestra":** Thomas, p. 619.

203   **"Lefty Clark's casino":** Beginning in mid-1957, the casino at the Tropicana was advertised as such in *Diario de la Marina* and other publications.

203   **Automobile giveaway:** Lowinger and Fox, pp. 281, 286–87.

10. CARNIVAL OF FLESH

205   **Deauville Hotel-Casino:** The facility opened on June 16, 1957, on the corner of Galiano, Malecón, and San Lázaro.

205   **Evaristo Garcia Jr.:** Ragano and Raab, *Mob Lawyer*, pp. 39–40, 348; Deitche, *Cigar City Mafia* (I), p. 89; Deitche, *The Silent Don* (II), p. 66.

205   **Trafficante applies for residency:** U.S. Treasury Department memo, Dade County OCB file #1–139, September 1961; Deitche (II), p. 69.

206   **John Martino:** Waldron with Hartmann, *Ultimate Sacrifice*, pp. 457–58.

206   **Ralph Reina:** Deitche (II), pp. 68–9.

206   **Dr. Ferdie Pacheco:** Author interview, Dr. Ferdie Pacheco, February 23, 2007.

206   **Trafficante and narcotics:** The subject of Trafficante's possible involvement in

drug smuggling in Cuba is covered in various FBN confidential memos dating from 1947 to 1957; see also U.S. Treasury Department memo, Dade County OCB file #1–139, September 1961; Ragano and Raab; Deitche (I); Deitche (II); Saenz Rovner, *La conexión cubana.*

207   **George "Saturday" Zarate:** U.S. Treasury Department memo, Dade County OCB file #1–139, September 1961; FBN RG-170, confidential memo, March 21, 1947; "Zarate Bolita Case to be Called Today Before Third Judge," *Tampa Tribune*, August 4, 1947; "George Zarate, Ex-Racketeer, Dies in Cuba," *Tampa Tribune*, August 25, 1955; Deitche (I), pp. 10–14.

208   **Cocaine at Sans Souci:** Ragano and Raab, p. 47.

210   **John F. Kennedy's presence in Havana:** Smith, *The Fourth Floor*, p. 222; Thomas, *Cuba: The Pursuit of Freedom*, p. 647; Dorschner and Fabricio, *The Winds of December*, p. 49; Waldron with Hartmann, p. 227.

211   **JFK orgy at Hotel Comodoro:** Ragano and Raab, pp. 39–40; Lacey, *Little Man*, p. 340.

211   **Sex in Cuba:** Havana's roots as a place of prostitution and vice are explored in Sublette, *Cuba and Its Music.* See also Tomás Fernández Robaina, "The Brothel of the Caribbean," in Chomsky and Smorkaloff, *The Cuba Reader*, pp. 257–59; Oscar Lewis et al., "A Prostitute Remembers," in Chomsky and Smorkaloff, *The Cuba Reader*, pp. 260–63.

211   **Show magazine:** I am indebted to author Rosa Lowinger, who allowed me to examine her impressive collection of *Show* magazines from the 1950s.

212   **Availability of showgirls:** The role of showgirls in the sexual climate of the times was commented upon by virtually everyone I interviewed, including Bernard Frank, Miami, March 3, 2006; Estela Rivas, Havana, August 15 and 17, 2006; Helio Orovio, Havana, August 24, 2006; José "Pepe" Rodríguez, Havana, August 24, 2006; Delio Valdes, Miami, October 17, 2006; Armando Jaime Casielles, January 24 and 26, 2007; Joe Stassi Jr., telephone, March 22, 2007; as well as other sources who asked to remain anonymous.

212   **Havana nightclubs:** Many of the clubs are profiled in various issues of *Show*; there are advertisements for the clubs in *Show, Confidencial de Cuba*, and other Cuban publications. The life and atmosphere at the smaller clubs is detailed in Acosta, *Cubano Be, Cubano Bop* and Lowinger and Fox, *Tropicana Nights.* The atmosphere of the era in general is also presented in various issues of *Cabaret* magazine, as well as "skin" magazines from the era; for example, "Sin—With a Rumba Beat!," *Stag*, November 1950.

213   **Bubbles Darlene in Havana:** *Cabaret Yearbook*, Winter Resort No. (1956).

215   **"The Americans from the South":** Lowinger and Fox, p. 206.

215   **Prostitution in Havana:** The subject was discussed in author interviews with Bernard Frank; Rosa Lowinger, Los Angeles, July 21, 2006; Estela Rivas; Helio Orovio; Delio Valdes; Armando Jaime Casielles; and Joe Stassi Jr. Additional

sources, especially in relation to Doña Marina and her brothels: "Sin—with a Rumba Beat"; Skylar, "Cuba's Lure-Legalized Filth!," *Suppressed,* February 1957; "Guide to After-Dark Havana," *Cabaret Yearbook* (1956); Robaina in Chomsky and Smorkaloff, pp. 257–59; Lewis et al., in Chomsky and Smorkaloff, pp. 260–63. Also of interest is an article by Lionel Olay in *Escapade* magazine ("Anna." June 1962, pp. 18, 38, 63-69). Olay, an American businessman in 1950s Cuba, writes, "Believe me when I tell you that so rampant was licentiousness, and so infectious, that [in Havana] it was the nonsinner, if he remained such for long, who felt forced to act in a clandestine manner."

216　**Havana's *mundo secreto*:** Author interview, José "Pepe" Rodríguez. Pepe, now seventy-six years old, lives with three dogs and five cats in a hovel in Vedado, where he is known by his neighbors as an "expert" on the subject of Havana in the 1950s. Pepe is also cited as a source in Lowinger and Fox, pp. 222, 295.

217　**Lesbian show at Hotel Comodoro:** Ragano and Raab, p. 46.

217　**Sexual preference of Ofelia Fox:** Lowinger and Fox, pp. 371–78.

217　**Shanghai Theater:** Author interviews: José "Pepe" Rodríguez; Ralph Rubio, September 16, 2006, and October 24, 2006; Bernard Frank; and Armando Jaime Casielles. See also Mallin, "The World's Rawest Burlesque Show," *Cabaret,* September 1956; "Havana Is a Man's Town," *Eye,* October 1956.

The legend of the Shanghai Theater is touched upon in many novels about the era, including G. Cabrera Infante's *Three Trapped Tigers,* Thomas Sanchez's *King Bongo,* and, most notably, Graham Greene's *Our Man in Havana,* in which Greene writes:

> The Shanghai was in a narrow street off Zanja surrounded by deep bars. A board advertised *Posiciones,* and the tickets for some reason were sold on the pavement outside, perhaps because there was no room for the box office, as the foyer was occupied by a pornographic bookshop for the benefit of those who wanted entertainment during the *entr'acte.*

219　**Exploits of Superman:** Author interviews: José "Pepe" Rodríguez; Bernard Frank, Ralph Rubio, Chris Ragano, Tampa, July 16, 2006, and March 1, 2007.

219　**"I know because he [Superman]":** Author interview, José "Pepe" Rodríguez.

220　**"Nig Devine was a sexual degenerate":** Author interview, Ralph Rubio.

220　**"Everything was geared towards sex":** Ibid.

221　**"We identified so completely":** Szulc, *Fidel: A Critical Portrait,* p. 439.

221　**"Batista was carrying on":** Ibid.

221　**"The guerrilla and the peasant":** Guevara, *Reminiscences of the Cuban Revolutionary War,* p. 102.

222   *The Story of Cuba's Jungle Fighters* (CBS documentary): The story behind this television documentary is detailed in Szulc; Geyer, *Guerilla Prince*; Thomas; and DePalma, *The Man Who Invented Fidel.* The documentary was viewed by the author at the Museum of Television and Radio, New York City.

222   "Sierra Manifesto": Bonachea and Valdes, *Revolutionary Struggle,* pp. 343–48; Szulc, pp. 465–66, 480–81.

223   Cuban Navy mutiny at Cienfuegos: Thomas, pp. 640–42; Sweig, *Inside the Cuban Revolution,* pp. 53, 61, 111, 122.

223   July 1957 murder of four boys: Thomas, p. 625; Franqui, *Diary of the Cuban Revolution,* p. 198.

223   Assassination of Frank País: Thomas, pp. 637–38; Sweig, pp. 47–49.

224   Arrival of Albert Anastasia: Cirules, *The Mafia in Havana,* pp. 7–8, 14–15; Fuentes, "Mafia in Cuba," *Cuba International,* August 1979; author interview, Ralph Rubio.

224   "We were warned about Anastasia": Author interview, Ralph Rubio.

225   "Lansky once told me": Author interview, Armando Jaime Casielles.

225   "The impression in my mind": Ibid.

11. TROPICAL VENGEANCE

226   Trafficante trip to NYC: Ragano and Raab, *Mob Lawyer,* pp. 29–30; Deitche, *The Silent Don* (II), pp. 77–78; Wald, "Mafia Link in Death of Anastasia?" *New York Herald Tribune,* October 28, 1957; "Anastasia Case Holds '150 Angles,'" *New York Herald Tribune,* October 30, 1957; Meskill, "Yen for Cuba Cash Doomed Anastasia," *New York World-Telegram & Sun,* January 9, 1958.

226   Trafficante letter to Anastasia: Deitche (II), pp. 77–78.

227   Meeting at Warwick Hotel: People Re: Umberto Anastasia, investigative memo (supplementary complaint reports), uncatalogued, NYC Municipal Archives; Ragano and Raab, pp. 29–30; Deitche (II), pp. 77–78; Lacey, *Little Man,* pp. 244–45; Wald, "Mafia Link"; "Anastasia Case Holds."

227   Chiri Mendoza: Investigator Whiteside, investigative memo, meeting with Roberto "Chiri" Mendoza and others, January 18, 1958, NYC Municipal Archives; Lacey, pp. 239–40, 244–45; Deitche (II), pp. 78–79; González Echevarría, *The Pride of Havana,* p. 330.

227   Meeting at Chandler's restaurant: Investigative memo, January 18, 1958; Lacey, p. 245; Deitche (II), pp. 78–79.

228   Joe Stassi arrival in NYC: Stratton, "The Man Who Killed Dutch Schultz," *GQ,* September 2001; *O.G.: Joe Stassi, Original Gangster,* documentary; author interview, Richard Stratton, New York City, February 15 and 21, 2007.

Stratton did time in prison with Joe Stassi and they struck up a friendship, which led to his writing a profile for GQ and doing a documentary on Stassi with filmmaker Marc Levin.

228   **"The Jews made the Mafia":** O.G.: *Joe Stassi.*

229   **Joe Stassi and Anastasia hit:** In his interview in O.G.: *Joe Stassi, Original Gangster,* the retired mobster is coy about his involvement in the Anastasia murder. Stassi admits that he was staying at the Park Sheraton Hotel on the day of the murder but declines to say anything further. Director Richard Stratton, who came to know Stassi well before his death in 1999, believes that Stassi's coyness on the subject was tantamount to a confession of involvement. Says Stratton: "If Joe didn't have anything to do with the Anastasia hit, he would have told me so, period."

There exist many theories on the hit, one being that Anastasia's murder had nothing to do with Cuba. Some believe the Mad Hatter's death stemmed from his rivalry with Vito Genovese. This theory was first put forth by Joe Valachi in his 1963 congressional testimony. Another theory fingers mafia boss Carlo Gambino. As recently as 2001, a prominent Mafia website named three hit men who allegedly carried out the murder on behalf of Gambino. In truth, as with many Mob rubouts, the facts have been obscured by decades of speculation. All these years later, Anastasia's entanglements with the Havana Mob remain the most compelling explanation for his murder.

229   **Anastasia murder:** The Anastasia hit is one of the most famous Mafia killings in U.S. history and, as such, is covered in Fox, *Blood and Power*; Raab, *Five Families*; Sondern Jr., *Brotherhood of Evil*; Peterson, *The Mob*; Ragano and Raab, *Mob Lawyer*; Maas, *The Valachi Papers.* Also the newspaper accounts detailed above: Wald, "Mafia Link"; "Anastasia Case Holds"; "Yen for Cuba Cash." In addition, details on events leading up to the murder, the murder itself, and the subsequent investigation are contained in Investigative Files Re: Umberto Anastasia, NYC Municipal Archives.

231   **Trafficante and Rivers at Havana airport:** Ragano and Raab, p. 35.

232   **Ragano conversation with Trafficante at Columbia Restaurant, Ybor City:** Ragano and Raab, pp. 33–37.

234   **Anastasia problem disappears:** Author interview, Armando Jaime Casielles, January 24 and 26, 2007.

234   *Confidencial de Cuba:* Issue dated January/February 1958. From the private collection of Rosa Lowinger.

235   **Mafia meeting at Apalachin, NY:** The bungled Mob gathering at Apalachin is another seminal event in organized crime history, covered at length in Fox, Raab, Sondern, Peterson, Maas, and others.

235   **Trafficante at Apalachin:** Deitche (II), pp. 80–83.

237   **Lansky role in exposing meeting:** Eisenberg, Dan, and Landau, *Meyer Lansky*, p. 248.

238   **"Nobody to this day knows":** Ibid.

238   **Sinatra–Ava Gardner honeymoon in Havana:** Kelley, *His Way*, p. 173; Summers, *Sinatra: The Life* (I), p. 162. Ava Gardner is quoted regarding the honeymoon:

> We went to Havana, in Cuba, and had a fight the first night. Who knows what we fought about? I remember standing up, pissed drunk, on the balcony of the [Nacional] hotel, on the edge. Standing there, balancing. Frank was afraid to go near me. He thought I was going to jump . . . God, I was crazy! . . . God almighty!

238   **Sinatra friendly with Lansky, Trafficante:** Summers (I), pp. 19, 21, 130, 135, 180; Lacey, pp. 146, 151; Ragano and Raab, pp. 20–21, 82, 115, 188, 214–17.

239   **Marlon Brando in Havana:** Marquez, "Marlon Brando: the Conga Man," *La Jornada*, July 7, 2004; Lowinger and Fox, *Tropicana Nights*, pp. 221, 284, 342.

239   **"Discovering Afro-Cuban music":** Brando, *Brando: Songs My Mother Taught Me*, photo caption.

239   **Graham Greene in Havana:** Bianchi Ross, "Graham Greene's Cuban Time," on www.CubaNow.net, undated; Greene, *Our Man in Havana*.

240   **Errol Flynn in Havana:** Cirules, *The Mafia in Havana* (1), p. 145; Szulc, *Fidel*, p. 504; *Cuban Rebel Girls* (1959): director Barry Mahon; screenwriter Errol Flynn. Using mostly outtake footage from *Cuban Rebel Girls*, Flynn also put together a documentary about the Cuban Revolution entitled *Cuban Story*. In this film—which wasn't available to the public until thirty-five years after it was made—Flynn makes an appearance and again professes his admiration for Fidel Castro.

240   **Hemingway in Cuba:** Author interview, Delio Valdes, Miami, October 17, 2006; Norberto, *Hemingway in Cuba*, entire book. Also Millman, "Hemingway's Ties to a Havana Bar Still Move the Mojitos," *Wall Street Journal*, December 8, 2006. Virtually every contemporary guidebook on Cuba has an entry on Hemingway's years on the island.

241   **George Raft:** Cirules (I), p. 146; Cirules, *La vida secreta de Meyer Lansky en La Habana* (II), pp. 124–25, 129; Lowinger and Fox, pp. 3, 292, 303, 329; Fuentes, "Mafia in Cuba," *Cuba International*, August 1979; "George Raft estrella absoluta en la gran revista de Abril," *Show*, April 1958; Yablonsky, *George Raft*, entire book.

243   **Cuban music and American culture:** Sublette, *Cuba and Its Music*, entire book. Also, Cruz, *Celia: My Life*; Orovio, *Diccionario de la musica cubano*.

243   **Desi Arnaz background:** Sublette, pp. 452–54, 534, 581–82.

244   **Afro-Cuban jazz:** Acosta, *Cubano Be, Cubano Bop*, entire book; Figueroa, "Israel Lopez 'Cachao,'" http://www.picadillo.com/figueroa/cachao; Figueroa, "Mario Bauza," http://www.cubanmusic.com. Also author interview, Helio Orovio, Havana, August 24, 2006. This interview with musicologist Orovio took place on the front porch of the UNEAC (Cuba writers' union) building during a thunderous tropical downpour.

For an explanation of the connection between Kansas City jazz and the corrupt political machine, see T. J. English, *Paddy Whacked*, pp. 213–24.

12.   A HANDMADE WOMAN

247   **Opening of Hotel Riviera:** Author interview, Ralph Rubio, September 16, 2006, and October 24, 2006; Lacey, *Little Man*, pp. 233–37; Schwartz, *Pleasure Island*, pp. 156–59, 177–78, 199–200; "*Ginger Rogers, en persona, super-estrella en su gran revista*," *Show*, December 1957.

248   **"She can wiggle her ass":** Lacey, p. 235.

248   *Steve Allen Show* **live at Riviera:** The entire show was viewed by the author at the Museum of Television and Radio, New York City; Schwartz, p. 161; Lowinger and Fox, *Tropicana Nights*, pp. 304–5.

249   **"Lansky reputation attracted high rollers":** Author interview, Ralph Rubio.

250   **Lansky affair with Carmen:** The details of Lansky's relationship with Carmen are presented in Cirules, *La vida secreta de Meyer Lansky en La Habana* (II) and, to a lesser extent, in Cirules, *The Mafia in Havana* (I). Facts were verified and expounded upon in author interview, Armando Jaime Casielles, January 24 and 26, 2007.

250   **"[She] was olive-skinned":** Author interview, Armando Jaime Casielles.

251   **Jaime and Lansky at Carmen's apartment:** This anecdote is detailed in Cirules (II), pp. 108–11; additional quotes and details, author interview, Armando Jaime Casielles.

254   **Rebels establish "liberated zone":** Szulc, *Fidel*, pp. 467–69, 490; Thomas, *Cuba: The Pursuit of Freedom*, pp. 620–25; Franqui, *Diary of the Cuban Revolution*, pp. 184–217; Bonachea and Valdes, *Revolutionary Struggle*, pp. 408–14; Guevara, *Reminiscences of the Cuban Revolutionary War*, pp. 196–227.

254   **William Gálvez Rodríguez background:** Gálvez, *Otro jinete apocalíptico*.

255   **"Fidel was putting into words":** Author interview, William Gálvez Rodríguez, Havana, March 8, 2007.

255   **"The fact that we were outnumbered":** Ibid.

255   **"Why We Fight":** Castro, "Why We Fight," *Coronet*, February 1958.

256   **"I know revolution sounds like bitter medicine":** St. George, "Cuban Rebels (Interview with Fidel Castro)," *Look*, April 3, 1958.

257   **Gran Premio and kidnapping of Juan Manuel Fangio:** This incident has become part of the lore of the Cuban Revolution and is detailed in Sweig, *Inside the Cuban Revolution*, pp. 103–4; Szulc, p. 482; Thomas, p. 651; Franqui, pp. 285–86; Schwartz, pp. 187–89.

259   **Burning of the sugar crop:** Szulc, pp. 453, 687–90; Bonachea and Valdes, p. 367; Franqui, pp. 284, 292–99.

259   **"I know well the heavy personal losses":** Castro, "Why We Fight."

259   **Action and Sabotage in Havana:** The activities of the 26th of July Movement and the civic resistance are detailed at length in Sweig, and Oltuski, *Vida Clandestina: My Life in the Cuban Revolution.* Oltuski was an underground leader of the civic resistance while at the same time working as an engineer for Shell Oil in Cuba.

259   **Burning of Belot oil refinery:** Sweig, p. 104.

259   **Creation of separate rebel columns:** Szulc, pp. 489, 493–97; Franqui, pp. 279–94; Thomas, pp. 620–23, 627, 632; Guevara, pp. 138–39.

260   **Raiding the National Bank of Cuba:** Schwartz, p. 190; Sweig, pp. 105–6.

260   **Attempted assassination of Raúl Menocal:** Franqui, p. 296.

260   **"Night of One Hundred Bombs":** Sweig, p. 112.

261   **Announcement of general strike:** Sweig, pp. 134–37; Franqui, p. 295; Bonachea and Valdez, p. 278. The strategy behind the strike is discussed at length in Oltuski.

261   **Cynthia (Schwartz) Duncan (Lansky's granddaughter):** Author interview, Cynthia (Schwartz) Duncan, Miami, May 4, 2006. Additional information on Richard Schwartz: Laccy, pp. 214, 289, 363.

262   **"I knew I was in Havana":** Author interview, Cynthia (Schwartz) Duncan.

262   **"We were treated like royalty":** Ibid.

263   **Lansky "pinched":** Lacey, pp. 241–46; Eisenberg, Dan, and Landau, *Meyer Lansky*, pp. 284–88, 290; Messick, *Lansky*, p. 215.

264   **Conversation with Detective Graff:** Lacey, pp. 238–46.

265   **Unwanted media attention for Lansky:** Havermann, "Mobsters Move in on Troubled Havana," *Life*, March 10, 1958.

265   **Lansky banned from Cuba:** Eisenberg, Dan, and Landau, pp. 288–91.

265   **"Batista played a little joke on me":** Eisenberg, Dan, and Landau, p. 290.

265   **Lansky-Batista relationship:** Author interview, Ralph Rubio; author interview, Armando Jaime Casielles; Cirules (II), pp. 161–71; "*Los encuentros de la mafia con el General Batista,*" *Juventude Rebelde*, July 4, 2004.

266   **Lansky-Batista meeting at Kuquine:** Author interview, Armando Jaime Casielles; Cirules (II), pp. 165–67; "*Los encuentros.*"

266   **"They were very, very close":** Lacey, p. 230.

267   **Cash payments to Batista:** Author interview, Ralph Rubio; author interview, Armando Jaime Casielles; Dorschner and Fabricio, *The Winds of December*, pp. 65–66.

13 . THE SUN ALMOST RISES

268   **Opening of Havana Hilton:** Schwartz, *Pleasure Island,* pp. 154–56, 178; Lowinger and Fox, *Tropicana Nights,* pp. 183, 256, 281, 327–30; Cirules, *The Mafia in Havana* (I), pp. 148–55; Deitche, *The Silent Don* (II), pp. 87–89; Smith, *The Fourth Floor,* p. 90.

269   **Nevada Gaming Commission decision:** Schwartz, pp. 162–63; Lacey, *Little Man,* pp. 256–57; Reiss, "The Batista-Lansky Alliance," in *Cigar Aficionado,* May/June 2001.

270   **Ragano visits Trafficante:** Ragano and Raab, *Mob Lawyer,* pp. 39–48.

270   **"Bartenders don't drink":** Ibid., p. 41.

271   **"This is the most important room":** Ibid., p. 42.

271   **"I became a different man in Cuba":** Ibid., pp. 43–44.

271   **"I sometimes wondered":** Ibid., p. 44.

272   **Ragano and Trafficante at *una exhibición*:** Ibid., pp. 44–45.

273   **Super-8-mm movie of Superman:** Footage of the famous Havana sex performer—made by Frank Ragano in 1958—was viewed by the author on March 1, 2007, in Tampa, courtesy of Chris Ragano, Frank's son.

273   **Ragano offered opportunity to buy in:** Ragano and Raab, pp. 47–48.

273   **"I'm sure Fidel will never amount to anything":** Ibid., p. 48.

274   **Failed general strike:** Oltuski, *Vida Clandestina,* pp. 139–54; Sweig, *Inside the Cuban Revolution,* pp. 136–48; Szulc, *Fidel,* pp. 484–85; Franqui, *Diary of the Cuban Revolution,* pp. 296–315.

274   **Operacíon Verano:** Szulc, pp. 490–91; Thomas, *Cuba: The Pursuit of Freedom,* pp. 663–68.

275   **Raúl Castro kidnapping of U.S. citizens:** Thomas, p. 666; Sweig, p. 171; Szulc, pp. 493–94; Smith, pp. 142–43.

277   **Captain Gálvez in Las Villas:** Author interview, William Gálvez Rodríguez, Havana, March 8, 2007; Dorschner and Fabricio, *The Winds of December,* pp. 259–60.

277   **"We could smell victory":** Author interview, William Gálvez Rodríguez.

278   **Lansky trips around Caribbean:** Cirules, *La vida secreta de Meyer Lansky en La Habana* (II), pp. 143–45; author interview, Armando Jaime Casielles, January 24 and 26, 2007; author interview, Richard Stratton, New York, February 15 and 21, 2007. Stratton mentioned that Stassi, during their interviews in the late 1990s, detailed various trips around the Caribbean to expand casino operations for the Havana Mob.

278   **International Hotels, Inc. looking toward expansion:** Author interview, Joe Stassi Jr., telephone, March 22, 2007.

278   **Lansky-Trafficante-Jaime trip to Dominican Republic:** Author interview, Armando Jaime Casielles; Cirules (II), pp. 150–60.

279   **"The first surprise I had":** Cirules (II), pp. 152–53.

280   **"Santo gave me a .45 pistol":** Ibid., p. 155.

281   **"It was the first time":** Ibid., pp. 155–56.

281   **"I had the feeling":** Author interview, Armando Jaime Casielles.

282   **Stassi Jr. sets up meeting for Pat Slots:** Author interview, Joe Stassi Jr.

282   **Stassi Jr. background and marriage:** Ibid.

283   **Trafficante hints to Ragano of assistance to rebels:** Ragano and Raab, p. 48.

284   **Norman Rothman meeting with José Aleman:** Findings of the House Select Committee on Assassinations, Vol. 5, Testimony of José Aleman, September 27, 1978.

285   **Rothman gun smuggling with Mannarino brothers:** Waldron with Hartmann, *Ultimate Sacrifice*, pp. 307, 329, 332, 347, 352. Authors Waldron and Hartmann suggest that a partner of Rothman's in this plot was U.S.-born Frank Fiorini, later known as Frank Sturgis, at the time a gun supplier for the 26th of July Movement. Fiorini/Sturgis would later switch sides and become a key player in various Mob and CIA attempts to assassinate Fidel Castro.

285   **Robert D. Weicha as CIA operative in Cuba:** Szulc, pp. 469–72. In *Ultimate Sacrifice*, Waldron and Hartmann curiously do not mention Weicha, though they do devote hundreds of pages to the CIA's supplying money and guns to the 26th of July Movement.

286   **Cuban government gun shipments from Dominican Republic and elsewhere:** Thomas, pp. 648–56; Szulc, pp. 451–52, 470–71.

286   **Cash couriers off the island:** The Ralph Reina–Trafficante relationship is detailed in Deitche, *The Silent Don* (II), pp. 68–69. Dusty Peters was a well-known figure in Havana Mob circles and is discussed in Lacey, p. 246; Messick, *Syndicate in the Sun*, p. 139; and Messick, *Lansky* (II), pp. 197, 217. Verification of Peters's role was provided by author interview, Ralph Rubio, Tampa, September 16 and October 24, 2006; author interview, Bernard Frank, Miami, May 3, 2006.

286   **Bank of Miami Beach:** Messick (II), p. 199.

287   **Castle Bank in the Bahamas:** Russo, *Supermob*, p. 208.

287   **Lewis McWillie background:** Lowinger and Fox, pp. 181–82, 335, 362–64; Waldron and Hartmann, pp. 301–2, 333, 343, 353–54.

287   **McWillie testimony:** Findings of the House Select Committee on Assassinations, Vol. 5, Testimony of Lewis McWillie, September 27, 1978.

14. "GET THE MONEY"

289   **Hotel Monte Carlo de La Habana:** Cirules, *The Mafia in Havana* (I), pp. 127–32; Cirules based his investigation of plans for the Hotel Monte Carlo on financial documents found in the Cuban National Archive.

289   **"Havana will be a magical city":** Author interview, Armando Jaime Casielles, January 24 and 26, 2007; Cirules, *La vida secreta de Meyer Lansky en La Habana* (II), pp. 183–84.

290   **Sinatra as investor:** Cirules (I), pp. 128, 131.

290   **"[Sinatra] wants to televise":** Ibid.

291   **Other investors, including William Miller:** Ibid.

291   **"Mr. Miller is considered":** Ibid.

292   **Articles in *Diario de la Marina*:** Dorschner and Fabricio, *The Winds of December*, p. 22.

293   **Los Tigres de Masferrer in Havana:** Ibid., pp. 98–99, 256–57, 363.

293   **Atmosphere in Havana late December 1958:** Dorschner and Fabricio, entire book.

293   **Behavior of Batista, December 1958:** An excellent source on Batista's final days is José Suárez Nuñez's *El gran culpable*—Suárez Nuñez was Batista's former press secretary. The book was self-published in Caracas in the early 1960s.

293   **Batista eating and vomiting:** Dorschner and Fabricio, p. 64; Suárez Nuñez, p. 16.

294   **Batista, affinity for horror movies and cheating at cards:** Dorschner and Fabricio, p. 67; Suárez Nuñez, p. 25.

294   **General Díaz Tamayo incident:** Dorschner and Fabricio, pp. 126–27.

295   **"Last night while I lay in bed":** Ibid., p. 159.

295   **Batista–Ambassador Smith meeting:** Smith, E., *The Fourth Floor*, pp. 170–76; Dorschner and Fabricio, pp. 189–93, 197; Thomas, *Cuba: The Pursuit of Freedom*, p. 680; Bardach, *Cuba Confidential*, p. 246.

296   **Batista secretly prepares for exit:** Dorschner and Fabricio, pp. 348–49; Thomas, pp. 681–93.

297   **Holiday atmosphere in Havana:** Dorschner and Fabricio, p. 157; Cirules (II), pp. 173–74.

297   **Lt. Col. Esteban Ventura at Riviera:** Author interview, Ralph Rubio, September 16 and October 24, 2006.

298   **Ventura background:** Garcia, "The White-Suited Hired Assassin," *Granma International*, May 31, 2001.

298   **Lansky's excuse for New Year's Eve:** Lacey, *Little Man*, p. 249; author interview, Armando Jaime Casielles; Cirules (II), pp. 172–94.

298   **New Year's Eve at Plaza Hotel:** The entire evening is described in detail in Cirules (II), pp. 172–94, and was further verified by author interview, Armando Jaime Casielles.

298   **Ownership of gambling concession at the Plaza:** Author interview, Joe Stassi Jr., New York, March 22, 2007.

302   **Reaction in the street to news of Batista departure:** Author interview, Armando Jaime Casielles; author interview, Joe Stassi Jr.; author interview, Ralph Rubio; Dorschner and Fabricio, pp. 371–86; Lowinger and Fox, *Tropi-*

cana Nights, pp. 309–21; Phillips, *Cuba: Island of Paradox,* pp. 395–401; *American Experience: Fidel Castro,* PBS documentary; Phillips, "Batista and Regime Flee Cuba," *New York Times,* January 2, 1959.

302   **Presence of Los Tigres:** Author interview, Armando Jaime Casielles.

303   **Attacks on parking meters and slot machines:** Author interview, Armando Jaime Casielles; Lowinger and Fox, pp. 316–17; Dorschner and Fabricio, pp. 688–89; Phillips, pp. 397–98.

303   **George Raft at the Capri:** The most detailed description of this incident is in Yablonsky, *George Raft.* It has become a famous anecdote and is also noted in W. Smith, *The Closest of Enemies;* Lowinger and Fox; Lacey; and other accounts of New Year's Eve 1959 in Havana. See also Miller, "Raft Not Natural After Cuba 'Fade,'" *Miami Herald,* January 9, 1959.

303   **"There she was, asleep":** Yablonsky, pp. 221–22.

303   **"Everybody working the hotel is yelling":** Ibid., p. 222.

304   **"I wasn't sure what to do":** Ibid.

304   **Trashing of the casinos:** E. Smith, pp. 188–91; W. Smith, p. 187; Lowinger and Fox, p. 317; Schwartz, *Pleasure Island,* pp. 194–96; Cirules (II), pp. 176–94; Dorschner and Fabricio, p. 423; author interview, Armando Jaime Casielles; author interview, Ralph Rubio; author interview, Joe Stassi Jr.

305   **Pigs at the Riviera:** Cohen, "The Lost Journals of Meyer Lansky," in *Ocean Drive,* January 2005. Teddy Lansky is quoted as telling journalist Paul Sann, "Pigs, for Christ's sake! You wouldn't believe it, in this gorgeous, gorgeous hotel."

306   **Mobsters gather at Joe Stassi's house:** Cirules (II), pp. 193–94; author interview, Armando Jaime Casielles.

307   **Wayne S. Smith:** Author interview, Wayne S. Smith, February 15, 2007.

307   **"It was hectic":** Ibid.

307   **Lansky granddaughter departs:** Author interview, Cynthia (Schwartz) Duncan, Miami, May 4, 2006.

307   **"We had been warned":** Ibid.

307   **Ralph Rubio departs:** Author interview, Ralph Rubio.

307   **Friends of Batista escape:** Thomas, pp. 687–88; Lowinger and Fox, pp. 309–15; Dorschner and Fabricio, pp. 414–17; Bardach, p. 246.

308   **Castro enters Havana:** Thomas, pp. 692–93; Dorschner and Fabricio, pp. 487–94; E. Smith, pp. 200–3; Szulc, *Fidel: A Critical Portrait,* pp. 516–17. The spirit of Castro's arrival is captured in the song *"En eso llego Fidel"* (And then Fidel arrived) by Carlos Puebla, in Chomsky and Smorkaloff, *The Cuba Reader,* pp. 337–39.

308   **"The people won this war":** *American Experience: Fidel Castro.*

308   **Political executions begin:** Szulc, pp. 53–54; Thomas, pp. 726–27; Ragano and Raab, *Mob Lawyer,* p. 54; DePalma, *The Man Who Invented Fidel,* pp. 150–53; *American Experience: Fidel Castro.*

309   **"two hundred thousand dead gringos":** Thomas, p. 729; Szulc, p. 531; De-Palma, p. 140. DePalma quotes Castro as saying "twenty thousand."

309   **"We are not only disposed":** Lacey, p. 252; Dispatch 1037, U.S. Embassy, Havana, to Department of State, March 19, 1959, State Department papers, National Archives, Washington, D.C.

309   **"The gamblers took their cue":** Lacey, p. 250.

309   **Lansky spokesperson telephones U.S. Embassy:** Lacey, p. 251.

309   **"Castro is a complete nut!":** Ragano and Raab, p. 51.

310   **Frank Sturgis (aka Frank Fiorini) appointed casino liaison:** "Frank Sturgis Talks to the FBI," April 11, 1959, Cuban Information Archive, document #0147, http://www.cuban-exile.com; "Background on Frank Anthony Sturgis," Cuban Information Archive, document #0157. The above-cited FBI memos detail Sturgis's approach to the FBI and CIA to offer his services as a double agent. Sturgis did, in fact, become a U.S. operative and begin a long career as a CIA affiliate. Waldron with Hartmann, *Ultimate Sacrifice*, pp. 308, 332–33, 343–44; Bohning, *The Castro Obsession*, pp. 133–34.

310   **Losses at Riviera, December 1958 to April 1959:** Schwartz, p. 199; Lacey, pp. 253–54.

311   *Rebels in the casinos:* Phillips, "Gamblers in Cuba Face Dim Future," *New York Times*, January 4, 1959; Schwartz, pp. 199–201; Lacey, pp. 252–55; Ragano and Raab, pp. 49–53.

311   **Incarceration of Trafficante:** Ragano, pp. 49–62; Waldron with Hartmann, pp. 375–76, 383–87, 390; "Cuba Acts to Deport Trafficante," *Miami Herald*, June 11, 1959; "Trafficante Feels the Heat," *Tampa Times*, June 12, 1959; "Trafficante Ouster May be Postponed," *Tampa Times*, June 12, 1959; "Trafficante Still Awaits Hearing on Deportation," *Tampa Times*, June 15, 1959.

311   **Trafficante testimony:** Findings of the House Select Committee on Assassinations, Vol. 5, Testimony of Santo Trafficante, September 28, 1978.

312   **Other mobsters incarcerated:** Fox and Lowinger, pp. 329–30; Lacey, p. 253; Waldron with Hartmann, p. 343, 394.

312   **Joe Stassi escapes arrest:** Stratton, "The Man Who Killed Dutch Schultz," *GQ*, September 2001.

312   **Joe Stassi Jr. arrested:** Author interview, Joe Stassi Jr. Stassi Jr. was incarcerated for three days at the G-2 jail in Miramar and then transferred to a prison in Las Villas Province, where he was held for 109 days until his release.

313   **Trafficante at Triscornia:** Ragano and Raab, pp. 51–62; Waldron with Hartmann, pp. 375–76, 383–87, 390; Findings of the House Select Committee on Assassinations, Testimony of Santo Trafficante.

313   **Marriage of Trafficante's daughter:** Ragano and Raab, p. 55.

313   **"A happy-go-lucky atmosphere had been replaced":** Ibid.

313   **"They're going to execute me":** Ragano and Raab, p. 56.

314   **Ragano negotiates for Trafficante's release:** Ibid., pp. 51–62.

314   **Cash bribe paid to Raúl Castro:** Ibid., pp. 60–61; Waldron with Hartmann, p. 390.

314   **"I met Raúl Castro one time":** Findings of the House Select Committee on Assassinations, Testimony of Santo Trafficante.

315   **Lansky's last trip to Havana:** Author interview, Armando Jaime Casielles. Cirules (II), pp. 203–5; Lacey, pp. 253–58.

315   **Lansky tries to find Carmen:** Cirules (II), pp. 204–10.

315   **Three hundred executions:** Lacey, p. 253.

315   **"When he invited me to go":** *La mafia en La Habana,* documentary.

316   **Jaime's last conversation with Lansky:** Ibid; also author interview, Armando Jaime Casielles.

317   **Cuban government confiscates Hotel Riviera:** Lacey, p. 258.

318   **U.S. economic embargo against Cuba:** The embargo (referred to in Cuba as *el bloqueo,* or "the blockade") was instituted on February 7, 1961.

318   **Batista's plundering of Cuba:** Thomas, p. 687; also "Batista Government Bank Accounts," *Libertad,* January 28, 1969, Cuban Information Archives, document #0115, http://www.cuban-exile.com.

318   **Financial losses of Havana Mob:** Lacey, pp. 258–59.

319   **Joe Stassi post-Havana:** Stratton, "The Man Who Killed"; O.G.: *Joe Stassi, Original Gangster,* documentary.

320   **"I haven't had an erection in forty years":** Ibid.

320   **Lansky leaves behind seventeen million dollars:** Eisenberg, Dan, and Landau, *Meyer Lansky,* p. 256.

320   **"I crapped out":** Lacey, p. 258.

EPILOGUE

321   **Bay of Pigs invasion:** There is considerable literature on the planning and execution of the invasion, including Peter Kornbluth's *Bay of Pigs Declassified: The Secret CIA Report on the Invasion of Cuba* and Victor Andres Triay's *Bay of Pigs,* an oral history.

321   **Lansky assassination contract on Castro:** Eisenberg, Dan, and Landau, *Meyer Lansky,* pp. 257–59; Waldron with Hartmann, *Ultimate Sacrifice,* pp. 310–11, 321–22, 343, 399–405. Waldron and Hartmann cite author Anthony Summers and his biography of Richard Nixon, *Absolute Power,* in which it is alleged that Lansky made contact with a representative of Vice President Nixon to coordinate his Castro assassination plot. Lansky's intermediary was Cuban-born Bebe Rebozo, a Nixon confidant whom Lansky knew from his casino days in South Florida.

322   **Frank Sturgis and Charles White:** Waldron with Hartmann, p. 343. Sturgis

knew White by his real name, Charles Tourine. Sturgis testified before the
Rockefeller Commission in 1975.

322   **"A number of people came to me":** Eisenberg, Dan, and Landau, p. 259.

322   **The Cuba Project and Operation Mongoose:** There is voluminous
information on both of these covert initiatives, including books and testimony from nearly half a dozen governmental hearings. The Senate's Church
Committee hearings of 1977, the 1975 U.S. President's Commission on CIA
activities within the United States, also known as the Rockefeller Commission, and the House Select Committee Hearings on Assassinations in 1978 all
cover aspects of the CIA-Mob partnership. Noteworthy books include Waldron with Hartmann; Bohning, *The Castro Obsession*; and Fabian Escalante,
The Cuba Project: CIA Covert Operations, 1959–62.

    In addition, in June 2007 the CIA released its so-called family jewels.
These previously classified CIA files contained—among other things—details
on the agency's plot to assassinate Castro using the aid of mobsters Johnny
Roselli, Sam Giancana, and Santo Trafficante. The release of the files constituted an unprecedented admission of culpability on the part of the CIA,
though the details of the plot were not new. In 1994 an internal report compiled by the CIA inspector general was declassified and published under the
title *CIA Targets Fidel* (Ocean Press, 1996). It remains the most cogent account of this dubious underworld alliance.

324   **Post-Cuba activity and death of Rolando Masferrer:** Waldron with Hartmann, pp. 186–87, 332, 342–45, 388; Masferrer, "*Comentario: Apendejation*,"
Libertad, October 24, 1975.

325   **Batista, post-Cuba:** Gardner, "Batista Lives in Constant Fear of Bullet," *Miami Herald*, October 25, 1959; Batista, *Cuba Betrayed*, entire book.

326   **Trafficante, post-Cuba:** Author interview, Chris Ragano, Tampa, July 18,
2006, and March 10, 2007; Ragano and Raab, *Mob Lawyer*, pp. 65–356; Deitche, *The Silent Don*, pp. 109–229.

327   **Lansky, post-Cuba:** Author interview, Cynthia (Schwartz) Duncan, Miami,
May 4, 2006; Cohen, "The Lost Journals of Meyer Lansky," *Ocean Drive*, January
2005; Eisenberg, Dan, and Landau, pp. 261–324; Lacey, *Little Man*, pp. 260–439.

328   **Castro, post-Batista:** "Castro Calls Head of the U.S. Diplomatic Mission in
Havana a 'Little Gangster,'" *South Florida Sun-Sentinel*, December 23, 2005.

APPENDIX

335   **Attendees at the Havana Conference (December 1946):** Gosch and Hammer, *The Last Testament of Lucky Luciano*; Eisenberg, Dan, and Landau, *Meyer
Lansky: Mogul of the Mob*.

This book is based on myriad sources, including interviews with firsthand participants and experts; archive research at libraries, museums, and research institutions in Cuba and the United States; books and magazine and newspaper articles in English and Spanish; documentary films produced in Cuba, Spain, and the United States; court documents, including testimony from U.S. congressional hearings, and documents acquired through the Freedom of Information Act; all of it backed up with reporting by the author in Havana, New York, Miami, Tampa, Washington, D.C., and Los Angeles.

INTERVIEWS

Even though the events of this book took place decades ago, some interview subjects did not want to be identified by name. For some Cubans, the reality of mafiosi or mobsters operating in Havana in the 1950s is still a touchy subject. Some people are living in denial, while others simply do not want to be identified with the subject. For those who chose to speak with me on condition of anonymity, I have agreed to honor their wishes.

Among the interviewees listed below, I have included Armando Jaime Casielles, though my communication with Meyer Lansky's driver and bodyguard was more in the nature of a correspondence than a formal interview. My dialogue with Armando Jaime took place via e-mail and telephone between Havana and New York. I was scheduled to interview him on a research trip to Havana, but ten days before my departure I was informed that he had passed away from natural causes at 8:15 A.M. on February 12, 2007. In my correspondence with Armando Jaime, I was able to cross-check information on his background and experiences in Havana that was provided in other sources, most notably *La vida secreta de Meyer Lansky en La Habana* by Enrique Cirules.

The following is a list of interviewees and the places and dates when the interviews with them took place: Bernardo Benes, Miami (May 3, 2006); Judge Bernard Frank, Miami (May 3, 2006); Max Lesnick, Miami (May 4, 2006); Cynthia (Schwartz) Duncan, Miami (May 4, 2006); Scott M. Deitche, Tampa (July 7, 2006); Chris Ragano, Tampa (July 18, 2006, and March 1, 2007); Cookie Garcia, Tampa (July 7, 2006); Henry Beltran, Tampa (July 7, 2006); Rosa Lowinger, Los Angeles (July 21, 2006); Estela Rivas, Havana (August 15 and 17, 2006); Chef Gilberto Smith Duquesne, Havana (August 23, 2006); Helio Orovio, Havana (August 24, 2006); José "Pepe" Rodríguez, Havana (August 24, 2006); Ralph Rubio, Tampa (September 16 and October 24, 2006); Delio Valdes, Miami (October 17, 2006); Armando Jaime Casielles, telephone and e-mail (January 24 and 26, 2007); Richard Stratton, New York (February 15 and 21, 2007); Marc Levin, New York (February 21, 2007); Wayne S. Smith, Washington, D.C. (February 15, 2007); Dr. Ferdie Pacheco, telephone (February 23, 2007); Comandante William Gálvez Rodríguez, Havana (March 8, 2007); Joe Stassi Jr., telephone (March 22, 2007); Roberto González Echevarría, telephone (May 21, 2007); Peter Anthony Karvjian, telephone (November 3, 2008).

BOOKS

Among the history books, memoirs, biographies, and novels listed below are numerous tomes on the subject of organized crime. The use of one book, in particular, requires an explanation. *The Last Testament of Lucky Luciano* by Martin A. Gosch and Richard Hammer was published in 1974, nine years after Charles Luciano's death. The book's publishers, Little, Brown and Company, promoted the book as being based on interviews conducted with Luciano before he died by lawyer and movie producer Martin Gosch. Notes from the interviews were then given to Richard Hammer, an author of numerous books on organized crime, who wove together Luciano's first-person remembrances with a historical narrative. Upon release, the veracity of the book was challenged by a reporter for the *New York Times* after it was revealed that there were no transcripts of the interviews that Gosch claimed to have done with Luciano. The book became something of a cause célèbre, with competing crime writers Peter Maas and Nicholas Gage denouncing the book as a fraud. With the passage of time, history has shown the book to be no less accurate than other organized-crime memoirs.

I relate the history of the book's publication here in the interest of full disclosure. Some organized-crime historians refuse to cite the book as a credible source, while others quote from it as if it were the Bible. I have chosen a middle ground, citing the book as a source when I was able to back up information found in its pages with one or more other sources.

Acosta, Leonardo. *Cubano Be, Cubano Bop: One Hundred Years of Jazz in Cuba.* Washington, D.C.: Smithsonian Books, 2003.

Anderson, Jon Lee. *Che Guevara: A Revolutionary Life.* New York: Grove Press, 1997.

Argote-Freyre, Frank. *Fulgencio Batista: From Revolutionary to Strongman.* Piscataway, NJ: Rutgers University Press, 2006.

Asbury, Herbert. *Sucker's Progress: An Informal History of Gambling in America.* New York: Dodd, Mead, 1938.

Atkins, Ace. *White Shadow.* New York: G. P. Putnam's Sons, 2006.

Bardach, Ann Louise. *Cuba Confidential: Love and Vengeance in Miami and Havana.* New York: Random House, 2002.

Batista, Fulgencio. *Cuba Betrayed.* New York: Vantage, 1962.

———. *The Growth and Decline of the Cuban Republic.* New York: Devin-Adair, 1964.

Bernstein, Lee. *The Greatest Menace: Organized Crime in Cold War America.* Boston: University of Massachusetts Press, 2002.

Bohning, Don. *The Castro Obsession: U.S. Covert Operations in Cuba, 1959–1965.* Herndon, VA: Potomac Books, 2005.

Bonachea, Rolando, and Nelson P. Valdez, eds. *Revolutionary Struggle 1947–1958: Vol. 1, Selected Works of Fidel Castro.* Cambridge, MA: MIT Press, 1972.

Bonnano, Joseph. *A Man of Honor: The Autobiography of the "Boss of Bosses."* New York: Simon and Schuster, 1983.

Brando, Marlon. *Brando: Songs My Mother Taught Me.* New York: Random House, 1994.

Cabrera Infante, G. *Three Trapped Tigers.* London: Faber and Faber, 1989.

———. *Holy Smoke.* Woodstock, NY: Overlook Press, 1998.

Campbell, Rodney. *The Luciano Project: The Secret Wartime Collaboration of the Mafia and the U.S. Navy.* New York: McGraw-Hill, 1977.

Casteñeda, Jorge G. *Compañero: The Life and Death of Che Guevara.* New York: Knopf, 1998.

Castro, Fidel. *La historia me absolverá.* Havana: Editora Política, 1964.

———. *My Early Years.* Melbourne and New York: Ocean Press, 1998.

Chester, Edmund A. *A Sergeant Named Batista.* New York: Holt, 1954.

Chomsky, Aviva, and Pamela Maria Smorkaloff, eds. *The Cuba Reader: History, Culture, Politics.* Durham, NC: Duke University Press, 2004.

Cirules, Enrique. *The Mafia in Havana: A Caribbean Mob Story.* Melbourne and New York: Ocean Press, 2004.

————. *La vida secreta de Meyer Lansky en La Habana.* Havana: Ciencias Sociales, 2004.

Cohen, Rich. *Tough Jews: Fathers, Sons and Gangster Dreams.* New York: Simon and Schuster, 1998.

Cruz, Celia. *Celia: My Life.* New York: Rayo, 2004.

Deitche, Scott M. *Cigar City Mafia: A Complete History of the Tampa Underworld.* Fort Lee, NJ: Barricade Books, 2004.

————. *The Silent Don: The Criminal Underworld of Santo Trafficante Jr.* Fort Lee, NJ: Barricade Books, 2007.

Demaris, Ovid. *The Last Mafioso: The Treacherous World of Jimmy Fratianno.* New York: Bantam, 1981.

DePalma, Anthony. *The Man Who Invented Fidel: Castro, Cuba, and Herbert L. Matthews of the New York Times.* New York: Public Affairs Books, 2006.

Dewey, Thomas E. *Twenty Against the Underworld.* Garden City, NY: Doubleday, 1974.

Dorschner, John, and Robert Fabricio. *The Winds of December.* New York: Coward, McCann & Geohegan, 1980.

Eisenberg, Dennis, Uri Dan, and Eli Landau. *Meyer Lansky: Mogul of the Mob.* New York: Paddington Press, 1979.

Epstein, Daniel Mark. *Nat King Cole.* New York: Farrar, Straus and Giroux, 1999.

Feder, Sid, and Joachim Joesten. *The Luciano Story.* New York: David McKay, 1954.

Flynn, Errol. *My Wicked, Wicked Ways.* New York: G. P. Putnam, 1959.

Fox, Stephen. *Blood and Power: Organized Crime in Twentieth-Century America.* New York: Penguin, 1989.

Franqui, Carlos. *Diary of the Cuban Revolution.* New York: Viking, 1980.

Fried, Albert. *The Rise and Fall of the Jewish Gangster in America.* New York: Holt, Rinehart and Winston, 1980.

Fuentes, Norberto. *Hemingway in Cuba.* New York: Lyle Stuart, 1984.

Gálvez Rodríguez, William. *Otro jinete apocalíptico: Una historia novelada sobre la mafia de EE.UU en Cuba.* Havana: Ediciones Unión, 2004.

Gellman, Irwin F. *Roosevelt and Batista: Good Neighbor Diplomacy in Cuba, 1933–1945.* Albuquerque: University of New Mexico Press, 1973.

Geyer, Georgie Anne. *Guerilla Prince: The Untold Story of Fidel Castro.* Boston: Little, Brown, 1991.

González Echevarría, Roberto. *The Pride of Havana: A History of Cuban Baseball.* New York: Oxford University Press, 1999.

Gosch, Martin A., and Richard Hammer. *The Last Testament of Lucky Luciano.* Boston: Little, Brown, 1974.

Greene, Graham. *Our Man in Havana.* New York: Viking, 1958.

Guevara, Ernesto "Che." *Reminiscences of the Cuban Revolutionary War.* New York: Monthly Review Press, 1967.

Hemingway, Ernest. *To Have and Have Not*. New York: Charles Scribner's Sons 1937.

———. *The Old Man and the Sea*. New York: Charles Scribner's Sons, 1952.

Jennings, Dean. *We Only Kill Each Other: The Life and Bad Times of Bugsy Siegel*. New York: Prentice Hall, 1967.

Katcher, Leo. *The Big Bankroll: The Life and Times of Arnold Rothstein*. New Rochelle, NY: Arlington House, 1958.

Kefauver, Estes. *Crime in America*. Garden City, NY: Doubleday, 1951.

Kelley, Kitty. *His Way: The Unauthorized Biography of Frank Sinatra*. New York: Bantam, 1986.

Kuntz, Tom, and Phil Kuntz. *The Sinatra Files: The Secret FBI Dossier*. New York: Three Rivers Press, 2000.

Lacey, Robert. *Little Man: Meyer Lansky and the Gangster Life*. Boston: Little, Brown, 1991.

Latour, Jose. *Havana World Series*. New York: Grove Press, 2004.

Lewis, Norman. *The Honored Society*. New York: Putnam, 1964.

Lowinger, Rosa, and Ofelia Fox. *Tropicana Nights: The Life and Times of the Legendary Cuban Nightclub*. New York: Harcourt, 2005.

Maas, Peter. *The Valachi Papers*. New York: Putnam, 1968.

Martí, José. *Selected Writings*. New York: Penguin, 2002.

Matthews, Herbert L. *The Cuban Story*. New York: George Braziller, 1961.

Mencia, Mario. *The Fertile Prison: Fidel Castro in Batista's Jails*. Melbourne and New York: Ocean Press, 1992.

Messick, Hank. *Syndicate in the Sun*. New York: Macmillan, 1968.

———. *Lansky*. New York: Putnam, 1971.

Montero, Mayra. *Dancing to "Almendra."* New York: Farrar, Straus and Giroux, 2007.

Moore, William Howard. *The Kefauver Committee and the Politics of Crime, 1950–1952*. Columbia: University of Missouri Press, 1974.

Nelli, Humbert S. *The Business of Crime: Italians and Syndicate Crime in the United States*. Chicago: University of Chicago Press, 1976.

Oltuski, Enrique. *Vida Clandestina: My Life in the Cuban Revolution*. New York: John Wiley and Sons, 2002.

Orovio, Helio. *Diccionario de la musica cubano*. Havana: Letra Cubanas, 1992.

Peterson, Virgil. *The Mob: 200 Years of Organized Crime in New York*. Ottawa, IL: Green Hill, 1983.

Phillips, Ruby Hart. *Cuba: Island of Paradox*. New York: McDowell, 1959.

Powell, Hickman. *Lucky Luciano: The Man Who Organized Crime in America*. New York: Barricade Books, 2000. First published 1939 by Harcourt Brace as *Ninety Times Guilty*.

Raab, Selwyn. *Five Families: The Rise, Decline and Resurgence of America's Most Powerful Mafia Empires*. New York: Thomas Dunne Books, 2005.

Ragano, Frank, and Selwyn Raab. *Mob Lawyer.* New York: Charles Scribner's Sons, 1994.

Roberts, W. Adolphe. *Havana: The Portrait of a City.* New York: Howard-McCann, 1953.

Russo, Gus. *Supermob: How Sidney Korshak and His Associates Became America's Hidden Power Brokers.* New York: Bloomsbury USA, 2006.

Saenz Rovner, Eduardo. *La conexión cubana: Narcotráfico, contrabando y juego en Cuba entre los años 20 y comienzos de la revolución.* Bogotá: Universidad Nacional de Colombia, 2005.

Sanchez, Thomas. *King Bongo.* New York: Knopf, 2003.

Sasuly, Richard. *Bookies and Bettors: Two Hundred Years of Gambling.* New York: Holt, Rinehart and Winston, 1982.

Schwartz, Rosalie. *Pleasure Island: Tourism and Temptation in Cuba.* Omaha: University of Nebraska Press, 1997.

Smith, Earl E. T. *The Fourth Floor: An Account of the Castro Communist Revolution.* New York: Random House, 1962.

Smith, Wayne S. *The Closest of Enemies: A Personal and Diplomatic Account of U.S.–Cuba Relations Since 1957.* New York: W. W. Norton, 1987.

Sondern, Frederick, Jr. *Brotherhood of Evil: The Mafia.* New York: Farrar, Straus and Cudahy, 1959.

Suárez Nuñez, José. *El gran culpable: ¿Cómo 12 guerrilleros antiquilaron a 45,000 soldados?* Caracas: self-published, 1963.

Sublette, Ned. *Cuba and Its Music: From the First Drums to the Mambo.* Chicago: Chicago Review Press, 2004.

Summers, Anthony, and Robbyn Swan. *Sinatra: The Life.* New York: Knopf, 2005.

———. *Official and Confidential: The Secret Life of J. Edgar Hoover.* New York: G. P. Putnam, 1993.

Sweig, Julia E. *Inside the Cuban Revolution: Fidel Castro and the Urban Underground.* Cambridge, MA: Harvard University Press, 2002.

Szulc, Tad. *Fidel: A Critical Portrait.* New York: William Morrow, 1986.

Thomas, Hugh. *Cuba: The Pursuit of Freedom, 1762–1969.* New York: Harper and Row, 1971.

Tosches, Nick. *King of the Jews.* New York: Ecco, 2005.

Turkus, Burton B., and Sid Feder. *Murder Inc.: The Story of the Syndicate.* New York: Farrar, Straus and Giroux, 1951.

Waldron, Lamar, with Thom Hartmann. *Ultimate Sacrifice: John and Robert Kennedy, the Plan for a Coup in Cuba, and the Murder of JFK.* Updated edition, New York: Carroll and Graf, 2006.

Wolf, George, with Joseph DiMona. *Frank Costello: Prime Minister of the Underworld.* New York: William Morrow, 1974.

Woon, Basil. *When It's Cocktail Time in Cuba.* New York: Horace Liveright, 1928.

Yablonsky, Lewis. *George Raft.* New York: McGraw-Hill, 1974.

ARTICLES, ESSAYS, TRANSCRIPTS, AND REPORTS

Adler, Barbara Squier. "The Mambo and the Mood." *New York Times Magazine*, September 16, 1952.

Ameringer, Charles D. "The Auténtico Party and the Political Opposition in Cuba, 1952–57." *Hispanic American Historical Review*, 1985.

Baez, Luis. "Interview with Cuban Colonel José Quevedo." *The Militant*, Vol. 60, No. 4, January 29, 1996.

Bianchi Ross, Ciro. "Graham Greene's Cuban Time." www.CubaNow.net. Undated.

Bohemia magazine. "En Cuba" section. December 8, 1946.

Brief Magazine, Vol. 3, No. 1. "Lovely Latin (Cuban Dancer Elvira Padovano)." January 1956.

Cabaret magazine. "Havana: Nightlife Guide." December 1956.

Cabaret Quarterly, Special Resort No. Vol. 5. "Betty Howard: Her Bumps to the Bongo Packed Havana Theaters," 1956.

———. "Cabaret Guide to Havana."

———. "Havana's Favorite Drink Is the Daiquiri."

Cabaret Yearbook, Winter Resort No. Vol. 1. "Bubbles Darlene," 1956.

———. "Guide to After-Dark Havana."

———. "Tropicana Is Most Beautiful."

Castro, Fidel. "Why We Fight." *Coronet*, February 1958.

CIA (Central Intelligence Agency). "Inspector General's Report on Plots to Assassinate Fidel Castro," April/May 1967.

Cohen, Gary. "The Lost Journals of Meyer Lansky." *Ocean Drive*, January 2005.

Confidencial de Cuba. "¿Operan en nuestros cabarets gangsters americanos?" January/February 1958.

Depestre Catoney, Leonardo. "Nat 'King' Cole at Tropicana." www.CubaNow.net. Undated.

Eye, Vol. 5, No. 5. "Havana Is a Man's Town." October 1956.

Figueroa, Frank M. "Israel Lopez 'Cachao': Highlights and Review of His Smithsonian Jazz Oral History Interview." www.picadillo.com/figueroa/cachao. Undated.

———. "Mario Bauza: Highlights and Review of His Smithsonian Jazz Oral History Interview." www.cubanmusic.com. Undated.

Friedlander, Paul C. J. "Not Paris, But Friendly." *New York Times*, March 22, 1953.

Fuentes, Norberto. "Mafia in Cuba." *Cuba International*, August 1979.

Gage, Nicholas. "Underworld Genius: How One Gang Leader Thrives While Others Fall by the Wayside." *Wall Street Journal*, November 19, 1969.

Garcia, Pedro A. "The White-Suited Hired Assassin." *Granma International*, May 31, 2001.

Gardner, Llew. "Batista Lives in Constant Fear of Bullet." *Miami Herald*, October 25, 1959.

Gente de la Semana, American Edition. "Brief History of the Cuban Labour Movement & Social Policy Since 1952," January 5, 1958.

———. "Havana Crossroads of the World 1958."

———. "Havana's New Tunnel."

———. "Investment in Cuba 1958."

———. "New Public Works Projects of the Batista Regime."

González, Angel Tomás. "*El mafioso que se fue con* Castro." *Crónica*, October 23, 2005.

Granma. "*El Padrino y las relaciones entre la tiranía de* Batista *y la mafia*," October 21, 1975.

———. "Lansky '*El Cejudo*' *no hace caso*," August 29, 1988.

Havermann, Ernest. "Mobsters Move in on Troubled Havana." *Life*, March 10, 1958.

House Select Committee on Assassinations, Vol. 5, Testimony of Lewis McWillie, September 27, 1978.

———. Testimony of José Aleman, September 27, 1978.

———. Testimony of Santo Trafficante, September 28, 1978.

Jacobs, Sam. "Prío Spent Most of His Career Fighting Cuban Dictatorships." *Miami Herald*, August 6, 1977.

Johnson, Malcolm. "Lansky Sails in Luxury for Italy; Expected to Confer with Luciano." *New York Sun*, June 28, 1949.

Juventude Rebelde. "*Los encuentros de la mafia con el* General Batista," July 4, 2004.

———. "*Yo fui guardaespalda de* Meyer Lansky," February 6, 2005.

Lahey, Edwin A. "Gamblers Find Cuban Paradise." *Washington Post*, January 9, 1958.

Mallin, Jay. "The World's Rawest Burlesque Show: Nowhere Can Public See as Ribald and Racy a Show as in Havana, Where Patrons See Combined Stag Movies and Strip Tease." *Cabaret*, September 1956.

———. "Cuba's Carefree Cabaret: Massive Injections of Money for Lavish Shows, Elaborate Gaming Facilities Have Made Sans Souci Cuba's Top Club." *Cabaret*, April 1957.

———. "Havana Night Life." Unpublished article, 1956–7, Cuban Information Archives, Doc. 0211, www.cuban-exile.com.

Marquez, Ernesto. "Marlon Brando: The Conga Man." *La Jornada*, July 7, 2004.

Masferrer, Rolando. "*Comentario: Apendejación*." *Libertad*, October 24, 1975.

Matthews, Herbert L. "Castro Rebels Gain in Face of Offensive by the Cuban Army." *New York Times*, January 9, 1957.

————. "Populace in Revolt in Santiago de Cuba," *New York Times*, January 30, 1957.

————. "Cuban Rebel Is Visited in Hideout," *New York Times*, February 24, 1957.

————. "Rebel Strength Gaining in Cuba, but Batista Has the Upper Hand." *New York Times*, February 25, 1957.

————. "Old Order in Cuba Is Threatened by Forces of an Internal Revolt," *New York Times*, February 26, 1957.

————. "Situation in Cuba Worsening; Batista Foes Gain," *New York Times*, June 15, 1957.

————. "Top Castro Aide Denies Red Tie; Leaders Say They 'Await Fidel,' " *New York Times*, January 4, 1959.

Meskill, Paul. "Yen for Cuba Cash Doomed Anastasia." *New York World Telegram*, January 9, 1958.

Miami Herald. "Cuba Acts to Deport Trafficante," June 11, 1959.

Miller, Gene. "Raft Not Natural After Cuba 'Fade.' " *Miami Herald*, January 9, 1958.

Millman, Joel. "Hemingway's Ties to a Havana Bar Still Move the Mojitos." *Wall Street Journal*, December 8, 2006.

Mormino, Gary R. "Rallying for the Revolution." *Tampa Tribune*, February 19, 2006.

Mortimer, Lee. "Frank Sinatra Confidential: Gangsters in the Night Clubs." *The New American Mercury*, August 1951.

Newsweek. "Batista at Work," March 24, 1952.

————. "Counting Batista's Days," December 22, 1958.

New York Herald Tribune. "Anastasia Case Holds '150 Angeles.' " October 30, 1957.

New York Times. "US Ends Narcotics Sales to Cuba While Luciano Is Resident There," February 22, 1947.

————. "Cuba Ousts 13 US Gamblers," March 31, 1953.

————. "Batista Insists He's No Dictator," April 23, 1957.

Olay, Lionel. *Escapade*, Vol. 7, No. 4. "Anna." June 1962.

Pardon, Pedro Luis. *"Amadeo Barletta, representante en Cuba de los negocios de la pandilla yanqui 'Cosa Nostra.' "* *Granma*, March 30, 1971.

Pageant Magazine, Vol. 12, No. 2. "Advanced Latin (Tybee Afra: Afro-Cuban Rhythm Dancer)." August 1956.

Phillips, R. Hart. "Cuba Is Betting on Her New Gambling Casinos." *New York Times*, November 6, 1955.

————. "Batista Charges Castro Is a Red." *New York Times*, March 11, 1957.

————. "Cuba Suppresses Youths' Uprising: Forty Are Killed." *New York Times*, March 14, 1957.

————. "Batista Suspends Civil Guarantees." *New York Times*, August 2, 1957.

————. "Batista Is Dependent on Loyalty of Army," *New York Times*, September 25, 1957.

————. "Batista and Regime Flee Cuba; Castro Moving to Take Power; Mobs Riot and Loot in Havana," *New York Times*, January 2, 1959.

————. "Gamblers in Cuba Face Dim Future." *New York Times*, January 4, 1959.

Ramírez-Rosell, Reinaldo. "*El razzle-dazzle, mala publicidad*." *Diario de la Marina*, April 12, 1953.

Reiss, Matthew. "The Batista-Lansky Alliance: How the Mafia and a Cuban Dictator Built Havana's Casinos," *Cigar Aficionado*, May/June 2001.

Santos Moray, Mercedes. "Havana—Hemingway's Muse." www.CubaNow.net. Undated.

Sargeant, Winthrop. "Cuba's Tin Pan Alley." *Life*, October 6, 1947.

Show magazine. "*Prende en La Habana el arte de la mujer eléctrica*," December 1956.

————. "*Ginger Rogers, en persona, super-estrella en su gran revista*," December 1957.

————. "*George Raft estrella absoluta en la gran revista de Abril*," April 1958.

Skylar, Richard. "Cuba's Lure-Legalised Filth!'" *Suppressed*, Vol. 4, No. 1, February 1957.

Stag, Vol. 1, No. 5. "Sin—With a Rumba Beat!" November 1950.

St. George, Andrew. "Cuban Rebels (Interview with Fidel Castro)." *Look*, April 3, 1958.

Stratton, Richard. "The Man Who Killed Dutch Schultz." *GQ*, September 2001.

Striparama, Vol. 2, No. 2, "Cutie from Cuba . . . Carmela," 1962.

South Florida Sun-Sentinel. "Castro Calls Head of U.S. Diplomatic Mission in Havana a "Little Gangster,'" December 23, 2006.

Tampa Times. "Trafficante Feels the Heat," June 12, 1959.

————. "Trafficante Ouster May Be Postponed," June 12, 1959.

————. "Trafficante Still Awaits Hearing on Deportation," June 15, 1959.

Tampa Tribune. "Zarate Bolita Case to Be Called Today Before Third Judge," August 4, 1947.

————. "Deputies Pick Up Trafficante and Bodyguard 'On Sight,'" January 23, 1954.

————. "George Zarate, Ex-Racketeer, Dies in Cuba," August 25, 1955.

————. "Cuba Will Deport Trafficante on US Narcotics Request," June 11, 1959.

Time. "Caribbean Tyranny," May 13, 1935.

————. "Lese Majeste," May 27, 1935.

————. "Senator from Daytona," April 12, 1948.

————. "A Game of Casino," January 20, 1958.

————. "High Wind in Havana," February 3, 1958.

————. "Death on the Malecón," March 10, 1958.

———. "The Mob Is Back," March 2, 1959.

Velie, Lester. "Suckers in Paradise: How Americans Lose Their Shirts in Caribbean Gambling Joints." *Saturday Evening Post*, March 28, 1953.

Wald, Richard C. "Mafia Link in Death of Anastasia?" *New York Herald Tribune*, October 28, 1957.

Whitney, Robert. "The Architect of the Cuban State: Fulgencio Batista and Populism in Cuba, 1937–1940." *Journal of Latin American Studies*, 2000.

DOCUMENTARIES AND TELEVISION PROGRAMS

American Experience: Fidel Castro. PBS documentary. Directed by Adriana Bosch, 2004.

Cuban Story. Documentary. Presented by Errol Flynn. 1959. DVD. Chatsworth, CA: Image Entertainment, 2002.

Face the Nation. CBS Television. Interview with Fidel Castro, January 24, 1959.

La Habana en los años 50s. DVD. Directed by Waldo Fernández. Produced by Marakka 2000.

The Jack Paar Show. NBC Television. Interview with Fidel Castro, January 13, 1959.

La mafia en La Habana. Documentary. Directed by Ana Diez. Produced by Marakka 2000.

O.G.: Joe Stassi, Original Gangster. Documentary. Directed by Marc Levin and Richard Stratton.

Person to Person. Edward R. Murrow interview with Fidel Castro, February 2, 1959.

The Steve Allen Show. NBC Television. Live from the Hotel Riviera, January 16, 1958.

The Story of Cuba's Jungle Fighters. CBS Television documentary, August 1957.

INSTITUTIONS

Essential research in the form of law enforcement documents, transcripts, criminal files, magazine and newspaper archives, documentary films, old television programs, and photographs were culled from the following institutions: U.S. National Archives in Washington, D.C., which house files from the Federal Bureau of Narcotics (FBN) and also files of the Kefauver Committee hearings and those of the 1978 House Select Committee on Assassinations; Biblioteca Nacional José Martí, Havana; Hotel Nacional, historical archive, Havana; Museo de la Revolucíon, Havana; University of Miami Library (Cuban Heritage Collection); *Tampa Tribune* photo archive; New York

City Municipal Archives; New York Public Library (Newspaper Division); Museum of Television and Radio, New York City.

FBI FILES

Using the Freedom of Information Act (FOIA), FBI documents were gathered on the following individuals: Albert Anastasia, Meyer Lansky, Frank Sinatra, Santo Trafficante, and George Raft.

ALSO BY T. J. ENGLISH

HAVANA NOCTURNE
How the Mob Owned Cuba . . . and Then Lost It to the Revolution

ISBN 978-0-06-171274-6 (paperback)

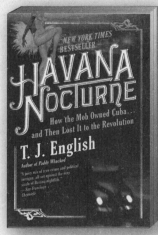

Havana Nocturne takes readers back to Cuba in the years when it was a veritable devil's playground for mob leaders. English deftly weaves the parallel stories of the Havana Mob and Castro's 26th of July Movement in a riveting, up-close look at how the Mob nearly attained its biggest dream in Havana—and how Fidel Castro trumped it all with the Cuban Revolution.

"A whiz-bang account of the Mafia's short-lived romp through 1950s Cuba." —*New York Times Book Review*

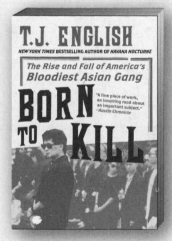

BORN TO KILL
The Rise and Fall of America's Bloodiest Asian Gang

ISBN 978-0-06-178238-1 (paperback)

T.J. English chronicles Vietnam war refugees who laid the foundation for a terrifying underworld of violence and power in 1980s New York City.

"A must for anyone interested in the emerging multiethnic face of organized crime in the United States."
—*Washington Post Book World*

PADDY WHACKED
The Untold Story of the Irish American Gangster

ISBN 978-0-06-059003-1 (paperback)

Bestselling author and organized crime expert T. J. English brings to life nearly two centuries of Irish American gangsterism. Stretching from the earliest New York and New Orleans street wars through decades of bootlegging scams, union strikes, gang wars, and FBI investigations, *Paddy Whacked* is a riveting tour de force that restores the Irish American gangster to his rightful preeminent place in our criminal history—and penetrates to the heart of the American experience.